Hillforts of the Cheshire Ridge

Investigations undertaken by The Habitats and Hillforts Landscape Partnership Scheme 2009–2012

Dan Garner

with sections by

Ian Brooks, Wendy Carruthers, Richard Chiverrell, Jill Collens, Heather Davies, Peter Marshall, Richard Mason, Sylvia Peglar, Mitchell Pollington and Rachel Pope

and contributions by

John Carrott, Alison Foster, Lindsey Foster, Gemma Martin, Barbara Mauz, David Mullin, George Nash, Susan Packman, Christine Prior, Helen Ranner, Ian Smith, Neil Suttie and Angela Walker

Edited by Jill Collens

ARCHAEOPRESS ARCHAEOLOGY

ARCHAEOPRESS PUBLISHING LTD
Gordon House
276 Banbury Road
Oxford OX2 7ED

www.archaeopress.com

ISBN 978 1 78491 466 0
ISBN 978 1 78491 467 7 (e-Pdf)

Cover: Aerial view of the eastern entrance at Eddisbury hillfort after excavation in 2010 © Greg Colley (Suave UAV Enterprises Ltd).

Printed in England by Holywell Press, Oxford
This book is available direct from Archaeopress or from our website www.archaeopress.com

Contents

List of Figures

Acknowledgements

The Habitats and Hillforts Project would not have been possible without the funding from the Heritage Lottery Fund under their Landscape Partnerships grant programme. The Project was developed by staff in the Natural and Historic Environment Team of the former Cheshire County Council. Ian Marshall, Team Manager, collated the bid; Alun Evans developed the 'Habitats' section; Jill Collens the 'Hillforts' section and the late Mike Wellman developed the training and community aspects of the bid. The implementation phase of the Project was made far easier through the co-operation and support of colleagues in the Project team: Ellie Morris (née Soper), the Project Manager and Colin Slater, the Ecological Project Officer. Grateful thanks are due to other former colleagues in Cheshire West and Chester, who assisted in various aspects of the project: Mark Leah, Development Control Archaeologist, provided advice and guidance on fieldwork methodology and oversaw the publication process; Rob Edwards and Moya Watson, Historic Environment Record Officers, provided assistance with the Cheshire Historic Environment Record and GIS; Elizabeth Royles and Laura Pooley, Cheshire West Museum Service, provided access to archaeological material in the archives and organised the display of some of the results of the Project in a temporary exhibition.

Thanks go to members of the Project Steering Group, which was chaired by the late Andrew Deadman who gave strong support to the archaeological programme. Regular members of the Steering Group included: Mark Hodgson, then Visitor Operations Manager for English Heritage at Beeston Castle; Christopher Widger, the National Trust Cheshire Countryside Manager; the late Dave Morris, Warden at Bickerton and Helsby hills; National Trust archaeologists, Carolanne King, Mark Newman and Jamie Lund; Tim Kirwen and Clare Davies (née Burnside) of the Woodland Trust; Vernon Stockton and Don Wilson of the Forestry Commission; and private landowners, Michael Platt (Eddisbury) and Mike Hardy (Kelsborrow) who allowed access to their land and supported the Project.

A number of English Heritage (now Historic England) staff provided specialist support during the Project including: Jennie Stopford the Inspector of Ancient Monuments for the southern half of the North West Region, who was involved with the project from the outset including discussions and negotiations over site management; Sue Stallibrass, Regional Science Adviser for the North West, who advised on sampling strategies; Stewart Ainsworth, Senior Investigator, who advised on commissioning the topographical and lidar surveys; and Pete Marshall, who provided valuable guidance and advice on radiocarbon dating.

Grateful thanks go to all the staff at Earthworks Archaeology and especially Will Walker and Leigh Dodd, for supervising the day to day running of the archaeological fieldwork, looking after the welfare and training of a multitude of volunteers and assisting with the post-excavation process. Thanks also to Owen Raybould from RSK Environment Ltd. who facilitated the inclusion of the report on developer-funded work carried out at Ince Marshes, which lie to the north of Helsby hillfort.

Finally, the Habitats and Hillforts Project was primarily a community project. Many people volunteered to help with the archaeological work and take part in the training events. People from the local community and students from Liverpool and Chester Universities supported the project with enthusiasm and commitment and are owed a debt of gratitude. Without their support the work presented in this volume would not have been possible.

It remains to dedicate my part in this work to my family, including those I lost whilst working on this Project: my father Peter Garner (d.2012), my grandmother Elizabeth Stubbs (d.2010), and my uncle Robert Stubbs (d.2011).

Dan Garner 2016.

Contributors

Chapter 1: Dr Jill Collens, formerly Manager of the Archaeology Planning Advisory Service, Cheshire Shared Services.

Chapters 1,2, 6–10, 12 and 15: Dan Garner, Project Officer (Archaeology) Habitats and Hillforts Project, Cheshire West and Chester. Now Partner, L-P: Archaeology (Chester).

Chapter 3: Dr Ian Brooks, Engineering Archaeological Services Ltd.

Chapters 4 and 11: Richard Mason, Field School Director (now Assistant Curator of Archaeological Collections, English Heritage) and Dr Rachel Pope, Senior Lecturer in European Prehistory, Department of Archaeology, Classics and Egyptology, University of Liverpool.

Chapter 5: Mitchell Pollington, Director (Operations, York), AOC Archaeology.

Chapter 13: Professor Richard Chiverrell, Professor in Physical Geography, Department of Geography and Planning, School of Environmental Sciences, University of Liverpool; Heather Davies, University of Liverpool and Dr Peter Marshall, Historic England.

Chapter 14: Wendy Carruthers, Archaeobotanist and Sylvia Peglar, Palynologist, on behalf of RSK Environment Ltd.

Finds studies: Dan Garner, Dr George Nash (University of Bristol), Dr David Mullin (University of Worcester).

Palaeoenvironmental analysis: John Carrott, Alison Foster, Lindsey Foster, Gemma Martin, Helen Ranner and Angela Walker (all Palaeoecology Research Services), Ian Smith (Oxford Archaeology North).

Dating: Dr Peter Marshall (Historic England), Dr Barbara Mauz (University of Liverpool), Susan Packman (University of Liverpool), Christine Prior, Dr Neil Suttie (University of Liverpool).

Illustrations: Dan Garner, Clare Statter (formerly L-P: Archaeology), Dr Ian Brooks, Mitchell Pollington, Dr Ben Edwards (Manchester Metropolitan University), Stephen Clark (formerly Cheshire West and Chester), Dr Meggen Gondek (University of Chester), Martin Roseveare (Archaeophysica Ltd).

Photography: Dan Garner, Leigh Dodd and Will Walker (Earthworks Archaeology), Greg Colley (Suave UAV Enterprises Ltd), Dr George Nash (University of Bristol), Colin Sharratt, Richard Mason.

Editing: Dr Jill Collens with Dr Peter Carrington (formerly Cheshire West and Chester).

Abbreviations

CALS Cheshire Archives and Local Studies

CCC Cheshire County Council

CHER Cheshire Historic Environment Record

CWaC Cheshire West and Chester

DTM Digital Terrain Model

OAN Oxford Archaeology (North)

PRO Public Record Office

SREP Sandstone Ridge ECOnet Partnership

Chapter 1
Background to the Habitats and Hillforts Project

Jill Collens and Dan Garner

The Cheshire hillforts (Figure 1.1) are some of the most conspicuous features of the prehistoric landscape in Cheshire. Outside of archaeological circles, however, they have almost become 'lost' in the landscape and in the awareness of the wider community, due to land use changes in the centuries following their construction. Various studies have been undertaken on the hillforts of Cheshire (see Chapter 2), but even so, there is limited information about these sites in terms of chronology, function, occupation history, economy and status. Considering that these hillforts stand as such important elements of the prehistory of the region, the lack of information about them is a major gap in our understanding.

The Habitats and Hillforts of Cheshire's Sandstone Ridge Landscape Partnership Project was focused on six of the Cheshire hillforts and their surrounding habitats and landscapes. It aimed to develop understanding of the chronology and role of the hillforts, raise awareness of these special assets and the issues affecting them, improve their condition and their physical linkages with the surrounding landscape and encourage more people to enjoy them and to take an active role in their management.

The Habitats and Hillforts Project was funded by the Heritage Lottery Fund through the Landscape Partnership Scheme programme, which focuses on areas of distinctive landscape character. The Project was based on the Cheshire Sandstone Ridge, which runs north to south in Central Cheshire and has been identified as a distinct character area by the Countryside Character volume for the Northwest of England (Countryside

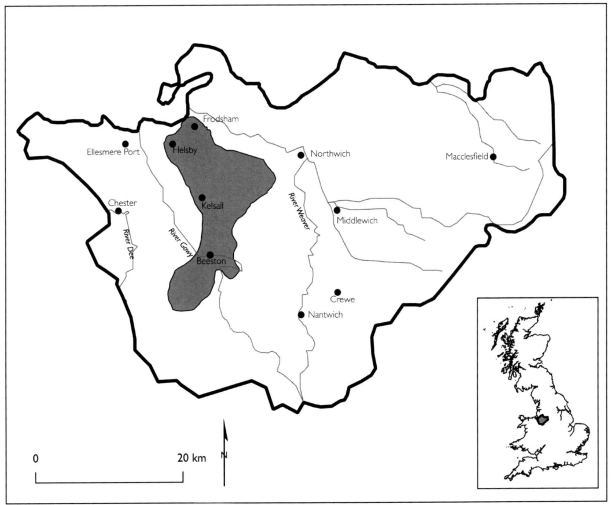

FIGURE 1.1 LOCATION OF THE STUDY AREA WITHIN CHESHIRE © CROWN COPYRIGHT. REPRODUCED BY PERMISSION OF THE CONTROLLER OF HMSO LICENCE NO. 100053067

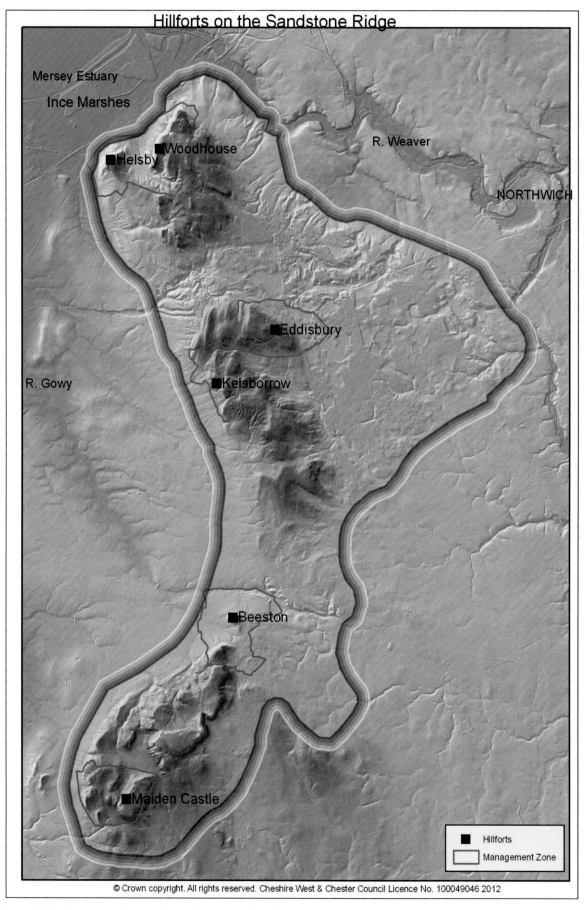

FIGURE 1.2 THE SANDSTONE RIDGE ECONET PARTNERSHIP (SREP) AREA AND THE HILLFORT MANAGEMENT ZONES OF THE HABITATS AND HILLFORTS PROJECT.

Commission 1998: 145–152). This area formed the limits for an EU LIFE ECOnet network which was given the title of the Sandstone Ridge ECOnet Partnership (SREP), formed as part of an initiative by Cheshire County Council (CCC) in 2005.

The SREP area (Figure 1.2) was used as the basis for the Habitats and Hillforts Project, which focussed on six hillfort management zones on the Ridge, rather than the entire SREP area. The Project was developed by specialist staff in the Natural and Historic Environment Team of the former Cheshire County Council and was granted Phase one funding in 2007. Following the award of Phase Two funding, it was launched as a three year project in October 2008. During the life of the project, local authorities in Cheshire were reorganised and so the Project was transferred to one of the new successor authorities, Cheshire West and Chester (CWaC), in 2009.

Towards the end of the initial three years it was agreed that a contingency sum within the original budget could be used to extend the project for an additional 12 months (ending October 2012).

The lead partner in the Project was CCC and then CWaC, and the partnership consisted of a range of organisations which came together to share approaches to managing environmental and heritage assets on the Sandstone Ridge. The partners were English Heritage (now Historic England), the National Trust, the Woodland Trust, the Forestry Commission and private landowners, all of whom owned, or had a management interest in, the six hillforts.

The project included six management zones, within which work would be focused (Figure 1.2). Each zone was centred on a prehistoric hillfort and running

Hillfort	Other names	NGR	National Heritage list for England name	National Heritage List for England number	Heritage category	Habitats & Hillforts Management Zone	Other prehistoric enclosure sites
Helsby hillfort		SJ 4926 7539	Promontory fort on Helsby Hill 250m northwest of Harmers Lake Farm	1013292	Scheduled monument	Frodsham	
Woodhouse hillfort	Woodhouses	SJ 5105 7572	Hillfort on Woodhouse Hill 500m west of Mickledale	1013297	Scheduled monument	Frodsham	
Eddisbury hillfort	Castle Ditch / Merrick's Hill	SJ 5532 6933	Eddisbury hillfort east of Old Pale Farm	1013295	Scheduled monument	Delamere	Oakmere promontory fort (No. 1013291 Scheduled monument)
Kelsborrow hillfort	Kelsborrow Castle	SJ 5315 6750	Kelsborrow Promontory Fort On Castle Hill 300m south west Of Castle Hill Farm	1013294	Scheduled monument	Willington	
Beeston Castle		SJ 5379 5919	Beeston Castle; Medieval Enclosure Castle and Site of Late Prehistoric Hillfort	1007900	Scheduled monument	Bickerton	Peckforton Mere promontory fort (No. 1013481 Scheduled monument)
Maiden Castle		SJ 4976 5289	Maiden Castle Promontory Fort on Bickerton Hill 700m west of Hill Farm	1013293	Scheduled monument	Bickerton	

FIGURE 1.3 THE HILLFORTS OF THE HABITATS AND HILLFORTS PROJECT.

3

from north to south these include: Helsby Hill; Woodhouse Hill; Eddisbury Hill; Kelsborrow Castle; Beeston Castle; and Maiden Castle. The management zone at Beeston Castle also included the suspected prehistoric enclosure on the edge of Peckforton Mere. All the hillforts have statutory protection as scheduled monuments (Figure 1.3).

During the Development phase of the Project, various surveys were undertaken in order to develop the detail of the Delivery phase. Two archaeological surveys were commissioned and delivered by Oxford Archaeology (North) during this phase - an Archaeological Desk-Based Assessment and an Archaeological Condition Assessment (OAN 2008a; OAN 2008b).

The Delivery phase of the Habitats and Hillforts LPS was divided in to four programmes of work:

- Programme 1: Habitats of the Ridge
- Programme 2: Hillforts of the Ridge
- Programme 3: Access and interpretation
- Programme 4: Training and volunteering

Within Programme 2 (Hillforts of the Ridge) there were two main threads of work which were divided between *Understanding hillforts* and *Restoring hillfort heritage*. The understanding hillforts work included a series of non-invasive surveys and training excavations for members of the local community, whilst the restoring hillforts heritage involved management work to improve the condition of the earthworks.

The Habitats and Hillforts Project team included three dedicated staff: Ellie Morris (née Soper) the project manager; Colin Slater the ecological project officer, responsible for the 'Habitats' element of the Project, and Dan Garner the archaeological project officer, responsible for the 'Hillforts' programme of the Project. The core team was supported by other council officers as required and most notably Jill Collens (archaeology) and Alun Evans (natural environment) from the Natural and Historic Environment Team. The Project had a dedicated steering group under the chairmanship of the late Andrew Deadman, with representatives of the various land owning bodies associated with the project, including representatives from English Heritage, the National Trust, the Woodland Trust and the Forestry Commission, as well as private land owners and other key stake holders.

Over the four year life of the project, archaeological investigation and management was carried out at six hillforts under Programme 2. Much of this work was interlinked with work in the other programmes which delivered:

- 40 hectares of new/restored habitats
- 1300 metres of restored hedgerows

- 700 metres of sandstone walls restored
- 700 metres of footpath improvements
- 4.1 kms of permissive access
- A range of promotional material, including booklets, leaflets, and on-site interpretational panels and a dedicated website.
- A range of events and activities including a guided walk programme, reminiscence workshop and community workshop
- Over 350 training and education days

The Habitats and Hillforts Project came to an end in 2012, but its legacy and that of SREP has been passed to the Sandstone Ridge Trust, which was formed in 2011, to secure funding to protect and manage the special landscape of the Ridge. The work of the Trust is based on the themes of improved understanding of cultural heritage, landscape-scale improvements for wildlife and increased awareness and access.

Methodology

All six of the hillforts in the Habitats and Hillforts Project were on the English Heritage 'At Risk' register at the start of the work, due to issues regarding erosion and lack of effective management. A Condition Assessment carried out in 2007 (OAN 2008b) identified agricultural activity, predominantly ploughing, erosion through visitor pressure and vegetation encroachment, causing root damage to sub-surface deposits, as the principal threats. Management recommendations were proposed, including a reduction in ploughing, control of visitor movement, removal of scrub, bracken and trees and control of burrowing animals, as well as the implementation of management agreements. Areas and opportunities for further archaeological investigations were also identified to evaluate the surviving resource and the potential damage to sub-surface archaeological deposits.

A programme of archaeological and management work was developed from the findings of the Condition Assessment and Scheduled Monument Consent was granted for this work at the start of the Project. In addition, each individual excavation was accompanied by an approved Project Design setting out the justification for undertaking the work. It was accepted that the primary justification was linked to ongoing management issues, identified during the Condition Assessment (OAN 2008b), such as rampart destabilisation through agents such as plant growth or animal burrowing. There was also an agreement that re-excavation of previous archaeological trenches was an acceptable proposition. Exposing original sections and conducting targeted sampling for scientific analysis had the potential to answer some of the questions of chronology that have hampered discussion of the hillforts for the last century and would result in limited fresh damage to the monuments. For this reason, all of the campaigns of excavation reported in this volume rely heavily on re-excavation of earlier trenches.

Excavation was carried out at four of the hillforts, the exceptions being Beeston Castle which had already been the subject of a campaign of excavation between 1968 and 1985; and Maiden Castle, where conducting excavation during the final year of the project would have had major impacts on finance and post-excavation. All the work was carried out as training excavations and was directed by Dan Garner with supervision from professional archaeologists provided by an archaeological contractor (Earthworks Archaeology); the bulk of the labour was carried out by, in excess of, 200 volunteers with varying levels of previous archaeological experience. In addition excavations were carried out at Merrick's Hill, part of Eddisbury hillfort, by the University of Liverpool Archaeology Field School with eighty students taking part.

Non-invasive work in the form of topographic and geophysical survey was attempted, to a greater or lesser degree, at all six hillfort sites, as well as on two mere side enclosures at Peckforton and Oakmere. Topographic survey was carried out by archaeological contractors (Archaeological Services, WYAS) and Liverpool University. Geophysical survey was carried out by a specialist commercial geophysics contractor (Archaeophysica Ltd); as training sessions led by an archaeological contractor (Engineering Archaeological Services Ltd), and as student training exercises by Liverpool University's School of Archaeology, Classics and Egyptology and by the History and Archaeology Department at Chester University.

It was acknowledged at the start of the Project that full publication would probably have to be achieved outside the project, due to the timescales inherent in archaeological post-excavation and the HLF policy at the time, of not funding post-excavation. However, grey literature reports were produced for all the work carried out, as part of the conditions of Scheduled Monument Consent and these are housed in the Cheshire Historic Environment Record (CHER).

At the end of the Project in December 2012, a popular publication on the results of the archaeological work was produced, entitled *Hillforts of the Cheshire Sandstone Ridge* (Garner 2012). This contains many of the essential pieces of new dating evidence accumulated during the four years of the Project, along with a brief consideration of the implications for the synthetic study of these hillforts.

There was also a need to try and place the hillforts within their landscape setting as part of the Project; however, the earlier desk-based research had demonstrated how difficult this was going to be owing to the lack

of demonstrable prehistoric features in the landscape. Cheshire has been heavily affected by agricultural improvement meaning that little in the way of extant earthworks survive in the landscape. The heavy clay soils which dominate the Cheshire Plain are also not conducive to revealing cropmarks of ploughed out archaeological features through aerial photography, nor are they well suited to large scale geophysical survey. Even with resources such as the Cheshire Historic Landscape Characterisation Project and a suite of aerial photographs spanning the 1940s to the early 21st century, much of the landscape remains a prehistoric blank. It was clear from the beginning that it would not be possible to achieve the sort of results seen on comparable projects such as the Wessex Hillforts Project (Payne, Corney and Cunliffe 2006), or the Hillforts of the Northumberland National Park (Oswald, Ainsworth and Pearson 2006). An alternative approach was therefore required.

Two possible avenues of enquiry were pursued by the Project to try and add new insights in to the landscape setting of the hillforts. The first was the acquisition of a lidar data set, but unfortunately large areas of the Ridge were not covered by existing surveys. As a result, in 2010 the Project commissioned a bespoke lidar survey for the entire SREP area (200 km²) at a resolution of 0.5m (Chapter 7, this volume). Secondly, some of the hillforts were very close to ancient mere sites which had not been fully studied from a palaeoenvironmental perspective; in particular there had been a lack of scientific dating to accompany previous palynological study. As a result, the Project worked in partnership with the Department of Geography at Liverpool University to extract and analyse fresh cores from both Peckforton Mere and Hatchmere (Chapter 14, this volume). To this was added some commercially funded palaeoenvironmental work undertaken on the Mersey estuary at Ince Marshes by RSK Environmental Ltd (Chapter 13, this volume), all of which has added to our understanding of the environment in the prehistoric period.

The papers presented within this monograph are all derived from the work undertaken as part of the *Understanding hillforts* thread within Programme 2 of the Habitats and Hillforts Project. As outlined above, this has involved a range of organisations and volunteers.

The papers are divided in to sections, according to type of work undertaken. They have largely been written or synthesised by Dan Garner, the Archaeological Project Officer, or by specialists and archaeologists working with the Project to bring an added dimension to the hillforts.

The introductory section contains a chapter on the previous archaeological work on the hillforts of the Sandstone Ridge (Chapter 2). Section 1 is a review of some of the main archive material relating to the Ridge, and includes a review of the large lithic collection from the area around Woodhouse hillfort by Dr Ian Brooks (Chapter 3) and a re-assessment of the archive of the excavations carried out at Eddisbury hillfort in the 1930s by W. J. Varley, by Richard Mason and Dr Rachel Pope (Chapter 4). Section 2 presents the results of non-invasive survey carried out on the ridge, including earthwork surveys of three of the hillforts by Mitchell Pollington (Chapter 5). Ten geophysical surveys were carried out as part of the Project and these are summarised by Dan Garner in Chapter 6. The full reports of these surveys are included in the online appendix. The results of the lidar survey of the ridge, commissioned by the Project, is summarised by Dan Garner in Chapter 7. Section 3 contains reports on the excavations on four of the hillforts, carried out by the project between 2009 and 2011, by Dan Garner (Chapters 8–10 and 12). An interim statement on the excavations carried out at Merrick's Hill, part of Eddisbury hillfort, by Liverpool University is presented in Chapter 11, by Richard Mason and Dr Rachel Pope. Section 4 contains reports on palaeoenvironmental work carried out as part of the project, including work undertaken to investigate the palaeoenvironmental record at two meres located just off the Sandstone Ridge, by Professor Richard Chiverrell, Heather Davies and Pete Marshall (Chapter 13). The final chapter in this section by RSK Environmental Consultants, was carried out as developer-funded fieldwork and is included to provide a wider environmental context to the hillforts on the Ridge (Chapter 14). The final discussion section summarises all the work carried out as part of the Project and the implications for our understanding of the Cheshire hillforts.

The archaeological work carried out as part of the Project also provided data which has implications for the management of hillforts and this is summarised for individual sites in the chapters in Section 3.

Landscape setting and natural topography

The Cheshire Sandstone Ridge is a small irregular ridge of Triassic sandstone overlain by brown sands and podzols (Furness 1978) which is aligned north to south across the Cheshire Plain from Frodsham in the north to Malpas in the south. The Ridge reaches heights of between 123m OD at Helsby in the north, and 227m OD at Raw Head in the Bickerton Hills to the south, but is still very prominent as it rises up sharply from the Plain. The Ridge is most dominant in the north but is discontinuous and becomes more broken to the south where it narrows to form small but abrupt ridges with gaps at Beeston and Bickerton. Glacial activity has had an effect by rounding off outcrops of sandstone and creating meltwater channels and lake beds; the northern part of the Ridge is flanked by fluvioglacial deposits of sands and gravels which have served to broaden and extend the elevated land to the east. These deposits are punctuated in places by a number of shallow meres and mosses which are prevalent in the Delamere area.

The modern landscape is largely pastoral and dominated by dairying which has encouraged a predominant land cover of grass with leys, improved grassland and permanent pasture offering grazing, silage and hay. Some arable and mixed farming is present on the more easily drained soils along the slopes of the Ridge where fodder crops are grown to provide winter feed as well as some commercial crops such as potatoes, cereals and rape. Hedges are predominantly of hawthorn and blackthorn with hedgerow trees being mainly mature oak with some ash and sycamore. Modern activity in the form of sandstone quarrying and the extraction by the aggregate industry of sands and gravels has substantially altered the land form of the Ridge in some places, most notably in creating new water bodies in the Delamere area.

Woodland cover is higher on the Ridge than the surrounding Plain, comprising ancient woodland and post medieval conifer plantations with broadleaved and mixed woodland on the steeper slopes or along the sides of watercourses. Around the central area of the Ridge, Delamere Forest contains extensive broadleaved and mixed woodland on the slopes and conifers on the gravelly soils to the east. Heaths and mosses are also common in this central area and are comprised of poorer quality pastures with woodlands of birch, oak, pine and alder and in places stretches of heath comprised of ling, gorse, bilberry and birch.

Chapter 2
The historical study of the Cheshire Hillforts

Dan Garner

This chapter is intended to provide a short review of the information available on the six hillforts located on the Cheshire Sandstone Ridge, prior to the commencement of the Habitats and Hillforts Project in 2008. The review does not detail every event, but is intended to cover the main areas of relevant research, highlighting the essential points of detail. This is not an exhaustive account but does contain references to all of the published literature on the subject. Much of the information is primarily drawn from the desk-based assessment produced by Oxford Archaeology North in 2008 (OAN 2008a). A broadly chronological approach has been adopted as this was felt to highlight how interpretation of some sites has been heavily dependent on prevailing trends; in some cases it is insightful in terms of the way interpretations have developed and changed over time.

Ormerod 1816–1819

The earliest record for many of the Cheshire hillforts was provided by George Ormerod in his *History of Cheshire* published between 1816 and 1819, with a second edition published in 1882. The *History* published in three volumes, contained both original work by the author, as well as transcripts of documents and reprints of earlier works including *The Vale Royal of England* by Daniel King, first published in 1656. Ormerod provides the earliest detailed plans for three of the Cheshire hillforts including Kelsborrow, Eddisbury and Maiden Castle (Figure 2.1). In the accompanying text, the sites of both Kelsborrow and Maiden Castle are described as 'strong British camp(s)' which are thought to be located with the intention of defending passes

through the Cheshire Ridge at Kelsall Hill and Larton (Larkton). The site of Eddisbury is however dismissed as a prehistoric monument in favour of it 'being formed by Ethelfleda in the year 915' (Ormerod 1882: 3). The hillforts at Helsby and Woodhouse are not mentioned in the text, however, another supposed 'British camp'

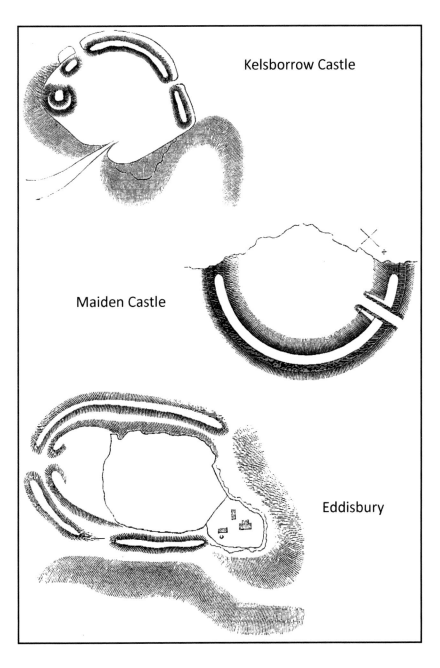

FIGURE 2.1 ORMEROD'S PUBLISHED PLANS OF KELSBORROW CASTLE, MAIDEN CASTLE AND EDDISBURY (ORMEROD, 1882: II 3)

known as Finnsborrow or Finness is referred to, though not accurately located (*ibid.* 3).

Shone 1911

William Shone published his *Prehistoric Man in Cheshire* in 1911 in which he included a comprehensive gazetteer, along with photographs of many artefacts and monuments. When describing the hillforts along the Cheshire Ridge, Shone relies heavily on Ormerod's earlier text and reproduces Ormerod's plans of Kelsborrow, Maiden Castle and Eddisbury. Contrary to Ormerod, he does identify Eddisbury as a prehistoric monument on the basis of 'its plan, and by the fact of so many tumuli being in its neighbourhood' (Shone 1911: 57). Shone also makes reference to the discovery of a number of urns containing calcined bones at the foot of Eddisbury hillfort (in the sand-pit field about half a mile south-east of the old ordnance cairn) in the spring of 1851; some fragments of which are in the Warrington Museum. To this he relates an account reported to him by 'an old man' in 1906 who worked at the quarry when young:

> 'In the disused quarry that is below the ruins of Eddisbury Castle to the east, he remembered when they cleared the soil from off the rock, they "found a lot of jars with old bones in them"; the jars were so rotten that "they fell to pieces when touched"' (Shone 1911: 58).

Shone also refers to a number of earthworks not mentioned by Ormerod which he considers likely to be British camps including Helsby Hill; The Foxhill, near Frodsham (Woodhouse); and the camp at Bradley, near Overton. He concludes that 'the earthworks of Cheshire would be a most interesting subject for future research' (Shone 1911: 81).

Varley 1934–1938

William Varley was the first archaeologist (based in the Department of Geography, University of Liverpool) to attempt excavation on any of the Cheshire hillforts. The first hillfort to attract his attention was Maiden Castle on Bickerton Hill upon which he conducted two seasons of excavation between 1934 and 1935. He then moved on to Castle Ditch, Eddisbury where he conducted three seasons of excavation between 1936 and 1938. The excavations at Eddisbury were not published until 1950, but this was in no small way due to the outbreak of World War II and its aftermath.

The Maiden Castle excavations 1934–5

The investigation of Maiden Castle was carried out under the title of the 'The Bickerton Camp Scheme' and published as two successive reports within the

Annals of Archaeology and Anthropology by Liverpool University, in successive years (Varley 1935; 1936). The excavations were supervised by Varley and J. P. Droop, while the work force was made up of high school pupils, members of the Liverpool Ramblers' Association and men from the Liverpool Voluntary Occupational Centres Association (Varley 1935: 108; Varley 1936: 112). The excavations were focused on the entranceway of the hillfort and provided sections through the main inner and outer ramparts (Figures 2.2 and 2.3). The results suggested a series of different rampart construction phases:

- A trench identified beneath the outer rampart (to the south of the hillfort entrance) and sealed by a turf-line, was interpreted as a palisade slot which was thought to pre-date the rampart construction (Varley 1935: 101);
- The inner rampart was described as comprising an inner core of timber and sand with a stone capping which covered the core and formed a revetment to the front and rear of the rampart (Varley 1935: 98). The timbers had survived in a carbonised state and this was seen as either the result of deliberately firing the ramparts or due to later heath fires, which had been spread beneath the surface by smouldering roots (Varley 1935: 109). Varley suggested the form of construction was similar to the *murus gallicus* style described by Caesar as a feature of Gaulish defences;
- The outer rampart was initially formed from a bank of sand and rubble over which a turf-line had formed. This turf-line was then covered by a layer of sand, above which another turf-line was noted and a stone revetment was present along the outer face. Varley suggested that the bank had either been built as a composite structure or that successive phases of rampart reinforcement were represented (Varley 1935: 101–2);
- The ditch between the inner and outer ramparts to the south of the entrance was observed to be an accentuation of the natural slope. However, several hollows were noted along the length of the ditch which had been quarried in to the sandstone bedrock (Varley 1936: 104–5). Varley suggested that these hollows might have been associated with water collection;
- Within the inturned entrance a pair of postholes were discovered which were suggested to have been gateposts recessed in to the rampart revetments (Varley 1936: 101). Guard huts or shelters were suggested to have been situated to the south and north of the entrance within the corners of the rampart inturns. The southernmost was described as an occupation floor and the northern one as an area of calcined bone and charcoal (Varley 1936: 101–2). One sherd of pottery was associated with the southernmost

floor and this was considered possibly to be late Iron Age (*ibid.* 106).

In conclusion, Varley considered that Maiden Castle had been initially constructed in the first half of the first century AD. This was based on the typology of the inner rampart construction (the *murus gallicus* style) and the presence of the inturned entrance which he considered to be a late development in the North West (Varley 1936: 106–111). The subsequent strengthening of the defences to the outer rampart were therefore interpreted as a response to the threat of Roman expansion in to the North West in the mid-first century AD (*ibid.* 107).

Varley and Jackson 1940

In 1940 the Cheshire Rural Community Council commissioned a series of historical handbooks. The first, *Prehistoric Cheshire,* was co-authored by William Varley and John Jackson and this contained the first attempt by Varley to synthesise the results of his excavation work on the Cheshire hillforts. In a section entitled 'The Hill-fort Dwellers' he suggested that the hillforts of Cheshire were linked geographically with the group which extended along the Welsh Marches southwards to the Severn Estuary. Varley also advanced a chronological evolution for the Cheshire hillforts from Palisade Enclosures (900–200 BC), to Simple Hillforts (200 BC–AD 1) and finally Multivallate Hillforts (AD 1–75) (Varley and Jackson 1940: 56).

The book included a map with an accompanying table entitled 'The Hillforts of Cheshire' (partly reproduced below as Figure 2.4). The hillfort at Beeston is omitted

as it remained unidentified as a hillfort until revealed by excavation during the 1970s and 1980s. The table is interesting as it characterises all of the hillforts as 'promontory camps' with the exception of Castle Ditch, Eddisbury.

The book included a brief account of the results of excavations at both Maiden Castle and Eddisbury, accompanied by photographs and line drawings from the excavations. It is noteworthy that Varley had revised his dating for Maiden Castle by this point, suggesting that the inner rampart and an outer 'counterscarp bank' dated to the second century BC; whilst the strengthening of the outer rampart dated to the first century BC (Varley and Jackson 1940: 70-1). The schematic section drawings produced in the 1940 publication for Maiden Castle are clearly an interpretative model rather than a close reproduction of the rampart sections published in 1936 (Figures 2.5 and 2.6).

The information on Eddisbury was effectively an interim statement on Varley's unpublished excavations which ceased in 1938. There was an attempt to promote his three phases of development for the hillfort consisting of: palisade structures (on Merrick's Hill); a contour fort; and then an enlarged contour fort with an extension added to the northwest. His proposed chronology linked the palisade enclosure with the urned cremation burials found in the adjacent sand quarry in 1851, which he attributed to the late Bronze Age (*ibid.* 64). The first contour fort was defined by an inner rampart, ditch and counterscarp bank with two entrances in the southwest and southeast corners. Behind the rampart was a 'cobbled walk' which was associated with occasional 'occupation-scatters' producing pottery of Iron Age

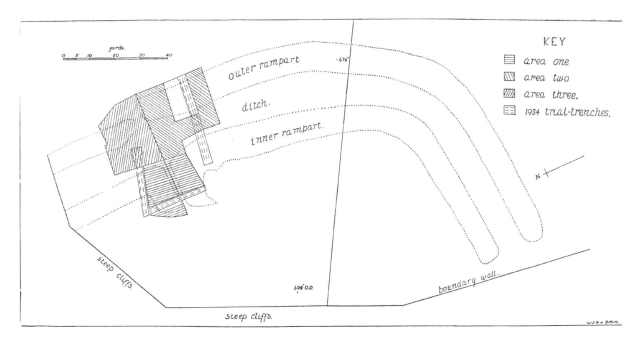

FIGURE 2.2 VARLEY'S PUBLISHED PLAN OF MAIDEN CASTLE SHOWING THE EXTENT OF HIS EXCAVATION TRENCHES (VARLEY 1936: FIG 1)

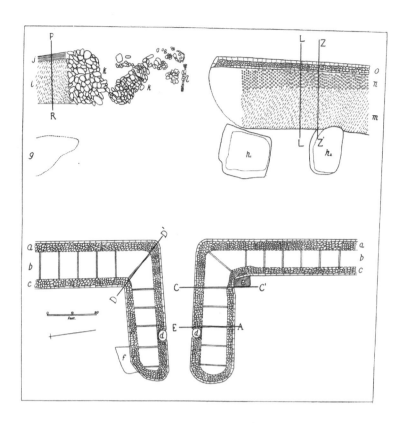

MAIDEN CASTLE. BICKERTON. PLAN OF AREA EXCAVATED IN 1935.

a. OUTER REVETMENT INNER RAMPART.
b. SAND AND TIMBER CORE.
c. INNER REVETMENT.
d. GATE-POST HOLES.
e. OCCUPATION FLOOR.
f. POSSIBLE OCCUPATION FLOOR.
g. ROCK OUTCROP.
h₁. & h₂. DITCH HOLLOWS.
i. SAND CORE OUTER RAMPART
NORTH OF ENTRANCE.

j. OUTER REVETMENT.
k. DISMANTLED RAMPART.
l. POSSIBLE END OF OUTER RAMPART.
m. SAND CORE OUTER RAMPART
SOUTH OF ENTRANCE.
n. RUBBLE ZONE
o. OUTER REVETMENT.
P.-R. D.-D.' ETC. LINES OF SECTION.

FIGURE 2.3 VARLEY'S PUBLISHED INTERPRETATIVE PLAN OF THE MAIN FEATURES IDENTIFIED AT MAIDEN CASTLE (VARLEY 1936).

type. The final enlarged fort included an extension to the northwestern end of the hill, with a new northwestern inturned entrance and the addition of a deep ditch outside the former counterscarp bank, making this in to a second rampart. The final phase of Eddisbury was attributed to between c.100 BC and AD 43 (*ibid.* 69).

Features of particular note with regard to Varley's plan of Eddisbury in the 1940 publication include a southwest entrance (Figures 2.7 and 2.8) and a counterscarp bank beyond the line of the northern ramparts which was made of earth with a stone revetment (Varley and Jackson 1940: 64–6). Amongst the black and white plates accompanying the text is an image of a circular stone structure located by the northwest hillfort entrance, labelled a 'Small Iron Age Hut' (Varley and Jackson 1940, Plate VIIA). There is also an image of a section through the inner ditch (Varley and Jackson 1940, Plate VIIB), which appears to suggest that it had been a segmental ditch created through the excavation of a series of compartments or pits (rather than as a continuous feature); although this was not commented on by the author.

The book also included a number of artefact illustrations relevant to the hillfort sites including a fragment

Site no.	Name	Altitude In feet O.D.	Area in square yards	Character
1	Bradley	120	9,482	Promontory camp defined by single ditch cutting off neck of land between two small tributaries of River Weaver. Without visible entrance.
2	Woodhouse Hill	483	17,670	Promontory camp defined by single rampart on eastern side cutting off scarp-bounded higher ground. Many breaks in rampart but no visible entrance.
3	Helsby Hill	450	20,250	Promontory camp defined by single rampart on eastern side cutting off scarp-bounded higher ground. No visible entrance.
4	Castle Ditch, Eddisbury	500	51,720	Contour-camp.
5	Kellsboro' Castle	400	43,238	Promontory camp defined by single ditch on eastern side cutting off scarp-bounded plateau. Ormerod's plan shows ramparts and breaks in ditch. No visible entrance.
6	Oakmere	260	18,964	Promontory camp defined by deep, irregular ditch lying between degraded ramparts, cutting off ground falling to eastern shore of Oakmere.
7	Maiden Castle Bickerton	694	14,488	Promontory camp defined by irregular ditch on east side, lying between two ramparts, cutting off scarp-bounded higher ground. Inturned entrance through inner rampart on north side.

FIGURE 2.4 THE HILLFORTS OF CHESHIRE (AFTER VARLEY AND JACKSON 1940: FIG 29).

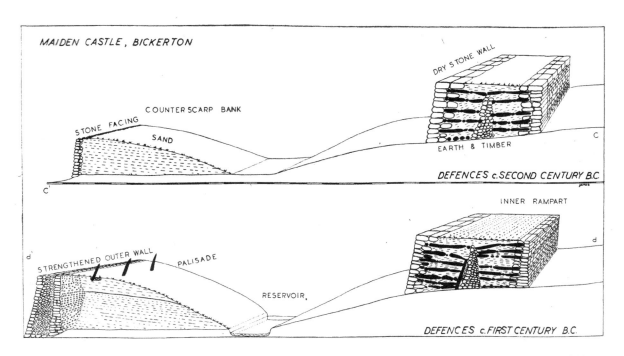

FIGURE 2.5 VARLEY'S PUBLISHED SECTIONS OF MAIDEN CASTLE SHOWING THE SCHEMATIC SECTIONS FIRST PUBLISHED IN 1940 (VARLEY AND JACKSON, 1940: FIG 12)

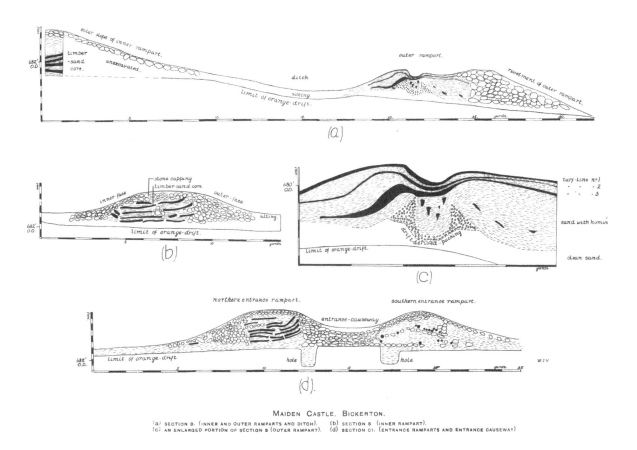

FIGURE 2.6 VARLEY'S ORIGINAL SECTIONS PUBLISHED IN 1936 (VARLEY, 1936).

of 'encrusted urn' from Eddisbury (*ibid*. figure 19E); this was the same fragment published by Shone and attributed to the cremation burials at the old quarry below the northeast side of the hillfort. Worked stone objects included 'The Beeston hoard' comprising a polished stone axe and a perforated stone axe-hammer (*ibid*. figure 3). Items of Bronze Age metalwork were illustrated in Appendix II and included: two looped and

and socketed spear heads from the cutting of the Manchester Ship Canal at Frodsham (*ibid*. figure 21.2); a looped and socketed spear from the 'missing' Broxton hoard (*ibid*. figure 21.3); and a palstave axe and chisel also from the Broxton hoard (*ibid*. figure 22a). The illustrations were mainly drawn by R. Gilyard-Beer and remain the only published illustrations of these objects.

Varley 1936–1938

The Castle Ditch, Eddisbury excavations 1936–8 (published 1950)

W. J. Varley's excavations at Castle Ditch, Eddisbury 1936–8 were eventually published in the Transactions of the Historic Society of Lancashire and Cheshire in 1950 (Varley 1950). In his preface, Varley states that both his excavations at Maiden Castle and Eddisbury were undertaken at the suggestion of Professor C. F. C. Hawkes 'to embark upon the systematic excavation of the hillforts of Cheshire'. Further detail is provided on the work force who were mainly volunteers from the clubs of the Occupational Centres Committee (Liverpool) who 'gave their labour to me from 8:30 am to 1 pm each working day, in return for which we fed, clothed, and housed them'; they were also allowed to continue to draw their benefits under several unemployment schemes at the time (Varley 1950: 1). Varley names himself as the overall director of the excavations and lists a number of assistants working with him, including his wife Joan Varley and the photographer Tom Jones; some assistance was given from Dr F. T. Wainwright in the final year (*op. cit.* 2).

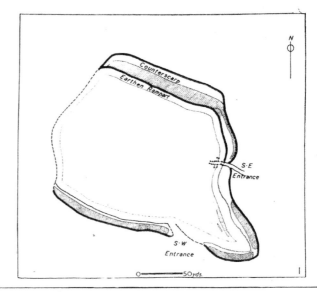

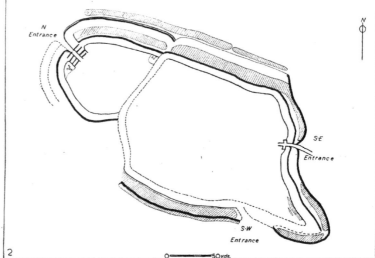

FIG. 8.   1. The original hill-fort at Eddisbury   W.J.V.
2. The reconstructed hill-fort at Eddisbury

(stone revetments solid black, ditches hatched)

FIGURE 2.7 VARLEY'S PUBLISHED PHASE PLAN FOR EDDISBURY
(VARLEY AND JACKSON, 1940: FIG 8)

The excavations consisted of four large trenches labelled 'Areas 1 to 4' and seven smaller trenches labelled 'a to g' (Figure 2.9). The locations of the four large areas were partly based upon the fact that much of the hillfort interior was down to crop during the summer seasons of excavation; however Varley listed specific reasons for the targeted locations as follows:

- Area 1 – the site of an entrance at the northwestern end of the earthworks;
- Area 2 – the junction between different parts of the earthworks;

- Area 3 – the suspected site of another entrance;
- Area 4 – 'Merrick's Hill' which had the remains of buildings protruding through the grass.

It is also stated that trenches a to e were only cut to confirm the nature and date of the earthwork with no special virtue attached to their siting; trenches f and g are omitted from the narrative. Varley did admit to certain failings in the excavation strategy, including not examining the hillfort interior owing to the presence of crops and not sectioning the defences on the southern side because they were scarped out of the rock. His main regret was not putting a section across the field boundary which bisected the summit of the plateau and formed the postulated northwestern limit of his 'original fort' (*op. cit.* 7).

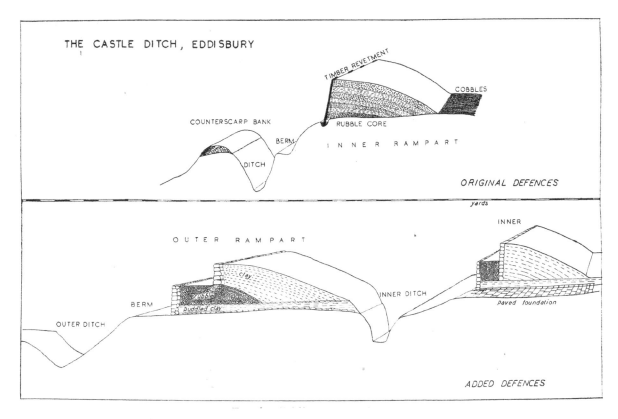

FIGURE 2.8 VARLEY'S PUBLISHED PLAN WITH SCHEMATIC SECTIONS THROUGH THE ORIGINAL AND ADDED DEFENCES
(VARLEY AND JACKSON, 1940: FIG 9)

The results suggested a series of different rampart construction phases spanning the prehistoric, Roman and Saxon periods:

- A timber palisade was suggested by two lengths of trench identified beneath a later rampart revetment in Area 4. Varley attributed this palisade phase to a date of *c.* 400–250 BC by analogy with other hillfort sites (Varley 1950: 52);
- The first hillfort defences formed a small univallate enclosure around the eastern half of the hill and consisted of an earth and stone inner rampart surrounded by a deep, narrow 'V' shaped ditch cut in to the solid rock. There was a length of counterscarp bank around the southeastern spur and a southeastern gap entrance with a guardroom on the south side. This phase was dated *c.* 200–100 BC; again through a series of suppositions rather than any firm dating evidence (*op. cit.* 53);
- The second hillfort defences extended the enclosure over the northwestern end of the hill and created a bi-vallate site. At this time an additional inturned entrance was added to the northwest, which was constructed with timber interlacing in the *murus gallicus* style (as seen at Maiden Castle). This phase was dated *c.* AD 1–50; again through a series of suppositions rather than any firm dating evidence (*op. cit.* 54–6);

- The hillfort defences were deliberately slighted: the southeastern entrance was blocked and sealed, the ditches filled up and the ramparts levelled to within a foot or so of their foundations. This was suggested to have been done by the Roman military in the late 1st century AD (*op. cit.* 57);
- The hillfort was re-occupied by a community that built huts over the ruined inner ramparts between the northwest entrance and the junction with the original defences in Area 2. The crude material culture associated with this occupation was definitely not Saxon and was attributed to the Dark Ages *c.* 4th to 6th centuries AD (*ibid.*).
- Later occupation was argued on the basis of a hut built over the inner ditch by the northwest entrance which produced an annular clay loom weight dating typologically to the 6th to 8th centuries AD (*op. cit.* 59);
- Reconstruction of the ramparts as evidenced in Area 2 was attributed to the Aethelflaedan burh documented in the Anglo Saxon Chronicle for the year AD 914 (*op. cit.* 61);
- Medieval and post-medieval occupation was reported at the southeastern end of the hilltop at Area 4 which is also known as 'Merrick's Hill' (*op. cit.* 63–8).

There are many inconsistencies within the Eddisbury report which have led a number of subsequent commentators to question its value (Cocroft *et al.* 1989); however, the most controversial part of the work centres on Area 2, the junction between the different parts of the earthworks (Figure 2.10 and 2.11). Varley used the evidence from Area 2 to support his theory about a primary hillfort only enclosing part of the hilltop, with a second larger hillfort being created by extending the ramparts to the northwest. Area 2 coincided with a change of alignment within the hillfort defences, which Varley suggested was either due to the presence of an entrance or two sets of defences built at separate times (Figure 2.10). The possibility of it being an entrance is quickly dismissed owing to there being no gap in the line of the outer ditch to facilitate one; however, there was a gap in the inner ditch but this was thought to be a feature of the later rampart extension. The stratigraphic relationships between the various sections of inner and outer rampart are discussed in terms of the extent of a stone pavement set in puddled clay, noted in this area (Varley 1950: 28) (Figure 2.12).

Details of particular note in Area 2 relate to the lower stratigraphic sequence of the outer rampart, consisting of an extensive pavement of flagstones set in puddled clay, a layer of puddled red clay, a layer of green clay and a second (less complete) layer of flagstones set in puddled clay. The upper layer of flagstones set in puddled clay was covered by a 'deposit of carbon-flecked, bone scattered occupation material devoid of relics except for masses of iron slag' (Varley 1950: 23). Varley's interpretation of the sequence was that everything beneath the 'occupation layer' was original and everything above it belonged to a later reconstruction (*op. cit.* 24). This occupation deposit was also identified on the inner rampart, where it was associated with a circular hut kerb and a hearth; the deposit here produced 'a great deal of pottery of peculiar and distinctive nature, which I [Varley] attribute to the Dark Ages' (*op. cit.* 28). Based upon this observation Varley suggested that the reconstruction of the inner and outer ramparts dated to the Aethelflaedan burh of AD 914. These details are significant in the re-

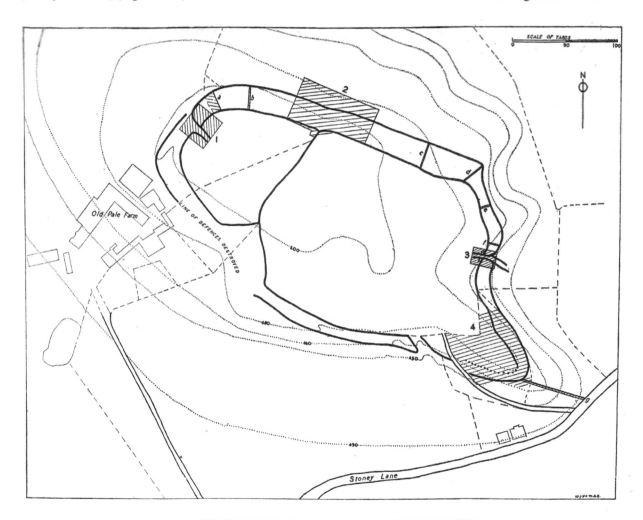

FIG. 3 : A CONTOURED PLAN OF EDDISBURY HILL.

Note.—The heavy lines denote ramparts. The areas of excavation are shown by hatching and are either enumerated 1, 2, 3 or 4 or lettered a to e.

FIGURE 2.9 VARLEY'S PUBLISHED PLAN SHOWING THE LOCATIONS OF HIS EXCAVATION TRENCHES (VARLEY 1950: 8). REPRODUCED COURTESY OF THE TRANSACTIONS OF THE HISTORIC SOCIETY OF LANCASHIRE AND CHESHIRE.

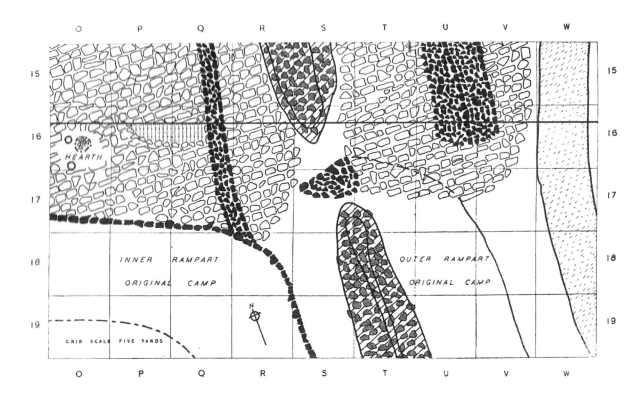

FIGURE 2.10 VARLEY'S PUBLISHED PLAN OF AREA 2 EDDISBURY (VARLEY 1950:24 FIG 8). REPRODUCED COURTESY OF THE TRANSACTIONS OF THE HISTORIC SOCIETY OF LANCASHIRE AND CHESHIRE.

FIGURE 2.11 VIEW OF VARLEY'S EXCAVATIONS IN AREA 2 LOOKING EAST (FROM THE COLLECTION OF THE LATE SANDY CAMPBELL).

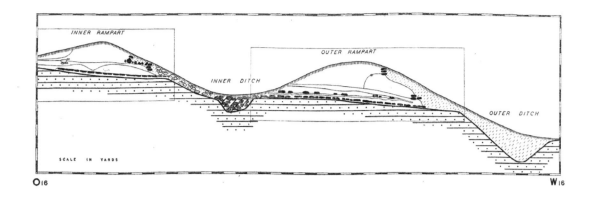

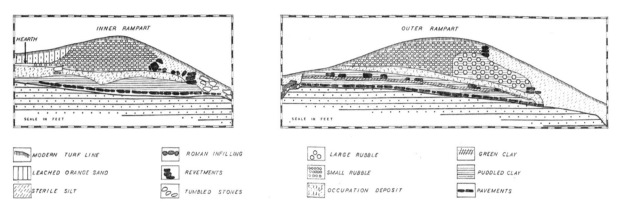

FIGURE 2.12 VARLEY'S SECTION THROUGH THE INNER AND OUTER RAMPARTS IN AREA 2 EDDISBURY (VARLEY 1950: 25 FIG 9).
REPRODUCED COURTESY OF THE TRANSACTIONS OF THE HISTORIC SOCIETY OF LANCASHIRE AND CHESHIRE.

examination of the Varley excavations at Eddisbury (See Garner, Chapter 10; Mason and Pope, Chapter 11, this volume).

The report deviates from the interim information published by Varley in 1940 (Varley and Jackson 1940) in that there is no longer any reference to a southwestern entrance and the small stone hut circle by the northwest entrance is now attributed to the Dark Ages (Varley 1950: 20–21). The report contains no proper finds section and none of the finds are illustrated, a fact that was compounded by the seeming disappearance of the entire Varley archive for both Maiden Castle and Eddisbury in subsequent years (see Mason and Pope, Chapter 4, this volume).

Varley 1964

Varley and Jackson's *Prehistoric Cheshire* saw only one edition because enemy bombing during World War II destroyed all the blocks and types from the first edition. By 1964 the Community Council approached William Varley to rewrite and update the original work and this was published under the title *Cheshire Before the Romans*. The book was more of a discussion of archaeological theory and artefacts in the UK as a whole with Cheshire designated as an area of little consequence (Morgan and Morgan 2004: 10). As with

the 1940 publication, Varley included a section on hillforts with a specific sub-heading of 'Cheshire Hill Forts'. This was a misnomer as the discussion only covered Maiden Castle and Eddisbury from the Cheshire forts with the hillforts of Almondbury (Yorkshire) and Old Oswestry (Shropshire) also included, because they were other sites that had been investigated by Varley. The book is notable for containing the only illustrations of Iron Age pottery from Maiden Castle and Eddisbury ever published (Varley 1964, figure 38), although the illustrations have been republished subsequently (Matthews 2002).

Webster and Powell 1949–51

Graham Webster (then based at the Grosvenor Museum, Chester) and Thomas Powell undertook a small excavation at Woodhouse hillfort in 1949, in an area where the rampart had been eroded by a well-used footpath on to the hilltop. The excavation however, consisted of little more than trimming back the eroded rampart to establish a formal section. It was reported that the section revealed a box-type rampart, revetted at the front and rear with stone walling. A 'hut' was also reported as being discovered during the excavation although this may have been a house platform of medieval or post-medieval date (OAN 2008a).

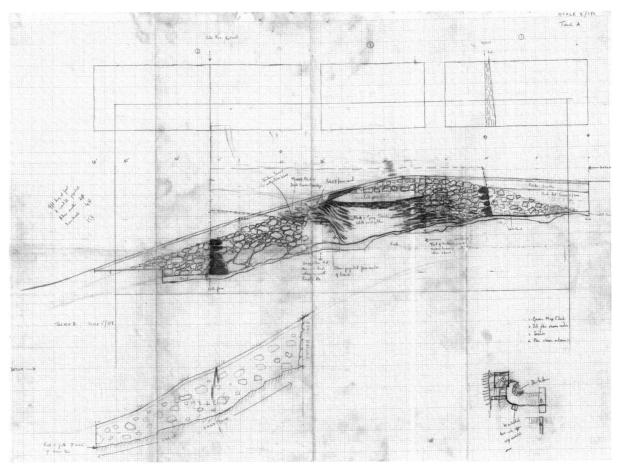

FIGURE 2.13 FORDE-JOHNSTON'S UNPUBLISHED PLAN AND SECTIONS FROM HIS EXCAVATIONS AT HELSBY 1963–4.

Bu'Lock 1955

A single excavation trench was opened on Helsby hillfort by James Bu'Lock (University of Manchester) in 1955, and the results were published as a three page article in the Transactions of the Lancashire and Cheshire Antiquarian Society the following year (Bu'Lock 1956). The trench was positioned to investigate a subsidiary bank on a stone ledge below the northern end of the hilltop, as excavation of a trench across the main ramparts of the fort was considered to be too formidable a task (Bu'Lock 1956: 108–9). The trench revealed a box-style rampart with front and rear stone revetments containing a core of rubble and sand. An occupation layer to the rear of the rampart contained charcoal and burnt stone which were interpreted as 'pot-boilers' (*ibid.*).

Forde-Johnston 1960–64

Between 1960 and 1962 James Forde-Johnston (Manchester Museum) carried out surveys of twelve hillforts in Lancashire and Cheshire including Helsby, Woodhouse, Eddisbury, Kelsborrow and Maiden Castle (Forde-Johnston 1962). He later published these in his book *Hillforts of the Iron Age in England and Wales: A Survey of the Surface Evidence* in 1976. In the preface

to the book he states that his original intention had been to take account of both surface and excavation evidence, but it soon became clear that this was too large an undertaking and his attention was confined thereafter to the surface evidence (Forde-Johnston 1976: v).

In 1963–64 Forde-Johnston undertook excavations at Helsby hillfort which included a trench across the inner rampart in the southwestern area of the fort; a trench within the entrance; and a trench against the outside of the inner rampart near the entrance. These excavations were never published but were described in letters which are held in the archives of the National Trust North West Region (OAN 2008a, 18). The main archive consists of an annotated plan and section drawing in pencil on graph paper (Figure 2.13).

The results of the excavations suggested that the main rampart consisted of an inner and outer stone revetment with a timber-laced core. No evidence for a ditch was encountered and Forde-Johnston maintained that there was no outer rampart either. No artefacts were recovered from the excavations and radiocarbon dating was not commonly used at the time. However, a tentative early Iron Age date was suggested on the grounds of the rampart style.

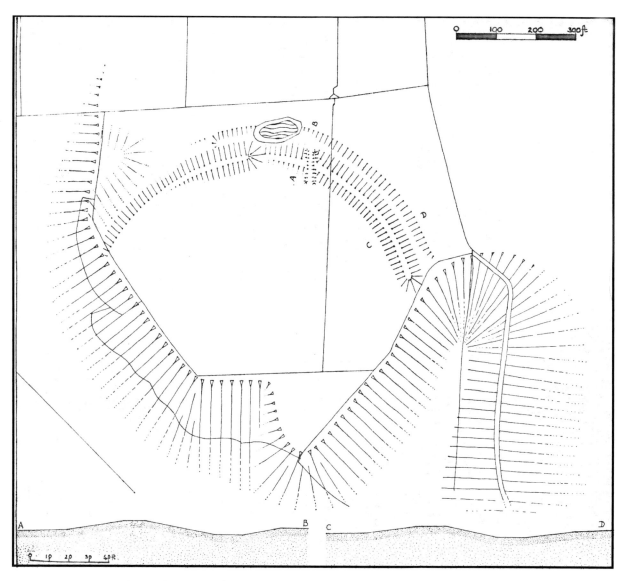

FIGURE 2.14 LONGLEY'S PUBLISHED PLAN OF KELSBORROW HILLFORT (LONGLEY 1979)

Coombs 1973

In June 1973, David Coombs (University of Manchester) excavated a section across the bank at Kelsborrow hillfort, immediately to the east of the field boundary hedge which cuts across the monument (Coombs 1988). The interior of the fort and any suspected entrances were not investigated and the trench was too narrow to provide anything beyond a cross-section through the rampart. The subsequent report was not published until 1988 and this was not comprehensive, only including a plan with no section drawing. The results described a line of three postholes running from the front to the back of the rampart which were interpreted as evidence for a timber revetment (*op. cit.* 65–6); the core of the rampart was a fine-grained white sand. The trench also encountered the edge of an outer ditch. No artefacts were recovered from the excavation and radiocarbon dating was not attempted.

Longley 1979

David Longley carried out topographic surveys of Helsby, Woodhouse, Eddisbury, Kelsborrow and Maiden Castle in 1979 and versions of these were later published in the first volume of the Victoria County History of Chester, in Longley's section on Prehistory (Longley 1987: 106). The plan of Kelsborrow hillfort produced by Longley in 1979 (Longley 1979: 53) shows a north-south linear feature cutting across the width of the rampart on the southeast side of the pond (Figure 2.14); this feature may have been detected during the Archaeophysica resistivity survey (see Chapter 6, this volume). For some time, this feature had been assumed to be associated with livestock erosion; however, during the Habitats and Hillforts Project, the landowner, Mike Hardy, produced an annotated plan from his family archives, which suggested the feature represented a formal excavation trench undertaken on the 8 April 1938 (Figure 2.15). This event is not recorded anywhere else, but the timing would fit with William Varley's last season of excavations at Eddisbury hillfort and it might have been a precursor to plans for more extensive excavations, following completion of his work at Eddisbury (thwarted by the outbreak of World War II).

Beeston Castle excavations 1968–73 and 1975–85

Two separate programmes of excavation were carried out at Beeston Castle, the first of which was directed by Laurence Keen between 1968 and 1973. These were primarily motivated by The Ministry of Public Works and Buildings who had been tasked with consolidating the structure of the medieval castle and preparing the monument for public access. The work was initially carried out using a labour force of ground-workers employed by the castle curator, as well as borstal and prison inmates supervised by archaeologists; later the work was carried out by a team of archaeologists. The second programme of excavation was undertaken between 1975 and 1985 under the direction of Peter Hough and a geophysical survey was conducted as part of the investigations in 1981 by Alister Bartlett. The results of both of the programmes of excavation were brought together as a single monograph edited by Peter Ellis and published in 1993 (Ellis 1993).

The results of this work demonstrated that the hilltop had evidence of archaeological features and artefacts dating from the Mesolithic onwards. The results suggested a series of different rampart construction phases:

- A linear series of postholes were found to the east of the medieval curtain wall in the large outer gateway trench and these were interpreted as a possible late Bronze Age palisade;
- Overlying these postholes was a bank of sand and stone. Traces of charred timbers within this bank might have suggested the presence of timber lacing and this wood charcoal produced a radiocarbon date of 1300–840 cal BC (2860±80 BP; HAR-4405) at the two sigma range (Ellis 1993: 87). The presence of two Ewart Park-type socketed bronze axes, found within the bank, suggest a date of 900–700 cal BC (Needham 1993: 45); it was thought that these objects might have been buried as a foundation deposit. This phase was attributed to Period 2B in the structural narrative;

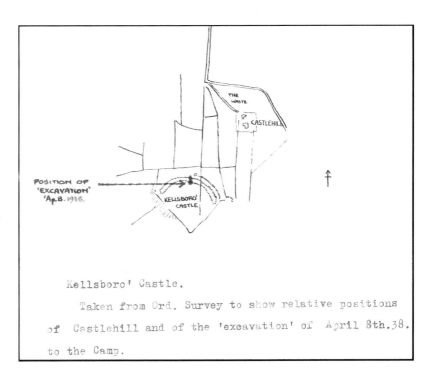

FIGURE 2.15 ANNOTATED PLAN OF THE 1938 EXCAVATION TRENCH AT KELSBORROW HILLFORT (COURTESY OF MIKE HARDY)

- The original Period 2B bank was buried beneath layers of sand to create a larger bank that was associated with the cutting of an outer ditch which terminated to the north of the medieval castle entrance. The primary fill of the ditch produced a radiocarbon date of 791–410 cal BC (2480±70 BP; HAR-8102) at one sigma (Macphail 1993: 84) suggesting a date in the early Iron Age. The upper deposits of the larger bank produced a La Tene I type dagger dated 450–325 BC. This phase was attributed to Period 3A in the structural narrative;
- The rampart bank was enlarged further with a line of stone boulders delineating the inner and outer edges of the bank and probably serving as revetments. A series of four postholes appeared to form part of a timber superstructure extending along and behind the rampart and the rampart core displayed signs of burning and vitrification. The postholes might be interpreted as evidence for an inturned entrance. Archaeomagnetic dates associated with the burnt stone around the postholes were 360–240 cal BC and 400–200 cal BC (Ellis 1993: 85–6). This phase was attributed to Period 3B in the structural narrative.

Aside from the evidence for a succession of rampart defences there were a total of 146 postholes excavated within the outer ward of the castle associated with late Bronze Age and Iron Age activity, although most of these were not closely dated (Ellis 1993: 35). Many of these postholes were thought to be associated with circular structures and at least nine buildings were suggested by the posthole alignments (*ibid.*). The excavations also produced a visible material culture with late Bronze Age pottery and Iron Age VCP (Very Coarse Pottery) being recovered from the hillfort interior along with additional items of metalwork, shale bracelets, saddle querns and a glass bead. Metal working of bronze and iron was also evidenced along with charred cereals suggestive of crop processing and storage. The results from Beeston Castle represent the most comprehensive and best dated evidence for late Bronze Age and Iron Age occupation so far published from any site in Cheshire.

Taylor 1980–81

In 1980 and 1981 Joan Taylor (University of Liverpool) undertook excavations at the southern end of the hillfort defences at Maiden Castle in advance of repairs to the ramparts, following erosion caused by pedestrian traffic along the footpath on the Sandstone Ridge, known as the Sandstone Trail. These excavations were small scale and intended to investigate burnt wood within the rampart which had become exposed. Samples were taken for magnetic susceptibility and thermoluminesence as well as pollen analysis and radiocarbon dating (Taylor 1980: 34–6). The overall results of the excavations have not been published, but a preliminary report was published by Taylor in 1980 and the results of the magnetic susceptibility analyses were compiled as an undergraduate dissertation at the University of Liverpool in 1982 (Krawieki 1982). Samples of carbonised wood were taken from the inner rampart and produced three radiocarbon dates (2350±60 BP; UB-2617), (2360±100 BP; UB-2618) and (2620±95 BP; UB-2619), which were calibrated by Matthews to 860–330 cal BC at two sigma (Matthews 2002: 5). Radiocarbon dating of samples of carbonised wood from the outer rampart produced two dates of 770–400 cal BC (2435±70 BP; UB-2615) and 380–10 cal BC (2130±70 BP; UB-2614) at two sigma as calibrated by Matthews (2002: 5).

The Eddisbury Topographic survey 1987

The Keele office of the Royal Commission on the Historical Monuments of England (RCHME) carried out a 1:1000 scale survey of Eddisbury hillfort in 1987. The results of this survey prompted a reappraisal of Varley's earlier interpretations regarding the constructional sequence of the site (Cocroft *et al.* 1989). This proposed that the whole plateau was enclosed by a univallate rampart which featured entrances to the north, northwest and east. A second rampart was then added on the northeast part of the hillfort and subsequently the fort was equipped with an outer rampart and ditch

around most of the circuit. The gap in the inner ditch, at the point where Varley suggested that the original and extended defences met, could therefore be an entrance (Cocroft *et al.* 1989: 135).

Quarterman 1996

A resistivity survey was undertaken at Kelsborrow hillfort by Alistair Quarterman in 1996 as part of his undergraduate dissertation at the University of Liverpool. This comprised a survey area of 2,160m² within the western part of the hillfort including the rampart and ditch. The results of the survey were summarised by Matthews (2002: 5–7). The survey provided further data regarding the extent of the bank and ditch of the rampart, as well as the suggestion of pits and structures on the interior. An entrance might be indicated by a gap in the bank and ditch roughly half way along the length of the rampart (*op. cit.* 7).

Rawson 1996–97

A resistivity and contour survey was undertaken at Helsby hillfort by S. Rawson, whilst a student at the University of Manchester, between 1996 and 1997. These surveys targeted the line of the possible outer rampart and a band of low resistance was observed that corresponded to a cropmark. The results are interpreted as possibly representing a ditch or palisade trench (OAN 2008a: 18).

Jecock 2006

A rapid field survey and assessment of the hillfort at Woodhouse were undertaken by Marcus Jecock in 2006 on behalf of English Heritage. The possible entranceway and the irregular form of the rampart were both ascribed to the effects of later quarrying, erosion, forestry and stone robbing at the site (Jecock 2006: 7–9). The defensive nature of the site was questioned by Jecock who observed that the site was situated in a dip slope, which would have exposed the interior of the hillfort to inspection from the eastern side.

Discussion

The research on the hillforts of Cheshire, undertaken prior to the Habitats and Hillforts Project, established a body of data which was reviewed and re-assessed in various attempts to develop our understanding of these sites in the prehistoric period. Excavations from the 1930s had focused on the ramparts and entrances of the hillforts and had established their structural composition and sequence of development. Dating and phasing of sites was based on the prevailing interpretations of the time. It was not until the excavations at Beeston Castle, between the 1960s and 1980s and the use of radiocarbon dating, that the early origin of some of these enclosed hilltops was recognised, when it was established that this was a hillfort which had its origins in the late

Bronze Age. Little was known about the interiors of the hillforts, although excavation at Beeston revealed traces of structures on the interior, whilst geophysical survey hinted at structures inside other hillforts.

In a relatively recent review of Iron Age studies the areas of Cumbria, Lancashire and Cheshire were described as a 'black hole' regarding the current state of archaeological knowledge (Haselgrove *et al.* 2001: 25). The archaeological research framework for North West England identified that there were only a few hillforts in the region and only a limited number had been examined through excavation or dated using radiocarbon techniques (Hodgson and Brennand *et al.* 2007: 51). The priority for future study of these monuments needed to include excavation of sites using a suite of scientific and artefactual analyses. This needed to be accompanied with attempting to place the hillforts within a wider context of landscape use and division. In particular, it was noted that there were only limited dating controls for many pollen diagrams in the south of the region, making it impossible to distinguish between episodes of clearance and farming from the Iron Age and Romano-British periods (*ibid*).

Chapter 3
The Lithic Collection from the area around Woodhouse Hillfort, Frodsham

Ian Brooks

Introduction

A large number of flint and chert artefacts were collected from fields in the general vicinity of Woodhouse hillfort, near Frodsham, in the 1950s by J. Adams. The assemblage demonstrates that this part of the Sandstone Ridge acted as a focus for prehistoric settlement from the early Mesolithic.[1] Unfortunately the original records associated with the collection are somewhat lacking; however, the majority of the artefacts have been labelled with a site name, and sometimes a date, which allows the collection to be separated into nineteen possible groups (Figure 3.1).

The majority of the artefacts can be assigned to a single site, that at Harrol Edge. Slightly more detail about this site is available in a partial text from the initial collection in 1953 that survives in the Cheshire Historic Environment Record (CHER) (Adams 1953). The precise location and extent of the other sites is uncertain, with the possible exception of Woodhouse Hill, which presumably relates to the immediate environs of the hillfort. It is also not certain whether some of the groups can be combined. For example, there are artefacts labelled 'Alvanley Fields',

'Alvanley Cliff Area' and 'Alvanley Cliff Fields', all of which are presumably in the same area, but precisely how these sites relate to one another is not recorded. In addition to the labelled artefacts, there are also 171 that are unlabelled and 32 which, although unlabelled, are probably from Harrol Edge on the basis of the raw material and the style of knapping.

Some estimate of the extent of the survey area can be can be estimated by examination of the Ordnance Survey 1:2500 Explorer map. Alvanley Cliff is marked at SJ 513737, Riley Bank at SJ 519745, Woodhouse Hill at SJ 511758, Kingswood Cottage at SJ 533727 and the hamlet of Manley at SJ 509716. The area covered, therefore, appears to extend east and south of Woodhouse Hill, covering an area of approximately 4km x 2km (Figure 3.2).

The methods of collection are unknown. It would seem unlikely that a systematic collection policy was adopted for all of the assemblages; rather, it is likely to have varied from site to site. Whilst the assemblage from Harrol Edge includes a range of knapping debris including a range of spalls, suggesting that intensive collection took place, others, such as that from Riley Bank Farm, contain a higher proportion of tools and larger artefacts than would normally be expected; a selective collection policy was probably adopted and thus these assemblages do not reflect the full potential range of material from the sites.

A mixture of flint and chert artefacts are represented within the collection. Flint is not natural to the survey area, with the nearest deposits of chalk containing flint being those of the Lincolnshire/ Yorkshire Wolds or Northern Ireland (Rawson *et al.* 1978). The Irish Sea Till and its associated gravels, however, also contain a limited number of flint nodules that could be a potential source for prehistoric groups (Mackintosh 1879). One of the concentrations of flint resources within the deposits associated with the Irish Sea Till recognised by Mackintosh in his survey of erratics of western England and eastern Wales was the valley of the River Weaver to the east of the survey area (*ibid.* 1879; Brooks 1989: 198). Chert deposits outcrop in the Carboniferous Limestones of the Peak District (Hind 1998) and those bounding both sides of the Vale of Clwyd (Berridge 1994: 95). These Welsh cherts are sometimes referred to as 'Gronant chert', although more strictly they are part of the Pentre Chert Formation.

Label	Flint	Chert	Total
399	1	0	1
A G Field	1	0	1
Alvanley Fields	7	0	7
Alvanley Cliff Area	1	0	1
Alvanley Cliff Fields	1	0	1
Aston	1	0	1
Close to Harrol Edge	4	0	4
Cross Roads Field	1	0	1
Harrol Edge	1428	135	1563
Kingswood	0	1	1
Manley	5	0	5
Norms? Waste Farm	1	0	1
Riley Bank Farm	76	1	77
Riley Bank Farm Field number 4	1	0	1
Shepherd House Field	1	0	1
Town Lane Field	3	0	3
Unlabelled probably Harrol Edge	26	6	32
Unlabelled	171	0	171
Woodhouse Hill	20	0	20
Total	**1749**	**143**	**1892**

FIGURE 3.1 SUMMARY OF SITES

---

[1] The assemblage was donated to the Grosvenor Museum in 1957 and given the accession code 75.P.57 (CHER 1023).

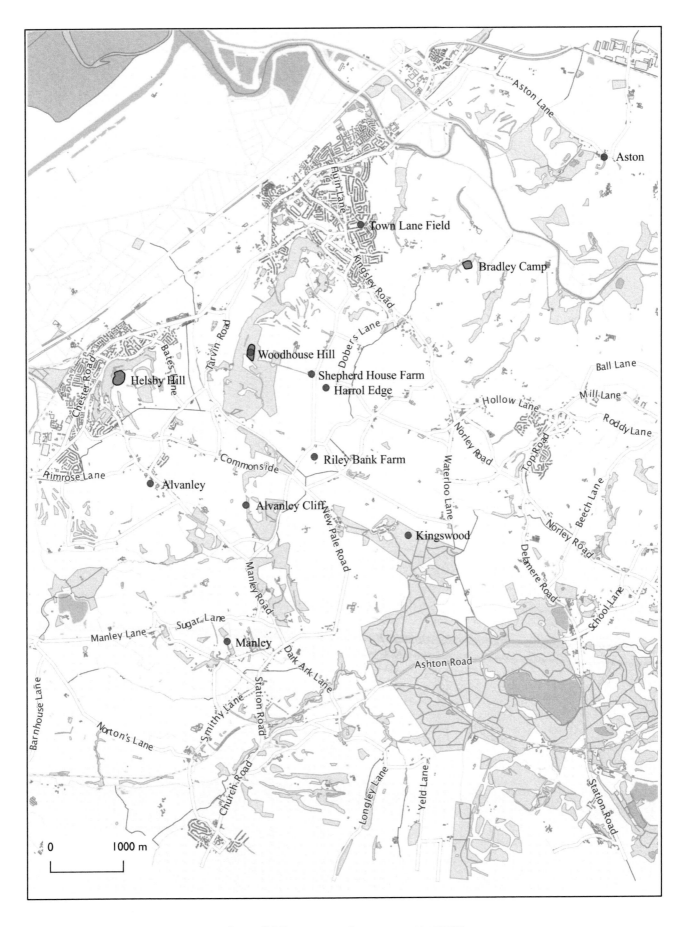

FIGURE 3.2 EXTENT OF THE ADAMS LITHIC COLLECTION

Harrol Edge

Harrol Edge is centred on SJ 52187544 and extends over an area of between 0.4 and 0.6ha (Adams 1953; Leah *et al*. 1997: 146). The note held by the CHER (Adams 1953) locates the main concentration to the east of Shepherd's House, with a marked concentration along the eastern field boundary.

A total of 1563 artefacts was labelled 'Harrol Edge', and a further 32, although unlabelled, are probably from Harrol Edge (26 of flint and 6 chert), based on the raw materials used and the style of knapping exhibited. It is assumed that the assemblage is the result of fieldwalking over a number of years, although Latham, (1987: 11) suggests there may have been an excavation on the site. If so, the artefacts are not labelled with any context information and no excavations records are known to exist.

The majority of the assemblage was of flint, although 135 artefacts (8.6%) were of a dark Carboniferous chert. The flint that dominates the assemblage is distinctive, with a series of dark and lighter bands. Whilst the texture of this material is a little coarse, it is not coarse enough to be the banded Gronant chert. Where the cortex survives it is worn, suggesting that it was collected from a derived source such as a till or gravel. The Carboniferous chert could have been imported to the site either from the Peak District or from North Wales (Hind 1998), both of which have suitable deposits. However, the macroscopic appearance of the chert used at Harrol Edge would suggest that Peak District sources are the most likely to have been exploited here, although North Wales cannot be ruled out.

The bulk of the assemblage consists of a range of flakes, blades and cores. The number of blades and blade fragments (232, 63 in dark chert) and the presence of a single crested flake in dark chert give an indication of the level of controlled knapping; their size suggests a late Mesolithic date for the majority. One of the cores was reused as a small hammerstone. The recovery of 246 spalls gives an indication of the intensive level of collection, which would appear to have been greater than on any of the other sites.

A total of 34 tools was recovered, largely of banded flint, the vast majority being fairly crude, small scrapers (Figures 3.3a and b, nos 1 and 2). The size and morphology of these tools suggest that they are largely late Mesolithic. It is noticeable that only one of the scrapers is of Carboniferous chert, with the rest being either banded flint or small pebbles of flint, probably from the Irish Sea Till or its derived gravels. The remainder of the tool assemblage contains small numbers of a range of tools and retouched pieces. Three truncated blades, eight small retouched fragments and a possible awl (Figures 3.3a and b, no. 4) are probably contemporary with the majority of the assemblage. However, a few artefacts suggest some later activity within the area. These include a plano-convex knife (Figures 3.3a and b, no. 3) and the fragment of a leaf-shaped arrowhead, both of which suggest a Neolithic presence. The arrowhead fragment is notable because it is made of dark, opaque chert of Peak District type.

Only one microlith was found, an obliquely blunted point on the distal fragment of a blade, together with a single microburin. However, the number of cores and worked lumps from the site (31 cores, 125 worked lumps) suggests that the production of microliths was being carried out on the site. The form and size of the one microlith collected would suggest an early Mesolithic component to the assemblage. An early Mesolithic presence may also be reflected in the marked difference in size between the cores of dark Carboniferous chert and those of banded flint. Only seven cores of dark chert were found, but they are much larger than those of flint, as are in many cases the blades struck from them. However, it is also possible that this difference reflects the size of the raw materials collected rather than a temporal/functional difference.

The assemblage is a good example of how not to treat lithics. Part of the assemblage had evidently been on display before being donated to the Grosvenor Museum and had been stuck to a hessian backing with epoxy resin, remains of which still adhere to some of the artefacts. Probably at a similar time some of the tools, particularly the scrapers, had their flake scars outlined in ink (Figures 3.3a and b, no. 2), although whether for display or as an aid for illustration is uncertain; this makes the reinterpretation of the knapping pattern very difficult.

Riley Bank Farm

The next largest group is labelled 'Riley Bank Farm'. A total of 77 artefacts was assigned to this group, all of which, except one, were of flint. The flint used for this group is different from that encountered at Harrol Edge, varying from an opaque light grey (N7) to a translucent light yellowish brown (10 YR 2/2). Where it survives, the cortex of all of the raw materials is worn, suggesting that a derived flint source was being exploited. It is most likely that this was the Irish Sea Till or one of its derived gravels, probably relatively local.

Unlike the Harrol Edge assemblage, this group is dominated by tools and other retouched pieces, with a total of 28 tools recorded. These include a hollow-based obliquely blunted point microlith, three leaf-shaped arrowheads (two of which are broken), a transverse arrowhead, a button scraper, two thumbnail scrapers, a core scraper, seven end scrapers, three side scrapers, two side/end scrapers and a point. In addition there are six flakes with some retouch and a truncated blade segment.

This is clearly not a consistent assemblage. No small fragments or spalls are present, suggesting that this is a selection of larger and retouched artefacts. The assemblage also spans several periods. The presence of a microlith suggests a level of early Mesolithic activity. However, the three leaf-shaped arrowheads and the transverse arrowhead are clearly of Neolithic forms (Green 1984: 19). The one complete leaf-shaped arrowhead (Figures 3.3a and b, no. 7) is small (14.3mm long) and squat (17.5mm wide) and corresponds to Green's group 4A (*ibid*. 21). The scrapers range in form, also suggesting a wide temporal spread amongst the assemblage. One large end scraper on a very high-quality translucent flint is probably early Neolithic (Figures 3.3a and b, no. 5). This artefact was labelled as Upper Palaeolithic by Adams, but there are no diagnostic artefacts of this date in the collection, and an early Neolithic date is more likely. Six of the scrapers (e.g. Figures 3.3a and b, no. 6) are small, well made and of forms which are classically assigned to the late Neolithic or early Bronze Age, particularly those with Beaker associations (Butler 2005: 168). Similar small scrapers can also occur in late Mesolithic contexts, but they tend to be less well made and not as rounded as the early Bronze Age forms (*ibid*. 105).

Woodhouse Hill

Twenty of the artefacts are labelled 'Woodhouse Hill', all of flint. The range of flint raw materials used in this group is similar to that from the 'Riley Bank Farm' group, and it is assumed that the same or similar derived sources were being exploited. Once again there is a predominance of retouched elements and tools within the group, with seven (45% of the assemblage) tools being recognised. These include an awl, three scrapers, a triangular arrowhead, a backed blade and a retouched fragment. A general impression of a largely late Neolithic or early Bronze Age assemblage is given by this group, although the backed blade (Figures 3.3a and c, no. 10) is probably early Neolithic in its associations. Once again, Adams labelled this artefact as possibly Upper Palaeolithic. Whilst it has some characteristics similar to some Upper Palaeolithic points (Butler 2005: 77; Pettitt and White 2012: 437), the damage along the leading edge is more consistent with use as a knife; interpretation as a large blade suggests an early Neolithic date.

Other Sites

The other sites in the collection (Figure 3.1) have very few artefacts associated with them, probably reflecting the casual acquisition of artefacts, rather than a systematic programme of research. There are also, however, a further 171 artefacts which are unlabelled and whose associations cannot be determined. This group contains 21 tools covering a wide temporal range. These tools include a broken, leaf-shaped arrowhead (Figures 3.3a and c, no. 8), a broken transverse arrowhead, the

fragment of an object with ripple flaking (probably an arrowhead fragment) (Figures 3.3a and c, no. 9), seven scrapers, two notches, two obliquely blunted points and six retouched or truncated flake or blade fragments. The presence of the obliquely blunted points would suggest an early Mesolithic component to the collection, whilst the arrowheads and scrapers are more consistent with a Neolithic to early Bronze Age date. The unlabelled group also contained 129 flakes or flake fragments and 20 worked lumps. As this component is missing from the other groups in the collection except Harrol Edge, it is possible that these artefacts were recovered from the other sites and that their labelling has been lost.

Two artefacts labelled 'Alvanley Cliff Area' and 'Alvanley Cliff Fields' are distinctive within the collection as being much larger than most of those collected. Whilst suitably sized nodules can occasionally be found within the Irish Sea Till and its associated gravel, it is possible that the flint for these two items may have been imported from further afield. The artefact labelled 'Alvanley Cliff' is a plano-convex knife of early Neolithic type (Figures 3.3a and c, no. 11). It is on an opaque grey flint, similar to the backed blade from Woodhouse Hill. Although flint of this type is known from the Irish Sea Till, it is more typical of that from the Lincolnshire/Yorkshire Wolds (Brooks 1989; Henson 1985). The artefact labelled 'Alvanley Cliff Fields' is a large tertiary flake with retouch along both of its sides forming a converging proximal end to this tool (Figures 3.3a and c, no. 12). This point is not sharp enough to be a piercer or awl; the damage would suggest it may have been use as a punch. Its size would suggest that it may be Neolithic in date.

Discussion

The Sandstone Ridge to the south of Frodsham would appear to have served as a focus for prehistoric activity, with elements from the early Mesolithic to the early Bronze Age represented within the collection. By far the largest group is that from Harrol Edge, which is largely Mesolithic with both early and late Mesolithic elements represented. Adams's is not the only fieldwalking campaign in the area. More recently Mayer carried out a programme of fieldwalking in the early 1990s over a very similar area. Although the project is yet to be published, an initial note on the first season's work suggests that a similar concentration of Mesolithic material was located at Castle Cob (Mayer 1990: 50), approximately 2.5km south of Harrol Edge, on a high point of the Sandstone Ridge. Cowell (1992: 6) also extended his fieldwalking programmes on the Wirral into north Cheshire, concentrating on an area of approximately 120ha around Sutton Weaver, in the valley of the River Weaver to the east of the Sandstone Ridge. This defined at least two possible areas of Mesolithic activity: one southeast of Aston, and the other at Sutton Weaver (*ibid*. 7).

Various stray finds and small collections, particularly of Mesolithic materials, have also been noted, both within the immediate area around Frodsham (Longley 1987: 37; Anon 1953; Anon 1975) and further south on the Sandstone Ridge, particularly at Ashton (Hodgson and Brennand 2006: 27; Morgan and Morgan 2004: 19). The attraction of the Ridge, particularly at its northern end, is clear. It provides panoramic views, particularly to the north over the lowlands of the Mersey and would have allowed the exploitation of a wide range of resources over a wide range of environments, with both the relative

uplands of the Sandstone Ridge and the wetlands of the Mersey easily accessible.

One of the key features of the collection is the types of raw materials used. The late Mesolithic component of the Harrol Edge assemblage is dominated by the use of a banded flint. This has somewhat variable knapping characteristics and probably would not have been the first choice if practical factors had been the sole consideration. The source of this material is not known but it does appear to have been preferentially selected. A similar pattern is hinted at by Mayer (1990: 48) for

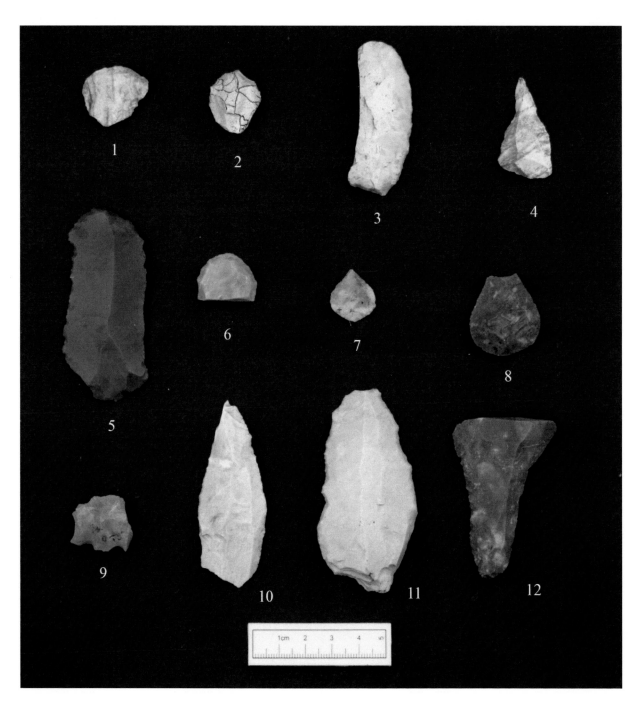

FIGURE 3.3A SELECTED LITHICS FROM THE ADAMS ASSEMBLAGE

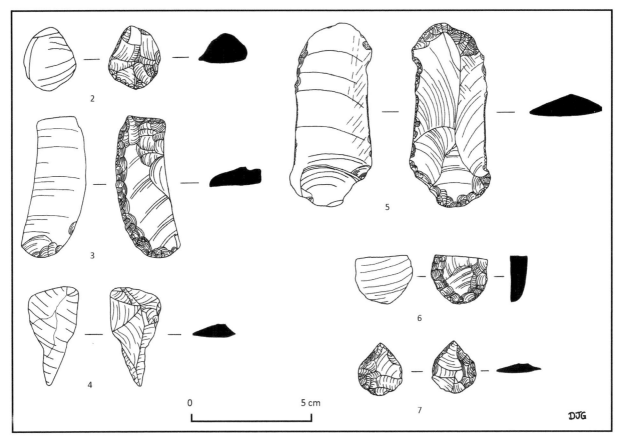

FIGURE 3.3B SELECTED LITHICS FROM THE ADAMS ASSEMBLAGE

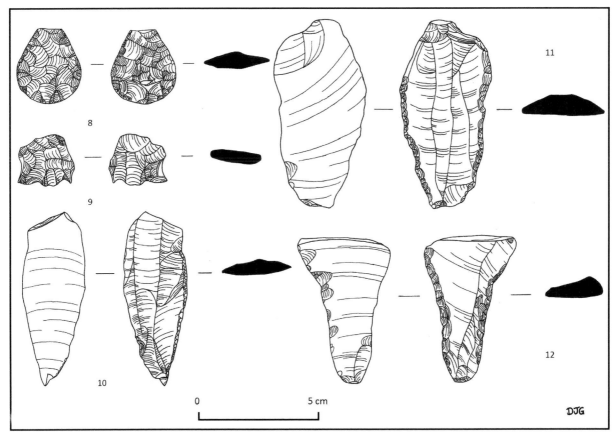

FIGURE 3.3C SELECTED LITHICS FROM THE ADAMS ASSEMBLAGE

27

other areas on the northern Sandstone Ridge. The use of imported chert at Harrol Edge appears to be largely associated with the early Mesolithic component of the assemblage. This pattern follows that previously noted on the Wirral (Cowell and Innes 1994: 34; Cowell and Philpott 2000: 24), where the use of chert, probably from North Wales, is also associated with early Mesolithic assemblages. This can be contrasted with the pattern to the east, particularly in the south and central Pennines, where the use of chert was more favoured in late Mesolithic assemblages (Myers 1989: 133; Hind 1998). However, the chert used at Harrol Edge has macroscopic characteristics similar to that from the Peak District, suggesting links with the east rather than the west, as is the case on the early Mesolithic sites of the Wirral.

It is assumed that the majority of the flint used in all of the assemblages was derived from the Irish Sea Till and its associated gravel deposits. Of particular interest is the concentration of flint erratics noted by Mackintosh (1879; Brooks 1989: 198) along the course of the River Weaver, which lies immediately to the east of the Sandstone Ridge. However, a few of the larger artefacts may have been made on flint imported from further afield. The use of flint from the Lincolnshire/Yorkshire Wolds has been suggested further north in Cumbria (Hodgson and Brennand 2006: 28), and a few of the artefacts in this collection are on an opaque pale grey flint that is common in the Wolds. On the other hand it is equally possible that these artefacts were made from the slightly larger nodules occasionally found in the Irish Sea Till, and the long-distance importation of raw materials remains speculative.

The nature of the prehistoric use of Harrol Edge is not certain, largely because the lack of records prevents us assessing the level and methods of collection. The assemblage is dominated by knapping debris with a range of cores and blanks, suggesting that a level of 'gearing-up' took place on the site. There are, however, also a limited number of tools, suggesting a level of domestic activity, so it is likely that the site acted as a home base. It is almost perfectly placed to act as a central point from which task groups could exploit the varying environments of the Mersey and the Sandstone Ridge. As noted above, the scatter appears to have covered an area of between 0.4 and 0.6ha, which would suggest that the site was probably one of Mellars' larger site types (Type II or Type III) (1976: 380). These he associated with social units equivalent to at least two or three nuclear families. The types of artefacts represented also fit within Mellars' Type C (scraper-dominated) assemblage type (*ibid.* 394), although given the probable method of collection it is more likely to have been a Type B (balanced) assemblage (*ibid.* 389).

Adams's flint collection from the Frodsham area is clearly important, but its history since recovery has reduced its value. The loss or lack of records as to the circumstances, methods of recovery and location of much of the collection and the fact that it had been misused before it was donated to the Grosvenor Museum, make it of less use than it might have been. The possible exception is the assemblage from Harrol Edge, although even here more information on the distribution and methods of collection would have been useful.

Acknowledgements

The material was loaned to the author by the Grosvenor Museum, Chester, and particular thanks are due to Elizabeth Royles for organising this and to Dan Garner for locating and supplying background information on the collection.

Chapter 4
The Lost Archive of Eddisbury: Rediscovering Finds and Records from the 1936–1938 Varley Excavations

Richard Mason and Rachel Pope

History of the archive

Ever since their publication in 1950, the findings and phasing of the excavations carried out at Eddisbury hillfort between 1936 and 1938 by Professor W. J. Varley (then Department of Geography, University of Liverpool), have been the subject of discourse (largely by Cotton 1954: 61; but subsequently also by Forde-Johnston 1962: 38; Challis and Harding 1975: 44–5; Longley 1987: 110–11; and Cocroft *et al.* 1989). A number of reinterpretations have been offered, with some calling for a reassessment of the finds assemblage (e.g. Griffiths 2001: 176), particularly as the finds were not published as part of Varley's report. Previous attempts to locate the Eddisbury archive – such as Ellis (1993) and Garner (personal communication) – had ended unsuccessfully, and it had been assumed that the archive was either lost or destroyed, perhaps during the Second World War (Hughes 1996: 47–8).

Excavations at Eddisbury hillfort, Merrick's Hill were conducted by the University of Liverpool Archaeology Field School in 2010 and 2011, as part of a working partnership with the Heritage Lottery-funded Habitats and Hillforts Project (see Mason and Pope, Chapter 11, this volume). Like all individuals who have conducted archaeological investigation in the region, we began our work at Eddisbury with a search of the National Monuments Record (NMR) (now the Historic England Archive). It suggested that the primary archive holder was a Mr Adrian Havercroft, and the finds were listed as in the possession of Bill Varley's second wife, Mary Varley (deceased 2006). Copies of Bill Varley's finds index were listed as being in the NMR, but a request for this material revealed that the documents have since been misplaced.

After tracing the whereabouts of Adrian Havercroft, a meeting was held to discuss Varley and the contents of the primary archive. This revealed a wealth of information on the 1930s work at Eddisbury. Havercroft first met Bill Varley when reading archaeology at Hull College of Education between 1968 and 1972 and, after graduating, became a close friend of the family. Upon Bill Varley's death in 1976, Havercroft – well aware of the sheer quantity of Varley's archives – assumed the role of 'archaeological executor' and offered to curate his archive, preserving it for future study. He managed

to retrieve a substantial quantity of archive material, including three boxes from Eddisbury hillfort but remained convinced that there was more to be recovered. Upon the death of Mary Varley in 2006, Havercroft returned to the Varley family home to search for any material that might have been missed previously. During this visit, he managed to recover further paper records (relating to other sites) and a few boxes of material that had been stored in a caravan. Shortly afterwards, he repacked much of the archive into paper bags and cardboard boxes; the original packaging was discarded. At the time of writing (2012), Adrian Havercroft had again been called to the Varley family home following the death of the person who had inherited the house from Mary Varley, to see whether any further archaeological material might be recovered.

What is clear from the volume of archive material recovered for Varley's excavations at both Old Oswestry and Almondbury hillforts, is that Varley had retained the majority of his archive material until his death in 1976 (Hughes 1996: 46; Rowan May personal communication). A recent discovery at Manchester Museum, however, suggests that not all material was returned to Varley following specialist analysis. An enquiry to the museum led to the curator highlighting a group of human remains deposited by Varley in the 1950s, supposedly from his excavations at Eddisbury. Examination of this assemblage by the authors soon discounted any association with Eddisbury. This prompted further research by the museum curators, who eventually established that these were in fact the human remains from Heronbridge (a Roman settlement south of Chester), also believed lost (Sitch 2012). Shortly after dismissing this group of material as coming from Eddisbury, a faunal remains assemblage was brought forward. Luckily the assemblage retained its original packaging, which gave contextual information that coincided with the grid references and features in Varley's (1950) Eddisbury publication. The bone identification labels, which date between 1938 and 1939, belong to the late Dr John Wilfrid Jackson, and prove that he was either involved during the excavation process or immediately after the final season in 1938 (Figures 4.1 and 4.2). Like the material held by Havercroft, the faunal assemblage at Manchester Museum had remained unpublished until its discovery in 2011.

FIGURE 4.1 EDDISBURY'S PREHISTORIC FAUNAL MATERIAL AS FOUND AT MANCHESTER MUSEUM.

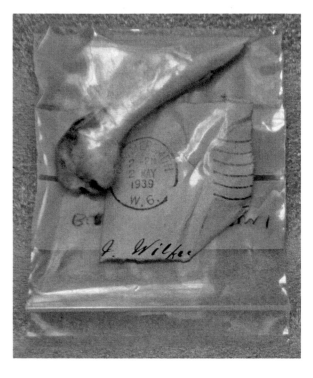

FIGURE 4.2 DR JOHN WILFRID JACKSON'S LABELLING OF THE POST-MEDIEVAL FAUNAL REMAINS.

Archive contents

Of immediate interest was the retrieval by Havercroft of thirteen photographs, four excavation record shots and nine working shots. The working shots in particular provide a unique insight into Varley's excavation methods, equipment and the individuals involved. We know that Tom Jones, of Mucking fame, was the site photographer at Eddisbury (Varley 1950: 2), and the Eddisbury record shots seem to have been processed by Jones during the post-excavation phase of the Mucking excavation; the excavations having taken place between 1965 and 1978 (Figures 4.3 and 4.4). Thus Jones was producing archive-standard photographs of Eddisbury for Varley 15 years after his 1950 publication. This suggests that Varley may have been preparing a second publication in the years prior to his death, in the same period when we know that he was preparing drafts for the full publication of his excavations at both Old Oswestry and Almondbury (Hughes 1996: 46; Rowan May personal communication). The Jones' Mucking archive has recently been worked on by Chris Evans (Cambridge Archaeological Unit), and it is our hope that some new Eddisbury material may come to light as part of that project. No drawn records were recovered as part of the Eddisbury archive held by Havercroft, with the 'finished' drawings for Eddisbury having been produced by Margaret Jones, née Owen (Varley 1950: 2). Margaret Jones – who went on to be Director of the Mucking excavations – had been a Geography student at the University of Liverpool and undertook her early field training with Bill Varley.

Unfortunately the Eddisbury archive contained no paper records, but thankfully Havercroft had retained the original finds card index from Eddisbury that he had copied and submitted to the NMR, which could not be located when we consulted the records (Figures 4.5 and 4.6). The finds records consist of typed, consecutively numbered individual record cards. These were apparently produced during the post-excavation process for every find that had been retained from the excavations. This practice is apparently consistent with Varley's finds recording methodology for Almondbury (Rowen May personal communication). The information recorded includes general location (occasionally measured) and associated features, the depth of discovery of the find, and sometimes a grid or section reference; the reverse normally includes a sketch of the find(s). The finds cards are occasionally edited with written amendments in ink, demonstrating changes made to the archaeological record, most likely during production of the 1950 article. Fortunately, this finds index was accompanied by no less than four boxes of finds, containing prehistoric, medieval and post-medieval material from the 1936–8 excavations.

FIGURE 4.3 1930S EXCAVATIONS AT EDDISBURY WITH SITE SUPERVISOR BETTY FURNISS.

PHOTOGRAPH BY

W. T. JONES F.S.A. A.R.P.S.

MUCKING POST - EXCAVATION
THURROCK MUSEUM 6 FLOOR
ORSETT ROAD,
GRAYS RM17 5DX Tel: 0375 76827 Ext. 52

FIGURE 4.4 TOM JONES' POST-EX STAMP FROM MUCKING ON THE
REVERSE OF AN EDDISBURY RECORD SHOT.

The majority of the Varley finds assemblage dates to the post-medieval and early modern period – the later occupation of Eddisbury, restricted to the southeastern tip of the hillfort in the area known as Merrick's Hill or Varley's (1950) Area 4. Initial assessment by Julie Edwards (Cheshire West and Chester) established that the post-medieval ceramics represent a maximum of 73 hollow-ware/flatware vessels, predominantly slipware, dating from the 16th to 18th centuries. A clay pipe bowl and stem fragment with leaf moulded seams, dated by Peter Davey (University of Liverpool) to the 19th century, and a fragment of a green-glazed brick were also found amongst the ceramic sherds. The glass assemblage assessed by Dr Hugh Willmott (University of Sheffield) consists of fragments belonging to a minimum of four glass vessels dating to the 16th and 17th centuries, and several fragments of 17th-century window glass, along with a section of lead window came, found stored in glass sample vials. The small finds assemblage consists of copper-alloy pin fragments, a 17th-century pewter spoon, and a rim fragment belonging to a pewter charger, probably of similar date. At Manchester Museum, examination of the faunal remains confirmed two boxes as belonging to the post-medieval deposits excavated on Merrick's Hill. An initial assessment by Dr Sue Stallibrass (University of Liverpool) has identified these as predominantly consisting of the remains of sheep and deer, with evidence too for the consumption of pig, poultry and fish.

Amongst the post-medieval ceramic assemblage were nine sherds of storage vessels dating to the 13th–15th centuries, including two fragments from a late medieval bunghole cistern. Preliminary x-ray analysis of the iron assemblage by the late Paul Courtney (University of

FIGURE 4.5 EDDISBURY FINDS CARD INDEX.

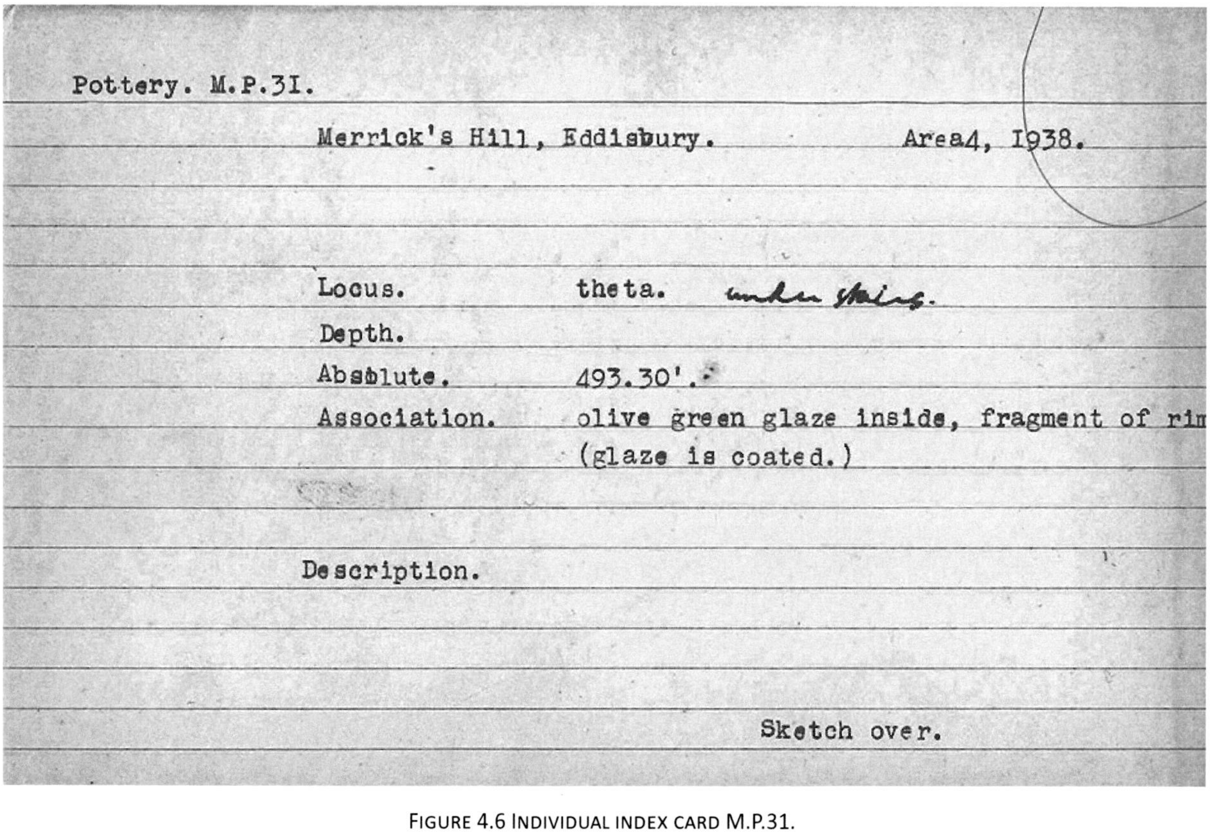

Pottery. M.P.31.

Merrick's Hill, Eddisbury.   Area4, 1938.

Locus.   the ta.   under staining.
Depth.
Absolute.   493.30'.
Association.   olive green glaze inside, fragment of rim
                    (glaze is coated.)

Description.

                              Sketch over.

FIGURE 4.6 INDIVIDUAL INDEX CARD M.P.31.

FIGURE 4.7 THE ANNULAR CLAY LOOM WEIGHT IDENTIFIED IN THE VARLEY ARCHIVE.

Leicester) also identified a terminal end fragment of an 11th–13th-century horseshoe (Clark Type 2). Aside from the numerous historical accounts, Varley's evidence for Anglo-Saxon occupation was based upon an annular clay loom weight found on the interior occupation surface of a 'Saxon' hut (Varley 1950: 10). Whilst the ceramic sherds are no longer present, the bun-shaped loom weight is in the archive and consists of two joining fragments (Figure 4.7). Varley's evidence for the Roman slighting of Eddisbury was based on two artefacts mentioned briefly in his publication: a fragment of *tegula* and a Roman pottery sherd (1950: 10; 24); both are present in the archive. Both the *tegula*, now in two joining pieces, and the pottery sherd have heavily abraded surfaces, typical of plough soil or water eroding conditions. A further two sherds of *c*. 2nd-century greyware were also found amongst the post-medieval ceramics.

Twenty-five sherds of Iron Age ceramic, including a piece of VCP complete with fingerprint impression, were included in the archive. Unfortunately, preliminary analysis suggests that these cannot be cross-referenced with the sherds recorded by Varley in the card index (see below). Discussion with Adrian Havercroft suggests that he is confident that he has no other material that could be from Eddisbury. This matter will be investigated further, ahead of the production of the final report on the work of the University of Liverpool at Eddisbury. Found amongst the prehistoric ceramics were two whetstones from the eastern entrance (Varley Area 3) and a siltstone whetstone or pallete from the northwestern entrance (Varley Area 1); all three retain information on the location of their discovery. The prehistoric faunal remains at Manchester

Museum consisted of a collection of labelled tobacco tins containing fragments of burnt animal bone. Analysed by John Wilfred Jackson in the late 1930s, the fragments have been kept within their broad contexts of discovery; either by area of excavation, by deposit, or by feature. The labels within the tins show that Varley's prehistoric or 'Dark Age' interpretations were current in the late 1930s. Varley's retention of faunal remains, and in some instances even wood charcoal, demonstrates his recognition of the value of scientific analysis at this relatively early date, in line with the activities of archaeological colleagues in 1930s Cambridge (see Pope 2011: 68).

Other objects found amongst the prehistoric ceramics included a stone spindle whorl, perhaps that published by Varley in *Cheshire before the Romans* (1964, figure 38), and a small flint bladelet (late Mesolithic to early Neolithic) found on Merrick's Hill (Varley Area 4). Of particular interest is a fossilised round of a clubmoss root *(Lepidodendron)*, hollowed out at one end to create what one can only assume is a small mortar, an unparalleled use of a fossil in this way, if prehistoric. The grid reference and recorded depth of the artefact suggest that it was found at the northwestern entrance (Varley Area 1), in close proximity to the hut (Varley 1950, figure 4). Perhaps the most astonishing discovery within the finds archive is the survival of iron gatepost fittings, which we currently believe to be pivots, discovered *in situ* at the front of the eastern entranceway during the 1937 season (Varley Area 3). The gatepost fittings were found inside two rock-cut postholes (Figures 4.8 and 4.9), and their extraordinary survival appears to be the result of the mineralisation of the timber uprights found above them, which were perhaps subsequently discarded. Following the death of Mary Varley in 2006, the fittings were found inside a caravan, stored in a cardboard box packed with sawdust. They are now almost completely corroded and in a very fragmentary state.

Methodology

The primary aim of the research into the lost archive of Eddisbury has been to produce a record, compliant with the standards of both the Historic England Archive and the Archaeology Data Service, of all the objects known to have been recovered from Eddisbury by the Varleys, during the period in which temporary access to the assemblage has been negotiated. The

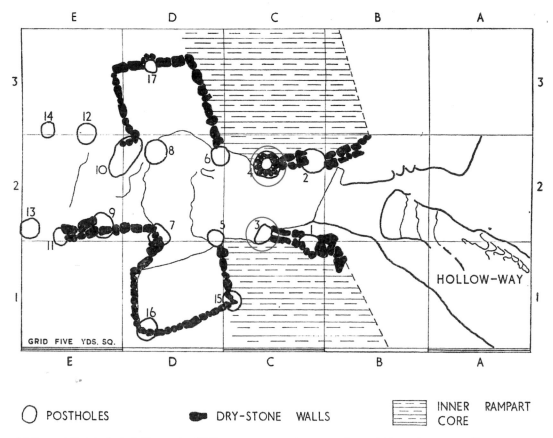

○ POSTHOLES   ● DRY-STONE WALLS   ▨ INNER RAMPART CORE

FIGURE 4.8 PLAN OF VARLEY AREA 3, EDDISBURY 1937 WITH THE LOCATION OF THE GATEPOST FITTINGS MARKED. REPRODUCED COURTESY OF THE *TRANSACTIONS OF THE HISTORIC SOCIETY OF LANCASHIRE AND CHESHIRE*.

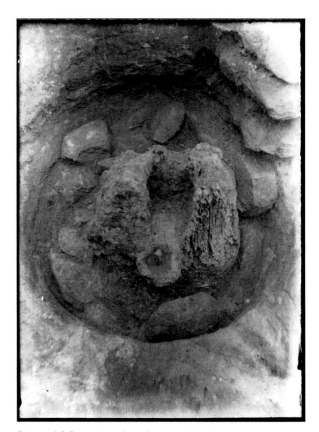

FIGURE 4.9 ONE OF THE IRON AGE IRON GATEPOST FITTINGS IN SITU. REPRODUCED COURTESY OF THE *TRANSACTIONS OF THE HISTORIC SOCIETY OF LANCASHIRE AND CHESHIRE*.

completed record will be submitted to the Historic England Archive. Adrian Havercroft has kindly transferred ownership of the finds assemblage and surviving archive to Manchester Museum, where it will be reunited with the faunal remains. A necessary part of the work has been to authenticate the objects, making sure that they did indeed originate from Eddisbury, as 'foreign' objects unnecessarily increase the financial burden of post-excavation analysis and potentially complicate the understanding of the site. Contamination is common in most antiquarian assemblages, and unfortunately, we have found it to be a problem with the Varley material (see below).

Assessment began with the creation of a digital catalogue for all recorded material, both present and missing, establishing both provenance and, where possible, any contextual information. The finds card index for Eddisbury contains a wealth of contextual information that was excluded from the 1950 publication. Using this contextual data alongside the published plans and sections, it has been possible to construct a data structure report for the excavated deposits that have recorded finds. This will begin to provide firm dating evidence for Varley's phasing and will be incorporated into the final Eddisbury report to be produced on the work by the University of Liverpool.

The stable condition of most of the finds has facilitated good progress, and preliminary results indicate that the original dating is largely accurate. Unfortunately, analysis of the iron gatepost fittings has been hindered by their extremely poor condition; their fragmentary and fragile state has even prevented physical examination. Thanks to recent funding from Historic England, the conservation required to stabilise and sample these objects is now being undertaken at York Archaeological Trust, under the supervision of Ian Panter. This is a costly and time consuming exercise but imperative for identifying their true function. The next phase of work will see Scanning Electron Microscopy (SEM) analysis of the samples by Edward Rule (University of Liverpool), which we hope will greatly inform on this unique example of Iron Age hillfort technology.

Issues

Whilst Varley's finds index is proving extremely informative, the consecutive numbering system demonstrates that both the index and the material archive are incomplete. The majority of the missing records and artefacts are prehistoric, predominantly the ceramics and a minimum of four whetstones.[1] The prehistoric ceramic records have also cast uncertainty on the provenance of certain sherds within the assemblage. Unfortunately, none of the prehistoric ceramics, most of which are individually marked, can currently be matched to the sketches on the index cards. We know from other records that the sketches are accurate and reliable; further, there are no clean breaks that might suggest that the discrepancies could be accounted for by more recent damage. The pot-marking is certainly Varley's, but we are reasonably confident at this stage that the sherds are not from Eddisbury, having confirmed one sherd derives from his excavations at Old Oswestry (1939–40), perhaps becoming mixed with the Eddisbury archive after his death. This theory is supported by the presence of at least 25 non-prehistoric vessels[2] found amongst the recorded overall total of 82 vessels, where the pot-marking confirms a 'mixing' of archive material, with one marked as being from Ousethorpe (a deserted medieval village site in Yorkshire excavated in 1964) and another from Etton Temple Garth (a medieval grange and manor site in Yorkshire excavated 1965–7). Similarly, one tin of bone at Manchester Museum was labelled as Maiden Castle, Bickerton. The remaining missing materials from the Eddisbury archive are mainly post-medieval small finds such as coins or dress accessories. Whilst their absence prevents re-analysis, the accuracy of the sketches has been sufficient to allow broad identification, mostly confirming the dates assigned by Varley.

Despite a standardised finds retention policy established by Varley, a copy of which we now hold by courtesy of Rowen May, it would appear that by far the greatest care regarding finds retrieval was taken when excavating prehistoric deposits. Figure 4.3 shows excavators sieving excavated spoil, utilising what appears to be a small tobacco tin as their finds tray (visible on the trench edge), probably one of the tins still containing finds at Manchester Museum. By way of contrast, finds retrieval for post-medieval deposits in Varley Area 4 appears to have been much more selective. The finds index and material archive contain nothing later than the early 19th century, the latest find being a complete clay pipe bowl dating to c. AD 1800–40. Our recent excavations, however, which included the re-excavation of much 1936–8 backfill and spoil, produced substantial quantities of 19th- and early 20th-century material. The disposal of early modern material is still a common practice to this day, but this deliberate jettisoning of anything post-dating the early 19th century by Varley's team may indicate more than a deliberately selective approach to finds retention. Rather, it may be evidence for Varley wanting the archaeological record to correspond with the written historical references to the site being abandoned in 1819 (Shaw and Clark 2003: 5).

This theory is further supported by Varley's acceptance of a medieval forester's lodge on Merrick's Hill (see Mason and Pope, Chapter 11, this volume). He showed such a structure on his phase plans, despite admitting that there was no archaeological evidence to support it (1950: 67). Whilst one could argue that its representation was conjectural, it could demonstrate Varley's desire to support the historical sources. With this in mind, it is necessary to question certain 'key' finds that have provided crucial dating to support his phasing: the Nuremburg jetton dated to c. AD 1550, found in a pit sealed by the primary phase of Building Two in Varley Area 4; a fob of c. AD 1800 found underneath a sealed floor from the later extension; the stereotypical Anglo-Saxon bun-shaped loom weight found on the floor of the 'Dark Age' hut; and the Roman pottery found in the hillfort ditch fill. Furthermore, it would appear that some of the finds records have been edited during post-excavation; record cards M.P.29-37 having been altered from 'found near stairs' to 'found under stairs' and thus perhaps nudging a *terminus post quem* for the date of construction. This desire to have the archaeology conform to the history was entirely in keeping with the work of others in the 1930s, perhaps especially that of Sir Mortimer Wheeler.

Discussion

Since the 1930s, archaeology has witnessed dramatic innovations in the analyses of material culture. The successful application of new techniques to older collections of material is providing a wealth of new

---

[1] Whilst we can quantify the minimum number of missing records, without knowing the original total we cannot speculate a maximum.
[2] 21 post-medieval, 2 medieval, 1 Roman, 1 of unknown date.

data, often helping us to reconsider previously accepted interpretations. Elaine Morris's (1996) re-assessment of Varley's ceramics from Old Oswestry, for example, demonstrated the inability at his time to differentiate correctly between so-called 'Dark Age' pottery and Iron Age VCP. It was on this basis that Higham and Hill (2001: 176) chose to reject Varley's phasing of the Anglo-Saxon occupation of Eddisbury – although interestingly we do now have well-dated evidence for Saxon activity at the site (Garner, Chapter 10, this volume). Most recently, a re-assessment of the much more complete Almondbury archive has been commissioned by the Tolson Museum, Huddersfield, ahead of proposed new excavations, and this, along with our own work on the Eddisbury archive and that of Hughes (1996) on Old Oswestry, provides a great opportunity to reassess Varley's work. As current investigators of Eddisbury hillfort, we can now combine a contemporary re-assessment of previous excavations with our own results. Being able to associate Varley's findings with a new C14-dated phasing of the hillfort contributes not only to new, dated material culture typologies for the region, but also to a developed understanding of prehistoric Cheshire.

When it comes to the excavation of hillforts, entrances have always been a preferred area for investigation because of their varying forms and thus their potential contribution to understanding the chronological development of the monument, yet none have produced a parallel for the iron gatepost fittings, or pivots, found by Varley at Eddisbury in 1937. Konstram (2006: 44) highlights this apparent absence, identifying the iron rings found in association with entrance structures at South Cadbury (Somerset) and Hembury (Devon),

possible hinge components, as the only known material from the United Kingdom. The potential pivot fittings from Eddisbury are therefore currently unique. Their remarkable survival offers the opportunity to reassess both the architectural design of hillfort entrances and the associated iron-working technology current in the Iron Age North West. Thanks to the resources provided by the Heritage Lottery-funded Habitats and Hillforts project, the Eddisbury archive will finally see the full assessment that it deserves. This archive is just a fraction of a much larger archaeological archive – a lifetime's dedication by one of Britain's foremost hillfort excavators in the early 20th century. Through the combined efforts of Gwilym Hughes (1996), our on-going research, and now the work of the Tolson Museum, we are providing a contemporary public record and archaeological synthesis for nationally significant material once assumed lost, and an epitaph for the early achievements of W. J. Varley and his team.

Acknowledgements

The authors would like to give special thanks to Adrian Havercroft – to whom this project is greatly indebted – for granting the authors temporary loan of the Varley archive and sharing his memories of Bill Varley. We would also like to thank Dan Garner (Habitats and Hillforts) and Ellie Morris (Cheshire West and Chester Council) for funding and advice. Thanks also to Bryan Sitch (Manchester Museum) for providing access to the Eddisbury faunal remains. Grateful thanks also to the specialists on the project for their expert work and advice: Paul Courtney, Chris Cumberpatch, Peter Davey, Gill Dunn, Julie Edwards, Fraser Hunter, Dawn McLaren, David Mullin, Sue Stallibrass, Colin Wallace, and Hugh Willmott.

Chapter 5
Earthwork surveys and investigations at Woodhouse Hill, Helsby Hill and Maiden Castle

Mitchell Pollington

Introduction

Between 2009 and 2012 Archaeological Services WYAS[1] undertook detailed earthwork surveys and investigations of three of the enclosures or hillforts situated along the Cheshire Sandstone Ridge: those on Woodhouse Hill and Helsby Hill, to the south of Frodsham, and Maiden Castle, Bickerton, as part of the Habitats and Hillforts Project. This paper presents an overview of the results of this work, providing a description and brief discussion of the surface remains at each site as they survive today. Full reports of the surveys are available in the Cheshire Historic Environment Record (CHER) (Pollington 2009; 2012a; 2012b).

Woodhouse Hill

Description

Woodhouse Hill is a ridge of high ground situated approximately 1.5km to the south of Frodsham, rising to a height of about 149m OD above the cliffs and terraces of the Sandstone Ridge escarpment on its western side. It is largely covered in birch woodland, together with extensive stands of rhododendron, although a recent programme of tree felling has exposed much of the underlying earthwork remains.

The enclosure on Woodhouse Hill is defined by a single rampart enclosing an internal area of approximately 1.6ha (Figure 5.1). This survives as a series of mounds and banks, which follow the natural contour at about 140m OD along a break of slope between the gradual incline of the hilltop and the steeper slopes to the north and east. At its southern end the rampart is marked by a low mound, and continues northwards as a terrace and low bank, forming an exterior facing scarp of up to 0.6m in height for a distance of around 20m. The rampart then continues as a series of substantial but fragmentary sections of bank, measuring between 10m and 28m long and up to 10.5m wide, with an internal scarp varying between 0.3m and 1.2m in height. Together these combine to form a substantial exterior rampart scarp which increases in height from about 1m at its southern end to 3.2m high along its most prominent central and

northern sections, before decreasing in height as the line of the rampart curves around the northern side of the hilltop. Exposed stone, visible protruding from the inner side of the rampart in a number of places, is likely to represent elements of the original underlying structure. There is no evidence for any external secondary rampart or ditch, and fragmentary sections of scarp recorded down slope are likely to be the result of slumping, and in some cases burrow collapse.

A possible entrance is situated at the northeastern corner of the enclosure, where a 7m wide break in the rampart is flanked by slight inturns in the bank. There is no surface evidence for a routeway leading up to the entrance, and any direct approach would have required a steep climb up the hillside to the northeast.

To the west the rampart continues as a substantial bank, forming an outer scarp nearly 2m high, although this becomes lower and less well defined as it curves around to form the northern side of the enclosure. Further concentrations of loose stone in this area are likely to represent the disturbed remains of the underlying rampart structure. The rampart terminates as it turns towards the southwest, marked by a large mound measuring 1.5m high on its exterior, northwestern side, and 0.6m on the interior. No further archaeological surface remains were identified to the south of this point that could represent a continuation of the rampart around the western or southern sides of the hilltop.

A number of amorphous depressions situated along the interior of the eastern section of the rampart may represent quarry ditches, used to provide material for the construction of the rampart. The largest of these is approximately 45m long and 16m wide, with a depth of up to 1.25m, and corresponds with the most substantial section of rampart to its immediate east. Indeed, where the quarry ditches are smaller, or absent, the existing rampart is less substantial. There is no further surface evidence for any prehistoric activity or occupation within the interior of the enclosure.

There is some indication of later activity along the rampart, to the north of where it is crossed by a modern footpath. Here, a level area measuring 6m by 4m, appears to have cut into the bank and could represent the site of a building, and a square depression to its southwest

---

[1] Formerly West Yorkshire Archaeology Services. The author is now with AOC Archaeology.

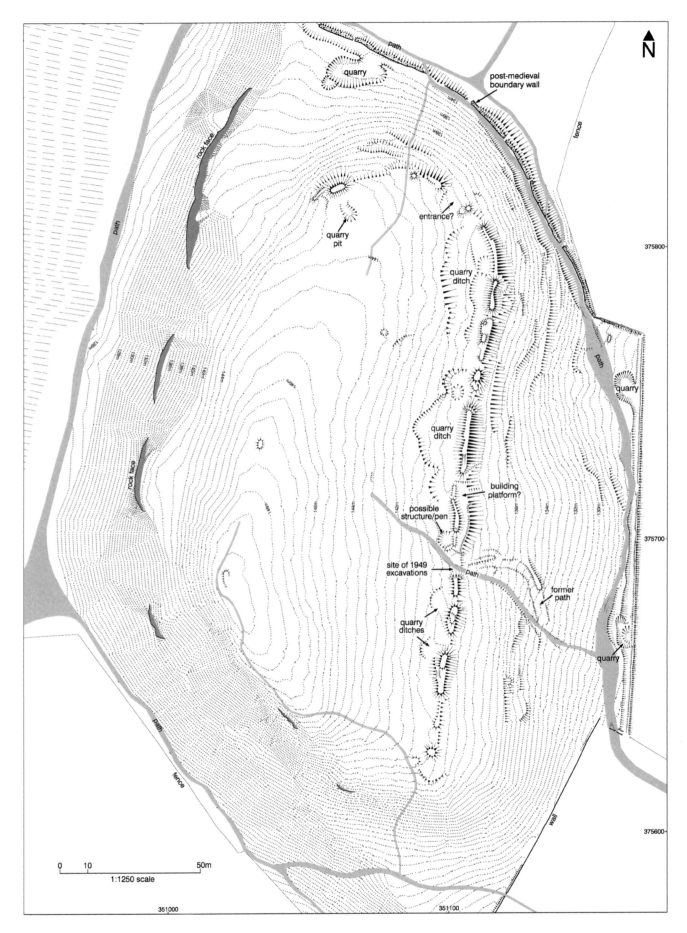

FIGURE 5.1 EARTHWORK SURVEY OF THE ENCLOSURE ON WOODHOUSE HILL (SCALE 1:1250).

could be the site of a structure such as an animal pen. It is possible that these features formed the site of a small dwelling, possibly accessed along a shallow hollow way, which curves up the eastern side of the hill towards this area. No buildings were recorded on this site on the Frodsham Tithe Map of 1846 (CALS EDT 163/2), or subsequent mapping, and any occupation here is therefore likely to pre-date the 19th century.

Discussion

It is unclear why the rampart of the enclosure on Woodhouse Hill exists in a fragmentary state, or whether this represents the remains of an original form, or is the result of later activity. The first edition Ordnance Survey twenty-five inch to the mile map of 1873 provides the earliest depiction of the rampart as a single unbroken bank, and it is not until after the Second World War that the Ordnance Survey Archaeology Division first recorded breaks through the rampart (Historic England Archive SJ 57 NW 5). This is unlikely to mean, however, that the breaks are the result of post-war activity. Indeed, the absence of breaks marked on the earliest Ordnance Survey maps may simply reflect the style of depiction of such earthworks, with the surveyors following a line along the base of the rampart and therefore producing a more cohesive representation of the enclosure than actually existed. It has been suggested that the breaks could be the result of small-scale quarrying (Jecock 2006: 7), and the blocks which form the underlying structure of the rampart would certainly have been a useful source of stone for field walls in the area. However, small stone quarries exist at the base of the hill, close to a post-medieval field wall which would have served this purpose, and minimised transport of material down the steep hillside. If these gaps do represent quarrying it would also seem illogical to quarry material from numerous different points, rather than remove a single length of bank, even if such activity was carried out at various different times. Disturbance could also have occurred due to forestry planting in the area, although only the southern half of the hilltop appears to have been commercially planted with coniferous trees during the 19th century, and this would not account for the breaks in the northern section of the rampart.

Alternatively, rather than representing areas of disturbance, it is possible that these breaks could be contemporary with the original construction of the site. Similar enclosures, such as Gardom's Edge, Derbyshire, have breaks along their banks which have been interpreted as entrances, and it has been suggested that this arrangement could perhaps represent an upland form of Neolithic causewayed enclosure (Ainsworth and Barnatt 1998; Barnatt et al. 2002). Segmented enclosure banks have also been shown to represent the remains of unfinished Iron Age hillforts at sites such as at Ladle

Hill, Wiltshire (Piggott 1931). There are also a number of examples of possible unfinished hillforts in Scotland and southern England (e.g. Feachem 1966; 1971), and James Forde-Johnston suggested that the enclosure at Woodhouse Hill may also be unfinished following his survey in the early 1960s (Forde-Johnston 1962). Indeed, at Woodhouse Hill the apparent correlation of the size of quarry ditches with the size of adjacent rampart bank sections, suggests that the rampart was intended to form a single bank that was never completed.

Although the most likely location of the entrance appears to be the break in the northeastern side of the rampart, this is not conclusive. It has been suggested that the enclosure could have been accessed through its northwestern side (Forde-Johnston 1962), where there is ease of access due to the gentler gradient leading up to the enclosure, which would provide a suitable route along which to herd livestock. There is, however, no archaeological surface evidence supporting the presence of an entrance in this area. The other substantial break in the rampart line, through which the modern footpath is aligned, may in part be the result of disturbance caused by an excavation in 1949 (Historic England Archive SJ 57 NW 5), compounded by erosion along the path itself.

Helsby Hillfort

Description

Helsby Hill is a prominent outcrop close to the northern end of the Sandstone Ridge, to the immediate east of Helsby, and situated 1.7km to the west of Woodhouse Hill. Its northern and western sides are defined by the steep sandstone cliffs of the escarpment edge, to the southeast of which the ground slopes gradually down towards the southeast. The hilltop is broadly divided into two halves by a field wall aligned southeast to northwest. To its west, the ground cover is primarily rough grassland, with areas of exposed bedrock along the cliff edges. The steeper slopes along the upper edge of the escarpment are covered by deciduous woodland. The eastern side of the hilltop comprises a single field of improved pasture, with a small plot in its northwestern corner containing a Cold War period Royal Observation Corps (ROC) monitoring post, and is in private ownership. Between 1915 and 1936 the area also formed part of a golf course.

The enclosure on Helsby Hill consists of a double rampart that curves around the hilltop, defining an internal area of approximately 1.4ha, with a probable entrance through its southwestern side (Figure 5.2).

The inner rampart survives as a prominent bank along its western end, forming the southern side of the enclosure, measuring up to 3.5m high externally and 1m high internally, with a width of 16.5m. A slight scarp aligned at a right-angle to the rampart bank, about 35m along its line from the west, marks the edge of Forde-Johnston's 1963–4 excavation trench, and the site of its re-excavation in 2010 (Forde-Johnston 1964; 1967; Garner, Chapter 9, this volume). This section of rampart is crossed by a modern footpath, aligned along the western side of the field wall, which runs through a break in the bank approximately 3m wide and 0.75m deep. This break is likely to be partially the result of the construction of the field wall, together with a combination of erosion, and probably deliberate levelling, along the route of the path over the last century. To the east, the inner rampart continues into the field of improved pasture where it survives as a bank with a prominent external scarp between 2.3m and 4.5m high. The internal scarp of this part of the rampart varies between 0.2m and 1.5m at it highest point along the northern section of the bank. Unlike the western side of the site, this area was historically ploughed, which has resulted in the spreading of the rampart bank to a width of 26m. The highest point along the eastern section of the inner rampart appears to be overlain by a wide mound. This may partially be a natural outcrop, but it corresponds with the site of a former golf tee, and may have been altered for this purpose. The inner rampart bank ends at the modern fence line bounding the northern side of the field, which runs along the escarpment edge. The remains of a parallel field bank and relict wall represent previous alignments of this boundary, and overlie the rampart. Disturbance around the northern end of the rampart may be the result of small scale quarrying, probably to provide material for the field bank and wall.

A further length of bank extends the line of the inner rampart down the steep escarpment edge, until it meets a modern footpath which cuts across the bank close to the cliff edge. This section of bank is around 52m long and up to 9m wide, and appears to have been positioned along a natural northeast facing scarp, to take advantage of the rise in the natural ground level. The internal scarp therefore measures between 0.1m and 0.3m high, while the northeast facing external scarp is between 2m and 4.5m high. Slumping along this side has caused the bank to widen, especially as it climbs the slope to the southeast. Exposed blocks of stone along the footpath are likely to have formed part of the underlying bank structure, although this stonework is now obscured by recent footpath surfacing work. A slight rectangular depression close to the centre of the bank marks the location of Bu'lock's 1955 excavation trench, re-excavated in 2010 (Bu'lock 1956; Garner, Chapter 9, this volume).

A short section of bank also survives below the southern end of the cliff edge, on the southwestern side of the site. This is orientated east-west and measures approximately 8m long, 3m wide and up to 0.6m high. As with the northern extension bank, it appears to have been positioned to take advantage of a natural scarp, in this case facing south. The bank roughly corresponds to a much more substantial bank recorded in the area by Bu'lock, Forde-Johnston and

Longley (Bu'lock 1956; Forde-Johnston 1962; see Longley 1987, figure 11), and extensive path erosion may have resulted in its now much degraded condition.

The outer rampart survives as a gradual scarp measuring up to 1.2m high along its western section, but survives as a sharper slope on the eastern side of the site, where it is between 1.5m and 3m high. A slight back-scarp along the rear of the northeastern end of the outer rampart represents the only surviving evidence of a possible bank along its length.

A probable inturned entrance is situated at the southwestern corner of the enclosure, formed by a 4.6m wide break in the rampart. Its southern side is bounded by the western end of the inner rampart, which is formed by a large mound, up to 4.8m high externally, and to the north by a continuation of the rampart scarp up to 3.5m high. This appears to continue as a low bank following the curving edge of the exposed rock along the cliff edge, with the external scarp decreasing in height as the natural ground level rises to the north. It is unclear whether this bank originally formed part of the hillfort enclosure itself, and sections of walling visible along its eastern side suggest it has at least been altered to form part of a later boundary. It is perhaps more likely that the rampart originally extended directly westwards from the northern side of the entrance to meet the cliff edge, which forms a natural barrier along which an additional rampart would, defensively, be unnecessary. Large boulders and concentrations of stone exposed by the path erosion in this area may have formed part of a collapsed rampart structure, but no bank survives.

There is no surface evidence for any prehistoric activity within the interior of Helsby hillfort. Two prominent rectangular platforms on the western side of the site appear simply to be the remains of golf tees. Other features are likely to relate to the use of the hilltop in the Second World War, during which the hill provided an important point from which to observe the approach of German bombers towards Merseyside. A sub-circular pit, about 0.7m deep and 6m wide, with a smaller rectangular pit on its southern side, has been dug into the rampart to the immediate south of the entrance. This may represent the site of an observation post from this period, which often consisted of a basic sandbag-revetted dugout. The remains of a possible cable trench, which extends eastwards from this area, could have held a telegraph or telephone cable to provide communication from the post. To the west, close to the footpath following the field wall, two rectangular platforms measuring approximately 4.5m by 6m appear to be cut into the top of the inner rampart. The cable trench appears to curve southwards towards these, and it is possible that they mark the sites of structures related to the observation post.

The Cold War period Royal Observer Corps (ROC) monitoring post, situated within a small plot at the highest point of Helsby Hill, also attests to the continuing

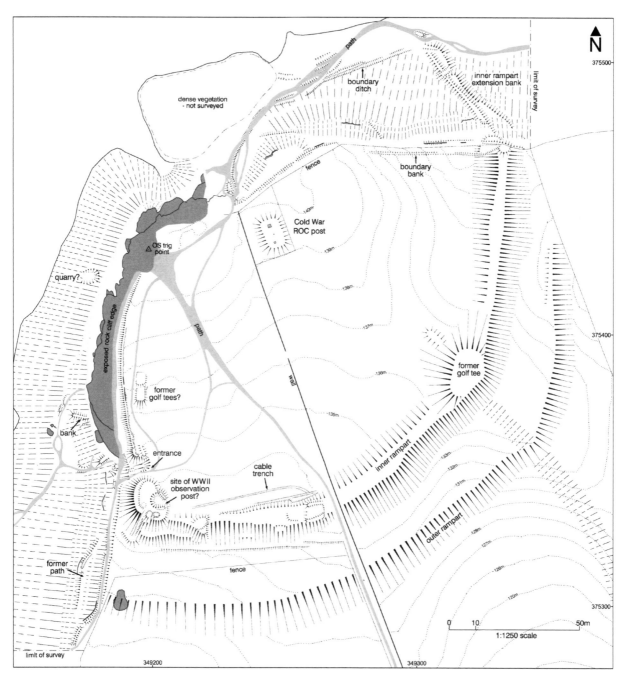

FIGURE 5.2 EARTHWORK SURVEY OF THE ENCLOSURE ON HELSBY HILL (SCALE 1:1250).

military use of the hill through the second half of the 20th century. On the surface, the entrance hatch, ventilation shaft and other fixtures for monitoring devices survive, surrounded by a low earthen mound. The post became operational in October 1962 and was decommissioned in September 1991.

Discussion

The discovery of Neolithic flints tools along the escarpment edge of Helsby Hill[2] together with the

identification of burnt deposits, possibly representing woodland clearance or other activity dating to this period (Garner, Chapter 9, this volume), suggests that Helsby Hill provided a focus for early prehistoric activity, and possibly occupation, pre-dating the construction of the enclosure. Indeed, the hill would have provided a prominent marker in the wider landscape, visible at a distance from northeast Wales and along the Mersey estuary, and this prominence could potentially have given the site a higher cultural or ritual importance. Although there is no structural evidence for a Neolithic origin to the enclosure itself, the significance of the site in the Neolithic period may not have been based on the

---

[2] Cheshire Historic Environment Record 1003 and 1005; National Trust Sites and Monuments Record 55101 and 55102.

presence of constructed monuments, but rather the hill itself may have been perceived as significant as part of a belief system that did not necessarily manifest itself archaeologically (see Welfare 2002: 74; Topping 1997). The most recent excavations of the site have demonstrated that the earliest phase of the enclosure itself is probably of a middle Bronze Age date, between 1435–1320 cal BC (NZA-37729) (Garner, Chapter 9, this volume), although it is not possible to infer the nature of any activity within the site during this period from the surface evidence. It is probable that activity or occupation continued on the site through the Iron Age and, palaeoenvironmental evidence retrieved from the inner rampart suggests that there was possible grain storage/processing on the site in the later Iron Age (210–90 cal BC (NZA-35496)) on the site in the 3rd century BC (Garner, Chapter 9, this volume).

It is unclear whether the enclosure originally comprised just a single rampart or if the inner and outer rampart were constructed as part of a coherent design. At present, excavation has been limited to the inner rampart, and no comparisons have been possible of the two. It would appear likely that the alignment of the inner rampart represents the earliest phase of development. This was positioned to take advantage of the natural topography of the hillside and is aligned along the top of a natural break of slope, broadly following the contour. This divides the gradually inclining interior of the enclosure from the steeper natural slope to the south and east. The outer rampart broadly follows the natural contours of the hillside, but does not appear to be aligned on a natural topographic feature, and its position is likely to have been determined simply by following the orientation of the inner rampart. The construction of the outer rampart may have provided additional defensive capability, but it would also have enhanced the monumental appearance of the enclosure. The increased visual impact of an additional rampart may not have been designed to impress those approaching the entrance to the site, as the rampart would not be clearly visible along a route following the top of the escarpment edge from the south. The double rampart would, however, have been highly visible across the farmland to the south and east, which may have formed part of a social or political unit associated with the site. It would also have been at least partially visible from Woodhouse Hill, and the development of the ramparts at Helsby could be seen as an expression of status and rivalry between the two, similar to that as suggested in the analysis of the relationship between Iron Age 'hillforts' in Northumberland (Oswald *et al*. 2006). It is, however, unclear whether any activity in the enclosure on Woodhouse Hill was contemporary with that of Helsby Hill or, indeed, whether the Woodhouse Hill enclosure was ever completed.

The bank extending the inner rampart down the escarpment edge appears in plan to have an awkward relationship with the main line of the rampart, suggesting a separate phase of development. Excavation across the bank has shown, however, that it is of almost identical construction to the inner rampart, and is likely to be contemporary (Garner, Chapter 9, this volume). It seems unlikely that this bank was constructed primarily for defensive purposes. The steep natural slope of the escarpment edge, and the cliffs to the southwest, would have made the northern and western sides of the hilltop naturally defensible and it would seem logical for any additional defences to be aligned along the upper edge of the escarpment. The bank could have enclosed the northeastern end of the terrace situated beneath the cliffs along the escarpment edge, with the short section of bank at the southern end of the terrace marking its southern boundary. There seems little defensive reason for enclosing this terrace, although it could possibly have been used for holding cattle or sheep outside of the interior of the hillfort. It has been suggested that the terrace could have been enclosed to define it as a significant area, perhaps with a ritual or religious function associated with the prominent rock outcrops (Stewart Ainsworth personal communication). This opens up the possibility that the original inner rampart incorporated the terrace into the circuit of the enclosure not for practical or defensive reasons, but because this area had other social or religious significance. Indeed, this could reflect the formalised enclosure of an area that had already been of some early significance, perhaps since the Neolithic period, with the Bronze Age enclosure builders asserting their control over this area, and through this, potentially imbuing a greater status and importance on the enclosure itself.

Maiden Castle

Description

Maiden Castle is an enclosure situated on the south side of Bickerton Hill, close to the southern end of the Cheshire Sandstone Ridge, approximately 1km to the west of the village of Bickerton. The site is bounded to the west by sandstone cliffs and the steep slopes of the escarpment edge, above which the ground level descends gradually towards the southeast from a maximum height of around 211m OD. The site is managed as heathland, with ground cover consisting of a mixture of grass, bracken and bilberry, with intermittent trees. The area is now used to graze cattle, which have been introduced to prevent the re-establishment of birch seedlings, and a programme of birch felling and bracken control has also been implemented. The Sandstone Trail footpath follows the escarpment edge along the western side of the enclosure, and crosses the ramparts at its southern and northeastern ends. During the second half of the 20th century the site was used for army cadet training and as a firing range by 33 Engineer Regiment, and a programme to clear any ordnance from the area was undertaken in the mid-1990s (Milln 1996). The remains of Maiden Castle primarily consist of two large well preserved sections of rampart divided by a ditch, which form an enclosure covering an interior area of approximately 0.7ha

(Figure 5.3). The enclosure also has a well preserved inturned entranceway on its northwestern side.

The inner rampart comprises a bank approximately 12m wide, with an external scarp of up to 2.5m high and an internal scarp surviving up to 1m high. The internal scarp of the inner rampart has been heavily disturbed by quarrying on the northeastern side of the enclosure, to the south of the entranceway, although it continues as a prominent bank to the north until it reaches the escarpment edge. The entrance is formed by inturned sections of the inner rampart, which are aligned east–west and extend into the interior of the enclosure. Together these define a narrow, corridor-like, entranceway approximately 0.8m wide and 17m long, with the banks on either side rising to a maximum height of 1.2m. Access to this must have been via a causeway over the inner ditch. A break in the bank of the outer rampart presumably marks the point of access from the east, although this break is substantially wider than its original form, largely as a result of archaeological excavations undertaken in the 1930s (Varley 1935; 1936).

A substantial berm is aligned along the exterior of the southwestern section of the inner rampart, which measures between 2.5m and 4.8m wide, with a front scarp of up to 1.2m high above the inner ditch, although this has been quarried into, in a number of places. The berm is partially visible continuing around the northeastern side of the enclosure, but in a more fragmentary form, and has been disturbed by later quarrying and excavation.

The ditch dividing the berm from the outer rampart bank measures up to 3m wide and is between 1.1m and 1.3m deep in relation to the natural ground level at its northern and southwestern ends respectively. The southern section of the ditch contains a number of large mounds created by quarrying into the berm, and other low banks to the northeast are associated with rectangular quarry cuts into the scarp of the berm. The ditch does not appear to continue to the north of the entrance way, although this area has again been heavily disturbed by archaeological excavation (Varley 1935; 1936).

The outer rampart bank is approximately 13m wide, with an internal height of between 0.9m and 1.3m. The bank is most prominent along its southern section, where its external height is over 2.4m. Part of its northeastern section has been disturbed by animal sets, small-scale quarrying and tree felling, but it survives as a large bank, up to 2m high, to the immediate south of the entrance way, at which point it is overlain by a low mound. The line of the outer rampart is continued to the north by a section of bank that has been disturbed by archaeological excavation and later military activity.

There is fragmentary evidence for an outer ditch around the enclosure, with a number of sections of a slight counter scarp visible to the south and east of the outer rampart. The presence of this ditch also appears to be confirmed by the recent lidar survey (Garner, Chapter 7, this volume). A number of amorphous mounds outside the northeastern side of the enclosure, to the east and southeast of the entranceway, overlie the line of this ditch and may represent spoil tips from Varley's excavations.

The interior of the enclosure has been heavily disturbed by quarrying, represented by substantial amorphous mounds and depressions. A larger quarry is also situated within the eastern edge of the inner rampart, to the south of the entranceway. It has been suggested that this quarrying may have been associated with the operation of the Bickerton Hill copper mines, which began in the late 17th century (Milln 1996: 4; see also Ashmore 1982). In places the quarry mounds are cut across by a boundary bank, which is aligned southeast to northwest through the centre of the enclosure, and measures approximately 0.5m high and 2m wide, and is in places revetted with a stone wall along its side. This boundary was probably constructed as part of the enclosure of the area in the mid-19th century (Bickerton Enclosure Map 1854, CALS QDE 1/36), and the quarrying is therefore perhaps most likely to date to the medieval or post-medieval periods. Another boundary bank, of similar construction, is aligned approximately northeast to southwest along the western edge of the enclosure, and follows the line of the former township boundary between Bickerton and Duckington to the west (Bickerton Tithe Map 1839, CALS EDT 46/2). Further stone quarrying has taken place along the cliff faces of the escarpment edge, on the western side of the site, although the date of this is unclear.

There is no evidence for internal occupation contemporary with the ramparts, and what may have survived is likely to have been destroyed or obscured by the quarrying, although subsurface prehistoric features could potentially survive in a relatively undisturbed area within the northern side of the enclosure (Garner, Chapter 6, this volume).

The site also contains the remains of a number of slit trenches, which were dug when the site was in use as an army training area in the second half of the 20th century. These survive as rectangular shallow depressions, measuring approximately 1m wide and between 1.7m and 2.8m long.

Discussion

Maiden Castle appears to represent a form of enclosure that is later than those at Helsby Hill and Woodhouse Hill, which are likely to have been constructed by the end of the 2nd millennium BC. Although superficially similar in plan to the Helsby Hill enclosure, Maiden Castle has an internal area only half of its size, while the ramparts and entranceway seem to represent a more complex and monumental form of construction than those surviving at

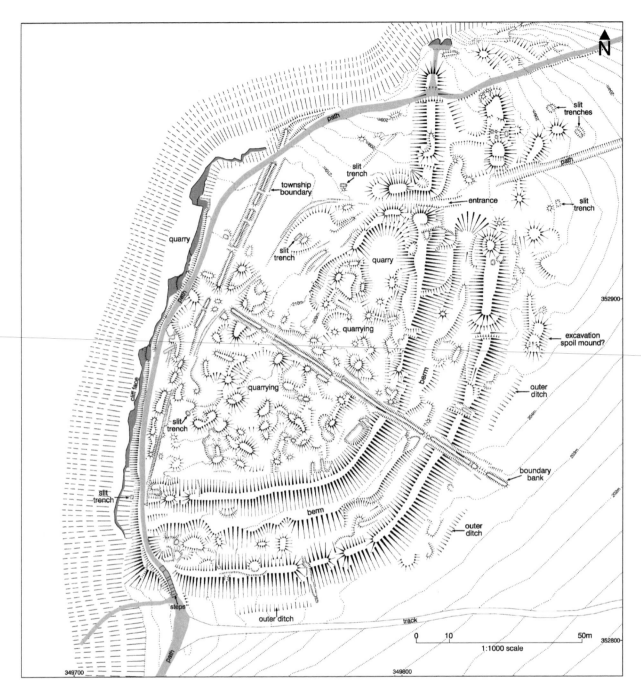

FIGURE 5.3 EARTHWORK SURVEY OF MAIDEN CASTLE (SCALE 1:1000).

Helsby Hill. The most recent radiocarbon dating evidence suggests that the inner rampart of Maiden Castle has a construction date between 860–330 cal BC, and that the date for the outer rampart is between 380–310 cal BC (Matthews 2002: 5; and Garner, Chapter 2, this volume). It is therefore likely that Maiden Castle represents a later, Iron Age, advance of the form of enclosure that developed during the late Bronze Age along the Cheshire Sandstone Ridge.

It is difficult to determine the phases of development of the enclosure from the earthworks alone, especially because of the extensive disturbance caused by

quarrying. It seems logical that the inner rampart would have formed part of the original design of the enclosure, rather than the interior of the enclosure being reduced by the later construction of the inner rampart, within a pre-existing circuit. Such a possibility is also supported by the radiocarbon results. The berm around the exterior of the inner rampart would have allowed the rampart to be constructed to a much greater height, reducing the possibility of slippage down the exterior scarp and providing a more stable platform on which any revetment or palisade could be constructed. The additional height would have allowed an increased defensive capacity, with the berm also producing an open area across which any attackers could easily be targeted from the rampart above. As well as this, it would have provided an impressive and monumental appearance, accentuating the importance of the site in the wider landscape, especially when viewed from the south and east.

The inturned entrance would also have provided visitors with an impressive route into the enclosure, with the length of the entranceway 'corridor' highlighting the divide between the high status interior and the surrounding area outside the ramparts. On a practical level, the length of the entranceway could potentially have acted as a defensive 'killing ground' in the event of attack.

Conclusion

Although the enclosures on Woodhouse Hill, Helsby Hill and at Maiden Castle all share similarities in their topographic positions, on prominent outcrops or ridges above steep escarpment edges, these sites vary in their form, date and potential function. Woodhouse Hill and Helsby Hill both appear to have their origin in the middle to late Bronze Age, and the size of the interior areas enclosed, suggest that they could have been designed to corral livestock, as well as potentially being focal points for other activities; they may not necessarily have had a primary function as defended settlements. The ramparts around all these enclosures would have provided them with a defensive capacity, but as has been seen at Woodhouse Hill and Helsby Hill, these do not always take advantage of the most defensible positions. It seems likely that the form of the enclosures was dictated not only by defensive requirements, but also potentially by a desire to include potentially culturally or ritually

significant areas, as at Helsby Hill, and to maximise the visual impact from the site.

Maiden Castle may originate a few centuries later than the other enclosures, and its smaller area, with limited room for herds of animals or communal activities, may suggest its principal function was as a defended settlement. The scale of the ramparts and complexity of the entranceway may imply the presence of a high status family group or local leader asserting their importance. Indeed, the construction of a secondary outer rampart at Helsby Hill could be seen as part of the same process of elaboration, with the occupants of the enclosure here 'updating' this older site to meet the changing social, cultural, and possible defensive requirements that may have influenced the form of Maiden Castle.

It is not possible to determine from the available dating evidence whether all, or any, of these sites were occupied at the same time, or for how long any activity within them continued. Indeed, the earthwork remains at Woodhouse Hill may even indicate that the enclosure was not completed and was never in use. We are also constrained in our understanding of activity within these enclosures due to the limited nature of any interior surface evidence.

The surface remains of all three enclosures cannot provide us with definite answers in relation to the date or role of these sites. However, detailed survey of the earthwork remains and analysis of their form has provided an opportunity to reconsider the layout, development and position of these enclosures within the wider landscape. It is hoped that this work has raised further questions regarding the function of these sites which could be addressed by future study.

Chapter 6
Geophysical Survey

Dan Garner

Background

The geophysical survey work carried out as part of the Habitats and Hillforts Project, between 2009 and 2012, amounted to a total of ten surveys covering seven scheduled monuments, including five of the six hillforts in the Project group. Woodhouse hillfort was not investigated using geophysics owing to the dense woodland covering the monument.

Prior to the commencement of the Habitats and Hillforts Project, limited attempts had been made to undertake geophysical survey on a number of the hillforts in the Cheshire group and often these surveys had been targeted to answer specific questions about a particular aspect of a monument. In 1981, a programme of geophysical survey was carried out by the Ancient Monuments Laboratory at Beeston Castle to investigate the area surrounding the excavations of the previous year in the outer ward and to locate a suspected ditch outside the main gateway (Bartlett 1981). At Helsby, part of what had been thought to be an outer rampart was targeted for a resistivity survey, the results of which suggested the line of a ditch or palisade trench (Rawson 1997). Two surveys were undertaken at Eddisbury: in 1990 both resistivity and magnetometry targeted the line of the possible early rampart which Varley suggested cut across the middle of the hilltop (Davies 1990); while in 2004, a resistivity survey tried to identify a geological fault line on the Merrick's Hill part of the hillfort (Pierce 2004). The most comprehensive resistivity survey on the Cheshire hillforts was undertaken on the western half of Kelsborrow hillfort by Alistair Quarterman in 1996 which identified possible pit clusters and building foundations within the enclosed area (Matthews 2002: 5–7).

In 2007, the local authority archaeological curators in the North West of England commissioned a review of the effectiveness of geophysical survey techniques in the region (Jordan 2007) funded by the Aggregates Levy Sustainability Fund. This was prompted by a series of poor survey results where subsequent open area excavation had identified archaeological features that had not been identified by geophysical survey. The nature of these features (such as a Roman pottery kiln at Middlewich, Cheshire) suggested that they should have been identified by these survey techniques. The results of the review were mixed, but it was accepted that the drift geology of the region was not ideal for geophysical prospecting. In the case of magnetometry this was owing to the high occurrence of erratics in the glacial tills which emit random magnetic signals and create a 'dotty' survey plot. The poor resistivity results were less easy to explain, but the extremes of moisture retaining properties on both clay-rich and sandy sub-soils were thought to be less than ideal. The review recommended a number of measures which could improve future returns on geophysical surveys, including ensuring that the geophysical contractor had access to detailed information on the underlying geology and increasing the number of readings being taken by reducing the width of transects from 1m intervals to 0.5m or even 0.25m.

The geophysical prospecting undertaken as part of the Habitats and Hillforts Project falls in to three categories:

- Volunteer training surveys – work undertaken as training exercises for local volunteers and overseen by specialist contractor Dr Ian Brooks of Engineering Archaeological Services Ltd.
- Student training surveys – work undertaken as part of student training programmes and overseen by lecturers from Chester and Liverpool Universities;
- Contractor surveys – work undertaken by specialist commercial geophysics contractor, ArchaeoPhysica Ltd.

Both magnetic susceptibility and electrical resistance surveys were carried out on all the investigated sites, with the methodology being designed to take on board the recommendations of the review undertaken by Jordan in 2007 and with the support of specialist advice from English Heritage. One site, Kelsborrow hillfort, was the subject of surveys by both students from Chester University and by the commercial contractor, allowing different approaches and methodologies to be compared.

This chapter presents a discussion of the possible archaeological features revealed by the surveys for each site, excluding features relating to the modern use of the site, such as drains or boundaries. Grey literature reports were produced for all surveys, from which the following summaries have been extracted. These can be accessed at the Cheshire Historic Environment record and through the online appendices.

Helsby Hillfort

Three areas of Helsby hillfort were surveyed by students from Liverpool University's School of Archaeology, Classics and Egyptology led by Dr Ben Edwards in 2009 and 2010 (Edwards 2011), (Figure 6.1).

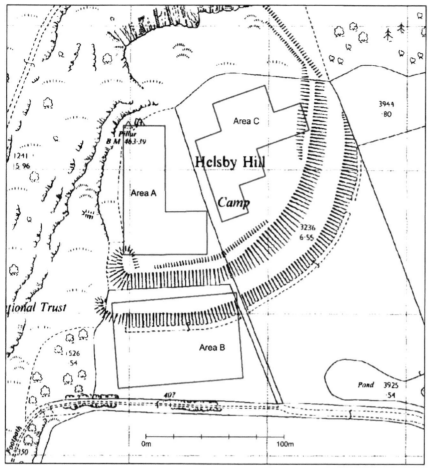

FIGURE 6.1 HELSBY HILLFORT SURVEY AREAS A TO C (EDWARDS 2011: 10 FIGURE 4).

the course of a large ditch, as ditches generally accumulate an increased concentration of magnetically susceptible elements. A low resistence linear anomoly running approximately 90m east to west probably also represents the course of the outer ditch as such features tend to produce low resistance anomalies, due to the better capacity for water retention afforded by ditch silts (Figure 6.2 [2]; Figure 6.3 [2]).

Curvilinear and associated linear low-resistance anomalies (Figure 6.2 [3] and [4]) identified in the resistivity survey are also likely to be composed of organic-rich soil elements concentrated in a cut feature. It appears that at least one of these linear anomalies post-dates the rampart anomaly (Figure 6.2 [1]), but their form and shape could indicate boundaries associated with the prehistoric settlement or pre-modern farming activities.

There are many constraints to geophysical survey on Helsby Hill due to the presence of large quantities of early 20th century to present day metallic debris both on the ground surface and in the turf layer. This is due to the use of the site since World War II for military purposes, and its current use as a recreational area. There was evidence for metallic rubbish and the setting of small fires. The picture is also complicated by the noisy magnetic background created by the iron-rich red sandstone bedrock. Despite these restrictions, it is possible to define a number of anomalies which may be associated with the use of the site as a hillfort.

In Area B (Figure 6.1) the outer rampart, running east to west, survives as a denuded bank badly truncated by agricultural improvement. This was revealed as a broadly linear diffuse area of generally magnetic response in the gradiometer survey and as a high resistance linear anomoly by the resistivity survey, probably composed of either packed earth or a mixture of free draining earth and stone (Figure 6.2 [1]; Figure 6.3 [1]).

There is no surface evidence of an accompanying outer ditch, but the anomolies representing the bank are closely paralleled by a linear diffuse area of generally positive magmentic response which probably represent

Several features were identified by the gradiometer survey in the western half of the interior of the hillfort in Area A (Figures 6.1 and 6.4).

Two circular anomalies (Figure 6.4 [1]), characterised by a central area of high magnetic susceptibility are surrounded by a slight pennanular positive anomaly, the whole area measuring c. 10m in diameter. The nature of these anomalies is unknown, but the intensity of the central values indicates the presence of metallic debris. Possible features associated with the entrance to the hillfort, perhaps small flanking ditches or gullies, may be represented by an irregular arc (Figure 6.4 [2]), c. 10m in diameter, which may actually be two opposing linear features to the north and south, with the apparent linking of the arc to the west, a consequence of the iron spikes and disturbance toward that edge of the plot.

Other features revealed by the surveys are perhaps related to land drainage or the provision of services to the World War II observation post on the hilltop.

Eddisbury Hillfort

Electrical resistance (Figure 6.5) and caesium magnetometer surveys (Figure 6.6) were carried out on

47

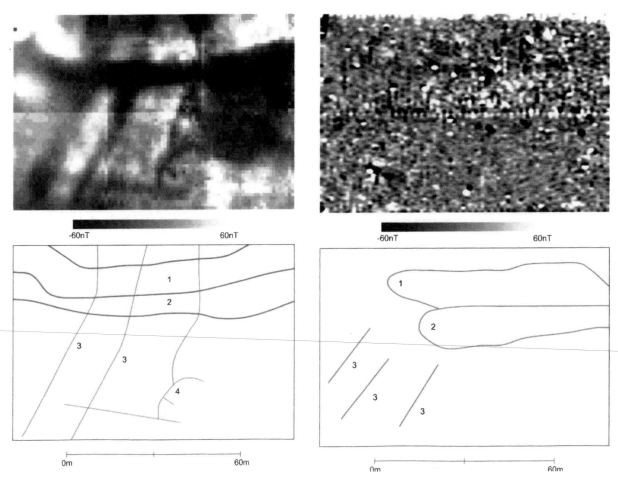

-60nT   60nT

-60nT   60nT

0m   60m

0m   60m

FIGURE 6.2 HELSBY HILLFORT SURVEY AREA B RESISTIVITY ANOMALIES (EDWARDS 2011: 10 FIGURE 4).

FIGURE 6.3 HELSBY HILLFORT SURVEY AREA B MAGNETIC ANOMALIES (EDWARDS 2011: 16 FIGURE 7).

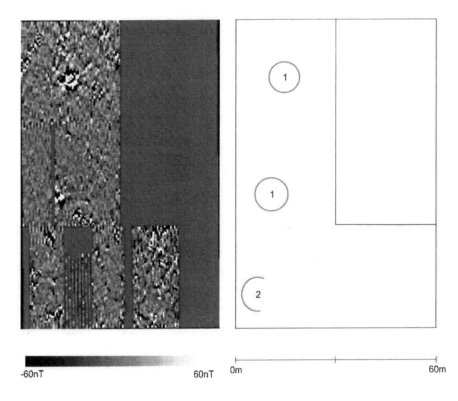

-60nT   60nT

0m   60m

FIGURE 6.4 HELSBY HILLFORT SURVEY AREA A MAGNETIC ANOMALIES (EDWARDS 2011: 12 FIGURE 5).

the interior of Eddisbury hillfort in 2009 and 2010, by specialist geophysics contractor ArchaeoPhysica Ltd (Roseveare *et al*. 2010a).

Geological variations are predominant in the survey results, with probable bedding or cracking of the sandstone bedrock detected close beneath the surface. Given the shallow nature of the overlying soils, it seems likely that archaeological features, which may have originally been present within the soils covering the hilltop, have been at least severely truncated, if not removed altogether. For this reason it is inevitable that potential rock-cut features (e.g. Figure 6.7 [9]) present the clearest anomalies in both data sets.

48

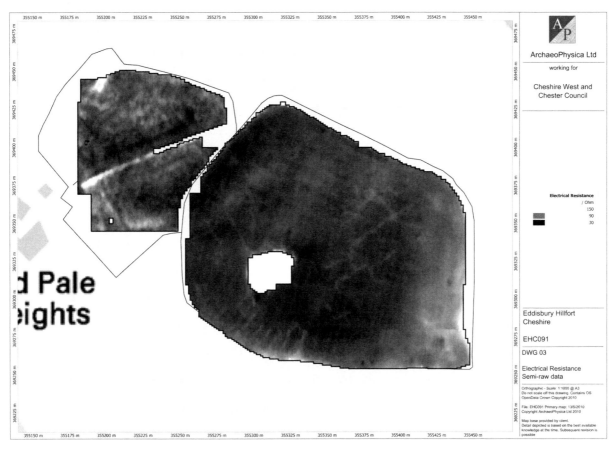

FIGURE 6.5 EDDISBURY HILLFORT RESISTIVITY SURVEY RESULTS (ROSEVEARE *ET AL.* 2010A: DWG 03).

FIGURE 6.6 EDDISBURY HILLFORT MAGNETIC FIELD SURVEY RESULTS (ROSEVEARE *ET AL.* 2010A: DWG 02).

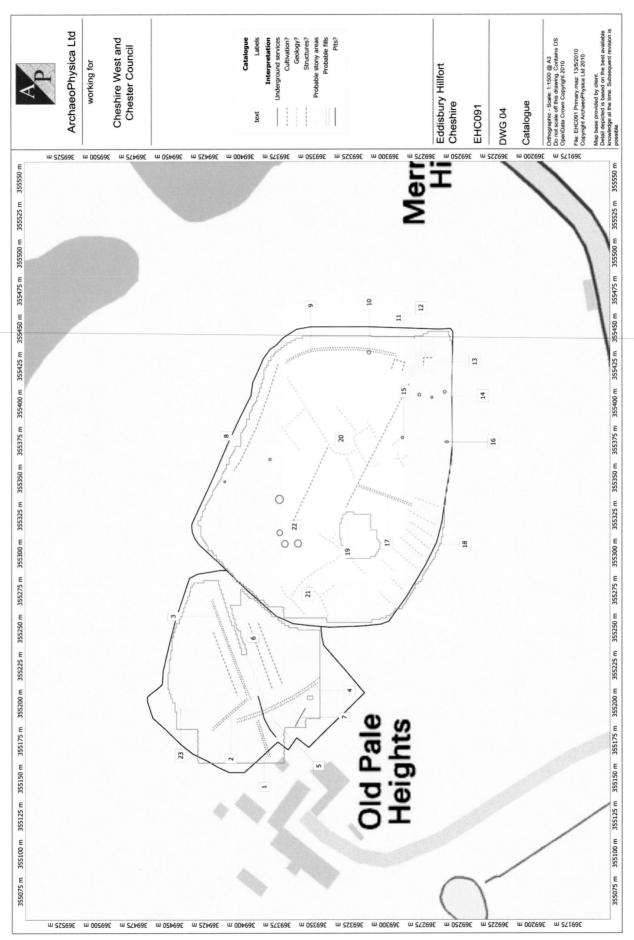

FIGURE 6.7 EDDISBURY HILLFORT SUMMARY OF THE SURVEY RESULTS (ROSEVEARE *ET AL.* 2010A: DWG 04).

Despite these restrictions, however, weak anomalies from features of archaeological interest were found. The clearest indications of past activity, are two probable ditch sections (Figure 6.7 [4] and [9]). The first lies below the western field and may well have formed the southern arc of the main hillfort enclosure (Figure 6.7 [4]), although a defensive purpose seems unlikely given the narrow width of the anomaly. Within the main enclosure, in the eastern field, the second ditch section (Figure 6.7 [9]) follows a smooth curve across much of the width of the field and could well have been the original eastern edge of the enclosure. Neither of these structures would appear to have been defensive as they are 3m or less in width. It is possible that these structures may be unrelated to the hillfort and if they are as late as medieval, their association with possible nearby rectangular structures (Figure 6.7 [11] – [13]) becomes interesting (see below).

The data presents a largely blank image for the interior of the hillfort, however, weak electrical resistance anomalies (Figure 6.7 [22]), all of a circular form, might suggest the presence of structures dug into the rock at this location. Large pits (in this case ranging in size from 3.5m to 5m diameter) are a common feature associated with prehistoric settlement and might be expected in this setting. The anomalies are not particularly diagnostic but are typical of moisture-retaining structures. In a prehistoric context, grain storage is a possibility within a settlement enclosure.

In the southeast corner of the survey area and possibly outside the circuit of the hillfort, and at least over or outside one of the probable ditch sections (Figure 6.7 [9]), are a pair of possible structures. Neither are well-defined but the southern one (Figure 6.7 [13]) appears as a broadly rectangular, low resistance area, bounded on its northern and eastern sides, and possibly the western, by an irregular area of high resistance (Figure 6.7 [12]). The latter could be natural, in which case perhaps [13] is cut into it; alternatively,

material [12] could have accumulated around an upstanding form of [13]. The lack of magnetic expression implies that if these structures are real then they are formed from earth and/ or stone, not brick and are perhaps fairly limited in depth. The northern structure (Figure 6.7 [11]) is less evident and may not be a structure at all, however, a similar form to [13] is implied. The rectangular nature might suggest the sites of buildings which may be related to the medieval or post-medieval use of the site as a forester's lodge (see Chapter 11, this volume). It is possible that these structures date from this time and could potentially have a medieval origin within an organised hunting and coursing environment. However, it is also possible that these represent the remains of 20th century wartime defensive structures.

Kelsborrow Hillfort

Surveys were carried out at Kelsborrow hillfort by students from Chester University's Department of History and Archaeology, led by Dr Meggen Gondek in 2009 (Gondek 2010) and by specialist geophysics contractor ArchaeoPhysica Ltd in 2010 (Roseveare et al. 2010b). Magnetometer surveys were carried out on three areas (marked Areas 1 to 3 on Figure 6.8) and resistivity on one area of the hillfort by Chester University (Figure 6.8), while an area of approximately 3.5ha, covering the interior and all of the ramparts was surveyed by electrical resistance (Figure 6.9) and caesium magnetometer surveys (Figure 6.10) by ArchaeoPhysica Ltd.

The site has been intensively ploughed in the past and given the apparently fairly shallow nature of the soil, it seems inevitable that shallow features have been truncated or destroyed. Good evidence for the form of the ramparts was recovered by the ArchaeoPhysica Ltd survey, including signs of a possible palisade trench or similar structure along the top of the rampart bank. The bank and ditch of the hillfort defences are clear in the data as high and low resistance anomalies respectively (Figure 6.11). However, the data is unusual in that the raised magnetic intensity anomaly corresponds to approximately the inner half of the bank, not the ditch fill as would normally be expected. The ditch itself does not exhibit a magnetic anomaly. The variation in width of these features apparent in the electrical resistance data is probably related to differences in drainage between the eastern and western halves of the site.

Along the top of the bank as evident by high resistance structures [3] and [10] (Figure 6.11), there is an irregular band of low resistance [4] and [9] which is discontinuous and of variable width although present over about half the length of the

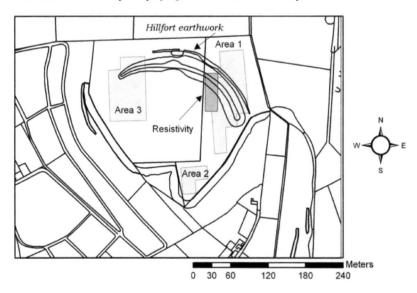

FIGURE 6.8 KELSBORROW: CHESTER UNIVERSITY SURVEY AREAS MAGNETOMETRY AREAS 1 TO 3 AND RESISTIVITY (GONDEK 2010:4 FIGURE 1).

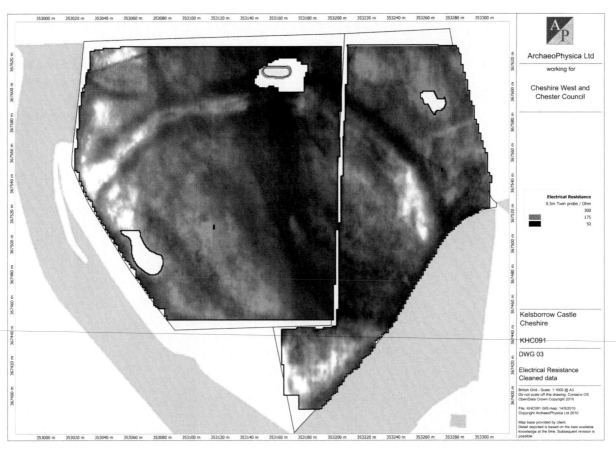

FIGURE 6.9 KELSBORROW: ARCHAEOPHYSICA LTD RESISTIVITY SURVEY RESULTS (ROSEVEARE *ET AL.* 2010B: DWG 03).

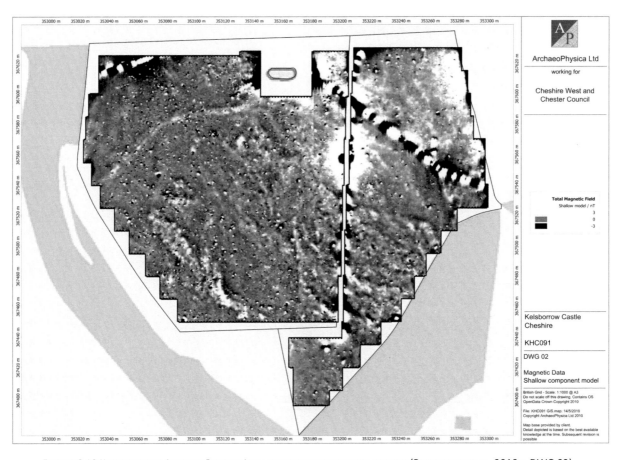

FIGURE 6.10 KELSBORROW: ARCHAEOPHYSICA LTD MAGNETIC FIELD SURVEY RESULTS (ROSEVEARE *ET AL.* 2010B: DWG 02).

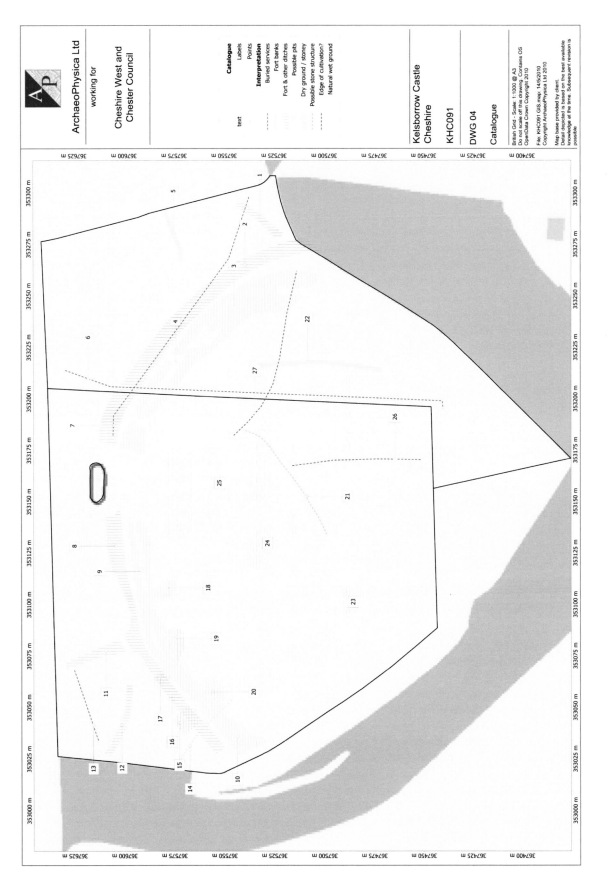

Figure 6.11 Kelsborrow: ArchaeoPhysica Ltd summary of the survey results (Roseveare *et al.* 2010b: DWG 04).

structure. Two interpretations are possible, both based upon the presumption that the anomaly is caused by damp fill within a feature cut into the bank itself. There may have been a trench to support a palisade or similar structure or the anomaly may be caused by fill within a former eroded channel, perhaps repairing earlier damage. Another possibility is that it relates to the construction of the bank itself, although this is perhaps less likely. If the bank has an earthen core covered by a stonier layer, then erosion of this outer material may have exposed the earthen (and presumably lower resistance) core. A magnetic anomaly coincident with the bank is hard to explain, however, it is unlikely to originate beneath the bank as there is no evidence that features cut into the natural ground here are exhibiting sufficient magnetic contrast to be detected and in any case, their depth of burial should result in a weaker and more diffuse anomaly than is present here. This implies the source has to be within the bank itself and taken with the discovery of a low resistance structure along the top suggests the bank to be a complex structure.

One possibility is that the inside face of the bank is covered with occupation debris, perhaps tipped there during settlement of the site, however, an alternative explanation might be that the bank or something within it has been burnt. Excavation by Dr David Coombs of Manchester University in 1973 across the bank in the eastern part of the site, revealed a line of three postholes which suggested the possibility of a timber revetment and if this has been burnt, then it is possible the magnetic susceptibility of the surrounding ground has become sufficiently elevated to be detectable at the surface. It is interesting that this anomaly occupies only the inner face of the bank, perhaps not what would be expected if a timber revetted bank had been burnt during conflict, for example. It is also possible that the interior of the hillfort is more magnetic than the exterior, although insufficient ground was covered outside to be certain and further work would be needed to explore this. It could be conjectured, that if the interior is more magnetic than the exterior and there is a burnt timber revetment, perhaps the whole fort has at some point experienced a serious conflagration. This is conjecture at this stage and further non-invasive work would be needed to examine this possibility.

A number of discrete low resistance structures lie along the course of ditch [8] (Figure 6.11) but seem wider or more substantial. It is uncertain whether these are natural and caused by the bedding of the underlying rock or are artificial structures like large pits. If the latter, they appear to lie under the bank [10] as there is a suggestion of pairing across the width of this structure, e.g. [15] with [20], [17] with [19]. During excavations at Kelsborrow, one of these possible pits was investigated (see Garner, Chapter 12, trench 3, this volume).

No clear indications of an entrance were found, although a gap filled by the present pond, could easily have accommodated a gate structure.

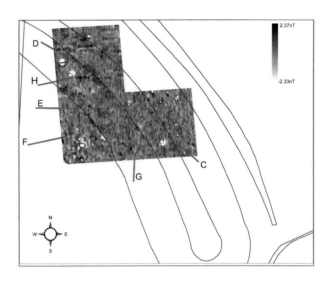

FIGURE 6.12 KELSBORROW: CHESTER UNIVERSITY SURVEY DETAIL OF THE AREA 1 SURVEY RESULTS (GONDEK 2010:12 FIGURE 7).

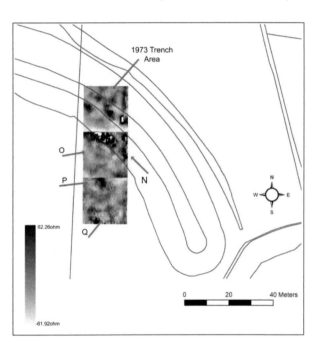

FIGURE 6.13 KELSBORROW: CHESTER UNIVERSITY SURVEY DETAIL OF THE RESISTIVITY SURVEY RESULTS (GONDEK 2010:17 FIGURE 11).

The bank and ditch did not show up well in Area One of the Chester University survey. Unfortunately, strong magnetic readings from a modern pipe or cable, running along the assumed line of the hillfort ditch, meant that the ditch was not detected. The rampart bank, although visible as an upstanding earthwork on site, did not show in the gradiometry results very clearly, if at all. Two very weak linear responses can be suggested (Figure 6.12 [C] and [D]), which do correspond to the Ordnance Survey demarcation of the top of the bank and where the 1973 excavation by David Coombs found rampart evidence. However, given the general northwest-southeast linear trends in the data, these linear anomalies may be deceptive. The inner edge of the bank appears most convincing in the northwest. Here it appears to have other features abutting it and a stronger magnetic signature.

The Chester University survey targeted a small area for resistivity in the eastern field, immediately to the west of Area One (Figures 6.8 and 6.13), to complement the magnetic survey. The grids for the resistivity survey appear to coincide in part with the 1973 excavation trench, which was 25m x 2m (Coombs 1988). The excavation trench may be identified by a northeast-southwest linear gap, which 'cuts through' a resistant anomaly that runs in an arc northwest-southeast, presumably part of the bank material. The bank material is noted to have contained sandstone as part of the revetment material (Coombs 1988: 66), which would contribute to a higher resistance. The bank (Figure 6.13[N]) appears as a band of resistant responses running northwest-southeast, but it is inconsistent and appears to have an interior band of less resistant signature within it. This less resistant signature may correlate with the top of the bank. Posthole or interior features are not visible on the top of the bank. The bottom of the interior bank is quite clearly visible as a break between higher and lower resistance. This difference between the top of the bank and its sides was also noted by the ArchaeoPhysica Ltd survey and was interpreted as potentially relating to a palisade on top of the bank (see above).

As with Area One, the results from Area Three of the Chester University survey, which was surveyed using gradiometry only and covers the western end of the rampart, were disappointing. There was no sign of the bank or ditch and it is likely that ploughing may have damaged features significantly in this area. The bank may be represented by a cluster of dipolar and slightly negative magnetic readings which might reflect the sandstone used in the bank structure as outlined by the 1973 excavation (Coombs 1988). The almost total absence of the ditch from the magnetic surveys carried out by Chester University corresponds to the survey carried out by ArchaeoPhysica Ltd and is probably due to soil conditions rather than a lack of survival.

Results from the surveys of the interior of the hillfort were rather different. ArchaeoPhysica Ltd note that there is certainly little or no evidence for internal form. Also absent are discrete sources typical of burning, e.g. hearths and pit-type anomalies typical of settlement. This could be due to a genuine lack of such structures, their loss through ploughing or simply insufficient contrast between the physical properties of the structures and their surroundings. It is possible that two large low resistance anomalies (Figure 6.11 [1] and [11]), typical of ditch fills could potentially form part of a northern annexe, but insufficient length was within the surveyed area to give an idea of form.

In contrast, the Chester University survey identified several possible features in Area One (Figure 6.8) inside the hillfort. Abutting the possible line of the rampart (D) (Figure 6.12)

is a possible roundhouse (E), a circular anomaly *c.* 8.5m in diameter. Inside is a slightly magnetic response forming a squared feature approximately 2.5m across, with some central magnetic activity in the interior. This could represent a roundhouse with a circular wall or eaves drip surrounding a square hearth, but this does not show a strong magnetic signature of burning; it may alternatively represent possible postholes forming roof supports. If this is a roundhouse, it is situated almost adjacent to the interior line of the rampart and is now covered by the spread of material probably related to ploughing out of the rampart itself. There is also a possible circular enclosure (F) abutting the interior line of the rampart surrounding this potential roundhouse, as well as other indeterminate features of slight magnetic response at (G) and (H).

Another possible roundhouse or enclosure feature was detected in Area Two of the Chester University Survey. This area lies south of the rampart (Figure 6.8), within the interior of the hillfort and was surveyed using gradiometry only. At approximately 11.4m in diameter, this circular feature of weak magnetic response with an interior dipolar response (I) (Figure 6.14), is perhaps more the size of an enclosure rather than a roundhouse. During excavations at Kelsborrow, this anomoly was investigated (see Garner, Chapter 12, trench 2).

In Area Three there are numerous examples of dipolar readings, which may represent near-surface metal or possibly archaeological features. These do not convincingly form coherent structures, but might represent stony filled pits. A few positive magnetic features might represent pits or possibly hearths. The most convincing coherent feature (and even this is a very slight signature) is a circular feature

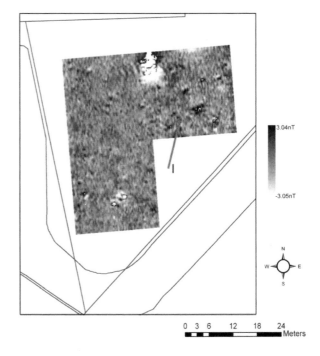

FIGURE 6.14 KELSBORROW: CHESTER UNIVERSITY SURVEY DETAIL OF THE AREA 2 SURVEY RESULTS (GONDEK 2010:14 FIGURE 8).

with potentially a concentric feature within it. This might be an enclosure ditch.

In the resistivity survey area in the eastern field, immediately to the west of Area One (Figure 6.8), the grids were laid out to target the potential roundhouse feature (E) identified through the gradiometry survey. An oval circular low resistance anomaly, *c*. 11m in diameter, was identified around a higher resistance reading (Figure 6.13 [P]). Potential interpretations might be an enclosure rather than a roundhouse, with packed earth (resistant) in the interior, perhaps relating to animal storage. To the south of this is a small circular low resistance anomaly (Figure 6.13 [Q]), which has a gap to the south. Just to the west is an east-west line of quite discrete closely spaced higher resistance anomalies, which may represent a series of pit or posthole alignments with interior packing material or rubble fill.

Figure 6.15 shows a schematic plot of potential archaeological features identified by the two Chester University survey sessions. Whilst the surveys do not definitely indicate an interior filled with the expected domestic and agricultural features of the later prehistoric period and all the interpretations should be treated with caution, there are hints that some archaeological features survive, albeit probably heavily truncated. The numerous dipolar anomalies peppered throughout the magnetic survey (not shown on Figure 6.15 for clarity) could represent pits or potentially hearth structures. These may be the only things to survive on heavily ploughed hillfort sites, where shallow features such as postholes or eaves drip gullies might be truncated or simply not registering a magnetic response (Payne 2006, 34).

Maiden Castle

As part of the volunteer training programme, the Habitats and Hillforts Project undertook geophysical survey at Maiden Castle in 2011, with local volunteers under instruction from specialist contractor Dr Ian Brooks, of Engineering Archaeological Services Ltd (Brooks 2011).

The fluxgate gradiometer survey covered an area of 0.33ha (Figure 6.16), while the resistivity survey covered an area of 0.25ha (Figure 6.17). The interpretation of both surveys is summarised in Figure 6.18.

Given the level of vegetation on the site and the restricted area of the undisturbed part of the hillfort, the results of the geophysical surveys are remarkably clear. The fluxgate gradiometer survey in particular has revealed some intriguing results, particularly in the difference in response between the two sides of the gateway (Figure 6.18). The inner rampart of the hillfort to the north of the entrance has a high magnetic signal (Figure 6.16) suggesting that there may have been some modification of the magnetic response, possibly through heating. The southern side of the gateway and the outer rampart do not give as strong a magnetic response, however, and the difference in magnetic response between the two sides of the gateway suggests that each of these ramparts is either constructed differently, or have been subject to a different history. The high responses recorded to the north of the gate are often associated with high temperatures, possibly the burning of the rampart. The rampart and gateway, as is expected, give a high resistance response, although this anomaly covers a larger area than the magnetic response to these features (Figure 6.17).

There are two linear magnetic anomalies between the inner and outer ramparts (Figures 6.16 and 6.18). The first skirts the end of the outer rampart before turning to run between the ramparts, whilst the second crosses the first roughly at right angles, blocking the gap between the two ramparts. The function of these anomalies is unknown, but it would suggest a level of activity associated with the entrance of the hillfort.

Inside the hillfort, the locations of possibly three roundhouses have been defined (Figures 6.16 and 6.18). Whilst only one has a full circle and a central anomaly which may be the response to a hearth, the others appear to be circles of suitable sizes to be roundhouses. The clearest of these forms a circle approximately 6.9m in diameter

Red features - gradiometry
Green features - resistivity

N
W–E
S

0   70   140 Meters

FIGURE 6.15 KELSBORROW: CHESTER UNIVERSITY'S SCHEMATIC PLOT OF POTENTIAL ARCHAEOLOGICAL FEATURES IDENTIFIED BY THE TWO SURVEY SESSIONS (GONDEK 2010:19 FIGURE 12).

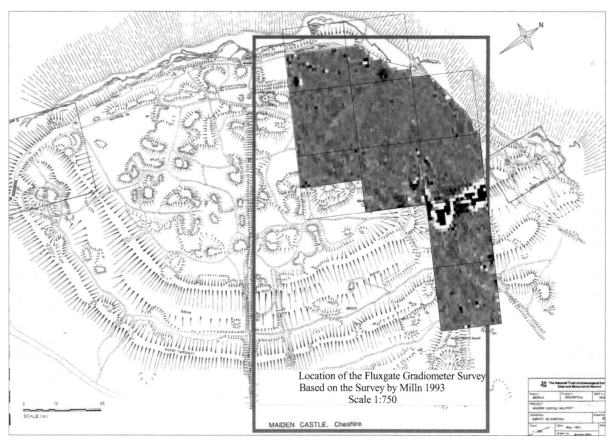

FIGURE 6.16 MAIDEN CASTLE GREYSCALE PLOT OF THE FLUXGATE GRADIOMETER SURVEY (BROOKS 2011: FIGURE 2).

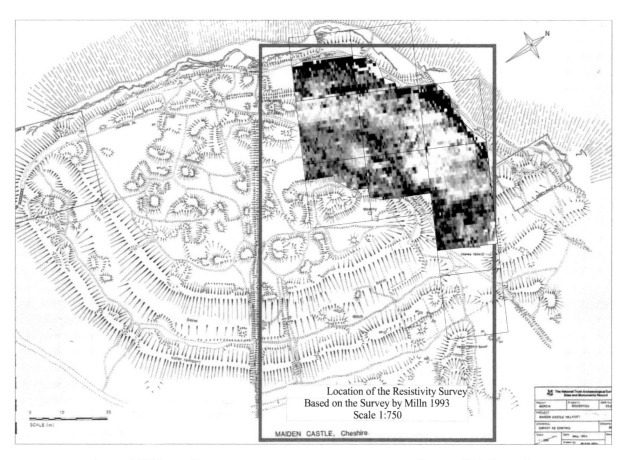

FIGURE 6.17 MAIDEN CASTLE GREYSCALE PLOT OF THE RESISTIVITY SURVEY (BROOKS 2011: FIGURE 3).

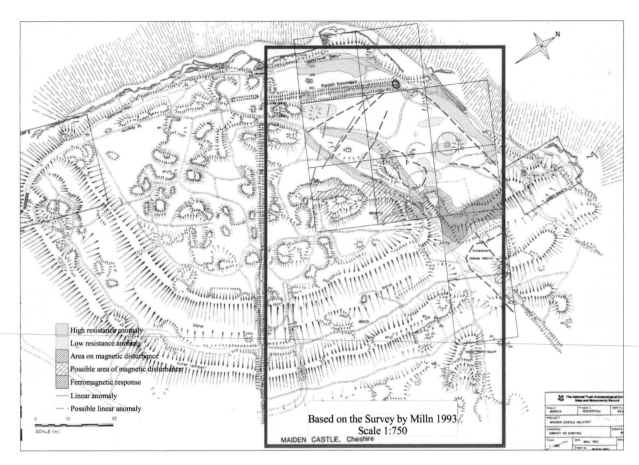

FIGURE 6.18 MAIDEN CASTLE SUMMARY OF THE GEOPHYSICAL SURVEY RESULTS (BROOKS 2011: FIGURE 12).

and has an area of magnetic disturbance at its centre. This response is typical of that expected from a roundhouse. In approximately the same area an enhanced resistance anomaly is recorded, together with a roughly circular, low resistance anomaly approximately 6.1m in diameter. Two other possible circular magnetic anomalies are just inside the gateway of the hillfort and may also mark the positions of possible roundhouses. They are approximately 8.2m and 7.8m in diameter, while another arc of low resistance appears to define part of an area approximately 7.5m in diameter. Unfortunately this does not correspond with any feature defined in the gradiometer survey.

Inside the hillfort, both magnetic and resistance linear anomalies were identified, some of which appear to correspond with modern footpaths and the boundary bank defining the parish boundary between the parishes of Bickerton and Broxton, all giving rise to enhanced areas of resistance.

Beeston Castle

As part of the volunteer training programme, the Habitats and Hillforts Project undertook geophysical survey at Beeston Castle in 2009 and 2010, with local volunteers under instruction from specialist contractor Dr Ian Brooks of Engineering Archaeological Services Ltd (Brooks and Laws 2009; Brooks and Price 2010a; Brooks and Price

2010b). Two separate survey areas were covered – in the outer bailey in June and August 2010 and at the outer gateway in November 2009 (Figure 6.19).

The Outer Bailey – June 2010

The geophysical surveys within the outer bailey of Beeston Castle carried out in June 2010, revealed a number of anomalies which possibly relate to the prehistoric, medieval and modern use of the site.

The results of the fluxgate gradiometer survey are shown as a greyscale plot in Figure 6.20, while the results of the resistivity survey are shown as greyscale plots in Figure 6.21. The interpretation of both surveys is summarised in Figure 6.22.

Two curvilinear magnetic anomalies have been defined in the fluxgate gradiometer survey. The first, although faint, appears to be a circular anomaly, approximately 7.6m in diameter (Figure 6.22). This may represent the position of a prehistoric roundhouse; however there were a number of sub-circular hollows in this part of the survey area which may also have given rise to this anomaly. The second is oval in shape with the southern half of this anomaly being clearer than the north. It encloses an area of 9.4m x 6.1m with its long axis running with the slope of the hillside.

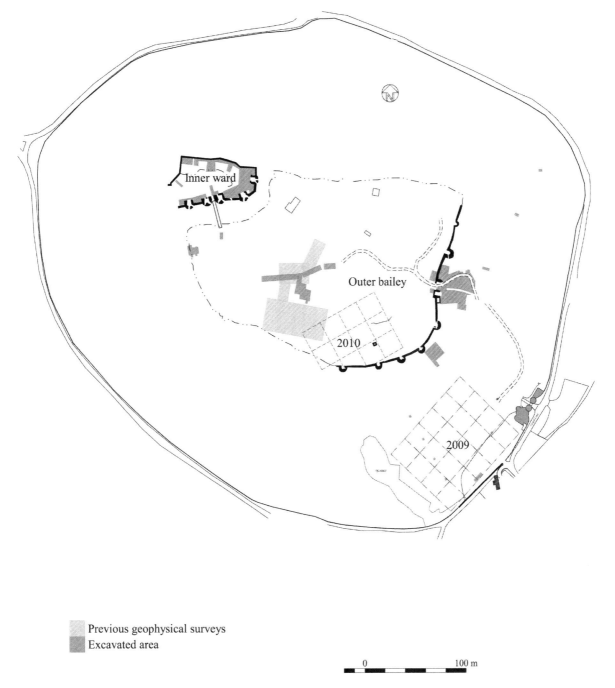

Inner ward

Outer bailey

2010

2009

Previous geophysical surveys
Excavated area

0   100 m

FIGURE 6.19 SHOWING THE AREAS OF THE 2009 AND JUNE 2010 SURVEYS IN RELATION TO EARLIER AREAS OF GEOPHYSICAL SURVEY AND EXCAVATION (BROOKS AND PRICE 2010A: FIGURE 2).

One feature of enhanced resistance is distinctive in that it too appears to define a circular anomaly, approximately 8.4m in diameter (Figure 6.22). It is possible that this may also represent the site of a prehistoric roundhouse; however it is curious that it does not appear to have a corresponding anomaly in the fluxgate gradiometer survey.

Three discrete anomalies have relatively high magnetic signatures suggestive of burnt features, possibly hearths or ovens (Figure 6.20). The full extent of the northern anomaly is not defined as it extends beyond the survey area, while the data covering the other two anomalies suggested that they have a dipolar structure, typical of

a burnt feature. Areas of burning such as furnaces or hearths, which are still in situ, give north-south oriented dipolar signals due to the relatively strong remnant magnetism of the feature.

The fluxgate gradiometer survey revealed a network of linear magnetic anomalies crossing the survey area of uncertain date (Figure 6.20); although it would appear likely that some may relate to the medieval or early post-medieval occupation of the site. Three anomalies are roughly parallel and run with the hill slope with a further two anomalies running roughly perpendicular to the others. Extending the line of the southern anomaly,

FIGURE 6.20 BEESTON CASTLE OUTER BAILEY AND OUTER GATEWAY FLUXGATE GRADIOMETER SURVEY RESULTS, NOVEMBER 2009 AND JUNE 2010 (BROOKS AND PRICE 2010A: FIGURE 3).

there appears to be a rectilinear enclosure, approximately 17.7m x 9.0m in size adjacent to the curtain wall of the outer bailey. It is possible that this anomaly may mark the position of a building against the curtain wall. Two anomalies adjacent to the curtain wall of the outer bailey are likely to be a response to the wall itself. It is possible, however that they may also be a response to the underlying prehistoric rampart (Figure 6.22).

The resistivity survey (Figure 6.21) identified three areas of very high resistance, one of which is likely to be archaeological in origin. It sits within a larger area of enhanced resistance on a terrace on the hillside, where the front of the terrace is marked by a rock outcrop.

Two linear anomalies form a band of enhanced resistance running parallel to the line of the curtain wall of the outer

FIGURE 6.21 BEESTON CASTLE OUTER BAILEY AND OUTER GATEWAY RESISTIVITY SURVEY RESULTS, NOVEMBER 2009 AND JUNE 2010 (BROOKS AND PRICE 2010A: FIGURE 4).

bailey. They are positioned at the foot of the hill slope along the northern edge of the flat area in front of the curtain wall. It is considered unlikely that these anomalies are the result of modern (footpath) features and possibly mark the position of an archaeological feature. A further two linear anomalies may have originally formed an enclosure approximately 18.7m x 23.0m in size, although this possibility remains speculative. Within the possible enclosure however, is an area of low resistance of uncertain origin, which sits on the lower terrace sampled by the survey (Figure 6.22).

The effect of the modern usage of the site can be demonstrated by areas of magnetic disturbance and high/

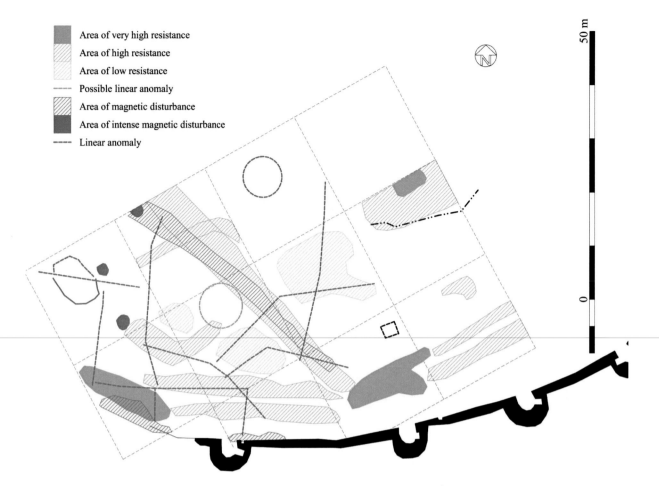

Area of very high resistance
Area of high resistance
Area of low resistance
Possible linear anomaly
Area of magnetic disturbance
Area of intense magnetic disturbance
Linear anomaly

FIGURE 6.22 BEESTON CASTLE OUTER BAILEY SUMMARY OF THE SURVEY RESULTS, JUNE 2010 (BROOKS AND PRICE 2010A: FIGURE 12).

enhanced resistance which correspond to a network of modern footpaths and wear associated with the use of a bench.

The Outer Bailey – August 2010

Both the fluxgate gradiometer and resistivity surveys carried out in the outer bailey of Beeston Castle in August 2010, have been particularly successful in locating and defining the nineteenth and twentieth century activity within this part of the castle.

The results of the fluxgate gradiometer survey are shown as a greyscale plot in Figure 6.23, while the results of the resistivity survey are shown as greyscale plots in Figure 6.24. The interpretation of both surveys is summarised in Figure 6.25.

The position of at least two assumed marquees has been defined together with details of the permanent works for securing the marquee guy ropes. The grey scale plot is dominated by a series of discrete ferromagnetic responses (shown in blue on Figure 16.25). The majority of these define two large rectangular areas which are at the edge of platforms cut into the hillside and probably represent permanent tether points for marquees for the Bunbury Temperance Fairs, which were held on the hilltop from

1851. A single iron ring attached to a sandstone block was noted during the survey and it is assumed that the other ferromagnetic responses are similar anchor points. The resistivity survey recorded two anomalies which align with these ferromagnetic anomalies and are similarly assumed to mark the anchor points of the marquees for the Bunbury Fair. Two sub-rectangular anomalies were also located. Their origins are uncertain, however they appear to align with the platforms assumed to be the sites of the fair marquees and therefore may be associated with this phase of activity on the site.

A third area with a concentration of ferromagnetic responses crosses the northern end of the surveys area. This has a concentration of discrete ferromagnetic anomalies within a zone of magnetic of disturbance. This anomaly aligns not only with the modern footpath crossing the site, but also with of one of the archaeological trenches excavated in the 1970s. Another large area of magnetic disturbance aligns with another of the main excavation trenches.

A further two anomalies appear to equate with the areas excavated between 1968 and 1985. Probably related to the latter is an area of mixed resistance including areas of high resistance, which may mark the position of the spoil heap for the excavation.

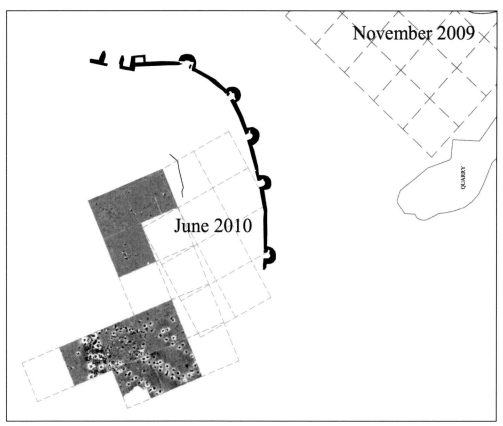

Figure 6.23 Beeston Castle Outer Bailey fluxgate gradiometer survey results, August 2010 (Brooks and Price 2010b: Figure 2).

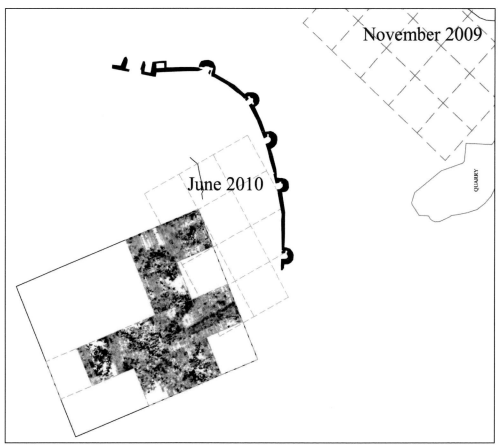

Figure 6.24 Beeston Castle Outer Bailey resistivity survey results, August 2010 (Brooks and Price 2010b: Figure 3).

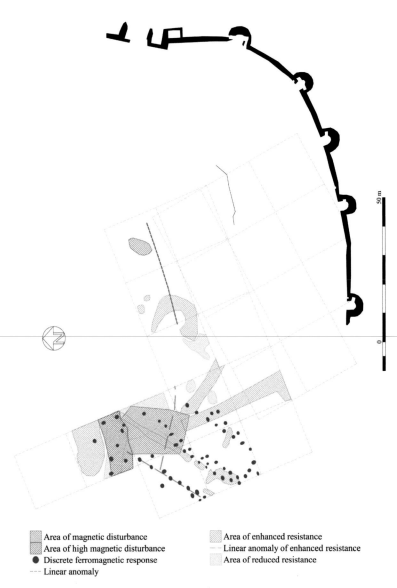

Area of magnetic disturbance
Area of high magnetic disturbance
● Discrete ferromagnetic response
--- Linear anomaly

Area of enhanced resistance
--- Linear anomaly of enhanced resistance
Area of reduced resistance

FIGURE 6.25 BEESTON CASTLE OUTER BAILEY SUMMARY OF THE SURVEY RESULTS, AUGUST 2010 (BROOKS AND PRICE 2010B: FIGURE 12).

Both the magnetometer and resistivity surveys revealed several anomalies which probably relate to known footpaths, access tracks, service trenches and a stone mason's yard. A distinct rectilinear shape, 11m x 5m in size could mark a platform cut into the hillside, possibly for a building.

Despite the extent of modern activity in this area, there are a number of anomalies both in the resistivity and fluxgate gradiometer surveys, which appear to relate to a possible earlier phase of agricultural activity.

Two magnetic linear anomalies are much fainter on the greyscale plots than the other anomalies and presumably represent possible archaeological features. The first crosses the slope at the western end of the survey area, whilst the second is an arc, with a projected diameter of approximately 6.6m. The origin of the latter is uncertain; however, the former appears to relate to a series of parallel anomalies. These are assumed to be the result of ploughing; therefore they may mark the southern extent of a field. A second area of possible ploughing has also been defined in the central area of the survey.

Similarly two bands of enhanced resistance which follow no known modern route and cut across the slope may represent slight terracing of the hillside, possibly for agriculture, although a geological origin cannot be excluded.

It is possible that the upper slopes of the survey area were slightly terraced and that ploughing took place on those terraces. There is a possibility of a platform having been cut into the slope, however the nature of this anomaly and the origins of the high magnetic anomaly can only be determined by excavation.

Peckforton Mere

Magnetic survey using a high sensitivity magnetometer with caesium vapour sensors (Figure 6.27) and twin probe electrical resistance survey (Figure 6.28) was commissioned to explore the promontory fort at Peckforton Mere. This was part of the Habitats and Hillforts Project aim to examine fortified sites of presumed Iron Age date in Cheshire. The survey work was undertaken in 2012

A marked high resistance anomaly runs approximately north-northwest to south-southeast in the southern section of the survey. This anomaly has a distinctive structure with higher resistance along its edges, which are well defined. The anomaly is approximately 5m wide suggesting it may be a track or road way.

The Outer Gateway – November 2009

The Outer Gateway area of the site is used for public events and picnics and so the results of any geophysical survey are likely to be influenced by modern disturbance.

The results of the fluxgate gradiometer survey are shown as a greyscale plot in Figure 6.20, while the results of the resistivity survey are shown as greyscale plots in Figure 6.21. The interpretation of both surveys is summarised in Figure 6.26.

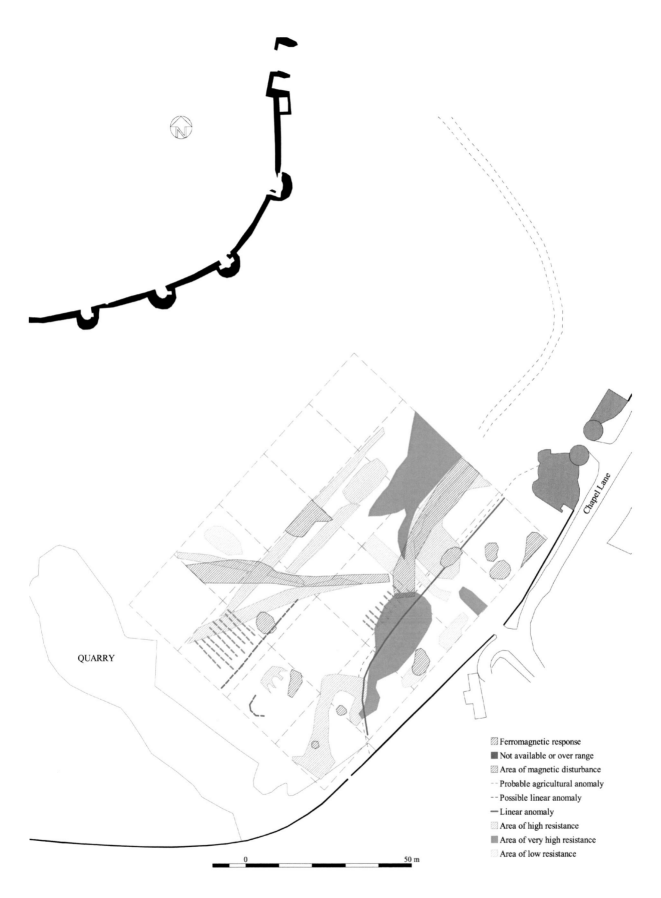

QUARRY

Chapel Lane

Ferromagnetic response
Not available or over range
Area of magnetic disturbance
Probable agricultural anomaly
Possible linear anomaly
Linear anomaly
Area of high resistance
Area of very high resistance
Area of low resistance

0   50 m

Figure 6.26 Beeston Castle Outer Gateway summary of the survey results, November 2009 (Brooks and Laws 2009: Figure 13).

PMF121 Peckforton Mere Fort, Cheshire
DWG 02 Magnetic Data

ArchaeoPhysica Ltd

Orthographic Centre X: 354266.00 m Centre Y: 357669.00 m Scale: 1:1500 @ A4 Spatial Units: Meter. Do not scale off this drawing
File: PMF.map from PERSEPOLIS 15/10/2012 Copyright ArchaeoPhysica Ltd 2012 OS OpenData Crown Copyright & Database Right 2012

FIGURE 6.27 PECKFORTON MERE MAGNETIC FIELD SURVEY RESULTS (ROSEVEARE 2012A: DWG 02).

surfaces buried beneath its debris. A further bank Figure 6.29 [12] may exist outside the southeast side of the enclosure which hints at multiple defensive structures at least on this side.

There is no direct evidence for an entrance, however, the passage of ground water into the enclosure from the pond to the southeast, might imply the entrance is in this corner. This might also explain the presence of a second bank along this side if there was a desire to reinforce this possible entrance.

Drainage into the ditch fill from the same pond might also explain the high resistance contrast between the fill and the ground to each side. The presence of trapped moisture Figure 6.29 [3] again implies bank material survives and also serves as a marker for the bank itself, where a clear anomaly for this was not observed relative to the background variation.

The site has been cultivated in the past as ridge and furrow crosses it and presumably this was the primary agent for the reduction of the earthworks. There is no sign of internal structures or features and whether this ploughing also accounts for the apparent lack of internal features cannot be ascertained at this stage.

by specialist geophysics contractor ArchaeoPhysica Ltd (Roseveare 2012a).

The most striking result is the clear detail of the defensive structure apparent in the electrical resistance data, but the near total absence of this from the magnetic data. The magnetic data was found to contain variation due to changes in soil chemistry and weak signs of ridge and furrow, but nothing resembling an enclosure was recorded. In contrast, the electrical resistance survey revealed clear anomalies typical of the bank and ditch of a fortified enclosure.

The whole circuit of the ditched enclosure is defined by a ditch Figure 6.29 [11] outside a high resistance area Figure 6.29 [10] which is typical of a spread bank. This implies that bank material still survives, i.e. there will be prehistoric

Oakmere

Magnetic survey using a high sensitivity magnetometer with caesium vapour sensors (Figure 6.30) and twin probe electrical resistance survey (Figure 6.31) was commissioned to explore the promontory fort at Oakmere. This was part of the Habitats and Hillforts Project aim to examine fortified sites of presumed Iron Age date in Cheshire. The survey work was undertaken in 2012 by specialist geophysics contractor ArchaeoPhysica Ltd (Roseveare 2012b).

The results from the Oakmere enclosure are intriguing. The lack of internal structures is not surprising; in this the results are similar to the site of Peckforton Mere. This may be due to the geology – at some sites the magnetic susceptibility would appear to be too low to permit magnetic means of

PMF121 Peckforton Mere Fort, Cheshire
DWG 03 50cm Twin Probe Electrical Resistance Data

ArchaeoPhysica Ltd

Orthographic Centre X: 354266.00 m Centre Y: 357669.00 m Scale: 1:1500 @ A4 Spatial Units: Meter. Do not scale off this drawing
File: PMF.map from PERSEPOLIS 15/10/2012 Copyright ArchaeoPhysica Ltd 2012 OS OpenData Crown Copyright & Database Right 2012

Electrical Resistance
50cm Twin probe / Ohm
Manually despiked
120
80
30

FIGURE 6.28 PECKFORTON MERE RESISTIVITY SURVEY RESULTS (ROSEVEARE 2012A: DWG 03).

prospecting, as at Peckforton Mere. Electrical resistance survey at Oakmere is dominated by large variations in resistance and it is possible that small internal structures are not resolvable against this variation.

The site at Oakmere is currently under pasture and there is no sign within either data set of cultivation within the monument itself. However, given the low magnetic susceptibility evident at the site it is not certain whether relict furrows would be visible in the magnetic data or not. Their absence in the electrical resistance data is more convincing, however, they might still be too subtle to be visible.

Where the survey coincides with the extant earthworks, e.g. Figure 6.32 [5], these are apparent as very high resistance

areas typical of well drained sandy and gravelly soil. A well-defined corner at [5] and also the inner edge at the southern end, might imply the existence of a revetment. The corner apparent at [5] and the lack of earthworks north of this (where the ground is lower) would suggest this may have been the original entrance. A 'causeway' and notch further south seems more likely to be a modern introduction associated with a service trench (Figure 6.32 [9]).

In addition, high resistance anomalies, Figure 6.32 [6] and [7] and a coincident ridge, would suggest the presence of an inturned entrance, although the significance, if any, of the low resistance region between them is uncertain. It is possible the high resistance area Figure 6.32 [3] is the site of another bank flanking [6] and [7] and thus defining the other side of an entrance passage approximately 7m wide at the inner end and apparently up to 14m wide at the outer end. This anomaly appears to run parallel to the lake edge rather than the ridge over [6] and [7]. There are other structures associated with these that are discussed later as they do not appear to relate to the prehistoric structure. The discovery of a likely inturned entrance provides useful evidence about the function and layout of the enclosure; it would clearly be defensible against the land although the lack of waterside defences would inevitably render it vulnerable to an offensive by boat. However, even here a simple palisade or thick hedge would offer significant protection. Anomaly Figure 6.32 [18] should not be confused with the defences and instead appears to be caused by the relatively better drainage off the slope above the lake creating a band of dry ground.

The interior has numerous variations of electrical resistance but most lack diagnostic form and many could simply be natural variations in the surface hydrology. Some discrete low resistance structures Figure 6.32 [12], [16] and [17] might mark the sites of medium-sized to large pits but there are no other anomalies that might indicate structural remains within a prehistoric context.

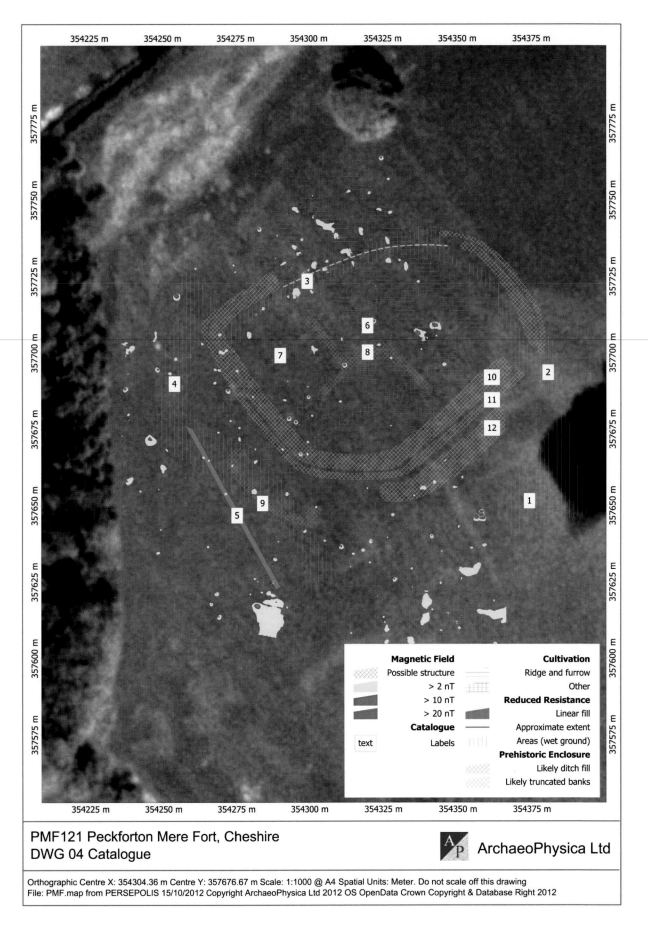

FIGURE 6.29 PECKFORTON MERE SUMMARY OF THE SURVEY RESULTS (ROSEVEARE 2012A: DWG 04).

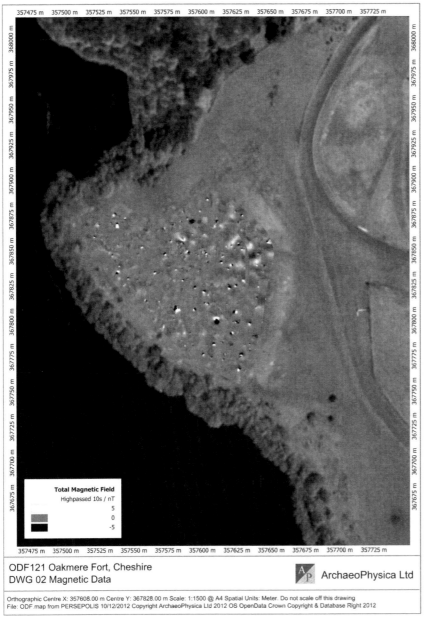

ODF121 Oakmere Fort, Cheshire
DWG 02 Magnetic Data

Total Magnetic Field
Highpassed 10s / nT
5
0
-5

ArchaeoPhysica Ltd

Orthographic Centre X: 357608.00 m Centre Y: 367828.00 m Scale: 1:1500 @ A4 Spatial Units: Meter. Do not scale off this drawing
File: ODF.map from PERSEPOLIS 10/12/2012 Copyright ArchaeoPhysica Ltd 2012 OS OpenData Crown Copyright & Database Right 2012

FIGURE 6.30 OAKMERE MAGNETIC FIELD SURVEY RESULTS (ROSEVEARE 2012B: DWG 02).

The most complex area is the northern end of the enclosure where, as has already been suggested, it seems likely there was an original entrance. However, there are a number of electrical resistance anomalies that make little sense in a prehistoric content and which might be indicative of a later phase of use. A parallel pair of high resistance linear anomalies Figure 6.32 [4] would be typical of wall footings given their length (14m) and separation (4m). If so, this would be a structure built within the entrance to the prehistoric enclosure. A rectangular shape enclosed between these, Figure 6.32 [5] and [7] seems likely to be related, although exactly how is uncertain.

There is a marked geometric layout to anomalies Figure 6.32 [2] to [6] and although these include structures likely to be of prehistoric date, it is possible that some

re-working has occurred. If so, perhaps the possible building [4] needs to be regarded as an element of a larger complex sheltered within and including elements of the likely prehistoric entrance.

This is partly reinforced by Figure 6.32 [2] which alone is just a low resistance area passing into the interior from the water's edge between higher resistance areas Figure 6.32 [1] and [3]. In this it is not particularly notable, except that it also forms the southwest edge of [6], continuing a clear straight course into the interior perpendicular to [4]. In doing so, it could bound what appears to be a discrete northern complex of features and could be of any date. The possibility of a later complex of structures sheltered within the probable prehistoric entrance is of interest as there was no evidence for this until this survey. The nature and purpose of this complex remains unknown, but clearly represents a phase of significant re-use of the monument, the prehistoric earthworks perhaps defining the extent of a smallholding or similar establishment.

There is perhaps evidence for artificial drainage within the monument, depending upon how anomalies Figure 6.32 [13] to [15] are interpreted. There is certainly evidence [9] for a drain or pipe having been laid right across it and associated with what appears to be significant modification of the earthworks where this passes through.

Conclusions

In most cases, the geophysical surveys have not been tested through sample excavation, with the exception of Eddisbury and Kelsborrow (the results of which are described in Chapters 10 and 12). However, it is clear that there is a limit to the effectiveness of these techniques of archaeological prospecting within the geological environment prevalent in Cheshire. Whilst substantial banks and ditches might be reliably detected, any finer detail in the interior, such as individual buildings or pit groups, would appear to be difficult to identify.

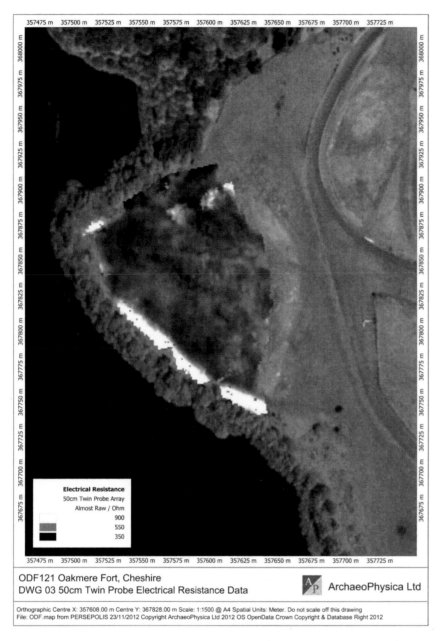

Electrical Resistance
50cm Twin Probe Array
Almost Raw / Ohm
900
550
350

ODF121 Oakmere Fort, Cheshire
DWG 03 50cm Twin Probe Electrical Resistance Data

ArchaeoPhysica Ltd

Orthographic Centre X: 357608.00 m Centre Y: 367828.00 m Scale: 1:1500 @ A4 Spatial Units: Meter. Do not scale off this drawing
File: ODF.map from PERSEPOLIS 23/11/2012 Copyright ArchaeoPhysica Ltd 2012 OS OpenData Crown Copyright & Database Right 2012

FIGURE 6.31 OAKMERE RESISTIVITY SURVEY RESULTS (ROSEVEARE 2012B: DWG 03).

Kelsborrow, Beeston and Maiden Castle by both student and volunteer surveys and in the main it was magnetic field surveys that produced these results, as opposed to resistivity. In contrast, the geophysics contractor surveys did not identify circular structures on any of the four sites investigated and indeed this included the site at Kelsborrow where circular anomalies were identified by the Chester University survey. The geophysics contractor suggested that the failure of the magnetic field technique was possibly due to the geology – at some sites the magnetic susceptibility would appear to be too low to permit magnetic means of prospecting (Roseveare 2012b). Differences in equipment and data processing could perhaps account for this variation in results.

It may be significant that two of the circular anomalies identified at Kelsborrow by the Chester University survey could not be identified in Trench 2, when tested by excavation. Furthermore, excavation at Trench 3, which was partly intended to target anomaly [19] from the ArchaeoPhysica survey, did identify a shallow pit in this area, but it was of far smaller dimensions than the geophysical results had suggested (see Garner, Chapter 12).

In summary, whilst the geophysical surveys have added new data to the seven monuments investigated by the Project, they have failed to elucidate convincing details about the layout and areas of occupation within the hillfort interiors. Whilst this may be a genuine reflection of the surviving below ground archaeology, this is unlikely, as excavations at both Eddisbury and Kelsborrow have suggested that internal features, such as postholes and pits, do still survive. Ploughing at Eddisbury, Kelsborrow and Peckforton has undoubtedly truncated many internal features. Similarly, the use of Helsby and Maiden Castle for military purposes has led to complications with the magnetic survey results. Future investigations of these and other monuments in the area, should therefore consider that high density sampling, with closer traverse separation, may be required and even then, limited return may be expected on geophysical prospecting using the techniques described above.

The surveys have produced useful data on the ramparts and ditches, including the suggestion of possible burning of the ramparts at Kelsborrow and the entrance at Maiden Castle, whilst the complexity of the bank construction at Kelsborrow has been highlighted. At Peckforton, a possible external bank was located which suggests the site may have had at least partial multiple lines of enclosure. At Oakmere a possible inturned entrance was identified, with indications of a complex of structures, suggesting re-use of the site at a later period.

When considering the results from the interiors of the hillforts, there is an interesting contrast between the surveys undertaken by the specialist geophysics contractor and the work carried out by volunteers and students. Possible 'roundhouses' were tentatively identified at Helsby,

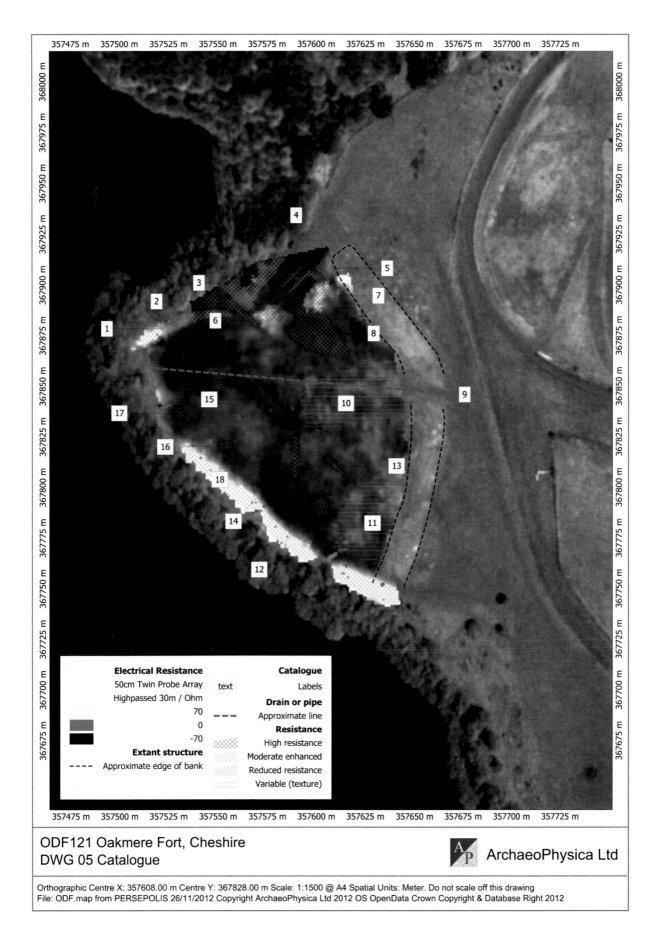

ODF121 Oakmere Fort, Cheshire
DWG 05 Catalogue

ArchaeoPhysica Ltd

Orthographic Centre X: 357608.00 m Centre Y: 367828.00 m Scale: 1:1500 @ A4 Spatial Units: Meter. Do not scale off this drawing
File: ODF.map from PERSEPOLIS 26/11/2012 Copyright ArchaeoPhysica Ltd 2012 OS OpenData Crown Copyright & Database Right 2012

Figure 6.32 Oakmere summary of the survey results (Roseveare 2012b: DWG 05).

Chapter 7
A lidar survey of the Cheshire Sandstone Ridge

Dan Garner

One of the aspirations of the Habitats and Hillforts Project was to place the prehistoric hillforts of the Cheshire Ridge within their wider historic landscape. This involved combining the results of the individual hillfort earthwork surveys (see Chapter 5, this volume) and existing datasets (such as the Cheshire Historic Environment Record, Cheshire Historic Landscape Characterisation and aerial photographs), with a site walk over of each of the wider hillfort management zones (as defined in Chapter 1, this volume).

In addition, it was recognised that lidar data would prove an invaluable supplementary data source, however, it was rapidly established that whilst some coverage of the area was held by the Environment Agency at 2m resolution, a complete data set did not exist for a large part of the Cheshire Ridge. The decision was taken to commission a new survey covering the entire area of the Sandstone Ridge Econet Partnership zone (approximately 200 square kilometres); and after discussion with Stewart Ainsworth (former Senior Archaeological Investigator with English Heritage), it was decided that the survey would be undertaken at a high density level of 0.5m resolution. This survey was commissioned and captured during May 2010 in order to avoid a fully developed leaf canopy in wooded areas. This chapter is not intended to provide a comprehensive account of the landscape history of the Ridge, but rather to explore the results of the lidar survey with regard to the hillforts and their immediate management zones. No attempt has yet been made to examine exhaustively the entire 200 square kilometres survey area; however, copies of the survey data are now held at the Cheshire Historic Environment Record and Chester University, where they are available as a resource for ongoing research.

The lidar data creates a three-dimensional terrain model which can be manipulated using computer-based software, to rotate selected areas of landscape through 360 degrees and to adjust the light source both vertically and horizontally, to alter the visual relief of the model. The hillfort specific areas of the lidar data set were analysed using the Quick Terrain Reader viewing software, but this did not reveal any new information that was not already visible on the topographic surveys or the two-dimensional hillshade images created from the data. The lidar imagery can be displayed two-dimensionally in a variety of ways, but the best results appeared to be gained using a greyscale hillshade with the light source set northwest-southeast. The results can be presented

as both a digital surface model (DSM) which shows vegetation and buildings, or as a digital terrain model (DTM) which is a 'bare-earth' model and removes modern vegetation and buildings (Crutchley and Crow 2009).

This chapter provides an overview of the information recovered from the Habitats and Hillforts lidar survey, with specific reference to the six hillfort sites and their immediate environs, from Woodhouse in the north to Maiden Castle in the south.

Woodhouse Hillfort

Woodhouse hillfort is perhaps the classic example of the use of lidar data as a topographic survey tool. Woodland is the main land use type where lidar has substantial advantages over other forms of survey, when the vegetation cover is stripped away and the features beneath are revealed. Woodhouse hillfort and its environs are owned by the Woodland Trust and managed as broad leaf woodland. The aerial photograph from 2010 (Figure 7.1) clearly illustrates that the hillfort (located in the centre of the photograph) and its immediate environs, are entirely hidden by the woodland leaf canopy. It is also useful to note that the photograph (top right) shows the southern part of Frodsham Golf Club, which was laid out over former agricultural land in 1990.

Towards the centre of the lidar DTM, (Figure 7.2) the removal of the tree canopy on Woodhouse Hill serves to reveal the line of the hillfort rampart (compare with the earthwork survey in Figure 5.1). The survey has also effectively captured many details of the landscape features associated with the modern golf course, such as the sand bunkers, tees and greens (top right). Furthermore, the survey has also managed to detect several of the underlying field boundaries associated with the agricultural landscape which existed prior to the creation of the golf course. These two examples clearly show that the 0.5m resolution survey has been effective in recording small topographic details, such as the golf course bunkers, as well as masked topographic details, such as the hillfort rampart. It is therefore reasonable to conclude that the data set is likely to have recorded much of the extant topographical detail visible in this landscape.

In terms of site setting, it is immediately apparent that the hillfort is occupying a raised knoll which is perched on the highest terrace of the adjacent cliffs. Fluvio-glacial out wash channels have formed deep scars in the adjacent landscape, with the example to the north of the hillfort (Figure 7.2, centre top) forming what is now known as Dunsdale; and the example to the south (centre bottom) leading to an area known as Snidley Moor. In both cases, these fluvio-glacial channels have been adapted as trackways, allowing passage from the high ground of the Ridge down to the lower lying ground bordering the marginal wetland of the Mersey Estuary. In the case of the northern channel, this route now passes down through Dunsdale to the lower lying medieval settlement of Netherton.

The lidar survey has been particularly successful at capturing a number of linear features within the landscape around Woodhouse Hill. For example, to the west of the cliffs (Figure 7.2, left) the modern agricultural field system is crossed by a slightly sinuous road running southwest to northeast, known as Tarvin Road. This road appears to cut across an earlier field boundary (top left) which represents the southern extent of the medieval town fields associated with the settlement of Netherton; suggesting that the present line of the road is an element of the post-medieval landscape. To the south of the hillfort, the lidar survey has detected field boundaries which are becoming increasingly masked by the encroaching woodland; reference to 19th and 20th century mapping can account for all of these boundaries as part of the post-enclosure agricultural landscape.

The farm complex to the east of the hillfort (Figure 7.2, centre right) is known as Mickledale Farm and incorporates elements of a stone built 17th century house and chapel; although documentary evidence suggests that the manor of Mickledale has its origins in the medieval period. It has been possible to establish the southern limit of the land associated with Mickledale Farm (prior to Parliamentary field enclosure) with reference to the Rock Savage estate map of 1778 (CALS DCH/E/416). This boundary can clearly be identified on the lidar survey as an east-west aligned linear (with a kink at the western end, skirting the northern end of the knoll on which Woodhouse hillfort sits) that terminates on the cliff edge (Figure 7.2). The land to the south of the Mickledale boundary remained common until it was enclosed by Act of Parliament in 1797 (CALS QDE 1/11) It is interesting to note that the site of the hillfort has been excluded from the Mickledale manor and would have remained part of the common.

In terms of more specific landscape features, the lidar survey has recorded a number of relatively small scale sand and stone quarries (for example, one adjacent to the Mickledale boundary, immediately north of the hillfort). There is also evidence for some landscaping associated with the 19th century house known as Foxhill and its associated arboretum (Figure 7.2, bottom left). Finally, a

possible mound or tumulus, appears to be present to the north of the hillfort within the wooded area; however, ground proofing through a site walk over has established that this is a natural geological out crop of the sandstone rock.

In summary, whilst the lidar survey has helped to substantiate the dominant position that Woodhouse hillfort occupies in the surrounding landscape, this has only confirmed the location of boundaries and features which are recorded on the historic mapping from the turn of the 18th century onwards. Once the modern, post-medieval and medieval landscape features are identified and accounted for, the remaining features appear to be of limited archaeological significance, beyond the hillfort itself. To some extent, this could be argued to be the result of the more recent land use in the area since the Enclosure Act of 1797. The c.1846 tithe map (CALS EDT 163/2) demonstrates that the entire area had been enclosed and turned over to intensive agriculture from the early 19th century; the smooth featureless areas making up the modern field system being testament to decades of cultivation using modern agricultural machinery. The only clues to how the contemporary prehistoric landscape might have been ordered appear to be the natural geological features, such as the cliff edge and the fluvio-glacial out flow channels. The modern use of these channels as routes from high ground to low ground may have originally been linked to the movement of livestock; the name Dunsdale meaning 'muck valley' (Dodgson 1971: 231) perhaps alludes to this. The use of the high ground for livestock grazing is demonstrated by the persistence of common land here until the advent of Parliamentary enclosure. Whilst this evidence only reflects the medieval or early post-medieval ordering and use of the landscape around Woodhouse, it may represent an ancient tradition of transhumance; one in which the sighting of Woodhouse at the confluence of two drove routes may have had particular significance. Indeed, it may account for the architectural design of the hillfort with the most imposing section of the rampart projecting eastwards on to the Mickledale valley and the route between Snidley Moor and Dunsdale Hollow.

Helsby Hillfort

The lidar survey data from Helsby demonstrate the success of this technique, in a similar way to Woodhouse. At Helsby, the landscape to the north and west of the hillfort is now heavily built up as part of the modern settlement of Helsby and for this reason, analysis of the lidar survey is focused more specifically around the hillfort itself. The aerial photograph from 2010 (Figure 7.3) shows the extent of the woodland leaf canopy around the steep slopes to the north and west of Helsby crag; which includes the northeastern annex of the hillfort on the lower ledge of the cliff. Whilst the hillfort itself is largely free of dense woodland vegetation, the

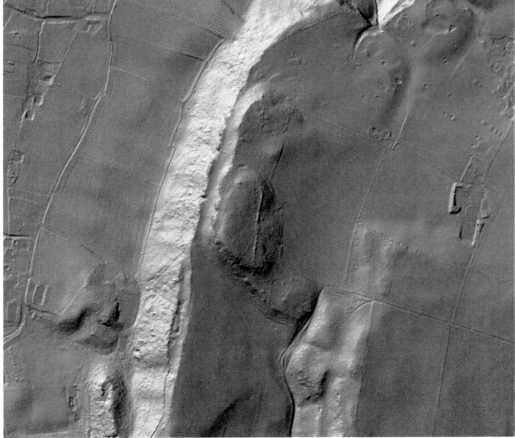

FIGURE 7.1 WOODHOUSE HILLFORT LANDSCAPE FROM THE 2010 AERIAL PHOTOGRAPHIC SURVEY (TOP) AND THE 2010 LIDAR SURVEY DTM (BOTTOM) © CHESHIRE WEST AND CHESTER COUNCIL.

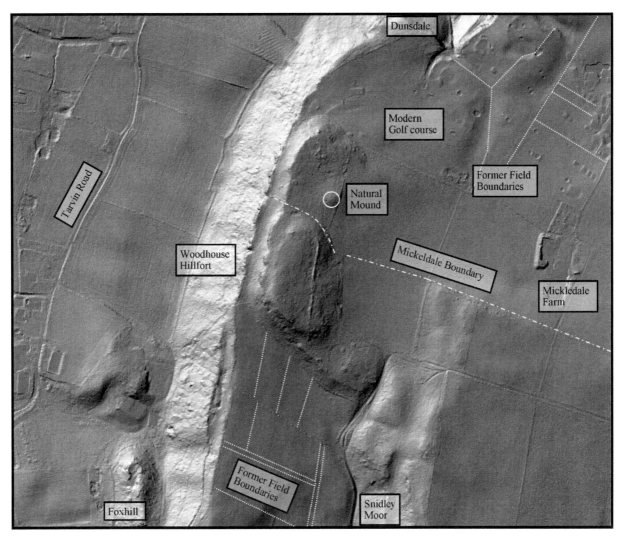

FIGURE 7.2 WOODHOUSE HILLFORT LANDSCAPE INTERPRETATION BASED ON THE 2010 LIDAR DTM © CHESHIRE WEST AND CHESTER COUNCIL.

eastern (right hand) half of the rampart circuit lies under agricultural land, which has previously been ploughed using modern agricultural machinery, resulting in the spreading of the rampart. The significant water body to the immediate south of the hillfort rampart is known as Harmer's Lake and has grown in size since its earliest rendering on the tithe map of *c*.1845 (CALS EDT 196/2). Nevertheless, it may be a significant feature as it is believed to be fed from a natural underground spring (Joyce and Foxwell 2011: 4).

The two linear field boundaries running northwest from Harmer's Lake across the hillfort ramparts and up to the cliff edge are associated with enclosure by Act of Parliament in 1797 (Figure 7.3 bottom, centre). Prior to this, the hilltop had been common land; it is interesting to note that the site of the hillfort remained common land following enclosure, as did the adjacent hillfort at Woodhouse. South of Harmer's Lake, part of the line of a former road is shown traversing the hilltop in an east-west direction. This road is still an adopted road leading from Harmer's Lake Farm downhill to a junction with

Bates Lane on the eastern flank of the hill (Figure 7.4, centre). The modern road is known as Hill Road North (previously it was called Amoss Lake Lane and later, Armers Lane) and on the western side of the hill there is a small cul-de-sac, known as Hill Road South. The two sections of Hill Road were originally linked as a route on and off the hilltop and the section which is no longer in use survives as a deep hollow track, leading to a dog-leg turn through a cutting in the sandstone rock, before emerging on the hilltop to the south of the hillfort. Whilst the route does not make use of fluvio-glacial channels (as seen at Woodhouse), it does make use of a natural topographic feature, in the form of a shelf along the cliff edge. There is, therefore, good reason to suggest that the Hill Road route is an ancient one and may well represent a droving route for livestock, allowing passage from the high ground of Helsby Hill down to the lower lying ground bordering the marginal wetland of Frodsham Marsh, on the Mersey Estuary.

More modern features are again easily identified on the survey results. To the west and north of the hillfort the

75

FIGURE 7.3 HELSBY HILLFORT LANDSCAPE FROM THE 2010 AERIAL PHOTOGRAPHIC SURVEY (TOP) AND THE 2010 LIDAR SURVEY DTM (BOTTOM) © CHESHIRE WEST AND CHESTER COUNCIL.

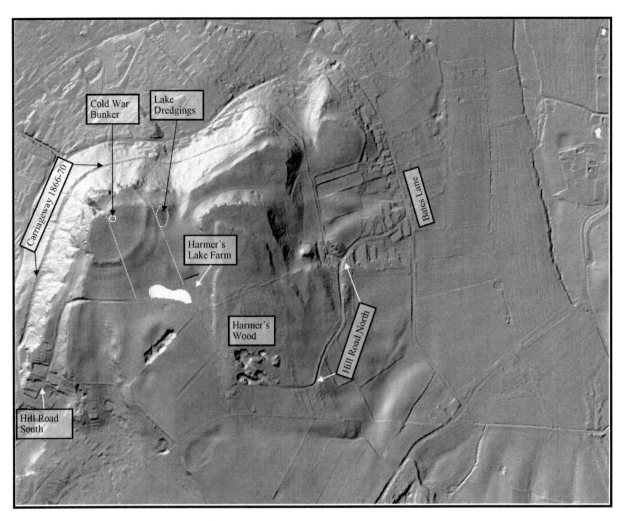

FIGURE 7.4 HELSBY HILLFORT LANDSCAPE INTERPRETATION BASED ON THE 2010 LIDAR DTM © CHESHIRE WEST AND CHESTER COUNCIL.

lidar survey has captured the course of a second road running along the natural contour of the cliff about half way down the slope (Figure 7.3 bottom, top and left; Figure 7.4). This route was a private carriageway built by the Marquis of Cholmondeley between 1866 and 1870 as a leisure drive for the local gentry. In addition, on the summit of the hill a small mound marks the location of a Cold War monitoring post which was built by the Royal Observer Corps and operated from 1962 (Pollington, Chapter 4, this volume; Joyce and Foxwell 2011: 22–25). To the south of Harmer's Lake, areas of 19th century sand and stone quarrying can be seen scarring the landscape. In particular, the group of stone quarries in Harmer's Wood date to the 1830s and 1860s when they were re-opened to quarry stone for the construction of the new Helsby church.

The lidar DTM (Figure 7.3 bottom) has effectively served to capture the full circuit of the hillfort defences, in spite of the negative impact from modern cultivation. This has managed to demonstrate not only the circuit of the main rampart, but also the presence of an outer counterscarp bank, or secondary rampart, which had been previously indicated by a parch mark on aerial photographs. The

northeastern end of the outer bank appears to abruptly end, where it meets the modern field boundary (Figure 7.3 bottom, centre). Immediately east of this field boundary, is an area of rough ground known to have been created in recent times by the deposition of dredgings from Harmer's Lake, located directly to the south of the hillfort. This is likely to have masked the original extent of the outer bank. However, the outer bank does not appear to mirror the main rampart's extension, which runs northwards down on to the lower ledge, to create the annex mentioned above. Extending the outer bank on to the lower ledge would have been a logical development if the main function of the outer bank was to strengthen the hillfort's defences. The fact that this did not happen suggests that the outer bank was primarily designed to increase the visual impact of the enclosure.

An area of noticeable rampart spread and flattening along the southeastern section of the main rampart could be interpreted as the location of a blocked entrance (Figure 7.3 bottom, centre). However, local history sources record the brief presence of a nine-hole golf course on the hilltop between 1915 and 1936 and the flattened section of rampart closely corresponds with the location of the third green and fourth tee (Joyce and Foxwell 2011: 13–15) (see Chapter 5). It is also noted that in 1922, the groundsman was granted permission to grow potatoes between the third green and fourth tee, which would have led to further erosion in this area.

At Helsby, as at Woodhouse, the use of the high ground for livestock grazing is attested by the persistence of common land here, until the advent of Parliamentary enclosure. Whilst this evidence only reflects the post-medieval or possibly medieval ordering and use of the landscape around Helsby, it may represent an ancient tradition of transhumance, in which the sighting of Helsby, overlooking a drove route and the site of a natural spring, may have had particular significance. Alternatively, the siting of Helsby hillfort serves to enclose the steep cliff at the northern end of a ridge, which ranks as the most distinctive feature of the surrounding landscape. The architectural design of the hillfort, with the most imposing section of the rampart projecting southwards down the ridge towards Alvanley Cliff, must have been a deliberate part of the design. It is also worthy of note that the primary rampart does not entirely respect the local topography, with its extension from the upper plateau down a steep slope to a lower ledge on the northeast end of the earthwork. The possible adherence to a preconceived design, which involved a simple semi-circular or crescent-shaped enclosure, created from a series of short linear sections with no obvious entrance, may be significant.

Kelsborrow Hillfort

The lidar survey data from Kelsborrow appears initially less informative than the previous two hillforts discussed in this chapter. The hillfort lies on the very edge of the lands which remained part of the royal medieval forest of Delamere, up until their eventual enclosure in 1819. The field boundary running north-south across the eastern (right-hand) side of the hillfort (Figure 7.5), can be traced to the first edition Ordnance Survey six inch to the mile map of 1874, but it is clearly an extension of the field boundaries imposed on to the landscape in 1819. Very little trace of the ordering of the pre-enclosure landscape can be discerned, but this may partly be explained by the deliberate 'gentrification' of the area by the Kenworthy family between 1892 and 1933. The most notable surviving feature of this development can be seen at the principal residence of 'Castle Hill' (Figure 7.6, top right) which was furnished with new formal gardens delimited by a stone built 'ha-ha', punctuated with semi-circular 'bastions' at the corners. To the south of the residence, at Birch Hill, a semi-circular folly had also appeared by 1897, marked on the second edition Ordnance Survey six inch to the mile map as 'stand'. Only the base of this now remains, but it may have originally functioned as a viewing tower. It is likely that these alterations were part of the development of the landscape as part of the

new 'Kenworthy Estate' which included a shire horse stud farm.

The lidar imagery clearly shows how the hillfort occupies a promontory with steep slopes and cliff edge delimiting the southern side (Figure 7.5 bottom). The small valley known as Boothsdale, on the southeastern side of the hillfort, has a narrow footpath leading up to the higher ground on the eastern side, which is revealed on the lidar survey (Figure 7.6, centre). This route seems too straight and narrow to have convincingly served as an earlier drove way. The name Boothsdale, however, is recorded as early as 1347 (as 'le Bothes') and means '(valley at) the herdsmens shelters' (Dodgson 1971: 213), implying some earlier form of livestock husbandry in the locality. To the north of the hillfort (FIgure 7.6 centre top) there is a small pit/pond adjacent to the 1819 field boundary, which is thought to be spring fed and is locally rumoured to have been previously used as a watering point by drovers (Joyce and Foxwell 2011: 63).

One distinctive feature from the survey is the oval shaped pit/pond which sits on the northern edge of the hillfort rampart. The origin of this feature is uncertain, but it is shown as a smaller pond on the first edition Ordnance Survey six inch to the mile map of 1874. It may have formed as a consequence of the partly infilled hillfort rampart ditch. The pond is seemingly not spring fed, as it has been known to completely dry up during dry, hot summers. Attention is drawn to this pond because immediately to the south of it, the rampart appears to be slightly spread or flattened, possibly indicating the presence of an entrance. However, this is problematic as it does not tally with either of the gaps in the rampart noted by Ormerod (see Chapter 2, this volume) and may be the result of livestock erosion associated with access to the pond for watering. Furthermore, the plan of the hillfort produced by Longley in 1979 (Longley 1979: 53) shows a north-south linear feature cutting across the width of the rampart on the southeast side of the pond (see Chapter 2); this feature may have been detected during the Archaeophysica resistivity survey (see Chapter 6, this volume). For some time, this feature has been assumed to be associated with livestock erosion; however, during the Habitats and Hillforts Project, the landowner, Mike Hardy, produced an annotated plan from his family archives, which suggested the feature represented a formal excavation trench undertaken on the 8 April 1938. This event is not recorded anywhere else, but the timing could fit with William Varley's last season of excavations at Eddisbury hillfort and might have been a precursor to plans for more extensive excavations, following completion of his work at Eddisbury. This detail may be significant, as Varley had targeted hillfort entrances on his previous two investigations at Maiden Castle and Eddisbury; and whilst this does not prove the location of an entrance at Kelsborrow, it might imply that its presence had been suspected.

At the western end of the hillfort rampart and within the interior of the hillfort, there is the faint trace of a circular mound (Figure 7.6, centre left). This feature was recorded by Ormerod (see Chapter 2, Figure 2.1), with his stylised representation clearly indicating an artificial feature of some prominence. The possibility remains that (as with the hillfort rampart itself), intensive ploughing of the hillfort interior has severely reduced the appearance of this mound. Geophysical survey (see Chapter 6) did not locate any features in this part of the hillfort interior which were suggestive of a ploughed-out barrow; the field name 'Kelsborrow' is derived from 'Kels-burh' (Kel's Stronghold) as opposed to being a reference to the location of a barrow (Dodgson 1971: 212). Nevertheless, the scatter of Neolithic and middle Bronze Age artefacts recovered from the hillfort since the early 19th century are suggestive of an earlier prehistoric presence on the promontory.

Whilst much of the surface evidence only reflects the late post-medieval ordering and use of the landscape around Kelsborrow, there are hints of earlier transhumance; suggesting that the sighting of Kelsborrow may have been overlooking a drove route and the site of a natural spring, as noted at Helsby. The architectural design of the hillfort with the most imposing section of the rampart projecting northwards along the ridge towards Kelsall Hill and the 'Kelsall Gap' seems to be a deliberate part of the design. The so called 'Kelsall Gap' is seen as one of only a few accessible east-west routes across the Cheshire Ridge and its proximity to Kelsall and Eddisbury was noted by earlier commentators (Ormerod 1882, Volume 2: 3). It was certainly exploited by the Roman military for one of the major roads through the region, linking the fortress at Chester (Deva) with the fort at Northwich (Condate). It is perhaps worthy of note that the hillfort rampart does not entirely respect the local topography, with its western extent running up hill across a visible contour in a southwestern direction, rather than extending northwest to the cliff edge along the natural contour. The possible adherence to a preconceived design which involved a simple semi-circular or crescent-shaped enclosure, created from a series of short linear sections with no obvious entrance, is comparable to the original design for the hillfort at Helsby.

Eddisbury Hillfort

The lidar survey data from Eddisbury has clearly succeeded in capturing much of the fine topographic detail recorded by the Royal Commission survey in 1987 (see Chapter 2). For this reason, a much larger area was investigated around Eddisbury in order to consider a number of disparate prehistoric, or suspected prehistoric, features in the landscape. As with Kelsborrow Castle, the hillfort lies within the lands which remained part of the royal medieval forest of Delamere up until their eventual enclosure in 1819. Furthermore, the hillfort is entirely contained within the bounds of a much larger enclosure known as 'The Old Pale' (to distinguish it from the New Pale near Manley, see below); it is not known precisely when the Old Pale was enclosed, but it certainly pre-dates a plan of 1627 (CALS DAR/D/33). According to a statement made by Sir John Done (d.1629) the purpose of the enclosure was 'to aid the feeding of the deer, and for the keeper's own beasts' (Green 1979: 176). The later development of the landscape of the hillfort is closely tied to the history of the Old Pale, as the southeastern end of the hilltop is associated with a medieval and post-medieval building complex/farmstead now known as Merrick's Hill (see Chapter 11, this volume). The present name is thought to be derived from a John Merrick, who was the tenant of the farmstead when plans to enclose the forest were first drawn up in 1812 (Dodgson 1971: 214). However, the site has been associated with the location of a royal hunting lodge known as 'The Chamber in the Forest' since as early as 1577 (*ibid.*) and a lodge building may have stood on the site from *c.* 1354 (Varley 1950: 65). Recent archaeological excavation and artefact analysis has suggested this phase of occupation on Merrick's Hill dates from at least the 16th century (see Chapter 11).

Much of the established field system around the hillfort can be seen on the 1819 enclosure map (CALS QDE 1/23); however, only a small area within the Old Pale is shown to be enclosed. This is primarily the site of Merrick's Hill which is shown as having a cluster of three buildings that broadly correspond to the buildings located by Varley's excavation (Varley 1950: 67). Adjoining the Merrick's Hill complex to the west is a larger enclosure, which is labelled 'The Chamber in the Forest'; and further west again is another building complex now known as 'Old Pale Heights'. From this comparison of the mapping it is possible to establish that the field occupying the eastern two thirds of the hillfort interior (which Varley argued to be the original hillfort – see Chapter 2), is the 'Chamber in the Forest' enclosure. This is interesting in providing a possible origin for the field boundary in the medieval period, but also in suggesting that the label 'Chamber in the Forest' actually refers to much of the hillfort, as opposed to a discrete cluster of buildings on Merrick's Hill. Nearly all of the other field boundaries within the Old Pale appear between 1819 and the first edition Ordnance Survey map of 1874.

There is a complex system of roads and tracks to the south and east of the hillfort and as with the other hillforts discussed in this chapter, it is tempting to look for evidence of early droving routes approaching the hillfort. The earliest routes at Eddisbury can be linked with the Roman road system, (Figure 7.8, solid lines) with a single road running east from the Roman fortress at Chester (Deva) and up in to the Kelsall Gap. The road appears to fork in an area of woodland now known as Nettleford Wood (Frere 1983: 297–9; Petch, 1987: 218); this feature has

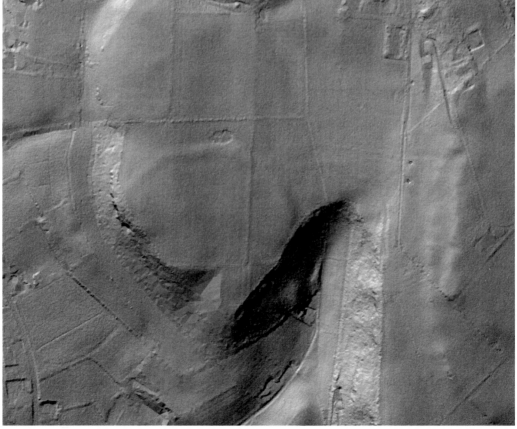

FIGURE 7.5 KELSBORROW HILLFORT LANDSCAPE FROM THE 2010 AERIAL PHOTOGRAPHIC SURVEY (TOP) AND THE 2010 LIDAR SURVEY DTM (BOTTOM) © CHESHIRE WEST AND CHESTER COUNCIL.

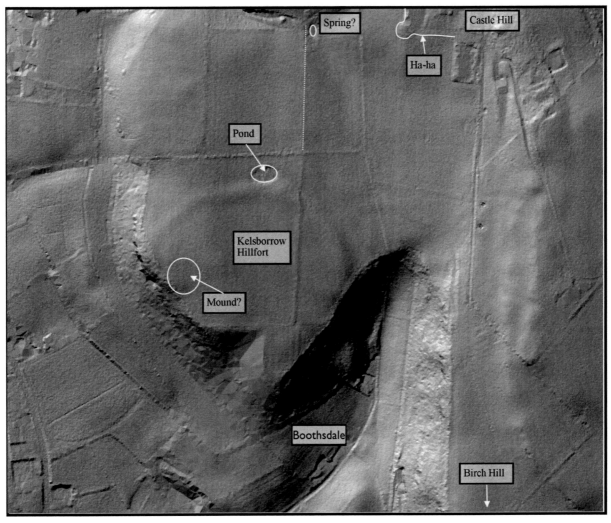

Labels in figure: Spring?, Castle Hill, Ha-ha, Pond, Kelsborrow Hillfort, Mound?, Boothsdale, Birch Hill

FIGURE 7.6 KELSBORROW HILLFORT LANDSCAPE INTERPRETATION BASED ON THE 2010 LIDAR DTM © CHESHIRE WEST AND CHESTER COUNCIL.

been captured by the lidar survey which shows the road junction as a fragment of two converging hollow ways (Figure 7.8, centre left). The lower road then continues southeast towards the Roman fort at Middlewich (Salinae) and much of its route is now followed by the modern A54 road. The upper road heads off in a more northeasterly direction across modern fields, skirting the edge of the plateau on which Eddisbury hillfort stands, before descending in to the lower lying moss lands. Then it passes through a narrow area of slightly raised ground known as the Pedlars Oak Gap, before continuing on to the Roman fort at Northwich (Condate) (Margary route 7a) (Petch 1987: 186). Only faint hints of the line of this road are given by the lidar survey (Figure 7.8 centre and centre right), with one small length exposed in an area of sandstone outcrop, which has previously been the subject of archaeological investigation (Petch 1987: 232); and a break in the line of a natural ridge directly to the southwest of Merrick's Hill. The route that the road originally followed descending the steep slope of Eddisbury Hill, has been obscured by later stone quarries which are also captured on the lidar survey (Figure 7.8 centre right). However, on the opposite side of Station

Road (the B5152) the Roman road is visible as a length of raised linear bank heading towards the northern end of Thieves Moss (ibid.). It is notable that the northern Roman road appears to completely disregard the site of Eddisbury hillfort in its planning.

To the north of the northern Roman Road there is another more sinuous track (now a modern footpath) which runs eastwards from the Nettleford Wood road junction on an almost parallel course to the Roman road (Figure 7.8, dotted line). However, this track does deviate slightly further to the north, eventually reaching the northern end of Stoney Lane; from this point the course of the track is now a modern road called Eddisbury Hill. The modern road passes directly to the south of the southeastern end of the hillfort at Merrick's Hill before descending to Station Road (B5152). This track is shown on an early plan of the forest dating to 1686 (PRO MR 1/640), where it is labelled 'Horse road from Chester to the Chamber'. Once the road reaches Merrick's Hill, the eastward section is labelled 'Road from the Chamber' and it continues on through Pedlars Oak to Crabtree Green and beyond. It is logical to suppose that this track way post-dates the Roman road and (as the 1686 plan suggests) its diversion north to the hillfort could be entirely related to the location of the medieval hunting lodge on Merrick's Hill. However, there is also the possibility that this track represents an earlier pre-Roman route, with the Roman road merely being an act of straightening out the section between the Kelsall Gap and Pedlars Oak, by the Roman military. In this latter case, the track could represent the line of a prehistoric drove way, running from the lower western plain and the uplands of the Ridge, via the hillfort at Eddisbury.

Another road is marked on the 1686 Forest Plan to the south of the northern Roman road and to the north of the southern Roman road. This track begins at the road junction in Nettleford Wood and initially follows the course of the Roman road to Middlewich, before deviating north to become the modern Chester Road (A556) to Northwich (Figure 7.8, dashed lines). This trackway is marked on the 1686 plan as 'Carryers Road from Chester to Northwich' and appears to have been created to provide an alternative route to Northwich, avoiding the need to traverse the steep slopes of Eddisbury Hill. The modern north-south road (B5152), to the east of Eddisbury hillfort, is also shown on the 1686 plan and is labelled as the 'Road from Frodsham to Cotebrook'. It is notable that there are no indications in the lidar data of roads or trackways to the north or west of the hillfort providing a route to the main northwestern entrance.

The lidar imagery clearly shows how the hillfort occupies a promontory with steep slopes and cliff edge delimiting the southern and eastern sides (Figure 7.7 bottom). This highlights the fact that, despite Eddisbury often being referred to as a contour fort, the choice for its location does appear to have been influenced by the existence of a promontory on the hill top. The most imposing sections of the hillfort rampart are set along the northern and western sides of the enclosure, with the impressive inturned entrance located at the northwestern end. The ramparts are an inverse 'L' shape (mirroring the shape of the cliff edges) and they create an enclosed space which is almost sub-rectangular in appearance. The architectural design of the hillfort, with the most imposing section of the rampart projecting northwestwards along the Ridge, towards the highest point on the Ridge at Pale Heights, appears to have been a deliberate intention of the builders. This high point at 176m OD was used for the site of an Ordnance Survey triangulation point and provides views across eight different counties; it is now marked by a modern circular monument consisting of a mound with surrounding standing stones. A closer look at the alignment of the hillfort's northwestern entrance, might suggest that it is actually aligned to the source of a natural spring which feeds a watercourse running downslope northwards, until it feeds in to Linmere Moss.

The plateau which the hillfort overlooks to the west is a naturally sub-rectangular shaped block of land, which largely defines the limits of the Old Pale medieval deer park; and it is tempting to see this as the basis for a much earlier boundary associated with the prehistoric hillfort landscape. To the north of this plateau are the southern limits of Linmere Moss, whilst to the east the natural topography is delimited by a series of post-glacial mosses and meres which persist southwards, until reaching the Bronze Age barrow cemetery at the Seven Lows. To the west, a natural boundary is again formed by a valley known as The Yeld, which now forms the township boundary between Eddisbury and Kelsall/Ashton. This boundary also demarcates the limits of the parish of Tarvin and is believed to be part of the pre-conquest boundary between the Anglo-Saxon Hundreds of Ruloe and Rushton. To the west of The Yeld, the lidar survey has captured traces of a co-axial field system at Longley Farm which is of uncertain date but is possibly prehistoric in origin (Figure 7.8, top left) (Longley 1987: 104; Scheduled Monument, National Heritage List for England list entry number 1018080).

The lidar survey for the Eddisbury area has also detected two other fragments of earthwork which will require further investigation in order to clarify their nature. The first is at the northern end of Nettleford Wood and appears to be a patch of ridge and furrow interrupted on the western side by a number of small areas of stone quarrying (Figure 7.8, centre left). Further west again, the ridge and furrow has been completely removed by modern agriculture associated with the post-enclosure landscape of small square fields; whilst on the eastern side it is bordered by the boundary of the Old Pale. The second feature is less easily explained and is located in the fork between the modern roads of the A556 and A54 to the west of Stony Lane. The feature has the appearance of a curving section of bank and ditch but it is entirely confined to the space between the two modern roads (Figure 7.8, centre) and requires further explanation, which at present is not forthcoming.

Beeston Castle

The lidar survey data from Beeston has clearly succeeded in capturing much of the fine topographic detail depicted on the hachure plan published in the report on the excavations at Beeston Castle (Ellis 1993: 99). The hillfort is entirely contained within the bounds of the medieval castle at Beeston, which was constructed by Ranulph III, Earl of Chester, from 1220 (ibid. 94). The castle and earlier hillfort occupy a prominent outcrop of rock overlooking the Cheshire Gap; the landmark is so strikingly visible that it is easily identifiable from the prehistoric hillforts which line the Clwydian Mountains of North East Wales. The hillfort itself makes use of the steep slopes and cliff edges of the promontory, with the rampart and ditch cutting off the more gently rising eastern approach (Figure 7.9).

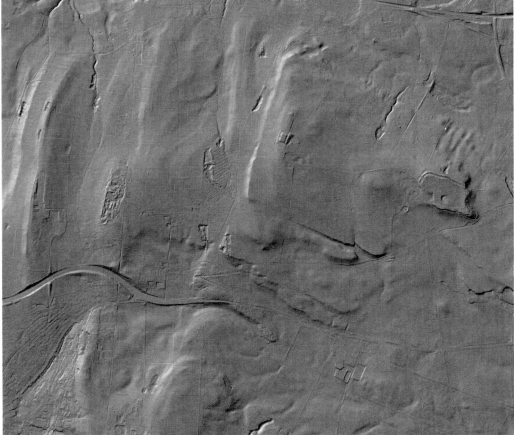

Figure 7.7 Eddisbury hillfort landscape from the 2010 aerial photographic survey (top) and the 2010 lidar survey DTM (bottom) © Cheshire West and Chester Council.

FIGURE 7.8 EDDISBURY HILLFORT LANDSCAPE INTERPRETATION BASED ON THE 2010 LIDAR DTM © CHESHIRE WEST AND CHESTER COUNCIL.

The area of land between Beeston Castle and Peckforton Hill to the south is marked by a number of springs and watercourses, which have now been drained and managed. However, prior to the 20th century, the spring water from this area was believed to have had curative properties and was compared favourably to mineral waters from the Malverns. Indeed, at the foot of Beeston crag, Castleside Farm (formerly known as Beeston Farm) was the location of the 'Beeston Spa' on the first edition Ordnance Survey six inch to the mile map of 1874 and this was still present by the third edition map of 1908 (Figure 7.10). Furthermore, at the base of Peckforton Hill, the lane known as Horsley Lane serves a small hamlet of houses including one with a rock cut plunge pool, shown as 'Horseley Bath' on the first edition Ordnance Survey map (Figure 7.10). This pool still survives, although the spring that fed it has long since run dry as a result of water pumping by the Staffordshire Water Board. There is a Latin inscription set above the pool and dated 1694. Refurbishment work undertaken at the site in 2007, uncovered the hilt and lower half of a late Bronze Age sword of Ewart Park type, dating to the 8th century BC (CHER 7003). The sword appears to have been deliberately broken in antiquity, possibly implying a ritual offering. This area is also the location of the so called 'Beeston Hoard' consisting of a Neolithic polished stone axe and an early Bronze Age perforated stone axe-hammer (Varley & Jackson 1940: 32). This connection between a network of natural springs and deposits of Neolithic and Bronze Age objects perhaps suggests that the hillfort at Beeston is set within a ritual landscape, which is hard to discern in the modern setting.

To the northeast of Beeston Castle is the site of Beeston Hall, which is shown to have the surviving elements of a moat on both the tithe map of 1846 (CALS EDT 43/2) and the first edition Ordnance Survey six inch to the mile map of 1874. Ormerod in his *History of Cheshire* records that 'The ancient hall was surrounded by a moat and suffered severely during the siege of the neighbouring castle, being fired by Prince Rupert's soldiers on March 19th 1644-5' (Ormerod 1882, Volume 2: 273). Whilst the lidar survey has not succeeded in clarifying the presence or absence of a medieval moat, it has detected the traces of an earlier field system to the south of the hall and to the north of the road known as Dean Bank (Figure 7.10, centre right). This field system does not appear on the tithe map or any of the earlier editions of the Ordnance Survey maps; and the alignment of the main east-west boundaries appear to respect the line of the Dean Bank road rather than the field enclosures associated with Beeston Hall. The origin of the Dean Bank road is unknown, but it appears to run in a slightly sinuous course from the modern A49 westwards, until it arrives at the base of Beeston

crag, finishing up directly beneath the site of what is thought to be the hillfort entrance.

A possible early curvilinear boundary is visible on the lidar survey to the north and west of Beeston crag, running from just south of Crimes Lane northwards to the north of Home Farm, before curving eastwards and running on to Bates Mill Lane (Figure 7.10, centre left). The feature can possibly be traced a little further east in surviving field boundaries. To the north of this feature is a fragment of a second linear boundary running parallel to the first, which is apparently associated with a more complex field system (top centre). This field system includes a patchwork of ridge and furrow earthworks which appear relatively straight and narrow, suggesting a post-medieval date. However, the earthworks are clearly earlier than a number of the marl pits occurring within this field system, as well as the line of the Crewe and Chester railway. The field system is bounded to the north by the meandering path of the River Gowy which is now largely replaced by the Shropshire Union Canal.

The architectural design of the hillfort with the most imposing section of the rampart and its entrance projecting southeastwards along a low ridge towards Bunbury and the 'Cheshire Gap' appears to have been an important factor. The so called 'Cheshire Gap' is seen as one of only a few accessible east-west routes across the Cheshire Ridge and Beeston crag is perfectly situated to give commanding views over the area. It was certainly exploited for such by the Norman Earls of Chester. It is perhaps worthy of note that the hillfort rampart appears to respect the local topography in its design with no particular hint of a preconceived architectural style in its appearance.

Maiden Castle

The lidar survey data from Maiden Castle has clearly succeeded in capturing much of the fine topographic detail seen on the earthwork survey presented in Chapter 5 (Figure 7.11). The hillfort perches on the summit of the steep cliff edge on the northeastern side of what is now known as Bickerton Hill, with the ramparts and ditches enclosing a relatively small area of the hilltop. Inspection of the tithe map of *c.* 1839 (CALS EDT 46/2) shows that the hill on which Maiden Castle is sited was previously known as 'Birds Hill', with the name changing to Bickerton Hill by the time of the first edition Ordnance Survey six inch to the mile map of 1874. Previous topographic surveys had identified a large and complex system of earthworks on the hillfort interior, which were convincingly argued to represent relatively small scale stone quarrying during the medieval or early post-medieval periods. The lidar survey has successfully captured this activity and has served to identify numerous similar clusters of quarry pits scattered across the

FIGURE 7.9 BEESTON HILLFORT LANDSCAPE FROM THE 2010 AERIAL PHOTOGRAPHIC SURVEY (TOP) AND THE 2010 LIDAR SURVEY DTM (BOTTOM) © CHESHIRE WEST AND CHESTER COUNCIL.

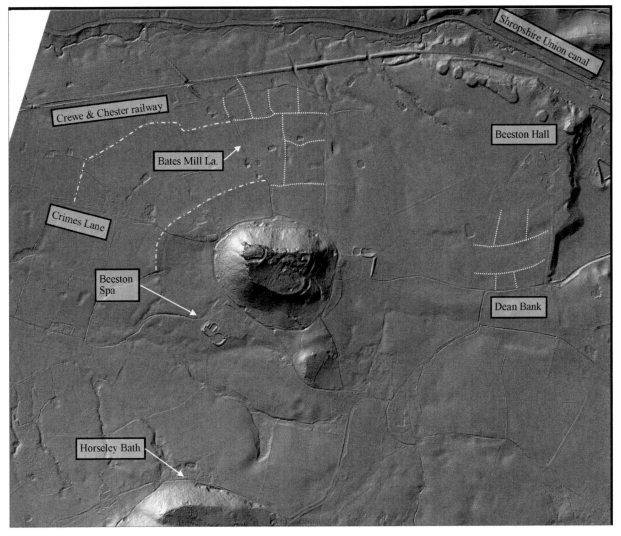

FIGURE 7.10 BEESTON HILLFORT LANDSCAPE INTERPRETATION BASED ON THE 2010 LIDAR DTM © CHESHIRE WEST AND CHESTER COUNCIL.

hilltop; suggesting that the hillfort was not deliberately targeted for the stone quarrying and was probably of no consequence to those quarrying the stone.

Birds/Bickerton Hill formed part of a common for the townships of Larkton, Bickerton and Duckington and local residents remember cattle grazing on Bickerton Hill as recently as the 1950s. Whilst parts of the hill were enclosed during the 18th and 19th centuries, this appears to have been carried out on a somewhat *ad hoc* basis, rather than as part of any systematic enclosure. Two township boundaries are shown on the hilltop from as early as the Egerton Estate map of 1735 (CALS DEO 1/5). The first runs along the southwest cliff edge of the hill and continues northeast until reaching Maiden Castle, it then follows the cliff edge on the northern side of the hillfort, before descending north from the hill top. This boundary marks the eastern extent of Duckington township and is clearly surviving as a bank on the lidar survey; particularly on the section running through Heather Wood (Figure 7.12, dot and dash line). The other boundary runs northwest to southeast across

the southwestern side of the hill top and marks the northern limit of Larkton township. This latter boundary does not appear to have left any surface traces for the lidar survey to capture; although the southeastern end is fossilised in the line of modern property boundaries.

The lidar survey has captured the line of a track which runs from the main inturned entrance of the hillfort in a northeasterly direction until it reaches the edge of a valley named on the Edgerton Estate map of 1735 as 'Pool Dale' (Figure 7.12). This track does not appear on any of the early mapping, but is now marked on the modern Ordnance Survey map as a 'track', which might imply that the route has no great antiquity. However, ground proofing of the lidar survey has shown that some sections of this track take the form of a fairly well defined hollow way and it could represent an early droving route on and off the hilltop. Two or three other trackways are possibly indicated on the southeastern side of the hill, providing access to the hilltop from the edge of Bickerton. It is notable that there is no apparent route on to the hilltop from

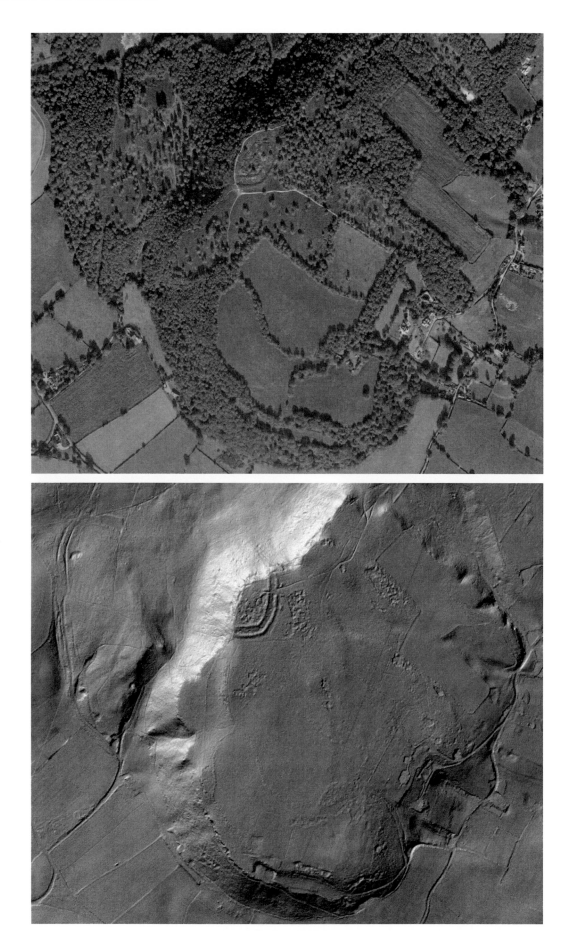

FIGURE 7.11 MAIDEN CASTLE HILLFORT LANDSCAPE FROM THE 2010 AERIAL PHOTOGRAPHIC SURVEY (TOP) AND THE 2010 LIDAR SURVEY DTM (BOTTOM) © CHESHIRE WEST AND CHESTER COUNCIL.

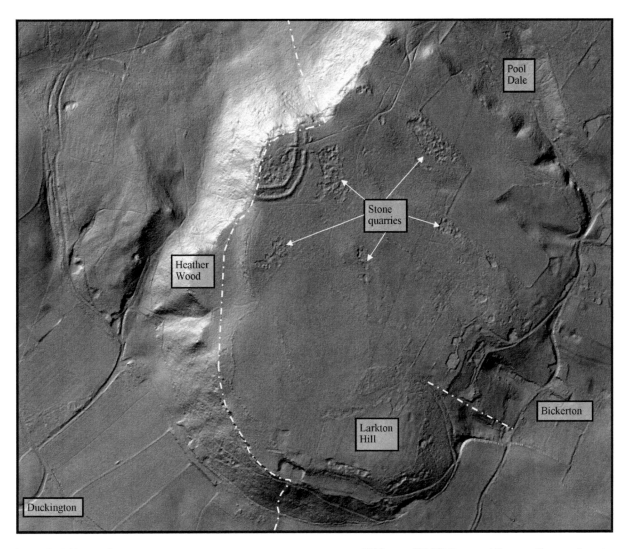

FIGURE 7.12 MAIDEN CASTLE HILLFORT LANDSCAPE INTERPRETATION BASED ON THE 2010 LIDAR DTM © CHESHIRE WEST AND CHESTER COUNCIL.

Duckington township. There are no known springs or natural water sources on the hilltop.

The most imposing sections of the hillfort ramparts are set along the southern and eastern sides of the enclosure with the impressive inturned entrance located at the northeastern end. The architectural design of the hillfort, with the most imposing section of the rampart projecting south and eastwards across the hilltop and towards the head of the Pool Dale valley, appears to have been deliberate. The hillfort it clearly designed to impress anyone approaching the hilltop from any accessible direction; the entrance perhaps facing the principal route on and off the hill. The design of Maiden Castle does not particularly make use of the existing topography and the line of the inner rampart is not as semi-circular or crescent-shaped as earlier commentators have suggested (see Chapter 2). The inner rampart is more of a reversed 'L' shape (mirroring the shape of the cliff edge) and creates an enclosed space which is similar to a parallelogram in appearance. The outer rampart does appear more curvilinear, but it is unclear whether this is

a deliberate adaption or simply an artefact of extending the line of the enclosure further out from the cliff edge. The inner rampart inturned entrance and a simple gap entrance in the outer rampart is identical to the northwestern entrance of Eddisbury hillfort.

Manley Common

It has not been possible to carry out a systematic, detailed examination of all the lidar data captured for the Sandstone Ridge Econet Partnership zone, as has already been stated. The summary analysis above has provided an indication of the nature of the data in the area of the hillforts and their immediate management zones. As an indication of the potential of the data from other parts of the Sandstone Ridge zone, the area around Manley Common and the New Pale was selected for comparison.

Manley Common lies to the northwest of Eddisbury hillfort and west of Delamere Forest. The limit of the New Pale deer park, enclosed in the 17th century, is still clearly visible in the modern field pattern, as a large

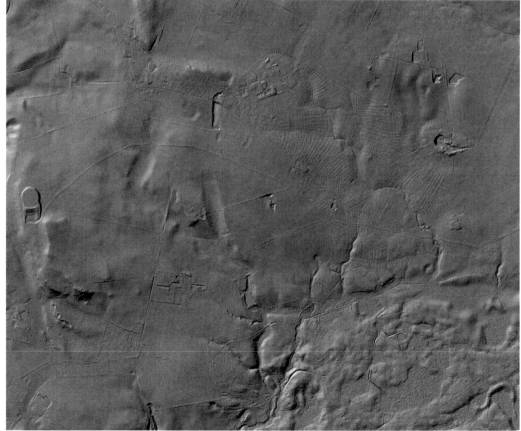

FIGURE 7.13 MANLEY COMMON LANDSCAPE FROM THE 2010 AERIAL PHOTOGRAPHIC SURVEY (TOP) AND THE 2010 LIDAR SURVEY DTM (BOTTOM) © CHESHIRE WEST AND CHESTER COUNCIL.

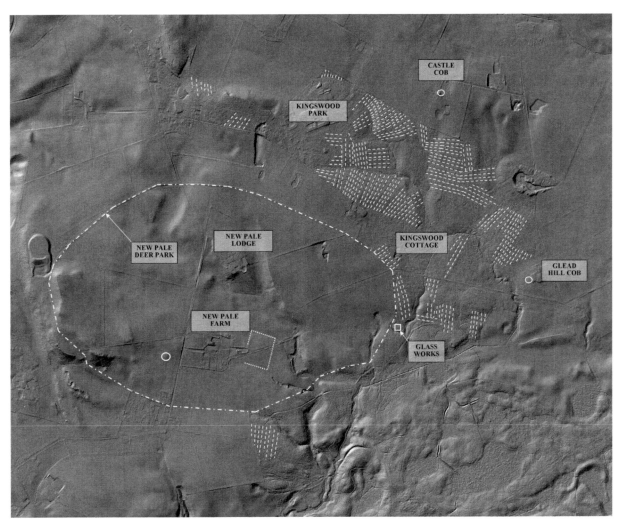

FIGURE 7.14 MANLEY COMMON LANDSCAPE INTERPRETATION BASED ON THE 2010 LIDAR DTM © CHESHIRE WEST AND CHESTER COUNCIL.

oval-shaped enclosure (Figure 7.14). The eastern side of the New Pale is bordered by woodland known as Kingswood, which has a large residential complex at its northern end called 'Kingswood Park' (formerly Crossley Sanatorium). The lidar survey shows this area without woodland and reveals surviving fragments of medieval ridge and furrow, representing part of a formerly unsuspected field system (Figure 7.14, dashed lines). This medieval field system ends abruptly at the edge of the New Pale enclosure, lending further support to the antiquity of the earthworks. The ridge and furrow had clearly been flattened within the area of Kingswood Park and in the area of a former nursery known as Castlehill Cottage (now Kingswood Cottage). However, what is most apparent is the sudden disappearance of the field system as soon as the limits of Kingswood are reached; it is a stark example of the impact modern ploughing regimes have had on the historic Cheshire landscape. The significance of the medieval field system is appreciated when it is viewed in relation to the surviving earthwork remains of a late medieval glass works (Scheduled Monument, National Heritage List for England list entry number

1020705) (Figure 7.14, centre right). Previously this monument was seen as an isolated site in the depths of the medieval forest; however, it can now be seen as part of an extensive medieval landscape.

Within the New Pale deer park itself, scrutiny of the lidar data suggests a rectangular enclosure on the eastern side of New Pale Farm (Figures 7.14, centre bottom). This enclosure is clearly earlier than the track running between the farmstead and the site of a fresh water spring; and it is tempting to see it as the site of a medieval moated manor house. This tentative identification requires further testing however, in order to validate this hypothesis.

Finally, the lidar survey suggests the presence of a small mound to the west of New Pale Farm (Figure 7.14, centre left). This feature also appears to be visible on the 2010 aerial photograph (Figure 7.13 top) and may simply be a natural feature. However, there are two known Bronze Age barrows to the east of Kingswood known as Glead Hill Cob (Hondslough Farm) and Castle Cob and further burial mounds in this area would not be unexpected.

Concluding remarks

The lidar data have captured the existing hillforts along the Ridge and have confirmed that no additional extant prehistoric enclosures are located beneath the wooded hill tops. The data have not provided any indication of additional lines of enclosure or internal structures in the hillforts, with the exception of Helsby hillfort, where the presence of an outer counterscarp bank has been confirmed; which had previously been suggested by a parchmark in the field south of the ramparts. Whilst further analysis of the results is required, there are clearly elements from a number of periods preserved within the landscape of the Ridge, as demonstrated by the examination of the data from Manley Common and New Pale. Further study of the lidar data will undoubtedly be repaid by the recognition of new landscape features of all periods and an enhanced understanding of the landscape of the Ridge.

Chapter 8
Excavations at Woodhouse Hillfort

Dan Garner

Introduction

The hillfort at Woodhouse Hill, Frodsham is situated at around 140m OD at the northeastern end of the Cheshire Sandstone Ridge (Figure 1.2). This chapter presents the results of archaeological excavation carried out at the hillfort between 6 July and 20 August 2009, under the overall directorship of the author. The work was conducted as a training opportunity for local volunteers under the supervision of professional archaeologists Gary Crawford-Coupe, Andy Lane and Leigh Dodd (Earthworks Archaeological Services); as well as fieldwork experience for students from the School of Archaeology, Classics and Egyptology (SACE) at Liverpool University, under the supervision of Dr Ben Edwards and Dr Rachel Pope.

The evaluation at Woodhouse hillfort was intended to provide additional data to inform a strategy for the long-term management of the scheduled monument, in line with the findings of the Desk-Based Assessment and the Condition Assessment carried out by Oxford Archaeology (North) prior to the start of the Project (OAN 2008a; 2008b) (see Chapter 1, this volume). The site was on the Heritage at Risk Register owing to inundation by birch woodland, rhododendron and bracken vegetation. The monument is in the ownership of the Woodland Trust and is currently managed by them as broad leaf woodland. The Trust signed a management agreement with English Heritage in 2008, under section 17 of the Ancient Monuments and Archaeological Areas Act 1979, which led to the systematic clearance of rhododendron from the interior of the hillfort and the felling of 65 trees along the line of the eastern rampart. These measures were very much seen as urgent remedial works and there is still a need to clearly define a more sensitive management strategy for the whole site.

Site location

This part of the Ridge comprises Middle Triassic Sherwood Sandstone (British Geological Survey 1980) overlain by Bridgnorth well-drained sandy and coarse loamy soils (British Geological Survey 1983). The site occupies part of an outcrop of the Ridge that slopes gently upwards from the southeast, before terminating at steep cliff-edges to the north and northwest. The promontory upon which Helsby hillfort is sited, is plainly visible from the site (Figure 1.2), and it is only the dense tree-cover at Woodhouse Hill that prevents wide views to the north,

west, and southwest from within the hillfort interior. The view to the east is interrupted by a rise in the Sandstone Ridge, and similarly a further rise to the south of the hillfort, in the area of Foxhill Wood, prevents extensive views in that direction. The hillfort utilised the natural slopes and sandstone scarps of the outcrop to the west and southwest, and little artificial modification is visible in these areas. The eastern and northern sides of the hillfort are delineated by a bank that varies considerably in size, with the larger sections being situated to the north. The total area of the fort is around 1.8 hectares (4.4 acres), with approximately 0.2 hectares (0.5 acres) being occupied by the ramparts (Forde-Johnston 1962: 19).

Methodology

The fieldwork at Woodhouse comprised seven excavation trenches as located on Figure 8.1. In the case of all trenches the approach, as defined by the Scheduled Monument Consent, was to cause minimal disturbance to the surviving archaeological deposits by either targeting a previous excavation trench or by only removing demonstrably recent surface litter and topsoil. All excavation was therefore undertaken by hand, using appropriate hand tools. Once root and rhizome penetration was encountered the evaluation exposed the extent of their coverage in plan. Subsequently, the upper root/rhizome layers were removed in order to establish the depth of penetration. Any indications of rampart slumping owing to the action of roots/rhizomes was recorded where possible without damaging the earthworks. All evaluation was undertaken with a view to avoiding damage to any archaeological features or deposits which appeared to be demonstrably worthy of preservation in situ. Excavated material was examined in order to retrieve artefacts to assist in the analysis of their spatial distribution.

Trench 1 was located at the southern end of the eastern rampart in the area believed to be the site of Graham Webster's 1949 excavation trench. The original excavation was in an area where a footpath passed through a gap in the rampart (OAN 2008a: 12); and Forde-Johnston subsequently reported that the section had revealed a box-type rampart revetted at the front and rear with stone walling (Forde-Johnston 1962: 19).

All trenches were reinstated at the end of the excavation process. In each case a sheet of geo-textile (terram) was used to line the base of the excavation and then the

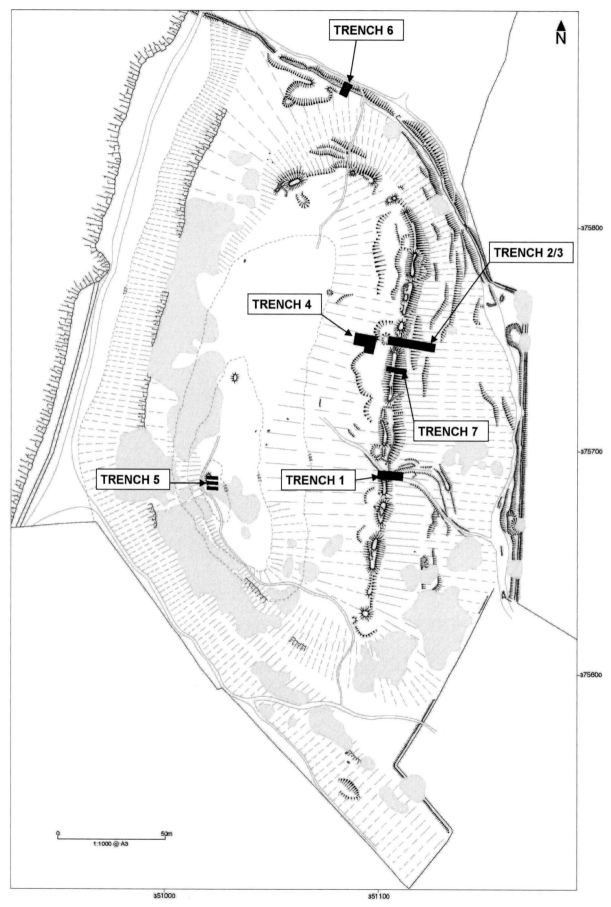

FIGURE 8.1 TRENCH LOCATION PLAN OVER-LAID ON TO THE HACHURE PLAN PRODUCED AFTER THE TOPOGRAPHIC SURVEY IN 2009 © ASWYAS.

trench was subsequently backfilled using the excavated material. In areas where earthwork reinstatement was required (such as Trench 1) there were enough large sandstone fragments within the excavated material to be able to recreate the original contour without the need for additional measures such as wire mesh gabions or sandbags. All trenches were given a top covering of the original topsoil which had been set aside for the purpose.

Arrangements were made for the long-term storage of the physical archive with the Cheshire West and Chester Museum Service with the unique accession number CHEGM 2009.83.

Results

A broad sequence of phases was developed for the whole site, in an attempt to maintain a basic chronological framework for all seven excavation trenches (Figure 8.2)

Phase	Summary
0	Pre-hillfort activity on the hilltop
1	Primary hillfort construction
2	Secondary hillfort activity
3	Post-hillfort modification, quarrying and erosion
4	Modern (20th century) hilltop activity

FIGURE 8.2 THE MAIN PHASES IDENTIFIED WITHIN TRENCHES 1 TO 7.

Trench 1 *(Figures 8.3 and 8.4)*

Trench 1, measuring 11 x 4m, was excavated at the southern end of the eastern rampart in the location believed to be the site of Graham Webster's 1949 excavation trench, as identified in the 2009 topographic survey (see Pollington, Chapter 5, this volume). It was primarily intended as an opportunity to re-examine and record a full section through the rampart and to recover material for scientific dating where appropriate. The trench would also serve to inform some of the more general management issues regarding tree and bracken infestation. The rampart was predominantly constructed from a core of sandstone rubble within a pale orange sand matrix, with traces of two courses of a stone retaining wall on the outer face. A possible secondary phase of rampart construction was detected on the inner face, which consisted of a deposit of sandstone rubble within a dark brown soil matrix.

Phase 0

The base of the earthwork had been constructed on top of a layer of grey silt-sand (107) up to 0.3m thick which contained small sub-angular fragments of sandstone and covered the entire trench. Beneath this sand was the upper surface of the sandstone bedrock (104) which was criss-crossed with naturally occurring fault lines.

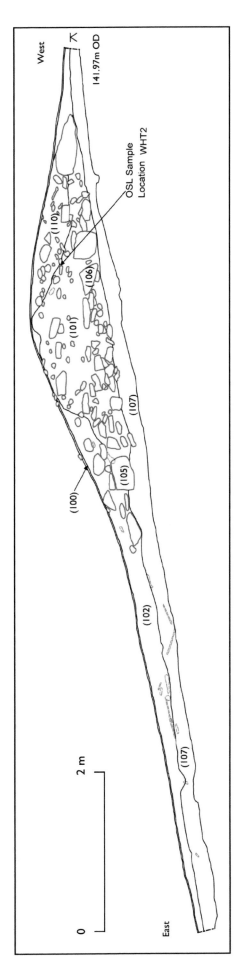

FIGURE 8.3 TRENCH 1 NORTH FACING SECTION THROUGH HILLFORT RAMPART.

Phase 1

The base of the earthwork consisted of a layer of fairly densely packed large angular sandstone fragments within a light brown sandy soil (106). The eastern edge of the earthwork base appeared to have been constructed as a fairly well-dressed drystone wall (105) which survived to a height of two courses and would have functioned as an outer retaining wall or revetment for the rampart's core (101). The core of the earthwork consisted of fairly loose orange sand (101) containing a high percentage of small and medium sized angular sandstone fragments.

Phase 2

The uppermost context within the surviving earthwork was a deposit of dark grey/brown silt-sand up to 0.4m thick (110); which contained a high percentage of small and medium sized angular sandstone fragments. Deposit (110) had the appearance of being a later addition to the inner face of the rampart. The interface between the base of layer (110) and the top of layer (101) was sampled by Professor Richard Chiverrell from the Department of Geography at Liverpool University for OSL dating (see below).

Phase 3

On the eastern side of the earthwork the external hill slope was covered by a dark grey/brown silt-sand (102) containing sandstone rubble. This was thought to represent a mixture of old topsoil and rampart tumble, downslope from the upstanding earthwork. The only artefact recovered from layer (102) was a prehistoric flint tool but this is likely to be a residual object.

Phase 4

A large part of the trench was covered by a dump of material comprising lumps of sandstone within a deposit of dirty grey sand (108). This was interpreted as a reconstructed section of the earthwork forming the backfill of the archaeological trench excavated by Graham Webster during 1949. The removal of backfill (108) exposed a vertical section through the earthwork (Figure 8.4) which was given a nominal cut number (109). The backfill material (108) produced the base to a glass bottle marked 'MORGAN'S POMADE' (the company first started producing hair and skin care products in 1873), as well as a number of spent .303 calibre rifle cartridges and a piece of shrapnel of 20th century date (see below and Figure 8.27).

FIGURE 8.4 SECTION THROUGH THE EASTERN RAMPART IN TRENCH 1 DURING EXCAVATION. LOOKING SOUTHEAST.

A linear gully (103) formed by footpath erosion had cut diagonally through (102) across the trench on a northwest-southeast alignment. In 1949 Graham Webster's original excavation trench had been located on a section of the rampart that was being adversely affected by footpath erosion. This footpath was detected during the topographic survey in 2009. Still visible as a scar on the approach to the eastern arm of the rampart, it continued through the break in the rampart and then could be further traced in to the hillfort interior. It was clear that the footpath had become increasingly unused since the time of Graham Webster's investigations and this is likely to be the result of the increasing tree cover on the summit of the hill and the loss of a dramatic view point. As a consequence, the old footpath scar (103) had become partially submerged in leaf litter, which seems to have created favourable conditions for the root systems of the freshly colonizing birch scrub.

The uppermost context within trench 1 was a dark brown peat-like layer (100) formed from relatively recent leaf litter from the extant vegetation.

Trench 2/3 *(Figures 8.5–8.7)*

Trenches 2 and 3 were originally separate, but were eventually joined to form one continuous transect, measuring 15 x 3m, across an apparent 'gap' in the hillfort rampart and the lower slope of the hill. The trench was excavated at a roughly central point on the eastern rampart and was designed to involve the removal of leaf litter and topsoil in order to expose the surviving surface of the eastern rampart base. The location was chosen as an area identified by the topographic survey as a 'gap' in the eastern rampart (see Pollington, Chapter 5). The northern edge of the trench was located immediately next to the stump of a birch tree felled in October 2008 as part of the Woodland Trust management agreement works. The stump had been treated with *glyphosate* immediately after felling but clearly exhibited a mass of fresh growth. The root system connected to this stump extended in to the area of trench 2/3 where it had extensively penetrated the surviving bank of the rampart and promoted the collapse of the outer rampart edge.

Phase 0

The base of the earthwork had been constructed on a layer of grey silt-sand (308) up to 0.3m thick which contained small sub-angular fragments of sandstone and covered the entire trench. The interface between the base of rampart (307) and the top of layer (308) was sampled by Professor Richard Chiverrell from the Department of Geography at Liverpool University for OSL dating (see below). Beneath this sand, the upper surface of the sandstone bedrock (305) had eroded along geological fault lines which formed natural terraces on the lower contours of the hill slope.

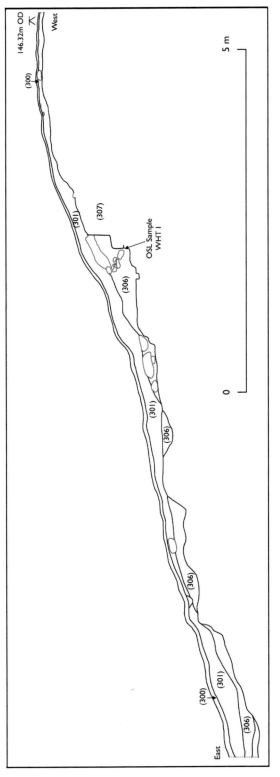

FIGURE 8.5 TRENCH 2/3 NORTH FACING SECTION THROUGH HILLFORT RAMPART.

Phase 1

As with Trench 1, the earthwork construction comprised a core of orange sand containing angular sandstone fragments with a more carefully constructed eastern edge. This appeared to have been constructed as a fairly well-dressed drystone wall that would have functioned as a retaining wall for the earthwork core. The intact base of the earthwork was given the context (307) but was not excavated as part of the fieldwork. No evidence for an external ditch was identified within Trench 2/3.

Phase 2

No deposits related to secondary hillfort activity were identified in this trench.

Phase 3

On the eastern external hill slope a layer of medium and large angular sandstone fragments (306) had been deposited over layer (308). This was interpreted as sandstone tumble, downslope from the upstanding earthwork. Layer (306) produced a single find in the form

of a decorated 19th century clay tobacco pipe bowl (see below and Figure 8.23). Overlying stone rubble layer (306) was a layer of dark silt-sand (302) that was 0.2m thick and probably represented hill wash and naturally occurring silt.

Phase 4

Overlying layer (302) on the eastern side of the earthwork was a dark grey/brown silt-sand (301) containing sandstone rubble that was rich in rhododendron roots and bracken rhizomes and probably represented a relatively modern topsoil. Above layer (301) and covering the entire trench was a dark brown peat-like layer (300) formed from relatively recent leaf litter from the extant vegetation.

Trench 4 *(Figures 8.8–8.16)*

Trench 4, measuring 10 x 5m, was excavated on the interior of the hillfort adjacent to Trench 2/3 and was deliberately located in a bracken rich area of the hillfort interior in order to investigate the level of damage that rhizome development might have caused to the buried archaeological resource. It was also intended to examine the edge of one of the internal quarry pits identified by the topographic survey (see Pollington, Chapter 5) and to identify internal features contemporary with the construction and use of the hillfort.

Phase 1

Overlying sandstone bedrock (204) was a light grey silt-sand (203) which covered the entire trench and contained fairly abundant fragments of small and medium sized sandstone. This deposit was approximately 100mm thick and it was characterised by numerous fragments of rounded sandstone which could be interpreted as 'rubble' probably generated through human activity. One minute flint flake was recovered from deposit (203), suggesting that it should be considered as an archaeological rather than a geological deposit.

Trench 4 was extended to the southeast in to one of the rampart

FIGURES 8.6 AND 8.7 THE EASTERN RAMPART IN THE AREA OF TRENCH 2 DURING EXCAVATION. LOOKING SOUTHWEST (TOP) AND SOUTH (BOTTOM).

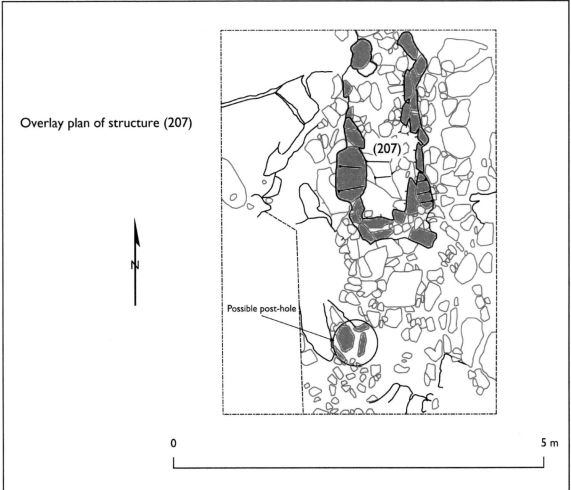

FIGURE 8.8 PLAN OF TRENCH 4 SHOWING LAYER (403) WITH THE TOP OF STRUCTURE (207) PARTLY EXPOSED.

FIGURES 8.9 AND 8.10 SHOWING THE UPPER SURFACE OF THE DENSE BRACKEN MAT LOCATED DIRECTLY BENEATH THE SURFACE LEAF LITTER.

Figures 8.11 and 8.12 Showing the depth of the bracken mat and the surface of the underlying grey podzol (403) which still exhibits some signs of rhizome penetration.

quarry pits identified by the topographic survey, in the expectation that such features would have facilitated the accumulation of deposits rich in cultural material. This quarry pit was allocated a nominal cut number (205) and had been cut directly in to the bedrock. Although a very thin covering of the light grey sand (203) extended down in to the rampart quarry pit there was no other indication of deposit formation in this feature and in consequence no accumulation of cultural material was present. Beneath (203) there were patches of black silt which were only present in one or two of the fissures of the underlying bedrock (sample <1>).

Phase 2

When the upper surface of layer (203) was first exposed, a line of four large sandstone fragments on a north-south alignment was noted on the western side of Trench 4.

FIGURES 8.13 AND 8.14 SHOWING THE GREY MINERAL SOIL (203) EXPOSED IN TRENCH 4. LOOKING EAST (TOP) AND LOOKING WEST (BOTTOM).

It was not possible to discern a cut at this level and a sample area of layer (203) was removed around the stone alignment, to establish whether or not they actually formed part of an archaeological feature. This revealed an arrangement of sandstone fragments which had been set on edge to form a rectangular-shaped structure (207), measuring 2m north-south and 1m east-west. Some of the edging stones had slumped on to their sides and there were also one or two gaps suggesting that the structure had been disturbed in antiquity; this may have been caused by an earlier phase of tree cover on the hilltop. The interior of the stone structure was largely filled with a deposit identical in appearance to layer (203); however, towards its base the deposit appeared to become darker and this was treated as a separate fill (206) which was bulk sampled (sample <4>). Structure (207) was apparently set on a naturally terraced step in the underlying bedrock and the interior was a maximum of 0.31m deep. Rather than being free-standing, it was clear that the structure would not have had any integrity if it had been built in this manner and it seems likely that it was set in a shallow cut, which would have originally been made through layer (403). The feature did not provide any cultural material or indication of date or function; however, the whole feature had a certain grave-like appearance and the apparent lack of evidence for the remains of a burial would not be unusual for Cheshire or the prevalent soil conditions.

To the south of structure (207) there was a second discrete arrangement of three sandstone fragments set on edge which may have indicated the location of a post setting that would also have been cut through layer (203).

Phase 3

At the western end of the trench overlying layer (203) was a mid-greenish-grey sand (202) containing occasional medium sandstone fragments. This might have represented the remains of relict topsoil.

Phase 4

Above layer (202) the entire trench was covered by a bracken mat (201), which was so dense that there was more rhizome than soil present. This demonstrated that the bracken on this part of the hill was a fairly old colony that had probably been established for several hundred years. The bulk of the bracken rhizome was restricted to the dense mat (201) and

FIGURES 8.15 AND 8.16 SHOWING THE GRAVE-LIKE TROUGH STRUCTURE (207) IN TRENCH 4 DURING EXCAVATION. LOOKING EAST (TOP) AND LOOKING SOUTH (BOTTOM).

beneath this level there was only occasional evidence for penetration in to the lower archaeological horizon represented by grey sand (203).

Trenches 5A–C *(Figures 8.17 and 8.18)*

Trench 5 was excavated on the western edge of the hillfort interior and consisted of three slit trenches (labelled 5A to 5C), each 1m wide and 6m long, excavated across a possible man-made mound identified on the summit of the hill during the topographic survey. The central slit trench (5B) was also sited to investigate the potential impact on the buried archaeological resource of a recent tree throw. Trenches 5A to C served to establish that a similar grey mineral soil layer (502) overlay the sandstone bedrock in all three locations. This grey soil was in turn covered by topsoil (501); however, there was no evidence to support the presence of a man-made mound on the summit of the hill.

FIGURES 8.17 AND 8.18 SHOWING THE IMPACT OF A BIRCH TREE-THROW ADJACENT TO TRENCH 5B.

Trench 6 *(Figures 8.19 and 8.20)*

Just to the north of the hillfort monument there is an old boundary in the form of a stone-revetted bank and back-filled ditch running on an east-west alignment for approximately 200m. This boundary has been identified as the southern edge of a medieval hamlet known as 'Mickledale'. The place-name Mickledale meaning 'big valley' is first recorded in documentary sources of AD 1351 as *'Mulkeldal'* (Dodgson 1971). A small trench, measuring 5 x 2m, was excavated across this boundary to establish how and when it was constructed.

Phase 3

The entire boundary could be separated in to two component parts: the bank and the retaining wall. The bank had a basal width of 2.4m and a surviving height of 1.4m. This consisted of a primary deposit of pale orangey pink sand (612) and an upper deposit of mid-brownish red sand (602); a worked prehistoric flint flake was recovered from upper deposit (602) (see below and Figure 8.28). The southern side of the bank was retained by a drystone wall (601) which was constructed from roughly shaped red sandstone blocks that survived to a height of six courses. The top three courses had the appearance of falling back towards the north, presumably owing to the soft nature of the retained bank deposits. It appeared that both the stone retaining wall (601) and the bank deposits (602) and (612) were broadly contemporary and that the entire boundary had been built in a single phase of construction. Unfortunately, no buried soil horizons were identified beneath lower bank deposit (612) and it lay directly above natural sand (613).

Phase 4

Parallel to the southern side of boundary wall (601), a shallow ditch cut (614) was identified which was 2m wide and 0.5m deep. Ditch (614) appeared to be cut up to the basal course of wall (601) and as such was probably a later addition to the original boundary. The primary fill of the ditch was a dark yellow-brown mottled sand (609) which contained no artefacts. Above this was a more consistent layer of orange sand (606), which produced a moulded glass bottle marked 'ELLISON & CORKER. FRODSHAM CHESHIRE' dated *c*. AD 1900 (see below and Figure 8.25). The upper ditch sediments were quite localised

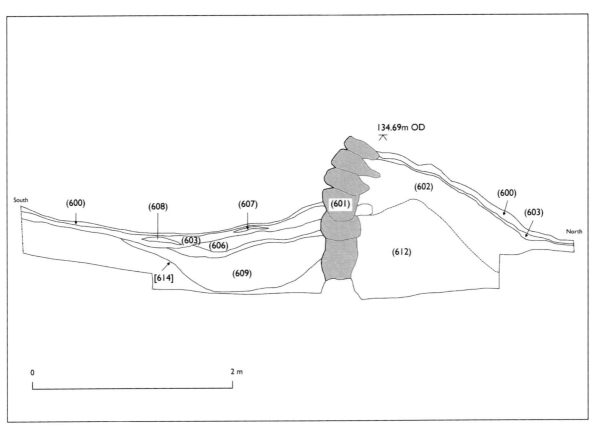

FIGURE 8.19 TRENCH 6 EAST FACING SECTION THROUGH MEDIEVAL BOUNDARY.

FIGURE 8.20 THE COMPLETED SECTION THROUGH THE 'MICKLEDALE' BOUNDARY AT TRENCH 6. LOOKING WEST.

and varied, with a deposit of sandstone blocks (610) on the eastern side of the trench probably representing tumble from wall (601), whilst deposits (607) and (608) were patches of charcoal/cinder possibly derived from a small camp fire.

The whole trench (including the upper fills of the ditch and the upper bank deposit) was covered by a layer of dark grey sand (603) above which was a thin layer of modern leaf mould (600).

Trench 7 *(Figures 8.21 and 8.22)*

Trench 7, measuring 8 x 2m, was located at a roughly central point on the eastern rampart in an area identified by the topographic survey as the best preserved section

of the rampart. The trench comprised a topsoil strip only, with the aim of learning more about the rampart construction. Like Trench 2/3 only the leaf litter and topsoil (700) was removed in order to expose the surviving surface of the eastern rampart (702).

Phase 1

The uncovered rampart structure (702) appeared too haphazard to be described as a 'box-rampart' but it was clearly a major piece of construction utilising some large irregularly shaped stone blocks (see Figures 8.21 and 8.22). As with Trench 2/3 the southern edge of the trench was located immediately next to the stump of a birch tree felled in October 2008 as part of the works carried out under the Woodland Trust management agreement. The stump had been treated with *glyphosate* immediately after felling, but exhibited some fresh growth. The root system connected to this stump extended in to the area of Trench 7, where it had extensively penetrated the surviving bank of the rampart (702) and promoted the collapse of the outer rampart edge (701) to such an extent, that it was no longer possible to identify the outer stone revetment which was encountered in Trenches 1 and 2. The interior edge of the stone rampart (702) also appears to have been affected by this outer rampart collapse as large voids were detected between the stone blocks suggesting relatively recent movement.

No deposits from any other phases were encountered.

The finds
Dan Garner

The clay tobacco pipe

One fragment of clay tobacco pipe was recovered from the excavation. This comprised a decorated 19th century clay tobacco pipe bowl combining an oak leaf motif with a sprig, possibly bearing acorns, from layer (306) Trench 2/3.

The glass

FIGURES 8.21 AND 8.22 TRENCH 7. THE EASTERN RAMPART AFTER REMOVAL OF LEAF MOULD AND TOPSOIL LOOKING SOUTH (TOP). THE INTERIOR EDGE OF STONE RAMPART (702), LOOKING EAST (BOTTOM).

A total of 46 fragments of post-medieval bottle glass were recovered from Trenches 1, 5 and 6 and these are summarised in Figure 8.24.

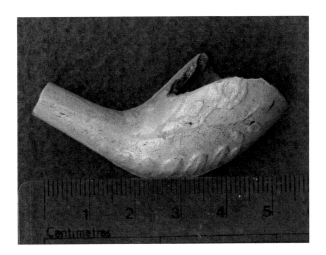

FIGURE 8.23 THE DECORATED 19TH CENTURY CLAY TOBACCO PIPE BOWL FROM LAYER (306) TRENCH 2/3. SCALE IN CENTIMETRES.

The bottle glass fragments recovered from the evaluation were derived from nine vessels of which the five more complete examples were manufactured using the mould-blown technique associated with later post-medieval/modern mass production. In terms of their contents, the most unusual item was the 'Morgan's Pomade' bottle from context (108) in Trench 1. The company first started producing hair and skin care products in 1873, which included hair darkening pomades. The remaining bottles are likely to have contained beverages, although the fragmentary nature of the assemblage makes the identification of the specific contents difficult to ascertain. The most complete example was recovered from ditch fill (606) in Trench 6 and appears to be of a flip-top variety dating to *c*. 1900; the legend cast on to the bottle alludes to a local company based in nearby Frodsham (Figure 8.25). The date range of the vessel glass was of late 19th century and later.

Copper Alloy

A total of six copper alloy objects were recovered from the evaluation (summarised in Figure 8.26) and all were derived from modern contexts in Trenches 1 and 7. Five of the objects were identified as gun cartridges of .303 calibre. One of these cartridges had not been fired, although there was no bullet present and the nose of the cartridge had been pinched closed; a standard way of manufacturing a 'blank round' of ammunition. The other object appeared to be a fragment of shrapnel perhaps derived from a mortar shell. These objects are likely to be derived from military training exercises during the earlier part of the 20th century (see Figure 8.27).

The worked flint

A total of four pieces of worked flint were recovered from the evaluation trenches and these have been ascribed a broad prehistoric date. This includes two tiny waste flakes from Trench 4 (203) and Trench 5B (501) which had clearly been burnt by exposure to excessive heat; exhibiting a discolouration to off-white and being covered with tiny fracture lines giving a 'crazed' appearance.

The piece of worked flint recovered from Trench 6 (602) was associated with the construction of a medieval boundary and is therefore judged to be residual. The object is manufactured from a honey coloured piece of flint and appears to be a waste flake which has been utilised as a small tool. Two of the edges have received treatment in the form of re-touch, which appears to have been intended to create a tapering point at one end of the flake (subsequently broken), perhaps for use as a small awl (Figure 8.28).

The fourth object was recovered from Trench 1 (102), which was interpreted as a modern topsoil deposit and it is therefore judged to be residual. The object is manufactured from a mottled pale grey piece of flint and appears to be a waste flake which has been utilised as a tool. Two of the edges have received treatment in the form of re-touch, which appears to have been intended to create serrated edges to the flake, perhaps for use as a small blade or scraper (Figure 8.28).

Trench	Context	Colour	Vessel	Date	Comment
1	108	Clear	Mould-blown Bottle	c. 1873+	1 neck fragment, 1 base fragment & 3 body fragments. 'MORGAN'S POMADE'
5	501	Green	Mould-blown Bottle	Post-medieval	1 base fragment & 4 body fragments. 'White H...'
5	501	Clear	Mould-blown Bottle	Post-medieval	1 base fragment & 8 body fragments. 'J.M ...'
6	606	Clear	Mould-blown Bottle	c. 1900+	1 base & body fragment, 2 neck fragments. 'ELLISON & CORKER. FRODSHAM CHESHIRE'
6	606	Green	Mould-blown Bottle	Post-medieval	2 base fragments & 17 body fragments
6	606	Green	Bottle	Post-medieval	1 base fragment
6	606	Green	Bottle	Post-medieval	1 base fragment
6	606	Brown	Bottle	Post-medieval	1 body fragment
6	606	Green	Bottle	Post-medieval	2 body fragments

FIGURE 8.24 THE GLASS BY CONTEXT.

Trench	Context	Date	Description
1	108	20th century	.303 calibre gun cartridge
1	108	20th century	.303 calibre gun cartridge
1	108	20th century	.303 calibre gun cartridge
1	108	20th century	.303 calibre gun cartridge (blank round)
1	108	20th century	Fragment of shrapnel
7	700	20th century	.303 calibre gun cartridge

FIGURE 8.26 SUMMARY OF COPPER-ALLOY OBJECTS RECOVERED FROM ALL CONTEXTS

Palaeoenvironmental sample assessment

Ian Smith

Aims and methods

Samples were delivered in 10L plastic tubs. After discussions with the site director regarding perceived poor preservation of remains and a paucity of datable finds, the aim was to establish the presence of any palaeobiological remains or dating evidence. Each sample was examined and three were judged to be suitable for flotation. Sample 2 was not processed owing to the demonstrably recent (1900+) nature of the deposit. None had evidence for waterlogging or the presence of well preserved organic remains, but it was thought possible that charred plant remains might survive.

FIGURE 8.25 A MOULD-BLOWN BOTTLE FROM DITCH FILL (606) IN TRENCH 6. THE BOTTLE IS CAST WITH THE LEGEND 'ELLISON & CORKER. FRODSHAM CHESHIRE' WHICH DATES TO C. AD 1900. SCALE IN CENTIMETRES.

FIGURE 8.27 A PIECE OF SHRAPNEL AND FOUR .303 CALIBRE RIFLE CARTRIDGES FROM TRENCH BACKFILL (108). THE CARTRIDGE ON THE FAR RIGHT HAS NOT BEEN FIRED BUT THERE IS NO EVIDENCE FOR A BULLET; THE NOSE HAS BEEN PINCHED CLOSED INSTEAD, INDICATING THAT IT WAS A BLANK ROUND. SCALE IN CENTIMETRES.

FIGURE 8.28 WORKED PREHISTORIC FLINT TOOLS RECOVERED FROM TRENCH 1, CONTEXT (102) (RIGHT) AND TRENCH 6 CONTEXT (602) (LEFT). SCALE IN CENTIMETRES.

Samples <1>, <3> and <4> were processed in water by flotation over a 500 micron nylon residue mesh and into a 250 micron flot bag. The resulting heavy residues and flots (or wash-overs) were dried. The flots were bagged once dry. The dried heavy residues were sieved into >4mm >2mm and <2mm fractions. The resulting groups of residue were laid out on trays and scanned for the presence of organic remains or artefacts.

Sample number	Trench number	Context number	Litres
1	4	203	7
2 (not processed)	6	608	3
3	1	107	50
4	4	206	7

FIGURE 8.29 THE SAMPLES BY CONTEXT AND UNPROCESSED VOLUME.

Results

The environmental potential of samples <1>, <3> and <4> was judged to be poor. The presence of so many modern roots is clearly problematic and indicates considerable bioturbation. Apart from occasional small fragments of charcoal, there appeared to be little palaeobiological material in these samples (Figure 8.30).

OSL (Optically Stimulated Luminescence) sample dating
Dan Garner

No suitable material was retrieved from any of the trenches for radiocarbon dating purposes. Two samples were removed for possible OSL dating by Professor Richard Chiverrell from the Department of Geography at Liverpool University. The first sample (WHT1) was taken from the top of the pre-rampart soil horizon (308) in Trench 2/3; whilst the second sample (WHT2) was taken from the section through the hillfort rampart in Trench 1 at the base of rampart deposit (110). Dr Barbara Mauz and Dr Andreas Lang from the Department of Geography at Liverpool University tested the two sample locations for background data.

The samples were subsequently ascribed laboratory sample codes LV387 and LV388 prior to testing. The sample testing was undertaken by Dr Barbara Mauz and Susan Packman. The results are summarised in Figure 8.31 as per English Heritage guidelines (Jones (ed.) 2008).

Discussion

In spite of the minimal invasive methods used during the trial excavation the results have proved informative in both increasing our understanding of the monument known as Woodhouse hillfort and in terms of gaining a greater understanding of the impact that the current management regime is having on the buried archaeological remains.

Sample number	Context number	Summary
1	203	<2mm fraction contains occasional seeds of a member of the Chenopodiaceae (possibly common orache *Atriplex patula*). The latter is a widely distributed species and occurs on arable land and in gardens. It is not clear whether these seeds are modern or ancient but their excellent condition strongly suggests the former. The presence of a clearly modern beetle (a member of the Curculionidae) abdomen in the same sample indicates that contamination by modern remains is possible.
1	203	>2mm dominated by circa 3mm fragments of sandstone and modern roots.
1	203	>4mm dominated by sandstone fragments.
1	203	Flot dominated by modern roots.
2	608	Contains frequent modern wood and charcoal.
3	107	<2mm dominated by sand.
3	107	>2mm dominated by sandstone fragments.
3	107	>4mm dominated by sandstone fragments.
3	107	Flot dominated by frequent modern roots but with rare fragments of wood charcoal 2 to 8mm.
4	206	<2mm to >4mm dominated by sandstone fragments, sand and modern roots.
4	206	Flot dominated by modern roots and with some delicate (and clearly modern) seeds visible.

FIGURE 8.30 SUMMARY OF THE SAMPLE RESULTS.

Sample name (field)	Sample Code	Luminescence Age (yrs before 2009)	Central Date	1 σ error (68% confidence)	Calendrical Bandwidth (68% confidence)	Calendrical Bandwidth (2 σ, 95% confidence)
WHT 1	LV387	2,900 +/- 210	891 BC	210 years	1101–681 BC	1311–471 BC
WHT 2	LV388	2,410 +/- 380	401 BC	380 years	78 –21 BC	1161 BC–AD 359

FIGURE 8.31 SUMMARY OF THE LUMINESCENCE AGE ESTIMATION FROM SAMPLES WHT1 AND WHT2.

Rampart form: In terms of 'understanding' the hillfort it has been informative to reinvestigate the structural form of the eastern rampart which was originally described by Webster and Powell in 1949 (OAN 2008a) as a 'box-type rampart'. In the section that was reinvestigated as part of the evaluation, it appeared that the rampart did originally have a drystone wall retaining its outer face (evidenced in both Trenches 1 and 2/3). The treatment of the inner rampart face was more difficult to define as no courses of drystone walling were identified in either Trenches 1 or 2/3. The evidence from Trench 7 would suggest that a fairly crude form of stone revetment had been added to the inner rampart face using substantial sandstone slabs; however, this could be evidence for a secondary phase of rampart building/repair on the inner side of the rampart, as suggested in Trench 1. The rampart core was filled with a mix of sandstone fragments and coarse sand, which is likely to have been derived from the internal quarry pits identified by the topographic survey in 2009 (see Pollington, Chapter 5). The overall impression was of a bank with only an outer stone retaining wall.

Earlier accounts had made no reference to an outer ditch at Woodhouse and more recent surveys (Jecock 2006: 7; Pollington, Chapter 5) could not identify any visible sign of a ditch. The extension of Trench 2/3 for a distance of about 15m downslope of the eastern rampart's outer face was able to demonstrate that no ditch-like sub-surface feature had ever existed in this location.

Date of rampart construction: The desk-based assessment concluded that the evidence recovered from the site to date suggested a single phase of rampart construction and that this was not closely dateable by typological comparison (OAN 2008: 16). The excavation has served to identify a secondary phase of rampart construction/repair on the internal face of the eastern rampart (deposit (110) in Trench 1). Whilst no suitable material was retrieved for radiocarbon dating purposes, an attempt has been made to date the two phases of rampart construction identified using the OSL dating technique. Whilst this technique has only provided a fairly broad range for the dating results, it does at least serve to confirm that the earthwork at Woodhouse is early; at least belonging to the earlier half of the first millennium BC and is perhaps even late Bronze Age in origin. There is significant

overlap between the two dating results and they could conceivably be interpreted as producing the same date; however, there is some suggestion that the secondary phase of rampart construction/repair belongs in the latter half of the first millennium BC. This new dating evidence perhaps suggests a broad chronological model which places the hillfort as a late Bronze Age monument that was enhanced/modified during the earlier part of the Iron Age.

The fragmentary nature of the rampart: The desk-based assessment and the topographic survey have both highlighted the irregularity of the surviving ramparts with several breaks identified along the eastern arm (OAN 2008a: 13; Pollington, Chapter 5). This has been used to suggest that the hillfort was perhaps 'unfinished' (Forde-Johnston 1962: 17–18), whilst others have preferred to ascribe this to the effects of later erosion (Jecock 2006: 7–9). The evaluation work in Trench 2/3 has provided direct evidence that at least one of the gaps in the eastern rampart can be attributed to recent collapse that was probably deliberately caused by stone-robbing or quarrying. The discovery of a 19th century clay tobacco pipe bowl amongst the collapsed rampart material provides a chronological context for this, and it seems likely that the surrounding 19th century field enclosure walls were, at least in part, created from the quarried material. This contradicts the interpretation of the evidence offered in the topographic survey (Pollington, Chapter 5).

There was also less direct evidence for further potential episodes of relatively modern damage to the ramparts in the form of the spent .303 gun cartridges and shrapnel recovered from Trenches 1 and 7. It appears likely that the earthworks were used for an episode of military training during the earlier part of the 20th century, which has remained largely unrecorded. Local anecdotal evidence suggests that nearby Dunsdale Hollow was used for firing and bomb throwing practice during World War II by Local Home Guard groups, including the 13th Cheshire Brigade Home Guard and the Frodsham Home Guard. It was also used for firing practice by American soldiers who were stationed in Warrington and at a camp in Delamere (Joyce & Foxwell 2011: 33–4). The presence of a fragment of shrapnel at Trench 1 suggests that the hillfort may have been used as target practice for live firing of mortars or similar heavy weapons and this could also account for some of the 'gaps' now present in the ramparts. Similar historical evidence is recorded regarding military use of Maiden Castle hillfort further to the south on Bickerton Hill.

Hillfort function: Information regarding the function of Woodhouse hillfort remains elusive with very little evidence being recovered from the interior of the hillfort. It was hoped that Trench 4 would provide a good representative sample of part of an internal quarry pit and a section of the interior. Surprisingly, it became rapidly apparent that beneath modern vegetation and topsoil levels there was only a very thin soil layer surviving above the top of the sandstone bedrock on the hillfort interior; this was confirmed in Trenches 1, 4 and 5. This soil layer had developed in to a homogenous grey podzol, bereft of features or stratigraphy; an inevitable consequence of the sandy free-draining soils. Whilst the thin soil layer may be explained as the result of ongoing erosion on the hilltop prior to the woodland regeneration, it is unusual that this has not led to the build up of colluvial deposits on the back of the rampart or within the internal quarry pits.

The only convincing internal feature identified during the evaluation was the stone-lined trough investigated within Trench 4. As has already been mentioned, this feature had a grave-like quality although no trace of a human burial or associated grave goods was present. This feature presented itself as a line of stone slabs set on edge, which protruded slightly above the surrounding grey podzol once the bracken rhizome mat had been removed; as such it seems likely that the original ground level on the hilltop had been lowered after the feature was created. On investigation, it was clear that this stone-lined trough had been disturbed in antiquity and this perhaps explains its seemingly empty nature. If the trough does represent a disturbed grave this raises a number of questions, foremost of which are: is it an isolated burial or are there a number spread across the hilltop; and is it contemporary with the hillfort? The trough was parallel with the eastern rampart but as both are on a north-south alignment this may be nothing more than coincidence. The lack of evidence for occupation within the hillfort in terms of cultural debris and structural remains may support the idea that Woodhouse was not intended for the same use as some of the other hillforts on the Cheshire Ridge such as Beeston Castle.

Management Review

A full consideration of the management work has been undertaken elsewhere (Garner 2011a) but the implications of the excavation results for the management of the hillfort are summarised below.

Bracken rhizomes: Investigation of the bracken rhizome infestation on both the eastern rampart (Trenches 1, 2/3

and 7) and the hillfort interior (Trench 4) has produced mixed results. The work on the eastern rampart has suggested that bracken has not yet reached an overbearing density as it is still competing with other flora such as the umbrella fern and young birch scrub. Trench 7 suggested that rhizomes had penetrated the outer stone of the rampart and it was observed that the rhizome was easily capable of regenerating new energy giving fronds and pinnae over a relatively short (two month) period. In terms of future management, this would suggest that an annual strim would have little effect on the long-term control of bracken growth on the ramparts, whilst it might have a negative effect on other flora such as the umbrella fern.

The area of bracken growth investigated on the interior (Trench 4) suggested that the bracken was not colonizing through spore dispersal but by rhizome encroachment. This had led to the formation of a dense bracken mat (201) formed mainly of rhizome, rather than soil. The rhizome colony was therefore fairly old and had probably been established for several hundred years. A site visit and inspection by Professor Rob Marrs (Liverpool University) resulted in the conclusion that the entire area was being covered by perhaps as few as half a dozen plants. The bulk of the bracken rhizome was restricted to the dense mat (201) with only occasional evidence for penetration in to the mineral soil beneath. The rhizome mat had formed in order for the bracken to create its own microenvironment above the unfavourable grey podzol soil and for this reason the bracken did not appear to be having too much of an adverse effect on the shallow underlying archaeology in this location.

Trees and roots: Investigation of the impact of scrub and tree root penetration on the underlying archaeology was attempted in all excavation trenches. On the eastern rampart (Trenches 1, 2/3 and 7) it was thought particularly informative to examine the impact of the recently felled birch trees that were considered to be less than 50 years old. At all three trenches evidence was found for rampart destabilisation caused by the outward pressure of the tree roots. This was particularly marked at Trench 7 where the outer face of the best preserved section of the rampart could not be positively identified, due to tree root infestation. It was also noted that voids had appeared on the inner rampart face, due to recent movement within the earthwork. Evidence at Trenches 1 and 2/3 suggested that tree root penetration would eventually cause the outer face of the rampart to be pushed outwards promoting collapse downslope. This would lead to the exposure of the less stable (soft and sandy) rampart core which would be more vulnerable to other forms of erosion.

On the hillfort interior the impact of a birch tree throw was investigated at Trench 5B. This clearly demonstrated that even though the birch tree had formed a relatively shallow root bole, the impact of the wind throw had resulted in a large hole (3m in diameter) which had removed all soil deposits and even sections of the underlying bedrock. Further evidence for the impact of birch roots was identified at the western end of Trench 2/3 where root penetration had caused the underlying bedrock to fracture and lift. This sort of bioturbation could lead to the introduction of modern contamination in to sealed archaeological deposits and features and this has clearly been identified with regard to the palaeoenvironmental sample assessment (see above). The fairly ephemeral surviving archaeological deposits and features identified within the hillfort interior are clearly threatened by the ongoing cycle of tree growth and regeneration.

Rhododendrons: Rhododendron growth across the hilltop had been identified as a relatively recent addition to the range of flora encountered. The colonisation across the hilltop was primarily through runners as opposed to seeding and the evaluation suggested that these runners were very shallow rooted. At Trenches 2/3 and 4 the rhododendron roots had not actually penetrated much beneath the leaf mould, topsoil or bracken rhizome mat. This should perhaps be seen as an indication of the recent arrival of the plant and not as a measure of the ongoing impact if the continued rhododendron colonisation went unchecked.

Conclusions

The trial excavation has served to provide a greater level of knowledge regarding the form, character and level of archaeological preservation on the monument known as Woodhouse hillfort. This has identified the monument as a rare early type of hilltop enclosure, which possibly owes its origins to the end of the Bronze Age rather than the previously suspected Iron Age. The hillfort interior has no above ground features to consider and whilst below ground archaeology is present, it can be classed as shallow, ephemeral and poorly preserved. Sampling has demonstrated that, within the confines of the evaluation, artefact and ecofact recovery has been very low with only hardy materials such as stone tools being identified from the prehistoric period. The visible remains (primarily the earth and stone ramparts) have clearly suffered from several earlier phases of detrimental use, including probably early post-medieval flattening of a section of the eastern rampart for the creation of a house platform, 19th century stone robbing and 20th century military bombardment.

The present woodland environment is a relatively recent development on the hilltop and this is dominated by birch scrub. The hilltop was previously covered by lowland heath within living memory and some heath species such as heather and bilberry continue to cling on beneath the encroaching woodland canopy. This vegetational change is essentially a natural progression, as lowland heath can only be maintained by human intervention such as through livestock grazing etc. The present management regime that has been adopted by the landowner, the Woodland Trust, is non-intervention and this will continue to favour the current woodland regeneration.

The surviving archaeological resource is clearly suffering a negative impact from the current land use and dense tree cover is clearly far from ideal when considering both the extant earthworks and the fragile buried archaeological remains. This is particularly acute where recent birch colonisation of the rampart is actively promoting destabilisation and collapse.

Chapter 9
Excavations at Helsby Hillfort

Dan Garner

Introduction

The hillfort at Helsby Hill, Helsby is situated at around 135m OD, at the northern end of the Cheshire Sandstone Ridge (Figure 1.2). This chapter presents the results of archaeological excavation carried out at the hillfort between 6 and 20 May 2010, under the overall directorship of the author. The work was conducted as a training opportunity for local volunteers under the supervision of professional archaeologists Gary Crawford-Coupe and Leigh Dodd (Earthworks Archaeological Services).

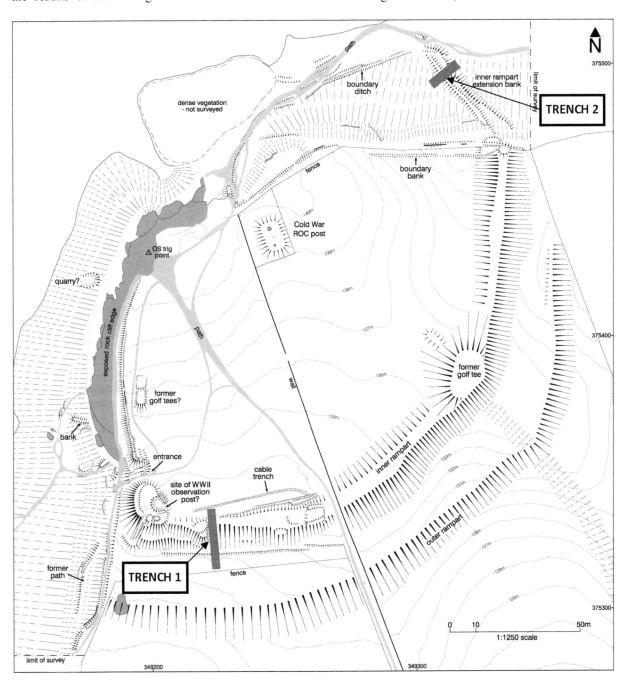

FIGURE 9.1 TRENCH LOCATION PLAN OVER-LAID ON TO THE HACHURE PLAN PRODUCED AFTER THE TOPOGRAPHIC SURVEY IN 2012 © ASWYAS.

The excavation at Helsby hillfort was intended to provide additional data to inform a strategy for the long-term management of the scheduled monument, in line with the findings of the Desk-Based Assessment and the Condition Assessment carried out by Oxford Archaeology (North) prior to the start of the Project (OAN 2008a; 2008b) (see Chapter 1, this volume). The site was on the Heritage at Risk Register owing to inundation by birch woodland, gorse and bracken vegetation. Approximately three fifths of the monument is in the ownership of the National Trust (acquired through several bequests since 1947) and is currently managed as open grassland. The remainder of the scheduled area is under the private ownership of Harmers Lake Farm, and is down to pasture which has in the past been intermittently ploughed, leading to significant spreading of the rampart. The Trust signed a management agreement with English Heritage in 2012, under section 17 of the Ancient Monuments and Archaeological Areas Act 1979, which led to the systematic clearance of much of the birch woodland from the interior of the hillfort. This was coupled with other remedial works, including the improvement of the main footpath leading on and off the summit of the hill and the removal of bracken along the rampart.

Site location

This part of the Ridge comprises Middle Triassic Sherwood Sandstone (British Geological Survey 1980) overlain by Newport 1 deep well-drained sandy and coarse loamy soils (British Geological Survey 1983). The site occupies an outcrop of the ridge that slopes gently upwards from southeast to northwest, before terminating at a steep cliff-edge on the northern and northwestern sides. The hilltop commands extensive views in all directions except due east, where there is a slight rise in a part of the promontory that is not occupied by the hillfort. These steep cliff-faces form a natural defence at the northern and western edges of the fort, and the gently sloping southern and eastern sides of the promontory were interrupted and protected by a curving rampart system. The rampart consists of an internal bank with a parallel external scarp (Forde-Johnston 1962: 16), which may represent the remains of a bank (CHER 1007/1; Bu'lock 1956: 108). No ditch is evident between the inner bank and the scarp, although an external ditch has been identified as a cropmark on aerial photographs. An additional area, consisting of a curving natural terrace in the cliff-edge to the north of the hilltop, was enclosed by the provision of banks that effectively comprised continuations of the main rampart line. An inturned bank at the western end of the site, running parallel to the steep cliff, represents the only apparent entranceway. The total area of the fort is around 4.25ha (10.5 acres), with approximately 1.4ha (3.5 acres) being occupied by the ramparts.

Excavation methodology

The fieldwork at Helsby comprised two excavation trenches as shown on Figure 9.1. In the case of both trenches the approach, as defined by the Scheduled Monument Consent, was to cause minimal disturbance to the surviving archaeological deposits by targeting previous excavation trenches. All excavation was therefore undertaken by hand, using appropriate hand tools and was generally limited to removal of topsoil and demonstrably modern backfill deposits only, using appropriate hand tools. Any indications of rampart slumping owing to the action of roots/rhizomes were recorded where possible without damaging the earthworks. All evaluation was undertaken with a view to avoiding damage to any archaeological features or deposits which appeared to be demonstrably worthy of preservation *in situ*. Excavated material was examined in order to retrieve artefacts to assist in the analysis of their spatial distribution. All investigation of archaeological horizons was by hand, with cleaning, inspection and recording both in plan and section.

Both trenches were reinstated at the end of the excavation process. In each case a sheet of geo-textile (*terram*) was used to line the base of the excavation and then the trench was subsequently backfilled using the excavated material. In areas where earthwork reinstatement was required there were enough large sandstone fragments within the excavated material to be able to recreate the original contour without the need for additional measures such as wire mesh gabions or sandbags. Both trenches were given a top covering of the original topsoil which had been set aside for the purpose.

Arrangements were made for the long-term storage of the physical archive with the Cheshire West and Chester Museum Service with the unique accession number CHEGM 2011.19.

Results

A broad sequence of phases was developed for the whole site, in an attempt to maintain a basic chronological framework for both excavation trenches (Figure 9.2).

Phase	Summary
1	Pre-hillfort activity on the hilltop
2	Construction of a stone rampart enclosing the top of the hill
3	Build-up of sand and silt colluvial deposits against the internal face of the stone rampart
4	A second episode of rampart construction or consolidation
5	Rampart collapse and subsequent formation of rather sterile soil layers suggesting abandonment
6	Post-medieval field boundaries and modern intrusions

FIGURE 9.2 THE MAIN PHASES IDENTIFIED WITHIN TRENCHES 1 AND 2.

Trench 1 (*Figures 9.3–9.17*)

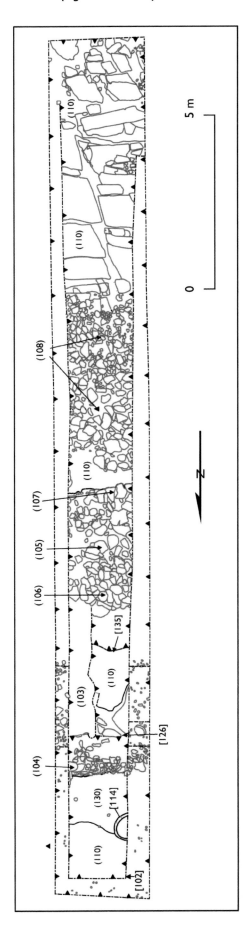

FIGURE 9.3 PLAN OF TRENCH 1.

Trench 1, measuring 24 x 2m, was excavated towards the western end of the southern side of the main rampart in the location of James Forde-Johnston's 1964 excavation trench 1 (see Chapter 2, this volume). It was primarily intended as an opportunity to re-examine and record a full section through the rampart and to recover material for scientific dating where appropriate. The trench would also serve to inform some of the more general management issues regarding tree and bracken infestation.

Phase 1

Potentially, the earliest feature within Trench 1 was located at the southern end of the trench beyond the outer limit of the hillfort rampart and consisted of a shallow linear feature (117) cut in to the top of the sandstone bedrock (110). Linear feature (117) had steep sides and a flat base; it was aligned east-west and was exposed for a length of 1.75m, with an average width of 0.75m and a depth of 0.3m. The primary fill (115) was a mid-red/grey sand 0.1m thick which was sealed by an upper fill of mid-brown silt-sand (116). The upper fill (116) was identical in character to overlying Phase 3 layer (129) and may have represented slumping in to the top of cut (117). Upper fill (116) contained flecks of charcoal and the fill was sampled as environmental bulk sample <10>; a charred wood fragment from (116) was sent for C14 dating. Linear feature (117) was initially thought to represent a possible pre-rampart timber palisade slot but identification over a greater length would be required in order to support this interpretation.

Phase 2

Forde-Johnston had originally interpreted the evidence from this trench as representing a single phase of rampart construction consisting of stone inner and outer walls with a timber inter-laced core. Re-examination of the evidence during 2010 suggested that this was an over simplified interpretation with little consideration of the stratigraphic sequence (see Figure 9.5 for a comparison between the 1964 unpublished section drawing and Figure 9.6 for a schematic view of the main rampart phases).

The earliest component of the rampart was a dry stone construction which was located to the north of rock cut slot (117) and at the southern side of the extant earthwork. Forde-Johnston had interpreted this as the rampart's outer stone revetment wall. On re-examination, this appeared to be a 'stand alone' primary stone-built rampart consisting of an outer stone facing wall (107) behind which was banked a stone rubble core (105). The internal face of this rampart (106) was fairly rough and appeared to have been constructed at an angle about 20 degrees from vertical; in the main there was no distinction between the rubble core (105) and internal

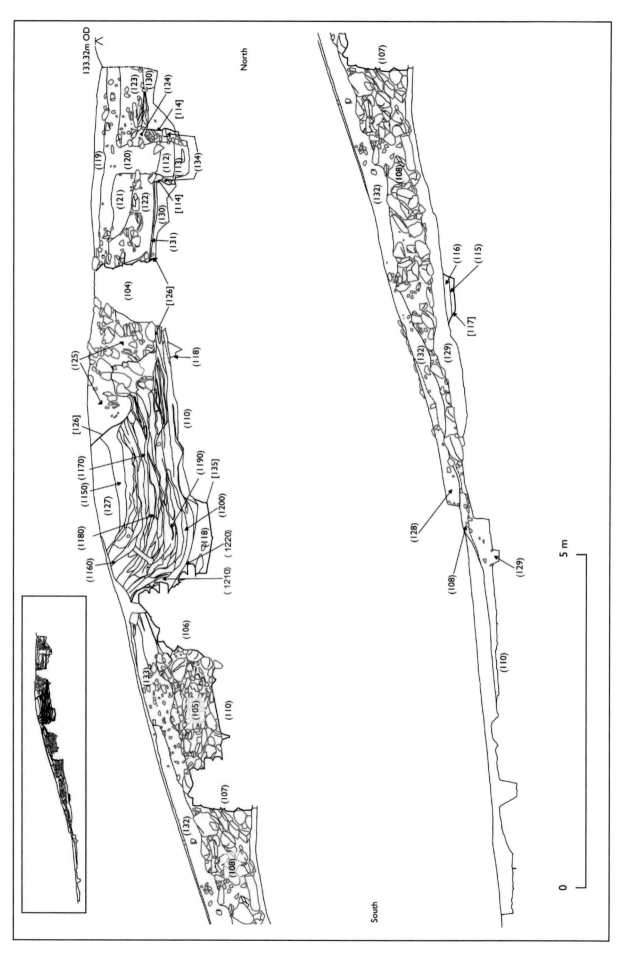

FIGURE 9.4 TRENCH 1 EAST FACING SECTION.

FIGURE 9.5 TRENCH 1 COMPARING FORDE-JOHNSTON'S EAST FACING SECTION THROUGH THE HILLFORT RAMPART WITH A COMPOSITE PHOTOGRAPH TAKEN DURING THE 2010 EXCAVATION.

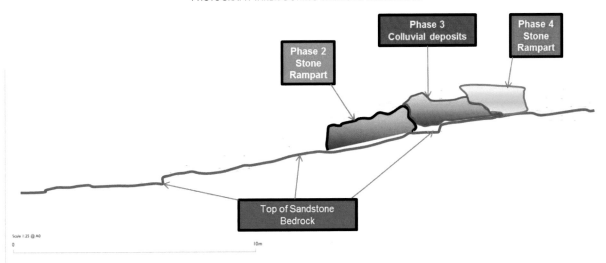

FIGURE 9.6 TRENCH 1 SCHEMATIC SECTION THROUGH THE HILLFORT RAMPART SHOWING THE REINTERPRETED STRUCTURAL PHASES.

face (106). Forde-Johnston had recorded the internal face (106) on his original 1964 section as a dashed line, but had annotated it as a "rough retaining wall" (Figure 9.5).

This primary rampart was exposed for a length of 1.75m and was 3.3m wide (north-south) at the base and had a maximum surviving height of 1.15m. It was built on a natural step in the sandstone bedrock, with the step appearing to form the basal course of the external rampart face (107). To the north of internal face (106) this step was recorded as cut (135) and this was primarily filled with a light grey silt-sand (118) which was bulk sampled as environmental sample <13>. Unlike the later rampart retaining wall (104) the primary rampart was constructed from irregular sized sub-angular and sub-rounded sandstone blocks which showed little evidence of being shaped. These blocks were bonded in a coarse grained, light yellow sand which appeared to have been specifically selected for

the purpose. External face (107) survived to a height of four courses above the utilised step in the sandstone bedrock (110).

Phase 3

A complex series of deposits had formed on the back of inner rampart face (106) above the fill (118) of foundation trench (135). Forde-Johnston had originally interpreted these deposits as charred *in situ* horizontal timbers which were thought to represent timber interlacing within the rampart core. In reality this block of deposits (111) consisted of overlapping lenses of black silt, interleaved with pale grey and yellow sands which had formed to a depth of 1.3m. These lenses had formed against the northern edge of internal stone rampart (106) (i.e. on the inside of the enclosed area) and in places they could be seen to have penetrated voids in the dry stone construction; suggesting that

FIGURE 9.7 TRENCH 1. SHOWING POSSIBLE PALISADE SLOT (117).

Phase 4

Forde-Johnston's inner revetment wall (104) was clearly the latest element in the rampart construction sequence and consisted of a single-faced dry stone wall, surviving to a height of 1.1m (roughly eight to ten courses). The wall was constructed from slab-like pieces of sandstone which appeared to have been specially selected and possibly even deliberately quarried for the purpose. Within the 1964 excavation trench, a 1.75m length of wall (104) was exposed and a vertical joint was noted in the construction towards its western end. This feature would have created a permanent weakness in the wall and it may be more than coincidence that posthole (114) is located 1.5m directly to the north of this joint. Wall (104) sat within construction trench (126) which was 2m wide at the top, tapering to 1m wide at the base, at a depth of 1m. On the northern side of wall (104) the construction trench (126) had cut in to colluvial deposit (131) whilst on the southern side it was cut in to the upper most deposit (127). Within construction trench (126) the space behind the formal dry stone wall construction (104) had been filled with a mixture of sandstone rubble and re-deposited silts and sands (125).

The remainder of the sequence in the northern part of the excavation largely revolved around posthole (114) and inner rampart revetment wall (104). The interpretation of this is somewhat complex. Furthermore, it appears that Forde-Johnston did not identify posthole (114) during his excavation and as a consequence the top 0.7m of the feature had been partly removed down to natural sand/bedrock whilst the lower 0.5m had survived *in situ* within the base of the 1964 excavation trench. The western section of the 1964 trench had provided a good half-section through the upper part of posthole (114) and its associated deposits; excavation was continued to the base of the posthole during the 2010 excavations.

Posthole (114) had been cut through colluvial deposit (131) to form a sub-circular pit 0.8m in diameter and 0.55m deep. After the insertion of a timber post (surviving as a post pipe) the edges of posthole (114) were filled with sandstone packing material (134) which indirectly suggested that the timber post had been approximately 0.45m in diameter. The stratigraphic relationship between posthole (114) and inner revetment wall (104) (see below) would suggest that they were broadly contemporary. After the erection of the timber post, the

the lenses were the result of colluvial deposition. To investigate the formation of these deposits further, a series of palynological samples were taken from seven silt lens horizons as part of a running core down the exposed section; from top to bottom these samples were attributed contexts numbers (1150), (1160), (1170), (1180), (1190), (1200), (1220) and (1210). All seven samples were found to be rich in fossilised pollen and small fragments of wood charcoal were selected from the top (1150) and bottom (1210) of the sequence for C14 dating. It was noted that some of the lenses within these colluvial deposits appeared to have formed over the uppermost surviving part of the internal stone rampart (106); however, this was hard to clarify owing to disturbance of the section at this point by animal burrowing. At the northern end of the trench, deposit (131) was thought to represent the remains of colluvial deposits (111) after being truncated by the insertion of inner revetment wall (104) (see Phase 4). The top of the sequence of colluvial deposits was sealed by a layer of compact mid-brown silt-sand (127) which was cut by wall construction trench (126).

To the south of external rampart wall (107) there was a layer of mid-brown silt-sand (129) which probably represented a natural accumulation of soil to the south of the rampart wall whilst the rampart was still in use (i.e. outside the enclosed area). Layer (129) was identical in character to Phase 1 slot fill (116) and the similarity may be explained as slumping in to the top of cut (117). Fill (116) was sampled as environmental bulk sample <10> and an indeterminate charred wood fragment was sent for C14 dating, producing a date of 400–370 cal BC (NZA-35495); this date is considered to be associated with the formation of layer (129) rather than the earlier filling of slot (117).

southern side of packing material (134) was covered by a deposit of red-brown silt-sand (122) that was rich in angular sandstone fragments and was up to 0.6m thick. The southern limit of deposit (122) had formed against the outer face of inner revetment wall (104) and was thought to represent tumble from the upper part of this structure. A layer of light brown silt-sand up to 0.3m thick (121) had sealed deposit (122) and in turn was sealed by layer (120). The northern side of packing material (134) was covered by deposit (124) which was very similar in character to deposit (122); and above this was a deposit of light brown silt-sand (123) that was rich in sandstone fragments that probably represent tumble from wall (104). The appearance of deposits (122), (121), (124) and (123) in section suggested that they had formed whilst the timber post within posthole (114) was still in place. After deposits (121) and (123) formed, the timber post appears to have been deliberately removed and the resulting cavity or post pipe then accumulated a series of fills. The lowest of these fills was a dark brown silt-sand (113) which contained a lens of dark grey silt and was 0.25m thick; above this was a mid-brown silt-sand (112) that was 0.25m thick. The upper 0.7m of the post pipe was filled by layer (120). The excavated components of lower fills (113) and (112) were entirely bulk sampled as samples <11> and <12> respectively; and two charred wheat grains from sample <12> were sent for C14 dating producing dates of 210–90 cal BC (NZA-35496) and 200–40 cal BC (NZA-35632).

FIGURES 9.8 AND 9.9 TRENCH 1. SHOWING ELEVATION OF THE INNER FACE (106) [TOP] AND OUTER FACE (107) [BOTTOM] OF THE PRIMARY STONE RAMPART. LOOKING SOUTH AND NORTH RESPECTIVELY.

Phase 5

At the northern end of the trench there was a sequence of archaeological deposits that had formed to a thickness of 1.2m. These were exposed within the excavation for a distance of 3m to the north of the stone inner face of the hillfort rampart (104) and so lay within the interior of the enclosed area of the hillfort. The top of the sequence consisted of a layer of firm red-brown clay-sand (119) which was up to 0.15m thick and contained small rounded pebbles and sandstone fragments. Beneath this was a layer of mid-grey silt-sand (120) which contained small sandstone fragments and was also 0.15m thick, except where it had formed the upper fill of the post pipe to posthole (114) where it was 0.7m thick.

FIGURE 9.10 TRENCH 1. SHOWING COLLUVIAL DEPOSITS (111) WHICH HAD FORMED BEHIND STONE RAMPART (106). LOOKING WEST.

FIGURE 9.11 TRENCH 1. SHOWING DETAIL OF COLLUVIAL DEPOSITS (111) WHICH HAD FORMED AGAINST (AND PARTLY OVER THE TOP OF) STONE RAMPART (106). LOOKING WEST.

FIGURE 9.12 TRENCH 1. SHOWING THE ELEVATION OF THE FACE TO INNER RAMPART REVETMENT WALL (104). LOOKING SOUTH.

FIGURE 9.13 TRENCH 1. SHOWING THE SECTION THROUGH THE INTERNAL STRATIGRAPHIC SEQUENCE TO THE NORTH OF RAMPART WALL (104) WITH POSTHOLE (114) (CENTRE). LOOKING WEST.

FIGURE 9.14 TRENCH 1. SHOWING THE REMAINS OF FIELD BOUNDARY (109)/(128) AFTER THE REMOVAL OF TURF AND TOPSOIL. LOOKING NORTH.

FIGURE 9.15 TRENCH 1. SHOWING THE SURVIVING IN SITU RAMPART STONEWORK AFTER THE REMOVAL OF THE 1964 BACKFILL. LOOKING SOUTH.

Figure 9.16 Trench 1 after topsoil removal revealing the backfilled 1964 trench. Looking south.

Figure 9.17 Trench 1. Inserted section of 'dry-stone wall' serving to shore an unstable part of the 1964 excavation. Looking west.

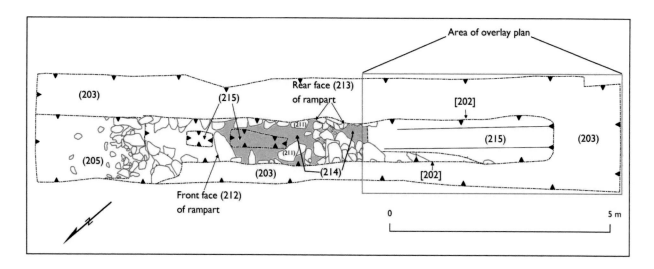

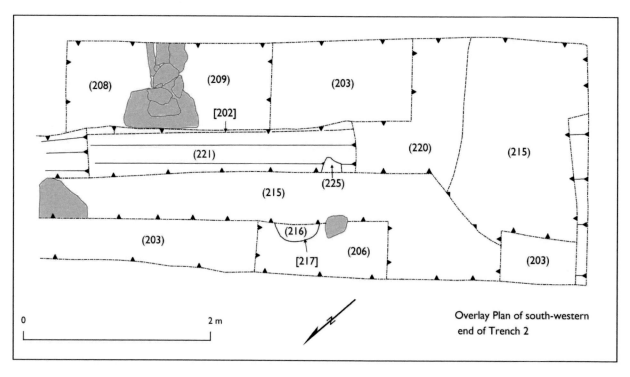

FIGURE 9.18 PLAN OF TRENCH 2.

To the south of external primary rampart wall (107) and so lying outside the enclosed area of the hillfort, was a series of layers which appeared to represent collapse and slippage from the rampart. The uppermost of these were sand-silt layers (132) and (133) which had progressively larger quantities of sandstone fragments present within their make-up. Beneath layer (132) was a large mass of sandstone rubble represented by layer (108) which covered an area 5.6m wide and at least 1.75m long, up to a maximum depth of 0.9m. Layer (108) was thought to represent the outward southerly collapse of the primary stone rampart (107)/(105)/(106). Beneath (108) was Phase 3 layer (129) which probably represented a natural accumulation of soil to the south of the rampart wall (107) prior to the collapse indicated by layer (108).

Phase 6

At the southern end of Trench 1, the remains of a field boundary had been preserved by the earlier excavations. This boundary was probably still an active land division at the time of the 1964 excavation, which would have promoted its survival within the excavations. It had been formed by a low retaining wall of sandstone blocks (109) which survived in places to a height of 0.3m (up to three courses). Behind this was a deposit of red-brown clay and angular sandstone fragments (128) which formed a low bank 2.4m wide and 0.2m thick. A study of the historic mapping for the area shows that this boundary was not part of the initial field enclosure in 1797 and indeed the boundary is not shown on any map up to (and including) the third edition Ordnance

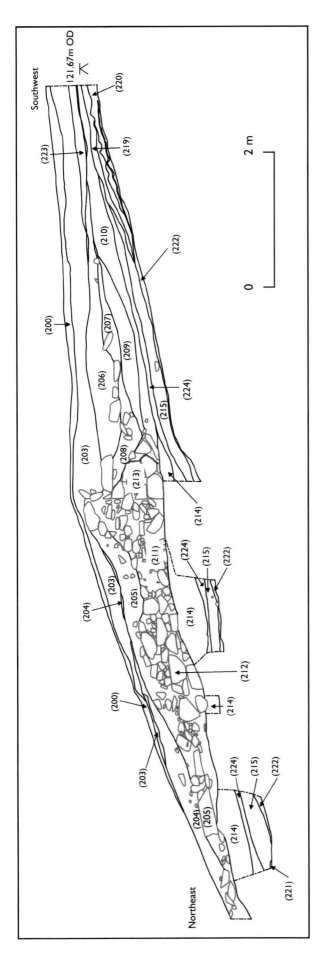

FIGURE 9.19 TRENCH 2 NORTHWEST FACING SECTION.

Survey twenty-five inch to the mile map of 1910. An early golf ball recovered from bank material (128) suggests that the field boundary was probably created at the time that Helsby hill top was being used as a nine-hole golf course between 1914 and 1937 (Joyce and Foxwell 2011: 13–15).

This boundary is still visible on the surface as a low terrace on the outer edge of the hillfort rampart, populated by several mature hawthorn trees. The modern field boundary is defined by a stock proof fence set 5m to the south of this feature, which was erected by the National Trust within the last ten years.

Once the 1964 backfill had been removed it became apparent that most of the stone elements of the hillfort rampart had been preserved *in situ* by Forde-Johnston with the exception of some elements of stone rampart core deposits (105) and (125) which are described more fully above. Under the terms of the Scheduled Monument Consent for the 2010 investigations the *in situ* stonework has been left in place. As a consequence, the stratigraphic sequence described above has been derived from the re-examination and selective sampling of the sections first exposed during the 1964 excavation.

The uppermost context within Trench 1 was a dark brown peat-like layer (100) formed from relatively recent leaf litter from the extant vegetation. Beneath this was a dense black mat of bracken rhizomes in a soil matrix of dark brown/black sandy-silt (101) up to 0.04m thick, which had an almost sponge-like quality when walked on. This layer of rhizomes had been cut by the 1964 excavation trench which was given the nominal cut number (102) and measured 24m north-south by 1.75m east-west. The 1964 excavation trench had been backfilled with the original excavation material which had become a homogeneous mid-grey silt-sand (103). During the removal of backfill (103) it was noted that bracken rhizome regeneration had taken advantage of the disturbed ground, effectively using the 1964 trench as a giant plant pot. As a result, bracken rhizome penetration appeared to be far deeper and more extensive within backfill (103) than in the undisturbed archaeological deposits visible in the trench sections.

The removal of backfill deposit (103) demonstrated that the 1964 excavation had not been as complete as the unpublished archive had suggested with the bulk of the stone elements of the hillfort rampart having been left *in situ*. There was also a previously unrecorded piece of stonework visible in the western section of the trench to the south of the rampart's outer face. This piece of stonework was a short section of dry-stone wall six courses high which appeared to overlie the *in situ* deposits associated with the collapse of the hillfort rampart. The stonework had not been recorded in Forde-Johnston's unpublished section and it was concluded that it had been inserted by the 1964 excavation team to shore up an unstable part of the excavation trench.

Trench 2 (*Figures 9.18–9.28*)

Trench 2, measuring 14 x 1m was orientated northeast to southwest and was excavated towards the northern end of the eastern section of what has been previously termed 'the subsidiary rampart', in the location of the trench excavated in 1955 by J. D. Bu'lock (see Chapter 2). Bu'lock had interpreted this as a later extension of the hillfort circuit on to a lower ledge of the cliff top. The 2010 excavation was primarily intended as an opportunity to re-examine and record a full section through the rampart and to recover material for scientific dating where appropriate. The trench would also serve to inform some of the more general management issues regarding tree and bracken infestation.

Phase 1

The following stratigraphic sequence was identified as pre-dating the construction of the hillfort rampart in

Trench 2. Sandstone bedrock (221) was exposed at both the northeastern and southwestern ends of the trench. At the southwestern end, the bedrock had been discoloured to a bright orange appearance as a result of having been exposed to intense heat. The eastern end of a shallow feature (225) was identified, cut in to the surface of bedrock (221) at this end of the trench, but was thought to be a natural hollow. The earliest deposit to have formed above the bedrock was an 80mm thick layer of black silt (222) which occurred throughout the trench and was sampled in three locations for palaeoenvironmental analysis as samples <3>, <6> and <8>. A palynological sample was also taken. Subsequently, the southern 2.8m of Trench 2 was covered by a layer of burnt and discoloured clay (220) which had apparently been heavily disturbed by the growth of modern tree roots in the vicinity. Both the top of bedrock (221) and burnt clay layer (220) were sampled for archaeomagnetic dating purposes by Neil Suttie from Liverpool University (see below). Burnt clay layer (220) was covered by a 50mm thick layer of black silt-sand (219) which contained lumps of burnt clay and was sampled for palaeoenvironmental analysis as sample <2>. Subsequently, layers of mid-brown silt-sand (215) and (224), which were rich in lumps of burnt clay and stone, had formed over the entire length of Trench 2 to a combined thickness of 0.3m. Finally, a layer of pale yellow/grey sand (214) up to 0.6m thick was deposited above layer

FIGURES 9.20 TRENCH 2. SHOWING THE TOP OF BURNT CLAY LAYER (220). LOOKING EAST.

FIGURE 9.21 TRENCH 2. SHOWING THE EXPOSED AREA OF THE 'BURNT' SANDSTONE BEDROCK (221). LOOKING SOUTHEAST.

FIGURE 9.22 TRENCH 2. SHOWING THE BUILD-UP OF DEPOSITS ABOVE THE BURNT SURFACE OF THE BEDROCK (BOTTOM OF SECTION) AND SAND LAYER (214) PRIOR TO THE INSERTION OF THE STONE RAMPART CORE (211) (TOP). LOOKING EAST.

FIGURE 9.23 TRENCH 2. SHOWING NORTHWEST FACING SECTION THROUGH THE STONE RAMPART. FRONT AND BACK OF THE RAMPART MARKED BY WHITE ARROWS.

(224) over the southern half of Trench 2. Layer (214) was sampled for palaeoenvironmental analysis as sample <1>; and a fragment of wood charcoal was subsequently selected for C14 dating, producing a date of 3950–3780 cal BC (NZA-35504).

Phase 2

After the deposition of sand layer (214) the next event in the Trench 2 sequence was the construction of a stone rampart. The rampart consisted of a relatively well-dressed stone outer face (212), a rubble core (211) and a roughly finished inner face (213); all of which were bonded in a coarse light yellow/orange sand. The outer face (212) survived to a height of two courses whilst the inner face (213) was constructed at an angle which was approximately 30 degrees from vertical. The whole rampart was constructed from irregular sized sub-angular and sub-rounded sandstone blocks which showed little evidence of having been shaped. The combined components of the stone rampart suggested that it had a basal width of 3.5m and a maximum surviving height of 1.2m. In every respect the stone rampart in Trench 2 was nearly identical in both dimensions and style of construction to the primary stone rampart in Trench 1 (recorded as (107), (105) and (106)).

Phase 3

After the rampart construction, a deposit of light grey/brown sand (210) formed against the inner rampart face (213), to a thickness of 0.3m. Layer (210) extended southeast from the inner rampart face as far as the limit of excavation and was subsequently covered by a layer composed of lenses of black/brown sand-silts (209). Layer (209) had formed against the inner face of the rampart to a thickness of 0.2m and was thought to be the "occupation layer" identified on Bu'lock's

published section drawing (Bu'lock 1955, figure 3). Layer (209) was sampled for palaeoenvironmental analysis as sample <5>. Above layer (209) was a layer consisting of inter-leaved lenses of black silt and pale orange/yellow sand (208) which was up to 0.3m thick. Layer (208) was formed against the inner face of the rampart and covered an area approximately 2m to the southeast of the rampart and was sampled for palaeoenvironmental analysis as sample <4>. A palynological sample was also taken. Layers (209) and (208) were very similar in character to the colluvial deposits assigned the group context of (111) in Trench 1 and are potentially part of the same formation process.

Phase 4

At the southwest end of the 1955 excavation trench, a feature (217) was identified cutting in to layer (208); this feature had been almost entirely removed by the earlier 1955 excavation. Cut (217) had almost vertical sides and surviving dimensions of 0.5m (north-south) by 0.15m (east-west) by 0.5m deep. The fill of the feature (216) was a dark grey-brown sand containing one large 'wedge' shaped sandstone block set vertically in to one side of the cut. The feature was thought to represent the remains of a large stone-packed posthole. Posthole fill (216) was covered by a layer of mixed grey and red/brown clay-silt (218) which was heavily disturbed by modern tree roots and was only present in the western section of the 1955 trench.

Phase 5

Colluvial deposits (209) and (208) were covered by a layer of light grey sand (207) which was up to 0.3m thick; above layer (207) was a layer of grey/brown silt-sand (206). Layer (206) reached its greatest thickness of 0.35m where it met the inner face of the rampart. This coincided with a quantity

FIGURE 9.24 TRENCH 2. SHOWING NORTHWEST FACING SECTION THROUGH THE COLLUVIAL DEPOSITS (209) AND (208) AGAINST THE INNER RAMPART FACE (213).

FIGURES 9.25 AND 9.26 TRENCH 2. SHOWING POSSIBLE POSTHOLE (217) WITH IN SITU LARGE PACKING STONE IN SECTION (TOP) AND IN PLAN (BOTTOM).

of large sandstone fragments within the soil matrix which probably represented tumble from the rampart. A similar layer (205) was recorded to the northeast of the rampart and here again the layer was rich in large sandstone fragments which probably also represented tumble from the collapsing rampart.

Phase 6

Above layers (218) and (205) there was a thin layer of dark grey/black silt (204) up to 60mm thick, which probably represented a relatively modern buried turf line; the layer was noted by Bu'lock in his published section drawing (Bu'lock 1955, figure 3). This 'buried turf' was sealed by a layer of red/brown clay (203) which was up to 0.4m thick and represented the uppermost context within Trench 2. This was a dark brown peat-like layer (200) 0.18m thick which had formed from relatively recent leaf litter from the extant vegetation. Beneath this it was possible to define the edges of the 1955 excavation trench which was attributed cut number (202); the trench did not appear to have been entirely backfilled and had survived as a linear depression on the surface of the earthwork. After the removal of backfill (201) it was possible to clean up the trench sections and re-record the stratigraphic sequence; taking samples where appropriate.

The finds

Dan Garner

The ceramics

Ceramic building material

Two fragments of 19th/20th century salt-glazed sewer pipe were recovered from the 1964 backfill deposit (103) in Trench 1. The same deposit (103) also produced a fragment of modern unglazed red earthenware tile with the letters '...ICE...' stamped on to the upper surface. There is no indication of where on the hillfort this material might have originally been derived.

Pottery

Two sherds of post-medieval pottery were recovered from backfill deposit (103) in Trench 1. The first was a body sherd of black and brown glazed earthenware, with glaze only present on the internal surface; the wall thickness would suggest that it

FIGURES 9.27 AND 9.28 TRENCH 2. SHOWING THE 1955 TRENCH AFTER THE REMOVAL OF BACKFILL (201). LOOKING NORTHEAST (LEFT) AND SOUTHWEST (RIGHT).

Trench	Context	Colour	Vessel	Date	Comment
1	103	Clear	Mould-blown Bottle	c. 1900+	1 neck fragment
1	103	Clear	Mould-blown Bottle	Post-medieval	1 rim fragment to a jar
1	103	Clear	Mould-blown Bottle	Post-medieval	1 body fragment
2	201	Clear	Mould-blown Bottle	c. 1900+	1 rim fragment, 7 body fragments. 1 fragment has a partial legend '...B...'

FIGURE 9.29 THE GLASS BY CONTEXT.

was derived from a large utilitarian vessel such as a storage jar or large bowl. The second sherd was a body sherd of pearl-glazed earthenware; the external surface was decorated with a pale blue transfer-printed design. Both sherds date to the 19th century and hint at some domestic occupation on, or near, the hillfort at this date.

The glass

A total of 11 fragments of post-medieval bottle glass were recovered from Trenches 1 and 2 and these are summarised in Figure 9.29.

The 11 bottle glass fragments recovered from the evaluation were derived from four vessels, all of which were manufactured using the mould-blown technique associated with later post-medieval/modern mass production. The eight fragments from context (201)

in Trench 2 are likely to be derived from a single milk bottle. The remaining vessels are likely to have contained preserves and beverages, although the fragmentary nature of the assemblage makes the identification of the specific contents difficult to ascertain. The neck fragment from (103) in Trench 1 appears to be of a flip-top variety dating to c. 1900+. The date range of the vessel glass is of late 19th century and later.

The metalwork – iron

A single iron object was recovered from the field boundary context (128) in Trench 1. The object was a complete iron chisel measuring 195mm long, with a rounded head 30mm in diameter and a hexagonal shaft, which tapered to a blade 22mm wide. The object is from a 20th century field boundary context and this is likely to indicate its date.

FIGURES 9.31 AND 9.32 TWO VIEWS OF THE SMALL BURNT PREHISTORIC FLINT CORE RECOVERED FROM TRENCH 2, CONTEXT (201).

FIGURE 9.30 AN IRON CHISEL FROM BOUNDARY BANK (128), TRENCH 1.

The worked flint

A total of two pieces of worked flint were recovered from the excavation trenches and these have been ascribed a broad prehistoric date. This included a tiny waste flake from Trench 1 (130) and a broken fragment of a small core from Trench 2 backfill context (201). The core fragment had clearly been burnt by exposure to excessive heat; exhibiting a discolouration to off-white and being covered with tiny fracture lines giving a 'crazed' appearance. There was evidence for part of the striking platform on the core fragment as well as three flake removals. The size of the flakes would suggest bladelet production. It is likely that the core fragment was disturbed during the 1955 excavation and was originally from the burnt layers pre-dating the rampart construction, which would suggest an early Neolithic date.

The golf ball

A complete golf ball was recovered from field boundary bank (128) in Trench 1. The object is an early type, although the precise manufacturer could not be identified. The ball is likely to be associated with the period between 1915 and 1936 when Helsby hilltop and part of the hillfort was used as a nine-hole golf course by the Helsby Golf Club.

Palaeoenvironmental Sample Summary

John Carrott, Alison Foster, Lindsey Foster and Helen Ranner (abridged by Dan Garner)

The following extract is abridged from an unpublished report by Palaeoecology Research Services (Report no.

PRS 2010/40) dated October 2010. The full report is available in the online appendix.

Ancient biological remains recovered from the samples were largely restricted to small fragments of poorly preserved, unidentified charcoal. Amongst the charcoal recovered from Phases 1 and 3 from Trench 2 were occasional fragments of charred root/rhizome which *may* have derived from turves used as fuel. These deposits appeared to have a significant ash content, which also suggests possible fuel waste.

The only other identifiable ancient remains were a few charred cleavers seeds and the charred orache/goosefoot seeds (perhaps from crop weeds) and charred grains/grain fragments recovered from Contexts (112) and (113) (the

FIGURE 9.33 THE GOLF BALL FROM BOUNDARY BANK (128), TRENCH 1.

Laboratory Number	Sample Number	Material & Context	Radiocarbon Age (BP)	d13C (‰)	Calibrated date range (95% confidence)
NZA-35493	Helsby [1210]	Charcoal, from lower colluvial deposit [1210]	2929±15	-25.5	1250–1050 cal BC
NZA-35496	Helsby [112] - A	Carbonised wheat grain from the secondary fill [112] of posthole (114)	2127±15	-22.5	210–90 cal BC
NZA-35632	Helsby [112] - B	Carbonised wheat grain from the secondary fill [112] of posthole (114)	2107±25	-23.6	200–40 cal BC
NZA-35504	Helsby [214]	Charcoal, from [214] deposit sealed beneath subsidiary rampart core material (211)	5048±20	-25.8	3950–3780 cal BC
NZA-35495	Helsby [116]	Charcoal from fill [116] secondary fill of rock cut slot (117)	2299±20	-27.5	400–370 cal BC
NZA-35494	Helsby [1150]	Charcoal from upper colluvial deposit [1150]	1620±15	-26.3	cal AD 400–530
NZA-37729	Helsby [1220]	Charcoal from lower colluvial deposit [1220]	3115±20	-26.6	1435–1320 cal BC

FIGURE 9.34 SUMMARY OF THE RADIOCARBON RESULTS FROM THE HELSBY SAMPLES.

secondary and primary fills of post-pipe to posthole (114) (Contexts (112) and (113), both Phase 4), from Trench 2. The grain fragments were poorly preserved (puffed and eroded), but a few were probably of a form of wheat and one (from Context 113) was perhaps of oat. These remains were too few to be of any interpretative value, however.

Radiocarbon Dating Summary
Pete Marshall (abridged by Dan Garner)

Seven single entity samples (Ashmore 1999) were submitted to the Rafter Radiocarbon Laboratory, New Zealand in 2010. The seven charcoal and carbonized plant remains samples were processed using the acid/alkali/acid protocol of Mook and Waterbolk (1985) and measured by Accelerator Mass Spectrometry (AMS) as described by Zondervan and Sparks (1997).

The radiocarbon results are given in Figure 9.34, and are quoted in accordance with the international standard known as the Trondheim convention (Stuiver and Kra 1986). They are conventional radiocarbon ages (Stuiver and Polach 1977).

Calibration

The calibrations of the results, relating the radiocarbon measurements directly to calendar dates, are given in Figure 9.34 and 9.35. All have been calculated using the calibration curve of Reimer *et al.* (2009) and the computer program OxCal v4.0.5 (Bronk Ramsey 1995; 1998; 2001; 2009). The calibrated date ranges cited in the text are those for 95% confidence. They are quoted in the form recommended by Mook (1986), with the

end points rounded outwards to 10 years or 5 years for errors < 25 years. The ranges in plain type in Figure 9.34 have been calculated according to the maximum intercept method (Stuiver and Reimer 1986). All other ranges are derived from the probability method (Stuiver and Reimer 1993) (Figure 9.35).

Interpretation

The radiocarbon results indicate that pre-rampart activity on the hillfort associated with several burning events took place in the early Neolithic (3950–3780 cal BC (NZA-35504)). The primary stone rampart built to enclose the whole promontory was constructed sometime prior to the formation of the windblown lenses, including [1210] dated to 1250–1050 cal BC (NZA-35493). The formation of these windblown deposits against the back of the rampart took place over 1470–1710 years (95% probability; Figure 9.35) and probably 1500–1640 cal BC (68% probability) ending in cal AD 400–530 (NZA-35494). Following formation of these windblown sands and silts, partial rebuilding of the rampart with a stone internal revetment wall (104) and erection of a timber post (114) took place.

The two measurements (2127±15 BP (NZA-35496) and 2107±25 BP (NZA-35632)) on samples from the fill (112) of post-pipe (114) are statistically consistent (T'=0.5; ν=1; T'(5%)=3.8; Ward and Wilson 1978) and could therefore be of the same actual age. This indicates that corn storage or processing was taking place in the interior of the hillfort in the late Iron Age, although it is possible that the grains are residual and therefore only provide a *terminus post quem* for the posthole.

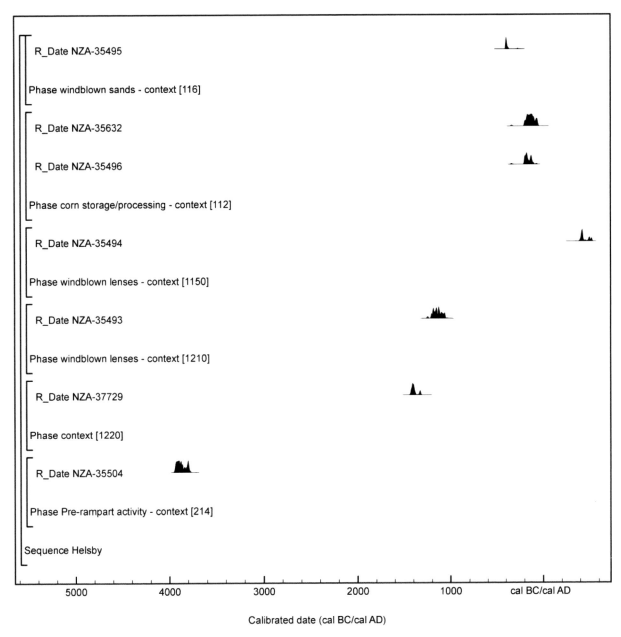

FIGURE 9.35 PROBABILITY DISTRIBUTIONS OF DATES FROM HELSBY. EACH DISTRIBUTION REPRESENTS THE RELATIVE PROBABILITY THAT AN EVENT OCCURRED AT A PARTICULAR TIME. THESE DISTRIBUTIONS ARE THE RESULT OF SIMPLE RADIOCARBON CALIBRATION (STUIVER AND REIMER 1993).

Palynological Summary

Richard Chiverrell (abridged by Dan Garner)

Pollen samples were taken from sections in both trenches at Helsby hillfort. The trenches provided evidence for six separate phases of activity, and materials suitable for palaeoenvironmental analyses were recovered from Phases 1 and 3.

A monolith was taken from Trench 2. Its base (the lower organic 6cm) equates to context (222) and the top to context (214). The whole sequence predated the rampart construction and belongs to Phase 1 of the site. Loss-on-ignition data for the monolith (Figure 9.36) confirm the organic nature of the basal 6cm, with >8% organic content, mostly in the easily combustible 180–350°C fraction. The unit appears an organic rich soil horizon, the top of a buried palaeosol. A further organic rich sample was taken from Trench 2, context (208) in Phase 3, a ditch infill resting against and postdating the construction of the rampart (Phase 2).

The second sequence sampled organic materials in the thick series of bedded sand and silt deposits laid down against the internal face of the stone rampart in Trench 1 and belongs to Phase 3 (contexts (1150), (1160), (1170), (1180), (1190), (1200) (1210), (1220)). The ~1m sequence consisted of bedded pale sands and dark organic silts (Figure 9.37). At

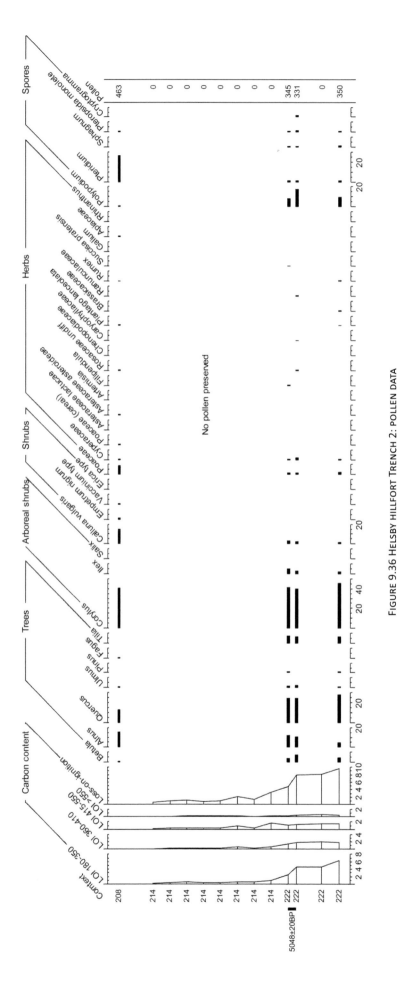

FIGURE 9.36 HELSBY HILLFORT TRENCH 2: POLLEN DATA

the time of the original excavation these organic silts were interpreted as the decayed remains of timbers. However, re-examination suggested that the silts and sands had accumulated in a ditch against the original stone rampart and therefore postdated its construction, although the beginning of the sequence could be almost contemporary with the latter. The preservation of organic material suggests accumulation in wet, perhaps intermittently waterlogged, anoxic conditions, with the sand layers perhaps indicating episodes of heightened erosion.

Methodology

Pollen analysis

Pollen samples were taken from the two monoliths. Sample preparation followed standard procedures, with the extracted material being stained with safranin and mounted in glycerol (Moore *et al.* 1991). Three hundred total dry land pollen grains were counted from each slide. Samples were counted using a Meiji MT5310H trinocular microscope at x400 magnification; a x1000 oil immersion lens was used for grains requiring closer scrutiny.

Identifications were made using the keys of Faegri *et al.* (1989) and Moore *et al.* (1991), supported by the University of Liverpool type slide collection. Taxonomic nomenclature follows the conventions of Stace (2010) and Bennett *et al.* (1994). Relative pollen diagrams were drawn using TILIA (Grimm 2010), plotted in context relative chronological order for each trench (Figures 9.36 and 9.37).

Geochronology

Age control for the two sequences is provided by radiocarbon dating. Seven single-entity samples (Ashmore 1999) from Trenches 1 and 2 were submitted to the Rafter Radiocarbon Laboratory, New Zealand, in 2010. The charcoal and carbonised plant remains samples were processed using the acid/

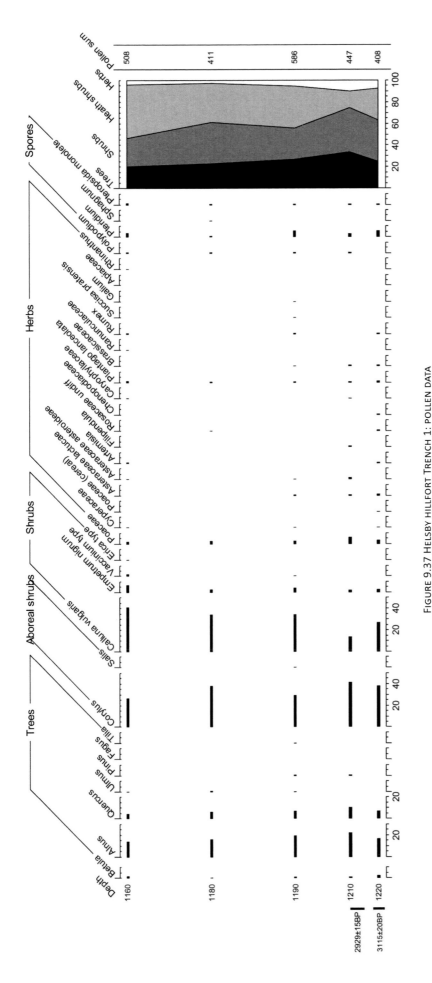

FIGURE 9.37 HELSBY HILLFORT TRENCH 1: POLLEN DATA

alkali/acid protocol of Mook and Waterbolk (1985) and measured by Accelerator Mass Spectrometry (AMS) as described by Zondervan and Sparks (1997). The results are given in Figure 9.34.

Results

The earliest pollen data for the site come from Trench 2, Phase 1, predating construction of the rampart. The spectra of the basal three samples in the monolith are dominated by the arboreal taxa, oak (*Quercus*) and hazel (*Corylus*). Lime (*Tilia*), a poor disperser of pollen, is also particularly abundant. Birch (*Betula*), alder (*Alnus*) and elm (*Ulmus*) are present in minor quantities. Herbaceous and dwarf shrub communities are almost entirely lacking, and the pteridophyte communities are limited to the arboreal parasite the polypody fern (*Polypodium*) and bracken (*Pteridium aquilinum*). This episode is dated to around 3950–3780 cal BC (NZA-35504).

From higher in the sequence in Trench 2, context (208), belonging to Phase 3, after construction of the rampart, is completely different in character (Figure 9.36), with greater frequencies of grasses (Poaceae), bracken and a diverse community of open ground herb taxa including some cereal grains. Nevertheless, arboreal pollen taxa remain abundant, with alder, oak and hazel the dominant components of the forest cover. The dwarf shrubs heather (*Calluna vulgaris*), crowberry (*Empetrum*) and bilberry (*Vaccinium*) are also more abundant.

Pollen spectra from Trench 1 also come from Phase 3 (Figure 9.37). As with context (208) in Trench 2, arboreal pollen taxa dominate, with alder, oak and hazel the most abundant components of the forest cover. The dwarf shrubs heather (*Calluna vulgaris*), crowberry (*Empetrum*) and bilberry (*Vaccinium*) are again also abundant, and there are high frequencies of grasses (Poaceae), bracken and a diverse community of open ground herb taxa including some cereal grains. Heather appears to increase in abundance as one moves up the profile, covering a period that extends from 1250–1050 cal BC (NZA-35493) through to cal AD 400–530 (NZA-35494).

Interpretation

The palaeovegetation sequence from Helsby hillfort is discontinuous but provides snapshot windows into the prehistory of the uplands of the mid-Cheshire Sandstone Ridge. The contexts from which pollen has been recovered – two colluvial sequences flanking the primary stone rampart and a soil beneath the rampart – typically received pollen from very local sources, and the vegetation that can be reconstructed is accordingly that of the immediate environs of the site, with limited influence from adjacent wetlands, such as Delamere. Prior to the construction of the hillfort, the underlying soils reveal a landscape dominated by oak, lime and hazel forest cover. The lack of open ground indicators suggests that this cover was complete. Comparison with the sparse radiocarbon-dated pollen data from the surrounding regions suggests that this impression is reasonable, with lime expansion dated at Crose Mere (North Shropshire) between 7400 and 3700 BP (Beales 1981). The two colluvial sequences reveal a much altered vegetation cover postdating construction of the hillfort. Lime is absent; oak and hazel remain significant but are much reduced from pre-hillfort times, while the wetland tree alder is more abundant, perhaps reflecting pollen transported a longer distance from the adjacent wetlands. The more abundant open ground communities show signs of human influence in the landscape, with cereal pollen and arable/pastoral weeds present in significant numbers (Behre 1981). In summary, construction of the hillfort and the materials associated with construction separate units rich with organic materials suitable for pollen analysis. The composition of the sub-fossil spectra shows a change from forested to a cleared, more open landscape with more substantial presence of humans reflected in the pollen-inferred land use.

Discussion

In spite of the minimal invasive methods used during the trial excavation, the results have proved informative in both increasing our understanding of the monument known as Helsby hillfort and in terms of gaining a greater understanding of the impact that the current management regime is having on the buried archaeological remains.

Pre-hillfort landscape: Previously, little was known about the landscape of Helsby outcrop prior to the construction of the hillfort beyond stray finds of a polished stone axe and a leaf-shaped arrowhead, both of which are attributed to the Neolithic period (OAN 2008: 18). Evidence recovered from Trench 2 has identified an ancient buried soil (222) containing fossilised pollen which has enabled a re-creation of the vegetation that prevailed on the hilltop in the late Mesolithic/early Neolithic period. This suggests a landscape dominated by oak, lime and hazel forest; the lack of open ground indicators suggesting a complete forest cover. There is also later evidence for a series of burning episodes in the area of Trench 2 which were sealed by a sterile sand layer (214) that has been dated to the early Neolithic (3950–3780 cal BC (NZA-35504)). These burning episodes are either localised evidence for occupation, or an indicator of woodland clearance on the hilltop.

Rampart form: In terms of 'understanding' the hillfort it has been informative to reinvestigate the structural form of the main enclosure of the rampart which was originally described by Forde-Johnston as a 'timber-laced box-type rampart' 8.4m wide. The excavation in 2010 reinvestigated Forde-Johnston's trench and demonstrated that the rampart could be broken down in to three broad phases of construction (see Figure 9.6). The earliest phase of rampart building consisted of a bank of sandstone blocks with a well-dressed outer face and an irregular inner face, which was built on a slight batter. This primary rampart was approximately 3.5m wide and bonded in light yellow sand; the form had a lot of similarities with the rampart construction of the adjacent Woodhouse hillfort (see Chapter 8, this volume).

Re-examination of 'the subsidiary rampart' occupying the natural stone ledge on the north of the site has confirmed that it survives as a single phase stone 'box-style' rampart, 3.5m wide. This consisted of a bank of sandstone blocks with a well-dressed outer face and an irregular inner face which was built on a slight batter and bonded in light yellow sand. In view of the re-interpretation of the main rampart enclosure, it is now clear that this rampart is identical in character to the primary stone rampart and is not a 'subsidiary rampart'. Rather, the northern part of the site was enclosed as part of the hillfort from the beginning and the two rampart sections are of the same phase.

Date of rampart construction: The central part of the rampart within Trench 1 had originally been interpreted by Forde-Johnston as a timber-laced core; however, this has now been identified as a complex sequence of colluvial deposits formed on the flank of the primary stone rampart. The earliest colluvial deposit in the sequence has been dated to the middle Bronze Age (1435–1320 cal BC (NZA-37729)) and the construction of the primary stone rampart must therefore pre-date this. A later phase of rampart construction was identified on the back of the colluvial deposits, comprising a stone retaining wall and associated posthole. The foundation cut for the retaining wall had truncated the uppermost colluvial deposits which have been dated to the sub-Roman period (cal AD 400–530 (NZA-35494)). The stratigraphic evidence therefore suggests an early medieval re-occupation of the hillfort at Helsby; it is perhaps the original 'farm on the ledge' alluded to in the Helsby place-name (Dodgson 1971).

The colluvial deposits: Perhaps the most unexpected result of the evaluation work has been the identification of a complex sequence of sand and silt lenses which appear to have formed against the flank of the primary stone rampart. These deposits have been identified within both excavation trenches and this might indicate that they survive (to varying degrees) along the whole inner circuit of the hillfort rampart. The mechanism for the formation of these lenses is likely to be colluvial deposition (a mixture of windblown and hill washed agents) and the whole block of deposits should be compared to the development of a sand dune; where there is an almost constant cycle of accumulation and erosion dictating the final appearance of the buried material. The deposits can vary in character from sterile white sands which are utterly devoid of any inclusions, to black silts with a somewhat desiccated appearance containing charred material indicative of human activity. The net result is a complicated sequence of inter-leaved lenses which would be virtually impossible to excavate with a traditional stratigraphic approach. Scientific dating from the bottom and top of the colluvial sequence suggests that these deposits formed over a period perhaps in excess of 1,500 years between the middle Bronze Age (1435–1320 cal BC BC (NZA-37729)) and the sub-Roman period (cal AD 400–530 (NZA-35494)). As such this represents a very rare archaeological resource not so far paralleled at any other Cheshire hillfort site. The composition of these colluvial deposits could suggest periods of occupation and abandonment within the hillfort; perhaps suggesting either seasonal trends or periods of intermittent use.

Palynological sampling of the more organic looking silts within these colluvial deposits has demonstrated a high level of fossilised pollen preservation. This has enabled a re-creation of the landscape in the immediate environs of the hilltop, after the hillfort rampart was constructed. In general, the pollen record suggests an open landscape dominated by heath type plants such as heather and bilberry, not unlike the current appearance of the National Trust property on Bickerton Hill. This probably indicates that the area around the hillfort was regularly grazed by livestock as the dominant heath taxa would otherwise have naturally reverted to broadleaf woodland quite rapidly. There is a slight trend towards the increasing dominance of heather through time; however, there are some less obvious trends in the sequence which may

benefit from further scrutiny in the future. The first of these is that cereal pollen is only present in the lowest sample (1220) of the sequence (dated 1435–1320 cal BC (NZA-37729)); perhaps suggesting that cereal was grown in the immediate vicinity of the hilltop shortly after it was initially enclosed. The next sample point in the sequence (1210) (dated 1250–1050 cal BC (NZA-35493)) indicates a slight resurgence of woodland taxa at the expense of heath type shrubs. This could have been caused by a variety of conditions but it is tempting to suggest that climate change may have been a factor in this, particularly as a sudden climate change event is proposed for the end of the Bronze Age (see the proposed event of 2650 BP, Van Geel *et al.* 1996) which led to a generally cooler and wetter climate. Subsequent recovery of the heath taxa in the sample record indicates continued livestock grazing on the hilltop, but no further indication of cereal pollen is present. This might perhaps suggest that cereal production had been moved off the hill to lower lying areas of the Cheshire Plain in the later prehistoric period.

Hillfort's function: Information regarding the function of Helsby hillfort remains elusive with very little evidence being recovered from the interior of the hillfort. The charred cereal grains recovered from post-pipe fills (112) and (113) perhaps indicate that corn storage or processing was taking place in the interior of the hillfort in the late Iron Age (210–90 cal BC (NZA-35496)). However, these charred grains are problematical as they were recovered from contexts that are potentially of sub-Roman or early medieval date and are therefore likely to be residual. It is possible that the charred cereals are derived from the colluvial deposits on the flank of the rampart which would have been disturbed during the construction of retaining wall (104). This would support the suggestion that any future investigations of the colluvial deposits should include the bulk sampling of charcoal rich lenses for the recovery of biological remains, other than fossilised pollen.

Management Review

The implications of the excavation results for the management of the hillfort are summarised below. A full review of management measures implemented through the Habitats and Hillfort Project has been presented in an unpublished Management Review Report (Garner 2011b).

Bracken rhizomes: Investigation of the bracken rhizome infestation on the southern part of the rampart (Trench 1) produced mixed results. It appears that the bracken was not colonizing through spore dispersal but by rhizome encroachment. This has led to the formation of a bracken mat that was so dense that there is more rhizome than soil present and this demonstrates that the bracken on this part of the hill was a fairly old colony that had probably been established for several hundred years. The bulk of the bracken rhizome is restricted to the dense mat and beneath this level there is only occasional evidence for penetration in to the lower archaeological stratigraphy. The rhizome mat had formed in order for the bracken to create its own microenvironment above the unfavourable sandy soil and for this reason the bracken did not appear to be having too much of an adverse effect on the deep underlying archaeological deposits in this location. There was some suggestion that the 1964 trench backfill had provided a favourable environment for fresh bracken rhizome growth.

Trees and roots: Investigation of the impact of scrub and tree root penetration on the underlying archaeology was attempted at both evaluation trenches. On the eastern rampart (Trench 2) evidence was found for rampart destabilisation caused by the outward pressure of the tree roots. Tree root penetration had also reached pre-rampart levels where it caused problems for archaeomagnetic dating of *in situ* burning.

Conclusions: The excavation has served to increase our knowledge of the form, character and level of archaeological preservation on the monument known as Helsby hillfort. This has identified the monument as a very rare early type of hilltop enclosure, which owes its origins to the middle Bronze Age rather than the previously suspected Iron Age. The hillfort interior has no above ground features to consider; however, sub-surface structures in the form of postholes have been identified within both excavation trenches. Sampling has demonstrated that, within the confines of the excavation, artefact and ecofact recovery has been very low with only hardy materials such as stone tools and charred plant remains being identified from the prehistoric period. The colluvial deposits which have accumulated on the flank of the rampart are clearly a valuable archaeological resource and serve to make Helsby a unique site amongst the Cheshire hillfort group.

The present woodland environment is a relatively recent development on the hilltop and this is dominated by birch scrub. The hilltop was previously covered by lowland heath within living memory and some heath species such as heather and bilberry continue to cling on beneath the encroaching woodland canopy. This vegetational change is essentially a natural progression as lowland heath can only be maintained by human intervention through livestock grazing etc. The surviving archaeological resource is clearly suffering a negative impact from the current land use and tree growth is clearly far from ideal when considering both the extant earthworks and the fragile buried archaeological deposits.

Chapter 10
Excavations at Eddisbury Hillfort

Dan Garner

Introduction

The hillfort known as Eddisbury hillfort, Delamere, that includes elements known as 'Castle Ditch' and 'Merrick's Hill', is situated at around 158m OD, on the eastern side of the Cheshire Sandstone Ridge (Figure 1.2). This chapter presents the results of archaeological excavation carried out over two seasons at the hillfort between 19 July and 30 September 2010, and 30 August and 21 October 2011, under the overall directorship of the author. The work was conducted as a training opportunity for local volunteers under the supervision of professional archaeologists Leigh Dodd, Gary Crawford-Coupe, Afon Bognar and David Higgins (Earthworks Archaeological Services).

The excavations at Eddisbury hillfort were intended to provide additional data to inform a strategy for the long-term management of the scheduled monument, in line with the findings of the Desk-Based Assessment and the Condition Assessment carried out by Oxford Archaeology (North) prior to the start of the Project (OAN 2008a; 2008b) (see Chapter 1, this volume). The site had been placed on the Heritage at Risk Register owing to ongoing erosion through repeated ploughing. The monument is in the shared ownership of the Forestry Commission, Mr Jon Batson of Old Pale and Mr Michael Platt of Eddisbury Hill Farm. The Forestry Commission acquired the northern section of the monument in 2000, while Mr Batson acquired the western section of the monument in 2001, when Old Pale Farm was converted into residential properties; these areas are managed as open grassland grazed by livestock. The remainder and largest part of the monument, owned by Mr Mike Platt, is ploughed on an annual basis, under the statutory constraint of the Ancient Monuments (Class Consents) Order 1994. The southeastern tip of the monument, known as Merrick's Hill, is not ploughed and has reverted to an area of natural scrub. There is no management agreement in place between the various landowners and English Heritage, under section 17 of the Ancient Monuments and Archaeological Areas Act 1979.

Site Location

The hill comprises an outcrop of Middle Triassic Sherwood Sandstone and Mercia Mudstone (British Geological Survey 1980) overlain by a light and sandy glacial till containing gravels, itself surmounted by Bearsted 2 deep, well-drained coarse and stony loamy soils (British Geological Survey 1983; English Heritage 2000: 2). The remains of the ramparts are most clearly visible in the northern and northwestern parts of the hillfort, where parallel banks and an inturned entrance are evident. On the eastern side of the fort, the defences become gradually slighter, and on the southern side, the natural cliff faces and scarps delineate the edge of the plateau. Eddisbury has the most extensive system of visible ramparts of all the hillforts of the Sandstone Ridge. With the exception of Beeston, Eddisbury is the largest hillfort of the Cheshire Ridge hillfort group, with around 2.8ha (7 acres) being enclosed and a further 3.4ha (8.5 acres) being occupied by the ramparts (OAN 2008a: 24).

Excavation methodology

The fieldwork comprised the excavation of fifteen trenches as located on Figure 10.1. Trenches 1, 14 and 15 were within the location of an area excavation (Area 2) undertaken by W. J. Varley (then of the Geography Department, University of Liverpool) between 1936 and 1938 (see Chapter 2, this volume and Figures 2.9 and 2.10). This work was intended to provide the opportunity to re-examine the sections through the inner and outer ramparts which were recorded by Varley in his Area 2 (see Chapter 2, Figure 2.12), with particular emphasis on recovering samples for scientific dating from the *in situ* 'occupation deposits' beneath the rampart construction. It was also hoped that these trenches would serve to clarify the presence of a postulated entrance (Cocroft *et al.* 1989) and provide samples for environmental analysis. It was unclear how much of the Varley Area 2 excavation was fully excavated between 1936 and 1938, as the published trench plan covered a smaller area than the larger scale trench location plan suggested. This conclusion is supported by an unpublished photogtraph of Varley's Area 2 excavation (Figure 2.11) which was brought to the author's attention by Roger Hones (the photograph was in the private collection of the late Sandy Campbell). It was clear from the published section however, that excavation in the western part of Varley's Area 2 was completed to the natural subsoil. It was intended that Trench 1 would be targeted at the western section of Varley's Area 2 and the features as shown on his figure 8 (Varley 1950: 24); whilst Trenches 14 and 15 would revisit the inner ditch and Varley's section through the outer rampart.

Trenches 2 and 3 were in the locations of Varley's trenches 'c' and 'd' (Figure 2.9). These trenches were located to investigate the impact of gorse root and bracken rhizome disturbance to the reinstated section of rampart in this location and the extent to which this is contributing to destabilisation of the earthworks. This work provided the opportunity to re-examine the sections through the outer rampart which were not published by Varley; with particular emphasis on recovering samples from the rampart construction for scientific dating. It was also hoped to establish phases of rampart construction and provide samples for environmental analysis. In the event, only Trench 3 was opened, as there were insufficient time and resources to open Trench 2.

Trenches 4 and 6 were in the location of Varley's Area 3 (Figure 2.9). These trenches were intended to investigate the survival of archaeological remains associated with the southeastern hillfort entrance. The intention was to revisit Varley's Area 3 with two trenches in order to compare the state of preservation between the two halves of the entrance with reference to the published records and the different modern land uses. Trench 4, outside the interior of the hillfort and the area of modern ploughing, would seek to relocate any remains of the *in situ* timber gatepost recorded by Varley, to assess the potential for scientific dating. Trench 6, in the western half of Varley's Area 3, was located within the annually cultivated field, owned by Mr Platt. Ultimately, the two trenches were linked to form a single open area excavation.

Trench 5 was in the location of Varley's Area 4. Trench 5 would investigate the survival of archaeological remains on the Merrick's Hill area of the hillfort. Varley's report implied that this area was entirely excavated between 1936 and 1938; however, stone building remains associated with a medieval/post-medieval farmhouse are still extant in the area and excavations by a local geologist during the 1990s and early 2000s suggested that some intact archaeology still survived. Merrick's Hill had become covered in alder woodland and scrub which was removed as part of the Habitats and Hillforts Project. The excavation of Trench 5 developed in to a two year student training 'field school' run by the School of Archaeology, Classics and Egyptology (SACE) at Liverpool University under the direction of Dr Rachel Pope. (Mason and Pope, Chapter 11, this volume).

Trenches 7 to 13 were situated within the large ploughed field owned by Mr Platt. Trenches 7 and 13 were located to test for the presence and preservation of hillfort rampart elements within the ploughed area, while Trenches 8 to 12, in the interior of the hillfort, were targeted to investigate the results of a geophysical survey undertaken by Archaeophysica during the winter of 2010 (Roseveare *et al.* 2010a). A summary of the geophysical results is presented in Chapter 6, this volume.

In the case of Trenches 1 to 6, 14 and 15 the approach as defined by the Scheduled Monument Consent, was to cause minimal disturbance to the surviving archaeology of the earthworks by targeting previous excavation trenches. All excavation was undertaken by hand and was generally limited to removal of topsoil and demonstrably

modern backfill deposits only, using appropriate hand tools. Excavation was undertaken with a view to avoiding damage to any archaeological features or deposits which appeared to be demonstrably worthy of preservation *in situ*. Excavated material was examined in order to retrieve artefacts to assist in the analysis of their spatial distribution. All investigation of archaeological horizons was by hand, with cleaning, inspection and recording both in plan and section.

All fifteen trenches were reinstated at the end of the excavation process. In each case a sheet of geo-textile (*terram*) was used to line the base of the excavation and then the trench was subsequently backfilled using the excavated material. The exception to this was Trench 4 which had six timber posts inserted in to the rock-cut postholes on the Forestry Commission owned part of the entrance prior to backfilling the trench with sterile sand from a local quarry. The six timber posts were intended to serve as a marker for the location of the southeastern entrance and to enhance interpretation of the site for visitors. In areas where earthwork reinstatement was required, there were enough large sandstone fragments within the excavated material to be able to recreate the original contour without the need for additional measures such as wire mesh gabions or sandbags. All fifteen trenches were given a top covering of the original topsoil which had been set aside for the purpose, and in the cases of Trenches 1, 3, 4, 14 and 15 they were then re-seeded with grass in order to return the areas to permanent pasture.

Arrangements were made for the long-term storage of the physical archive with the Cheshire West and Chester Museum Service with the unique accession number CHEGM 2011.20.

Results

A broad sequence of phases was developed for the whole site, in an attempt to maintain a basic chronological framework for all excavation trenches (Figure 10.3).

Trench 1 *(Figures 10.4–10.9).*

Trench 1, measuring up to 18 x 5m, was located at the northwestern end of the hillfort in an area that Varley had suggested was a later annex or extension to the original hillfort. The excavation re-exposed Varley's section through the inner rampart in order to recover samples for scientific dating and to re-examine a pre-rampart 'occupation layer'. The trench would also serve to inform the more general management issues regarding gorse infestation.

Varley had originally suggested that the earliest event in this part of the hillfort was the laying of a 'flagstone' pavement set in 'puddled clay' which was subsequently covered by a thick layer of puddled clay that he

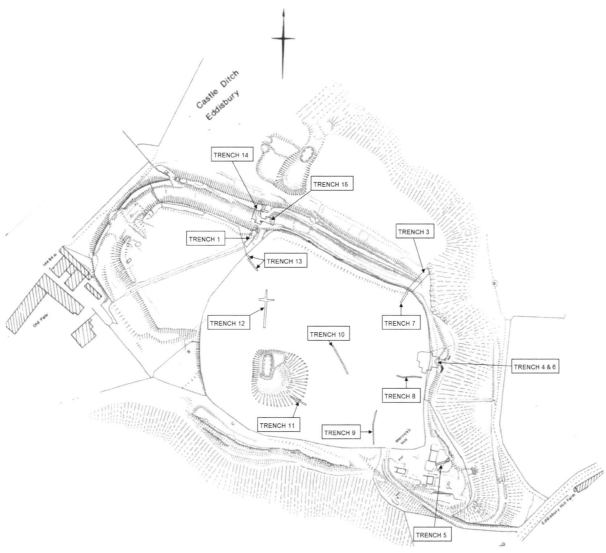

Figure 10.1 Trench location plan over-laid on to the hachure plan produced by the RCHME in 1987 (Cocroft *et al.* 1989).

interpreted as the earliest hillfort rampart (Varley 1950: 24). This part of the sequence was only investigated in a small area of the 2010 trench owing to the excessive depth at which the layers were encountered; however, it was concluded that both the flagstone pavement and overlying 'puddled clay' were of geological rather than archaeological origin. The main phases of archaeological activity encountered are outlined below:

Pre-rampart activity (Phases 1 to 3)

The earliest archaeological events in Trench 1 were represented by a number of discrete features excavated in to the top of the natural clay subsoil (Varley's 'puddled clay' layer). The first was a shallow feature (120) 1.6m wide and 0.25m deep that was sealed beneath the heart of the later hillfort rampart; this feature was filled by (119) and it was only seen in section so it was impossible to suggest whether it represented a discrete pit or a linear slot/ditch. The second feature (129) lay beneath the inner edge of the hillfort rampart and was fully exposed in plan

during the excavation (Figure 10.7); consisting of a sub-circular pit (measuring 1 x 0.7 x 0.2m) filled with a black charcoal-rich silt (122) that may well represent a hearth (dated 1870–1640 cal BC (NZA-36669)). One side of hearth (122) was subsequently cut by a second sub-circular cut (125) that was filled by a series of silt-sand deposits (123) and (124). These features were covered by a layer of grey silt-clay (114) that Varley had identified as an 'occupation layer'; unfortunately, the date of this layer remains speculative as no cultural material was recovered from the limited sampling of the soil.

Towards the centre of the trench was a thin lens of pale grey silt (115) which was delimited to both the east and west by large sandstone boulders (116/117). These boulders probably represent part of a curvilinear stone kerb which was recorded by Varley and which he interpreted as a 'Dark Age hut' (Varley 1950: 24-7, figure 8 and plate 9). In the section it could be seen that the two boulders were separated by a distance of 5m and the area between them was filled with brown clay (118) that was

141

FIGURE 10.2 AERIAL VIEW OF EDDISBURY © EARTHWORKS ARCHAEOLOGY.

Phase	Event	Dating
1	Pre-rampart occupation represented by a pit and possible hearth	3422±25 BP (1870–1640 cal BC)
2	Pre-rampart occupation represented by an 'occupation layer'. Early hilltop enclosure by timber palisade and counterscarp bank.	2483±25 BP (770–410 cal BC) & 2560±230 BP (OSL)
3	Pre-rampart activity represented by a curvilinear stone kerb for a hut or cairn.	
4	Primary inner rampart and segmental inner ditch.	
4a	Occupation within primary rampart including the laying of an internal cobbled track.	2347±20 BP (410–385 cal BC) & 2297±25 BP (410–260 cal BC)
5	Primary outer bank and ditch. Construction of the eastern entrance?	
6	Secondary inner bank deposits and re-cut of inner ditch. Silting of the outer ditch.	2260±25 BP (400–200 cal BC) & 2251±25 BP (400–200 cal BC)
7	Internal posthole alignment. Burning of the southern guardroom within the eastern entrance.	2203±20 BP (375–195 cal BC) & 2176±25 BP (360–160 cal BC)
8	Secondary outer rampart & re-cut of outer ditch	1930±30 BP (cal AD 10–130)
9	Rampart slighting/collapse & hillfort abandonment?	
10	Romano-British occupation of interior	250–350 AD (Pottery)
11	Post-Roman/early medieval features cut in to ramparts/ditch fills	860 ±70 AD (cal AD 745–980) (Arch.mag.)
12	Medieval/post-medieval plough soil	
13	Post-medieval field enclosure ditches	
14	Varley excavations 1936–8	

FIGURE 10.3 THE MAIN PHASES IDENTIFIED WITHIN TRENCHES 1 TO 15.

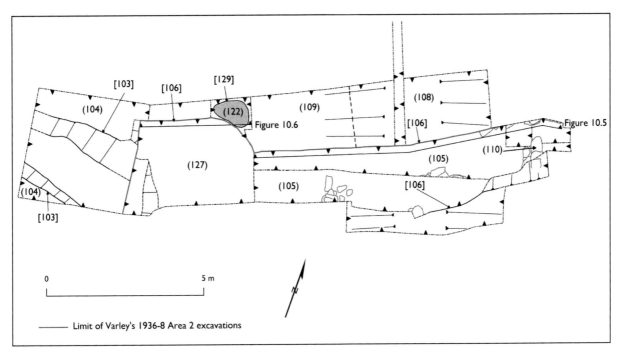

FIGURE 10.4 PLAN OF TRENCH 1.

0.25m thick (perhaps representing an internal floor?). The lack of dateable artefacts from this sequence makes the interpretation difficult, but as it was sealed by the construction of the hillfort's inner rampart, a 'Dark Age' date seems unlikely. An alternative explanation might suggest that the pale grey lens (115) was the remains of an old turf line which was preserved because it was buried by a low mound represented by brown clay (118); the mound being defined and retained by the stone kerb (116/117). This reinterpretation of the evidence might suggest the presence of a burial cairn (rather than a hut) beneath the hillfort rampart.

A monolith sample was taken through the sequence, which was analysed for pollen and material suitable for radiocarbon dating, in order to help develop the chronology of the site. Two samples were also taken for OSL dating: the first from the fill (119) of pit (120) and the second from the upper horizon of brown clay (118). The OSL sample (LV448) from pit fill (119) failed to provide a date; but the sample (LV447) from brown clay horizon (118) produced a date of 5340–1340 BC with 95% confidence. Whilst the OSL date from layer (118) is very wide it is likely that it is later than hearth/pit fill (122) and thus a date at the early/mid Bronze Age end of the spectrum seems probable.

The inner hillfort rampart (Phases 4 and 6)

The primary hillfort rampart was represented by a large mass of redeposited red clay and sandstone fragments (108) which formed a solid bank 9.5m wide at the base and still surviving to a height of 1.3m. The most likely

source for the bank material would have been the quarry for a corresponding external ditch; this was investigated by the 2011 excavations as Trenches 14 and 15. The front or outer edge of this clay bank had been revetted with a dry stone wall of mudstone blocks (110) which still survived to 0.8m in height, represented by five courses of stone. This stone revetment wall sat in a construction trench (111) that had been cut in to the pre-rampart 'occupation layer' and had been backfilled with the same clay and mudstone material that was used to form the primary rampart bank; this indicated that the wall and bank were contemporary. No evidence was found for a corresponding rear or internal revetment wall to the primary rampart.

A layer of mixed silt-clay (113) had subsequently formed on the interior of the rampart and this partly overlay the tail of the primary clay bank (108). After the formation of layer (113), a secondary phase of rampart construction was represented by the subsequent addition of a mass of yellow silt-sand (109) on the internal side of the original clay bank (108). This would have had the effect of increasing the width of the rampart base by a further 2m (total width 11.5m) and would perhaps have enabled the original height of the rampart to have been increased. A bulk sample was taken from deposit (109) in the hope that material suitable for radiocarbon dating could be recovered but this was unsuccessful (Figure 10.9).

Post-rampart activity (Phases 12 to 14)

A layer of cultivation soil (104) had subsequently formed on the interior of the secondary rampart to a depth of

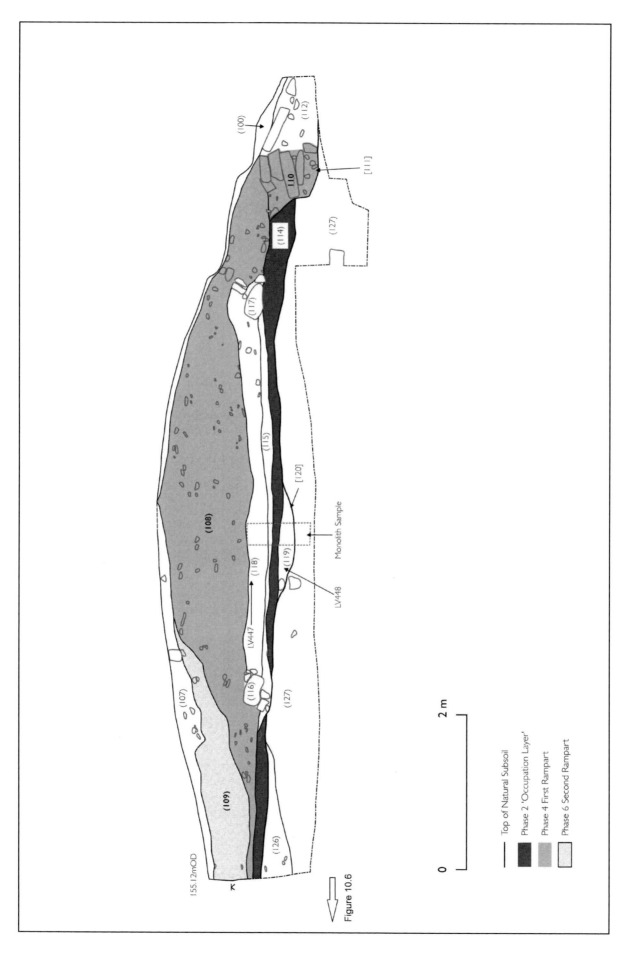

FIGURE 10.5 TRENCH 1 SOUTHEAST FACING SECTION (NORTHEAST).

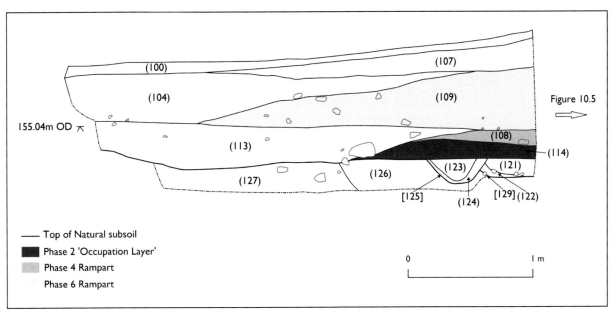

FIGURE 10.6 TRENCH 1 SOUTHEAST FACING SECTION (SOUTHWEST).

FIGURE 10.7 VIEW OF HEARTH PIT FILL (122) PRIOR TO EXCAVATION (SCALE 1M). LOOKING NORTHWEST.

0.4m. Two events post-dated the formation of the cultivation soil: the first was the excavation of a linear field boundary ditch (103) which had been backfilled with soil containing post-medieval artefacts; the second was the deposition of a layer of sandstone and clay (107) on the back of the inner rampart. It is thought that the boundary ditch might pre-date enclosure and that layer (107) probably represented the base of Varley's spoil heap from his 1936 excavation. The original cut of Varley's excavation trench was allocated context (106) and is shown on Figure 10.4 where it was identified.

Trench 3 *(Figures 10.10–10.17).*

Trench 3, measuring 24 x 4m, was located on the northeastern side of the hillfort defences in an area that

FIGURE 10.8 PHOTO MOSAIC OF THE SECTION THROUGH THE INNER RAMPART IN TRENCH 1 LOOKING NORTHWEST (SCALES 1M X 3 AND 2M X 1).

Varley had suggested was part of the original hillfort. The trench was located to re-expose Varley's 'trench d' section through the inner ditch, outer rampart and outer ditch (Varley 1950: 8, figure 3) in order to recover samples for scientific dating and to re-examine the construction sequence. Although Varley had recorded excavating a trench in this location he did not publish a section drawing or any photographs of the trench. The closest published evidence came from Varley's 'trench e' which comprised a photograph of an excavated section through the inner ditch which suggested that the ditch had been excavated in segments rather than as a continuous trench (Varley and Jackson 1940, plate VIIB; Varley 1950: 31, plate 11).

Varley clearly re-evaluated his interpretation of the rampart sequence in this location, because in his 1940 publication 'Prehistoric Cheshire' he suggests that the original hillfort defences consisted of an inner rampart, ditch and outer 'counterscarp bank' furnished with a stone revetment. He goes on to show the outer rampart (without a stone revetment) and outer ditch being added when the hillfort was enlarged with his postulated annex; he also shows the outer ditch terminating in the vicinity of 'trench d' (Varley and Jackson 1940: 64–6). However, by the time he published his full report in 1950 he appears to have abandoned the notion of an original 'counterscarp bank' altogether and does not specify whether there was

FIGURE 10.9 VIEW OF THE PALE YELLOW SILT-SAND (109) FORMING THE SECONDARY RAMPART BANK (SCALE 2M). LOOKING NORTH.

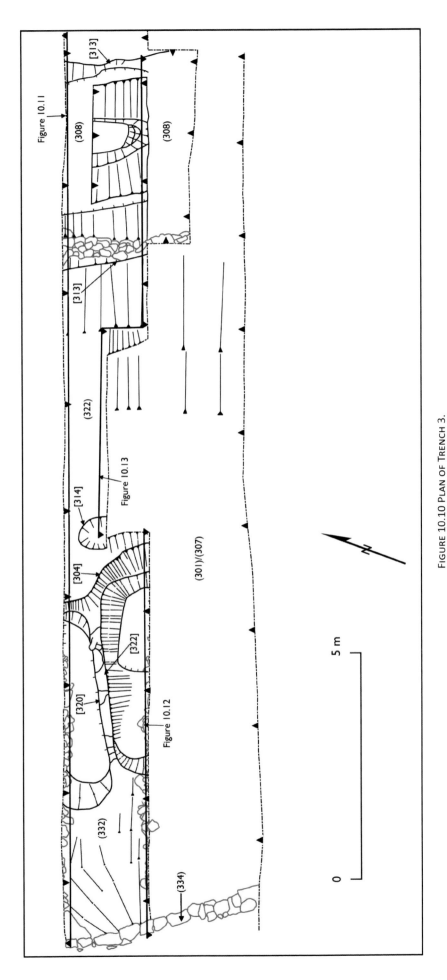

FIGURE 10.10 PLAN OF TRENCH 3.

a stone revetment to the outer rampart here, or if there was any evidence for the terminus of the outer ditch (Varley 1950: 32).

As the excavation of Trench 3 progressed it became increasingly apparent that there was no real evidence for the location of Varley's 'trench d' and it remains a distinct possibility that he did little more than remove the turf and topsoil during his excavation. Further excavation during 2010 was limited to cutting smaller slots through the bottom of the partially excavated trench in order to test the principle features making-up the hillfort ramparts and recover samples for scientific analysis. The main phases of archaeological activity encountered are outlined below:

Pre-rampart activity (Phase 1)

The earliest archaeological event recorded in Trench 3 was a shallow oval pit (314) cut in to the top of the natural clay (332) (Figure 10.10). The fill (315) was a yellow-brown clay-silt with rare flecks of charred material. The pit was sealed by the remains of a possible 'counterscarp bank' and was only partially exposed within the excavation. However, it is possible that it had been truncated during the earliest phase of hillfort construction and as such it might have represented a posthole. No evidence for a pre-rampart 'occupation layer' was found in Trench 3.

The possible 'counterscarp bank' (Phase 2)

Along the line of Varley's outer rampart evidence was present for a sequence of deposits (331) and (330) that

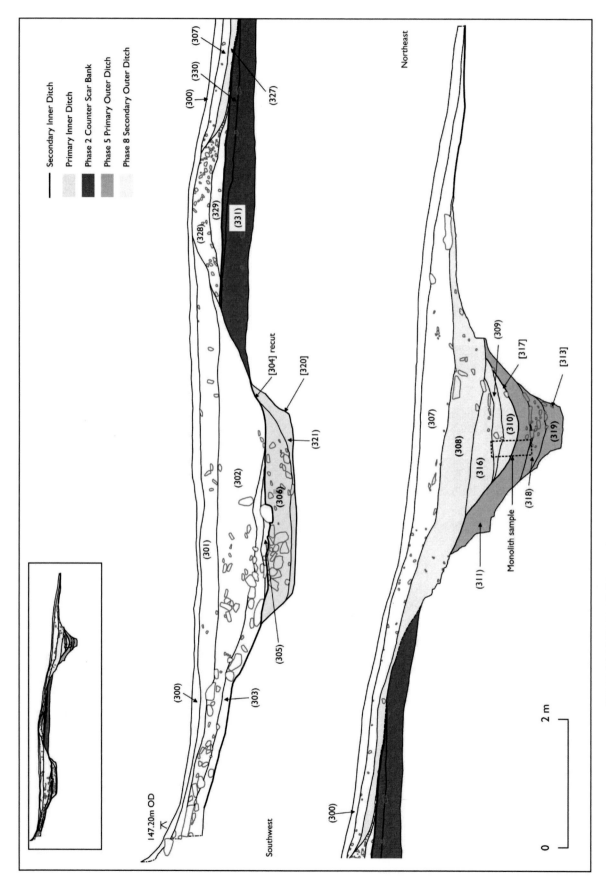

FIGURE 10.11 TRENCH 3. SOUTHEAST FACING SECTION THROUGH INNER DITCH, OUTER RAMPART AND OUTER DITCH.

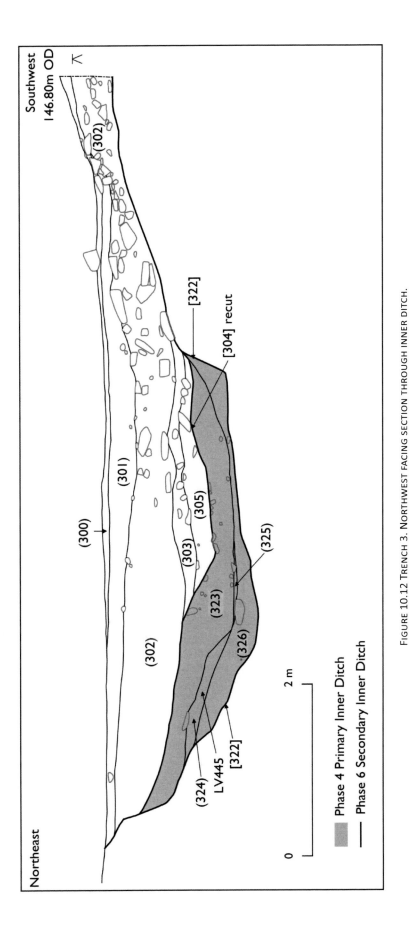

FIGURE 10.12 TRENCH 3. NORTHWEST FACING SECTION THROUGH INNER DITCH.

combined to form a bank 7.7m wide at the base and surviving to a height of 0.7m (Figures 10.11 and 10.14). This bank was distinct from the later outer rampart material and had been partly removed by the excavation of the earliest surviving phase of the inner segmental ditch (see below). It is possible that this bank represents the 'counterscarp bank' referred to by Varley in his 1940 publication. Unfortunately, it was not possible to reconcile the position of this 'counterscarp bank' with the stratigraphic sequence of the corresponding inner rampart in Trench 7; however, it is likely to belong to the earliest phase of the hilltop's enclosure. An OSL sample (LV444) from the top of deposit (331) produced a date of 1010–90 BC with 95% confidence.

The inner ditch (Phases 4, 6 and 9)

The inner ditch lay between the inner and outer ramparts as shown on Varley's published plan. The stratigraphic sequence in the area of the inner ditch proved to be very complex, as it became apparent that rather than being excavated as a continuous trench, the earliest phase of the ditch was segmental and had been created by quarrying a series of separate pits or 'compartments' on a parallel alignment to the ramparts. This can be seen in Varley's Trench 'e' photograph (Varley and Jackson 1940, plate VIIB; Varley 1950: 31, plate 11). Within Trench 3 two of these 'compartments' (cuts (320) and (322)) were partly revealed and could be seen to have removed part of the inner face of the 'counterscarp bank' deposits (see Phase 2 above) during their excavation; penetrating down in to the underlying sandstone bedrock to create a broken ditch roughly 5.5m wide and 1.8m deep. Each compartment was of variable size and they did not quite interlink, resulting in a thin ridge of upstanding bedrock which looked rather like a narrow bridge across the ditch (Figure 10.15). This method of ditch digging

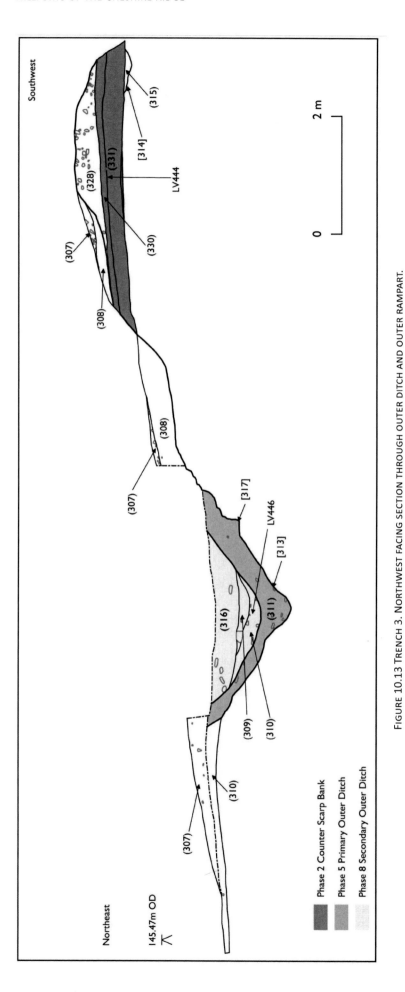

FIGURE 10.13 TRENCH 3. NORTHWEST FACING SECTION THROUGH OUTER DITCH AND OUTER RAMPART.

has been noted at other enclosure sites in the Welsh Marches and it is generally thought that the main aim was to quarry material for rampart construction with the resulting ditch being a secondary bi-product. It is also thought that the individual compartments might have been quarried by separate 'work gangs', perhaps providing an insight in to the way the local community could have been organised for the construction of the monument (Wigley 2007: 184).

The two compartments were initially filled with deposits of sterile red clay and sandstone fragments: fills (321) and (306) for pit (320) and fills (326), (325), (324) and (323) for pit (322). These fills are likely to be derived from erosion of the freshly created inner rampart bank (see Trench 7 below). The time span associated with the formation of these deposits is a matter of conjecture; however, it would appear that after a period of prolonged silting the inner ditch was re-cut as a continuous trench (304). The re-cut created a shallow, 'flat bottomed' ditch profile, 6m wide and 1.2m deep. Subsequently, the re-cut ditch also became silted up with a series of clay silts (305), (303) and (302) that contained increasingly frequent quantities of sandstone blocks that are likely to represent tumble from the outer face of the inner rampart. An OSL sample (LV445) from primary ditch fill (324) failed to produce a date (Figure 10.12); however, wood charcoal recovered from the primary fill of the ditch re-cut (305) produced a radiocarbon date of 390–210 cal BC (Beta-319723).

The outer ditch (Phases 5, 6 and 8)

The outer ditch lay beyond the 'counterscarp bank' and possibly cut its outer tail, although this was hard to ascertain. The ditch (313) was largely cut in to the underlying sandstone bedrock, creating a steep sided 'V'

FIGURE 10.14 PHOTO MOSAIC OF THE SECTION THROUGH THE INNER DITCH IN TRENCH 3 LOOKING NORTHWEST (SCALES 1M X 1 AND 0.5M X 2).

FIGURE 10.15 TRENCH 3. VIEW OF THE PRIMARY INNER DITCH LOOKING NORTHEAST.

shaped profile with a flat base, being 4.5m wide at the top and 2.5m deep (Figures 10.11 and 10.16). The rock-cut sides of the ditch exhibited tooling marks which appeared to have been made by a pick or chisel; demonstrating that a considerable amount of effort had gone in to the creation of the ditch. The outer ditch was initially silted up with a series of fairly sterile clay silts (319) and (318) after which a lens of charcoal-rich silt (312) was deposited before being sealed by a further fill of clay silt (311); charcoal-rich silt (312) produced a date of 400–200 cal BC (NZA-36654).

The outer ditch clearly formed a rounded terminus on the southeastern side of Trench 3; this is the same as the outer ditch terminus originally indicated by Varley in 1940 (Varley and Jackson 1940: 64–6).

Subsequently, it appears that the outer ditch was re-cut to create a slightly shallower ditch (317) approximately 4.5m wide but only 1.75m deep (Figures 10.11 and 10.13). The primary fill of this secondary ditch cut was a brown silt (310) which was sampled for both palaeoenvironmental remains and a possible OSL date (sample LV446, which failed to produce a date). The second phase of the outer ditch was then filled by a series of sterile clay silts (309), (316) and (308/327). The lower secondary fill (309) of the ditch re-cut produced a radiocarbon date of cal AD 10–130 (Beta-319724).

The outer rampart (Phases 5 and 8)

Very little of the outer rampart remained in the location of Trench 3, although further to the northwest the upstanding remains are visible as a sizeable bank. In the stratigraphic record it appeared that the outer rampart largely consisted of a deposit of sandstone fragments (328) that was derived from the up-cast of waste material from the creation of the earliest phase of the outer ditch. However, at the northern side of the excavation it could be seen that a primary deposit of grey silt-clay (329) formed the base of the outer rampart construction. The outer rampart was in the same location as, and had entirely buried, the 'counterscarp bank' (described above); it survived as a low (probably plough truncated) base 4m wide and 0.3m high. There was no evidence to suggest that the outer rampart had ever been furnished with either a front or rear stone retaining wall in this location.

Post-rampart activity (Phases 12 and 13)

A layer of post-medieval cultivation soil is probably represented by (301/307). Local anecdotal evidence suggests that the area of the hillfort examined by Trench 3 was cultivated for a potato crop during World War II (Mike Platt personal communication). At the southwestern end of the trench a dry-stone retaining wall (334) had been constructed in to the top of the relict plough soil (301) creating a misleading stone face to the front of the hillfort's inner rampart; this is more fully described under Trench 7 (below). The entire trench was subsequently sealed by a modern layer of turf and topsoil (300).

Trenches 4 and 6 *(Figures 10.18–10.35)*

The combined Trenches 4 and 6 measured up to 20m east-west x 16m north-south. Trench 4 was located on the site of the hillfort's eastern entrance which had previously been excavated by Varley during his final year of excavations in 1938. Varley recorded a passage way (approximately 8ft wide) defined by two parallel alignments of seven postholes, inter-spaced by short lengths of drystone walling and flanked by 'guardrooms' to the north and south, approximately half way along its length. He had proposed that there were two phases of construction within the entranceway; the first being entirely of timber and the second being a partial rebuild in stone with some remodelling of the timber gate posts. Varley published the excavation in his 1950 report as Area 3, in which he included a scale plan of the excavated entrance and a photograph of the northern 'guardroom'; along with three un-scaled photographs of an *in situ* timber 'gatepost' (Varley 1950: 29–34, figure 11, plates 12–14). Within Varley's 1950 account of the excavation, he suggests that the northern 'guardroom' was a later addition to the arrangement (Varley 1950: 29) and that the entrance along with both of the 'guardrooms' had been deliberately filled/ blocked up with sandstone rubble during the Roman period. The southern 'guardroom' is also described as having a layer of collapsed 'wattle-and-daub' covering the floor, which Varley suggests could have been part of the original superstructure (Varley 1950: 33).

The relationship between the construction of the eastern entrance and the construction of the inner rampart, through which it passes, was only fleetingly addressed by Varley in his 1950 report. In fact only two details are revealed: first, that the drystone walling associated with the southern 'guardroom' was bonded in to the rear stone revetment of the inner rampart; and secondly that Varley interpreted this to mean that the original inner rampart did not appear to have been stone revetted (Varley 1950: 29).

The main purposes of re-excavating the eastern entrance during 2010 were to establish whether or not there were any surviving deposits that would be suitable for radiocarbon dating and to confirm the stratigraphic relationship between the entrance and the inner rampart. The main phases of archaeological activity encountered are outlined below:

FIGURE 10.16 TRENCH 3. VIEW OF THE OUTER DITCH LOOKING NORTHWEST.

FIGURE 10.17 TRENCH 3. VIEW OF THE OUTER DITCH LOOKING SOUTHWEST.

Pre-rampart activity (Phases 1 to 3)

The earliest archaeological deposit encountered within Trench 4 was a light grey silt-sand (443) that had formed directly above the natural sandstone bedrock to a depth of up to 50mm and contained flecks of charcoal, heat-fractured stone and an animal tooth. Deposit (443) was

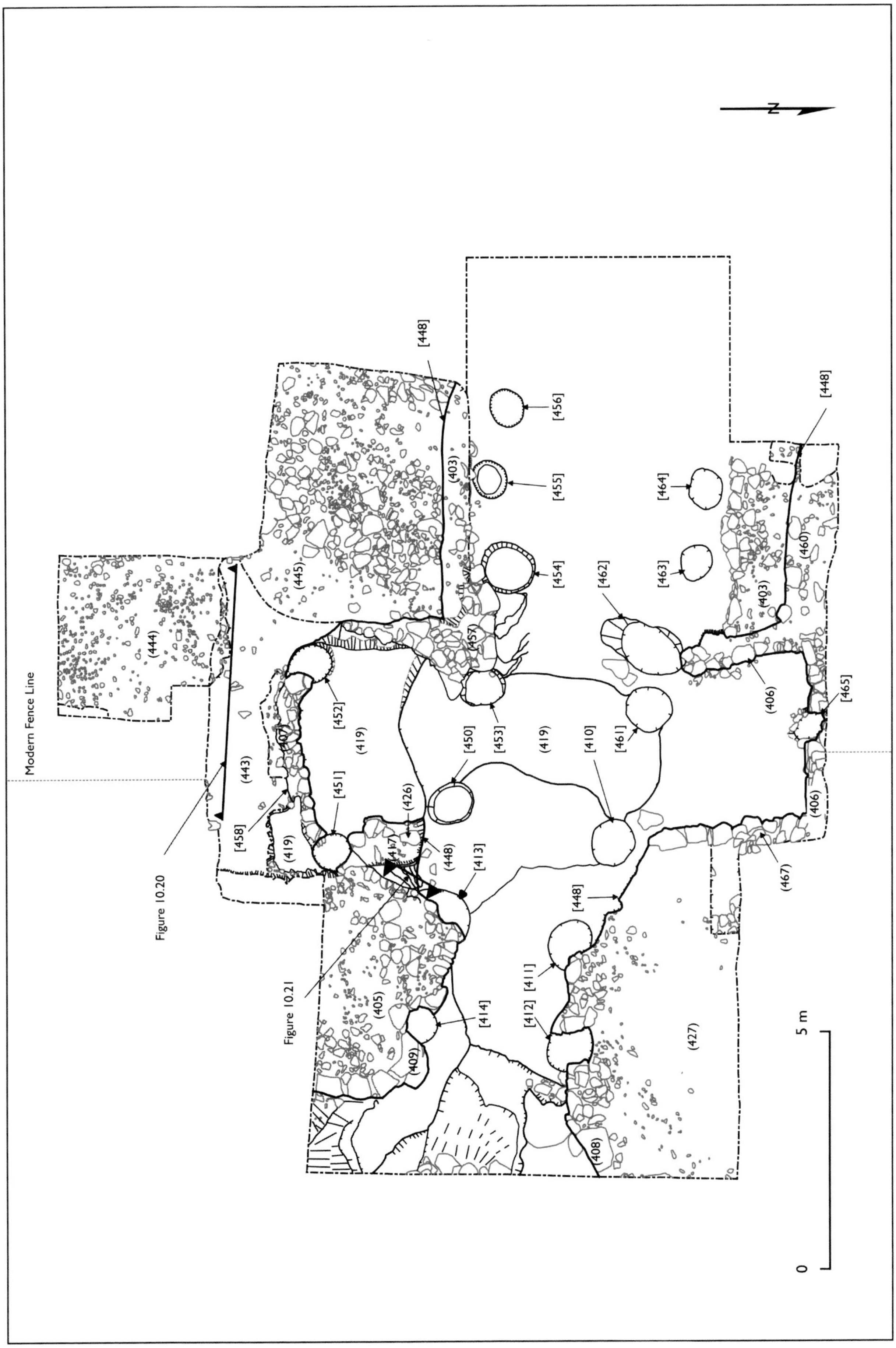

FIGURE 10.18 PLAN OF TRENCH 4.

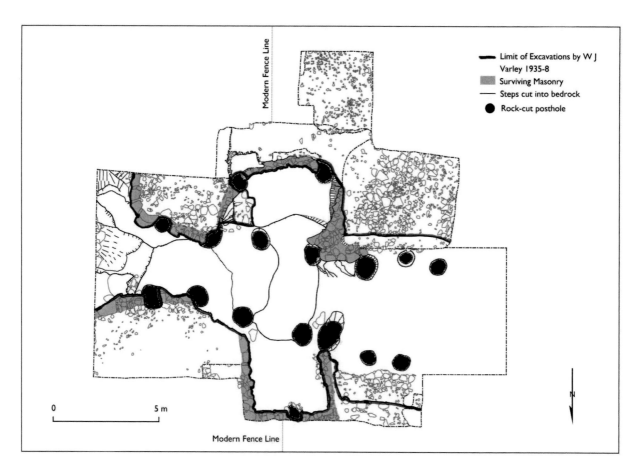

FIGURE 10.19 PLAN OF TRENCH 4 SHOWING THE EDGE OF VARLEY'S EXCAVATION AND SURVIVING MASONRY.

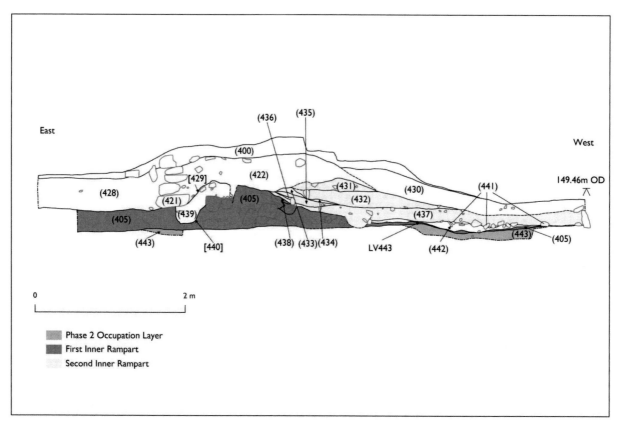

FIGURE 10.20 TRENCH 4. NORTH FACING SECTION THROUGH THE INNER RAMPART.

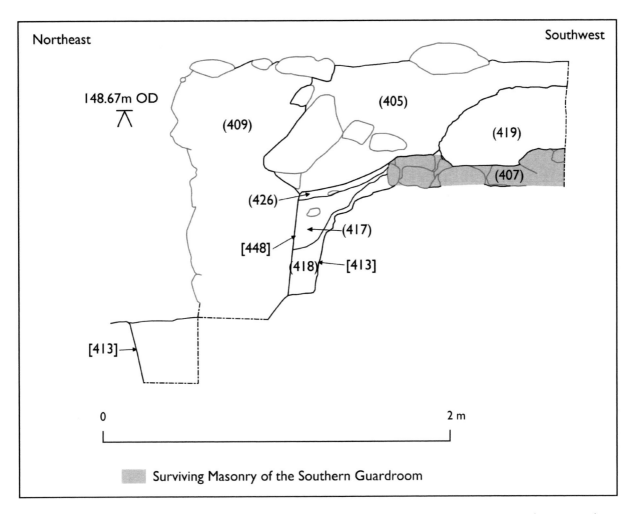

only exposed to the south of the southern guardroom where it appeared to pre-date the construction of the inner rampart (Figure 10.20). In terms of physical relationships, the deposit was cut by both the postholes of the eastern entrance and the southern 'guardroom'. A very similar deposit of silt-sand (513) was identified beneath the inner rampart in Trench 5 (on Merrick's Hill) from which two sherds of prehistoric pottery were recovered.

The inner hillfort rampart (Phases 4, 4a and 6)

The inner hillfort rampart was only examined on the southern side of the eastern entrance during the 2010 excavations, primarily to re-evaluate the conclusions drawn by Varley in 1938. A combination of truncation by Varley's excavations and post-Varley modification of the rampart (associated with its use as a modern field boundary), had resulted in the severance of the stratigraphic relationship between the entrance and the inner rampart. Furthermore, it appears that the location that Varley had marked the 'inner rampart core' on his plan of the eastern entrance was somewhat stylised; his use of the word 'core' seemingly chosen because the limits of the rampart were hard to ascertain.

Immediately south of the entrance, the contour of the hilltop turns quite sharply to the southwest and the line of the inner rampart would logically have followed the topography owing to the steepness of the hill slope. It is therefore probable that the original line of the rampart would have run on a southwest to northeast alignment at the location of the southern guardroom; as opposed to the north-south alignment proposed by Varley.

A section through the inner hillfort rampart to the south of the southern guardroom (Figure 10.20) suggested that the primary inner rampart had been constructed from a deposit of orange silt-sand (405) containing occasional fragments of angular sandstone up to 250mm in size. This deposit formed a bank that still survived to a width (east to west) of at least 5m at its base and a height of 0.65m at its highest point. The eastern limit of deposit (405) was not exposed but it conceivably extended to the eastern edge of the entrance way, whilst the western tail was roughly parallel with the western end of the southern guardroom. A similar deposit (447), that is also likely to represent the primary inner rampart, was identified in a small area to the north of the entrance and to the east of the northern guardroom. An OSL sample (LV443) was taken from the western tail of rampart deposit (405) (Figure 10.20) and produced a date of 840–160 BC with 95% confidence; however, some caution should be attached to this sample as it is likely to include elements of underlying deposit (443).

On the eastern side of rampart deposit (405), there was a feature cut in to the top of the bank that was only exposed in section. This feature (440) had the appearance of a timber slot or possibly a posthole and was filled with a brown silt-sand (439). Without seeing more of this feature in plan it is difficult to attach too much weight to any conclusions about its function but it might suggest that a timber revetment was inserted in to the front of the inner rampart, after the formation of the bank. This arrangement was originally suggested by Varley further to the south on Merrick's Hill (Varley and Jackson 1940: 65–6, figures 8 and 9) (see Figure 2.8) and later described as a pre-stone rampart palisade slot (Varley 1950: 34).

The western tail of rampart deposit (405) was overlain by a sub-circular deposit of charcoal rich silt (442) that was 2m in diameter and 0.1m thick. Initially, deposit (442) was thought to be the base of a hearth, but the lack of evidence for *in situ* burning might suggest that it was a dump of burnt material derived from hearth sweepings elsewhere. Four sherds of pottery (including three sherds from a bowl) were recovered from deposit (442); however, these are thought to be late Bronze Age in character and are suggested to be residual finds (see Mullin below). The deposit was bulk sampled (sample <20>) and produced charred remains of emmer/spelt wheat as well as weed seeds of nettle and goosefoot. Two dates were recovered from this material: 410–385 cal BC (NZA-36656) and 410–260 cal BC (NZA-36591).

A fairly rough cobbled surface (441/444) was laid over the western tail of rampart deposit (405) and charcoal-rich deposit (442). The surface extended at least 3m east-west by 3.4m north-south and consisted of a mixture of water worn cobbles, sub-rounded sandstone fragments and heat-fractured stone. To the west of the southern 'guardroom' a second area of cobbling (445) may have represented a continuation of surface (441/444), however, this additional part of the surface had a far higher concentration of sandstone fragments that gave a far more uneven appearance to the surface (Figure 10.23). A further patch of cobbled surface (460) was partially uncovered on the northern side of the entrance

FIGURE 10.22 TRENCH 4. SECTION THROUGH THE INNER RAMPART LOOKING SOUTH FROM THE SOUTHERN 'GUARDROOM' (SCALE 1M).

FIGURE 10.23 TRENCH 4. SANDSTONE AND COBBLE SPREAD (445) LOOKING EAST (SCALES 1M AND 2M).

to the west of the northern 'guardroom'. This northern area of cobbling was very similar in character to surface (441/444) on the southern side of the entrance. It is tempting to see these patches of cobbling as evidence for an internal track following the line of the inner rampart and indeed Varley originally reported evidence for such a feature further to the south on Merrick's Hill (Varley and Jackson 1940: 65–6, figures 8 and 9) (see Figure 2.8).

On the inner edge of the rampart a second patch of charcoal-rich silt (449) was deposited over part of cobbled surface (441/444). This was sampled (sample <22>) and produced charred remains of emmer/spelt wheat as well as weed seeds of grasses and goosefoot. This deposit was covered by a series of grey/brown sand-silt deposits represented by contexts (438) to (431); which appear to represent a second phase of rampart construction on the western side of the inner rampart. The addition of this series of deposits would have served to widen the base of the inner rampart by at least a further 1m and probably served to increase the original height.

No evidence for a rear stone revetment was identified in the surviving archaeology and it seems likely that such a feature would have left some trace in the stratigraphic sequence described above. A question mark must

therefore be raised about Varley's interpretation and in particular his reference to the stone walling of the southern guardroom being contemporary with the rear stone revetment of the inner rampart.

The eastern entrance (Phases 5 to 8)

In view of the conclusions drawn from the examination of the construction of the inner rampart (above) it is not stratigraphically possible to accurately place the origins of the eastern entrance within the chronology of the hillfort's development. What can be said with some confidence, is that the southern guardroom post-dates pre-rampart deposit (443).

As the majority of the entrance had been previously excavated by Varley in 1938 the construction sequence must remain largely dependent upon his original observations. The whole structure appears to have originated as a 'hollow way' (423) carved in to the natural sandstone bedrock. This hollow appears to have been formed deliberately although the possibility of this being the formalisation of a pre-hillfort route on to the hilltop remains a tantalising possibility.

Subsequently, two parallel lines of rock-cut postholes were carved in to the sides of the 'hollow way' forming an east-

FIGURE 10.24 TRENCH 4. AERIAL VIEW OF THE EASTERN ENTRANCE AFTER EXCAVATION IN 2010.

FIGURE 10.25 TRENCH 4. VIEW OF THE EASTERN ENTRANCE LOOKING WEST (SCALES 2M AND 1M).

PLATE 12 : THE SOUTH-EAST ENTRANCE GATEPOST. (*in situ.*)
The post holes belong to the original camp, the gatepost
and drystone walling belong to the reconstruction.

Eddisbury : Area 4, 1938.   W. J. V.

FIGURE 10.26 TRENCH 4. VIEW OF POSTHOLES (411) AND (412) WITH DRYSTONE
INFILL (408) LOOKING NORTH (SCALE 1M). COMPARE WITH VARLEY'S PUBLISHED PLATE
OF THE IN SITU GATEPOST (VARLEY 1950: 35, PLATE 12). REPRODUCED COURTESY OF
THE TRANSACTIONS OF THE HISTORIC SOCIETY OF LANCASHIRE AND CHESHIRE.

the largest and deepest postholes being at the eastern end of the alignment. In some cases the postholes still exhibited quite fine chisel marks demonstrating the level of workmanship that had gone in to their creation. In spite of earlier excavations, postholes (414), (413) and (412) still had their respective post-packing fills (446), (415) and (416) surviving *in situ;* which allowed for some estimation of the original post-pipe dimensions. This combined with the *in situ* timber post photographed by Varley has led to the conclusion that the posts were on average 0.5m or 0.6m in diameter and more than capable of supporting a substantial superstructure above the passage (Figure 10.26).

At the eastern end of the entrance, sections of drystone wall (408) and (409) had been inserted between postholes (412) and (411) on the northern side and (414) and (413) on the southern side (Figure 10.29). A thin layer of sand lay between the base of the drystone wall sections and the top of the sandstone bedrock in the hollow way. This was sampled (sample <30>) in one location beneath wall section (409) and ascribed the context (466). The sample produced charred fragments of emmer/spelt wheat. It was quite clear that the packing stones associated with all four postholes had been incorporated in to the drystone wall sections and that the walls had been constructed

west passage about 2.4m wide and 16m long. This passage consisted of a northern alignment of postholes running east-west of (412), (411), (410), (461), (462), (463) and (464); and a southern alignment of postholes running east-west of (414), (413) (450), (453), (454), (455) and (456) (Figures 10.18, 10.24 and 10.25). These postholes varied in diameter from 0.8m to 1.2m and in depth from 0.4m to 0.9m; with

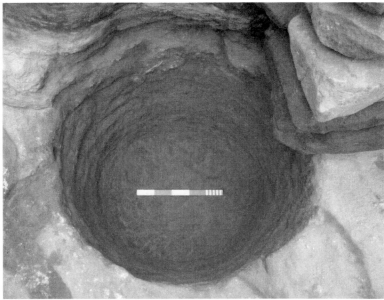

FIGURE 10.27 TRENCH 4. (A) VIEW OF POSTHOLE (411) LOOKING NORTH (SCALE 2M); (B) DETAIL OF THE BASE OF (411) CARVED IN TO THE SANDSTONE BEDROCK (SCALE 0.5M).

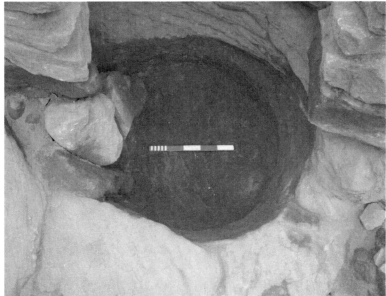

FIGURE 10.28 TRENCH 4. (A) VIEW OF POSTHOLE (412) LOOKING NORTH (SCALE 2M); (B) DETAIL OF THE BASE OF (412) CARVED IN TO THE SANDSTONE BEDROCK WITH IN SITU POST PACKING MATERIAL ON WESTERN SIDE (SCALE 0.5M).

around what would have been the *in situ* timbers. It seems logical to conclude that the stone walling was an embellishment to the timber structure and may well have been broadly contemporary with the postholes rather than a later phase of re-building.

To the east of the first two postholes (412) and (414) the drystone walling curved to both the northeast and southeast and continued to rise up the sides of the hollow way to form an outer stone revetment to the front of the inner rampart, on both the northern and southern sides of the entrance. Unfortunately, no stratigraphic relationship could be established between these sections of walling

and the rampart deposits (described above under phases 4, 4a and 6).

Several odd features can be highlighted in association with the eastern entrance passage. In the first case, on the northern alignment between postholes (411) and (410) (immediately east of (410)) there is a recess carved in to the side of the hollow way that has the appearance of being designed to accommodate a post of similar size to the others in the alignment. It is not of the same depth, however, as the other postholes and did not penetrate the lower bedrock (Figure 10.31). To the south of posthole (410) was a square depression that Varley felt may have

FIGURE 10.29 TRENCH 4. VIEW OF POSTHOLES (413) AND (414) WITH DRYSTONE INFILL (409) LOOKING SOUTH (SCALE 1M).

FIGURE 10.30 TRENCH 4. (A) VIEW OF POSTHOLE (414) LOOKING SOUTH (SCALE 2M); (B) DETAIL OF THE BASE OF (414) CARVED IN TO THE SANDSTONE BEDROCK WITH IN SITU POST PACKING MATERIAL ON SOUTHERN SIDE (SCALE 0.5M).

been intended to carry a strut supporting the gate (Varley 1950: 29), however, on reinvestigation this appears to be part of a natural fault in the sandstone bedrock. The proximity of postholes (461) and (462) is at odds with the spacing of the other postholes in the group and posthole (462) is much larger than the others. Varley's explanation for this was that posthole (461) had been filled in when the northern guardroom was added and posthole (462)

Figure 10.31 Trench 4. View of the carved recess appearing to adjoin the eastern side of posthole (410) looking northeast.

had been re-cut at this time to accommodate a secondary gate (Varley 1950: 29). Certainly, the corresponding posthole (454) on the southern side of the passage is slightly larger and more oval than the others in that alignment; perhaps lending support to the notion of a gate between (462) and (454). The lack of evidence for drystone walling between postholes (411) and (410) or (413) and (450) is also noticeable and will be returned to with regard to the guardrooms described below.

The southern guardroom (Phases 5 to 8)

The southern guardroom consisted of a sunken chamber that had been carved through layer (443) and in to the underlying sandstone bedrock to a depth of 0.6m. The floor of the guardroom was flat and apparently accessed from the adjoining passage to the north between postholes (450) and (453). The floor of the passage was 0.7m lower than the floor of the guardroom, meaning that access involved negotiating a fairly high step up. The southern extent of the guardroom was defined by postholes (451) and (452) and as with the entrance passage the spaces between the postholes had been filled with sections of drystone wall (407). The back of the construction trench for this wall was filled with sterile brown sand (459). This walling superseded the cutting of the postholes but appears to have respected the locations of the timber posts; again suggesting that the stone and timber elements were part of a contemporary construction.

The main item of interest within the southern guardroom was that Varley had wrongly identified the eastern return wall, which he shows running between postholes

(451) and (450). On reinvestigation the wall actually ran between (451) and (413). This discovery leads to a number of observations of which the most obvious is that the southern guardroom was not 'rectangular' as described by Varley (Varley 1950: 33), but is in fact more of a curious oval or rounded parallelogram in plan. Furthermore, posthole (450) no longer makes sense as part of the southern guardroom structure and may well not be contemporary with it. The other important consideration is that Varley had used the location of the southern guardroom to argue for the original gate being between postholes (410) and (450) (Varley 1950: 29). This is no longer a feasible suggestion and a gate between postholes (411) and (413) seems a far more likely location for the original gate. This is the location proposed by Varley for the later gate associated with the second phase of the entrance.

The error in the Varley excavation of the southern guardroom had resulted in a small triangle of intact archaeological deposits surviving within the northeast corner of the guardroom. This sequence began with a deposit of pale grey sand (418) up to 50mm thick which may have formed a floor deposit within the guardroom. Overlying this was a 0.3m thick deposit of charcoal-rich silt (417/424) containing large fragments of carbonised wood and lumps of burnt clay. This was sampled (samples <6>, <7>, <8>, <23> and <24>) and produced charred remains of emmer/spelt wheat, barley, black bindweed, sedge, pale persicaria, hazel, bramble and ribwort plantain; dated 360–160 cal BC (NZA-36592). This deposit was sealed by a layer of sand that appeared to be discoloured by heat and contained a large

FIGURE 10.32 TRENCH 4. VIEW OF THE SOUTHERN GUARDROOM WITH POSTHOLES (450) AND (453) IN THE FOREGROUND AND THE BLOCK OF INTACT ARCHAEOLOGICAL DEPOSITS SEEN TO THE EAST BEHIND POSTHOLE (450) LOOKING SOUTH (SCALE 2M).

passage the northern dry stone wall (406) had incorporated the packing stones and respected what would have been the extant timber post (Figure 10.34). The western wall was very poorly preserved with only the basal course of stone surviving along much of its length; however, in the northwest corner, the wall survived to a height of two courses that were bonded in to the western end of the northern wall (406). The third element was the eastern wall (467), which proved very peculiar in relation to the rest of the structure. The wall survived as five courses of stone that reached a height of 0.8m; however, there was a gap in the northeast corner meaning that there was no physical join with wall (406). Eastern wall (467) also seemed to have been constructed back to front, in that no attempt had been made to dress the internal western side, whilst the eastern side appeared to have been dressed for external display. The appearance of wall (467) did not tally with Varley's photograph from 1938 and this casts some doubt as to whether any of the original eastern wall had survived later 20th century developments on the site. The floor of the guardroom was in effect the top of the sandstone bedrock, although in one corner this was apparently covered with a layer of redeposited clay; perhaps the remnants of the puddled clay floor described by Varley (Varley 1950: 33).

number of sub-angular sandstone fragments (426). It seems likely that deposit (417/424) is the layer of 'wattle and daub' which Varley refers to as lying on the floor of the guardroom (Varley 1950: 33); it is also likely that this deposit represents the destruction of the guardroom through conflagration. It is of stratigraphic interest that deposits (418) to (426) appeared to have slumped in to the northeastern side of posthole (413); indicating that the posthole had been cut before the accumulation of these deposits (Figures 10.21 and 10.32).

The northern guardroom (Phases 5 to 8)

The northern guardroom was constructed in a different manner to the southern one with no evidence for quarrying in to the sandstone bedrock (Figure 10.33). The guardroom was accessed from the entrance passage between postholes (410) and (461); the access involving a step up from the passage to the level of the guardroom floor of 0.35m. The northern guardroom was rectangular in plan and was formed from three distinct structural elements. The first element was a single posthole (465) set in a central location along the northern wall of the guardroom; the post-packing material for this post was still *in situ* and as with the entrance

FIGURE 10.33 TRENCH 4. GENERAL VIEW LOOKING FROM THE SOUTHERN GUARDROOM TO THE NORTHERN GUARDROOM LOOKING NORTH (SCALES 1M AND 2M).

Varley had suggested that the northern guardroom was a later addition to the entrance and not part of the original design (Varley 1950: 33). Eastern wall (467) would appear to be part of a later structure and was perhaps rebuilt as part of the boundary reinstatement after the 1938 excavations (see description of structure (420)/(421) below). Varley had suggested that wall (467) coincided with the inner edge of the inner rampart, but this could not be tested owing to the suspected later interference with the structure.

20th century activity (Phase 14)

The western edges of Varley's original excavation trench, along with parts of the southern and northern limits, were identified during the 2010 excavations and were attributed cut context (448) (Figure 10.19). From this it became apparent that the Varley trench was not the rectangular area presented within the 1950 report as Area 3, but in fact more of a wall following endeavour; hence large portions of Varley's E1 and E3 grid squares were found to contain intact archaeology. The limits of Varley's excavations in his A–C1 and A–C3 grid squares were not confirmed during the 2010 excavations, but it remains probable that he did not formally excavate much beyond the limits of the entrance passage (to either the north or south) on the eastern side of his Area 3 plan. The backfill of Varley's trench was attributed the context (403)

PLATE 14 : THE NORTHERN GUARDROOM, S.-E. ENTRANCE.
Eddisbury : Area 3, 1938.   T. Jones.

FIGURE 10.34 TRENCH 4. VIEW OF THE NORTHERN GUARDROOM WITH POSTHOLE (465) AND DRYSTONE INFILL (406) LOOKING NORTH (SCALE 1M). COMPARE WITH VARLEY'S PUBLISHED PLATE OF THE NORTHERN GUARDROOM (VARLEY 1950: 37, PLATE 14). REPRODUCED COURTESY OF THE TRANSACTIONS OF THE HISTORIC SOCIETY OF LANCASHIRE AND CHESHIRE.

and this was found to contain a sizeable portion of large sandstone fragments that are likely to be derived from the material 'filling the entrance' in Varley's original excavation report (Varley 1950: 33). Varley's backfill (403) contained several items of interest including a number of worked stone fragments, such as a fragment of saddle quern stone and a fragment of a stone mortar. Of greatest interest, however, was a boulder decorated with a series of 'cup marks' which represent prehistoric rock art of Bronze Age date. The backfill also produced some ceramic objects including fired daub/clay that was probably derived from the southern guardroom and a fragment of Roman tile.

Along the line of the modern property boundary (between land owned by the Forestry Commission and land owned by Mr Platt), an earthwork had been constructed over the top of Varley's trench backfill. This earthwork took the form of an earthen bank (422) with a dry stone retaining wall (420/421) on the eastern side, which sat within a shallow construction trench (429). It is likely that this earthwork was a replacement/reinstatement of what had originally marked the field boundary prior to Varley's excavations and therefore dates to post 1938 (Figure 10.35).

To the east of the field boundary a layer of grey-brown silt-sand (427/428) had formed against the front of

FIGURE 10.35 TRENCH 4. VIEW OF THE EAST ENTRANCE DURING RE-EXCAVATION IN 2010. NOTE THE ELEMENTS OF POST-1938 DRYSTONE WALL (420/421) TO THE SOUTH AND NORTH OF THE ENTRANCE AND THE BOULDER RICH BACKFILL (403) OF VARLEY'S EXCAVATION.

drystone wall (420/421) to a depth of 0.4m. This was in turn covered by topsoil and turf layer (400). To the west of the field boundary earth bank (422) was partly covered by modern plough soil (430).

Trench 7 *(Figures 10.36–10.38)*

Trench 7, measuring 13 x 2m, was located as a southwestern extension to Trench 3 and was intended to examine the remains of the inner rampart within the modern ploughed field. The inner rampart had not been examined by Varley in this location owing to the field being under crop at the time of his excavations.

Pre-rampart activity (Phases 1 and 2)

The earliest archaeological deposit encountered within Trench 7 was a layer of sterile pale brown silt-sand (719) that was up to 0.27m thick. This was covered by a layer of mid-grey silt-sand (718) up to 0.13m thick which contained a distinct area of charred material, including fragments of burnt bone. This charred and bone-flecked part of layer (718) produced three sherds of prehistoric pottery and was bulk sampled (sample <34>), the sample producing charred hazelnut shell. A

separate bulk sample (sample <29>) was taken from the wider layer (718) context, and this produced charred seeds of barley, which produced a date of 770–410 cal BC (NZA-36648). Layer (718) was also sampled for OSL dating (sample LV449) but this produced a negative result.

The inner hillfort rampart (Phases 4 and 6)

The base of the primary hillfort rampart was represented by a layer of redeposited red-brown clay (722), which was 11.22m wide and up to 0.22m thick. An east-west alignment of large sandstone fragments (705) had been added to the upper part of layer (722) approximately mid-way across its width. These sandstone fragments were subsequently covered by red-brown clay-sand deposit (721) which contained large sandstone fragments and lenses of brown silt. Deposit (721) was 5.38m wide and 0.5m thick. It was thought that contexts (722), (705) and (721) combined to form the bank of the primary inner rampart and there was some evidence at the northern end of deposit (721) to suggest that the bank had originally had an outer stone revetment. In many respects this primary rampart bank was very similar in character to the inner rampart deposit (108) in Trench 1.

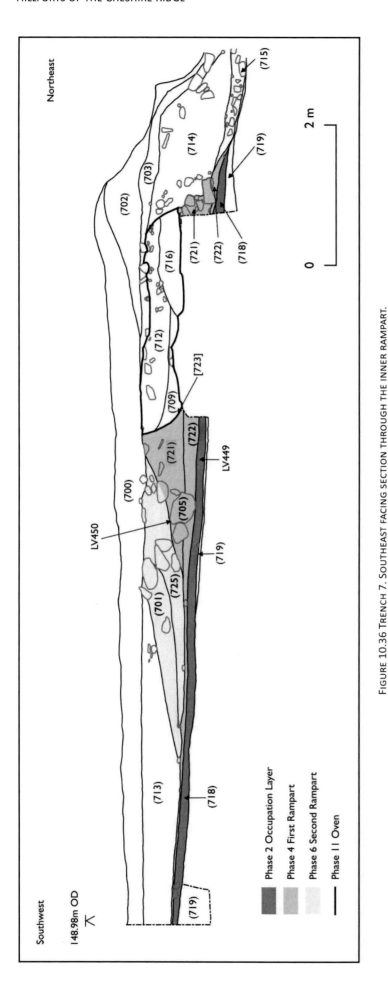

A subsequent phase of rampart building was represented by the addition of deposits (725) and (701) on the southern side of the primary inner rampart. The earlier deposit (725) consisted of a mid-grey-brown silt-clay that was flecked with charred material and sandstone fragments; this was sampled (sample <35>) and produced fragments of charred barley and wheat. This material produced two dates: 770–410 cal BC (NZA-36646) and 400–200 cal BC (NZA-36593); the earlier date could well represent contamination from underlying deposit (718). Deposit (725) was sampled for OSL dating (OSL sample LV 450) but the degree of error was too great to provide a meaningful result. Upper deposit (701) was a yellow-grey silt-sand which contained flecks of charred material and was bulk sampled (sample <15>) which produced charred fragments of emmer/ spelt wheat. Deposit (701) was very similar in character to secondary rampart deposit (109) in Trench 1.

Abandonment (Phase 9)

At the northern end of the trench there was a layer of sandstone rubble (715), which was thought to be equivalent to inner ditch fill (303) in Trench 3. Deposit (715) probably represents tumble from the outer stone revetment of the inner rampart. This is likely to be the result of natural erosion rather than deliberate slighting and may indicate abandonment of the site.

Clay oven (Phase 11)

The upper part of the primary inner rampart had been removed by construction pit (723) which was only partially exposed within Trench 7, being 2.8m north-south by 0.45m east-west and 0.45m deep. Pit (723) had been lined with a clay deposit (724) which had subsequently been fired to a biscuit hardness with a yellow-grey to red-pink colour (Figure 10.38). Deposit (724) was sampled for archaeomagnetic dating, which gave the date of the last/hottest firing as 745–980 AD (95% confidence) or 860 AD ± 70 (65% confidence). This burnt clay lining has led to the interpretation of the feature as an oven. The oven base was subsequently covered

166

FIGURE 10.37 PHOTO MOSAIC OF THE SECTION THROUGH THE INNER RAMPART IN TRENCH 7 LOOKING NORTHWEST (SCALES 1M X 4).

FIGURE 10.38 TRENCH 7. VIEW OF CLAY OVEN DEPOSIT (724) LOOKING NORTHWEST (SCALE 1M).

by a series of fills beginning with charcoal-rich black silt (727) that was bulk sampled (sample <32>) and sampled for pollen (sample <33>). Associated with the primary fill (727) was a concentration of carbonised material that was given a separate context (726) and was bulk sampled (sample <31>) and produced fragments of round wood charcoal. Above the primary fills was a deposit of red-brown clay (716) which may represent part of the collapse from the oven superstructure. This was sealed by deposits of brown clay-silt (709) and (711) which may have represented silting after the oven had gone out of use. Deposit (709) was bulk sampled (samples <18> and <19>) and deposit (711) was bulk sampled (sample <17>); both samples <17> and <18> produced charred seeds of goosefoot/orache. The upper fill of the oven was a deposit of charcoal-rich sand-silt (712) which was bulk sampled (sample <16>) and produced charred fragments of roundwood and grass seed. The location of this oven feature (set in to the top of the inner rampart) suggests that the inner rampart was no longer performing a defensive function at the time.

Cultivation soil (Phase 12)

A deep deposit of brown silt-sand (713) had formed on the southern side of the inner rampart, probably representing a medieval or early post-medieval cultivation soil.

Field boundary and cultivation soil (Phase 13)

Further to the evidence mentioned under Trench 3 (above), for a late modification to the outer face of the hillfort rampart in the form of drystone retaining wall (334), the evidence from Trench 7 suggested that wall (334) was retaining an earth bank which had been added to the outer face of the prehistoric inner rampart. This bank was primarily represented by a mid-brown sand-silt (714) which produced fragments of post-medieval brick. Overlying this was a layer of pink-red clay (703) and a layer of brown-grey clay (702). This post-medieval 'widening' of the inner rampart has created a false impression of where the prehistoric remains survive and the modern boundary fence is in fact sited to the east of the rampart, entirely on top of the post-medieval bank.

This in effect means that the entire inner rampart sequence is now within the plough zone of the cultivated field and this is represented by modern plough soil (700). The western end of the inner rampart is essentially protected by the buffer of relict plough soil (713); however, Trench 7 clearly demonstrated that the eastern end of the rampart was being actively eroded by ploughing and this could have a significant impact on the Phase 11 clay oven (described above).

Trench 8

Trench 8, measuring 20 x 1m, was located on the hillfort's interior within the modern cultivated field and was aligned roughly east-west. It was located to test the southern end of geophysical anomaly [9] (Chapter 6, Figure 6.6; Roseveare et al. 2010a). The trench was excavated using a mini-digger with a 1m wide toothless ditching bucket. The uppermost context encountered was the modern plough soil (800) which was up to 0.4m thick. Beneath this was a layer of mid-yellow/brown clay-silt (802) which was up to 0.3m thick and covered the entire trench. At the eastern end of the trench there was a deposit of rounded sandstone fragments and cobbles (801) which extended westwards for about 3.5m; this was thought to represent the edge of the internal metalled surface (444) encountered in Trench 4.

About 11m from the eastern end of Trench 8 there was a shallow deposit of buff/grey silt-clay (803) which was 3.7m wide and 0.2m thick. This clay appeared to have formed against a shallow step in the underlying bedrock (804) and was thought to be natural in origin. Deposit (803) was possibly the geophysical anomaly [9] identified in the 2010 survey.

Trench 9

Trench 9, measuring 28 x 1m, was located on the hillfort's interior within the modern cultivated field and was aligned roughly north-south. It was located to test geophysical anomaly [14] which possibly represented a group of pits (Chapter 6, Figure 6.6; Roseveare et al. 2010a). The trench was excavated using a mini-digger with a 1m wide toothless ditching bucket. The uppermost context encountered was the modern plough soil (900) which was up to 0.35m thick. Beneath this was a layer of mid-orange/brown clay silt (901) which was up to 0.35m thick and covered the entire trench. Natural sandstone bedrock (903) was encountered beneath layer (901) over the southern half of the trench; but the northern half of the trench located an intermediary layer of clay (902) which was thought to be a natural deposit. No archaeological features were encountered within Trench 9 and no explanation for the geophysical anomalies could be readily identified.

Trench 10

Trench 10, measuring 27 x 1m, was located on the hillfort's interior within the modern cultivated field and was aligned roughly northwest-southeast. It was located to test geophysical anomaly [20] which possibly represented natural features in the underlying rock (Chapter 6, Figure 6.6; Roseveare et al. 2010a). The trench was excavated using a mini-digger with a 1m wide toothless ditching bucket. The uppermost context encountered was the modern plough soil (1001) which was up to 0.35m thick and produced a rim sherd from a Roman mortaria. Beneath this was a layer of mid-orange/brown clay silt (1002) which was up to 0.35m thick and covered the entire trench. Natural clay (1004) was encountered beneath layer (1002) over most of the trench; but there were two patches of red/brown sand (1003) lying above the natural clay at between 6m to 8m and 21m to 24m along the trench from its northwestern end. These sand deposits were between 2m and 3m wide and up to 0.2m thick. Deposit (1003) was thought to be natural in origin and possibly indicates the source of the geophysical anomaly. No archaeological features were encountered within Trench 10.

Trench 11

Trench 11, measuring 15 x 1m, was located on the hillfort's interior within the modern cultivated field and was aligned roughly northwest-southeast. It was located to test geophysical anomaly [17] which possibly represented a north-south aligned linear feature (Chapter 6, Figure 6.6; Roseveare *et al.* 2010a). The trench was excavated using a mini-digger with a 1m wide toothless ditching bucket. The uppermost context encountered was the modern plough soil (1100) which was up to 0.4m thick. Beneath this at the northwestern end of the trench was a layer of mid-orange/brown clay silt (1101) which was up to 0.4m thick and appeared to increase in depth towards the northwest. Natural clay (1102) was encountered beneath layer (1101) and extended over the entire trench. Deposit (1101) was thought to be the edge of backfilling associated with the large open quarry feature still extant to the northwest of Trench 11 and it possibly indicates the origin of the geophysical anomaly [17]. No archaeological features were encountered within Trench 11.

Trench 12 *(Figure 10.39)*

Trench 12, measuring 26 x 1m, was located on the hillfort's interior within the modern cultivated field. It was the only evaluation trench targeting geophysical anomalies on the interior of the hillfort which produce archaeological features of any kind.

Posthole building(s) (Phase 7)

An alignment of five postholes was identified on a roughly north-south alignment, all cut in to the natural subsoil and sealed by post-medieval plough soil layer (1201). The southern three postholes (1204), (1206) and (1208) were similar in size and character (being 0.4 to 0.5m in diameter and 0.1 to 0.15m deep) and were filled with a red-brown silt (1203), (1205) and (1207). All three fills were sampled (samples <12>, <11> and <10>). Fill (1203) produced a charred seed of goosefoot/orache; fill (1205) produced charred seeds of barley, wheat, goosefoot/orache, stitchwort and grasses; and fill (1207) produced charred seeds of stitchwort and goosefoot/orache.

The northern two postholes (1209) and (1212) were each about 0.4m deep and contained secondary fills. Posthole (1209) was sub-circular (0.56 x 0.65 x 0.38m); the primary fill (1211) was a light grey sand and the secondary fill (1210) was a brown sand-silt which was sampled (sample <13>). The bulk sample from fill (1210) produced charred seeds of barley, wheat, blinks and pale persicaria as well as a prunus fruitstone; this produced a date of 375–195 cal BC (NZA-36653). Posthole (1212) was circular (0.4m in diameter and 0.43m deep); the primary fill (1213) was a red-brown silt-sand which was sampled (sample <14>). The bulk sample from fill (1213) produced charred seeds of wheat and pale persicaria.

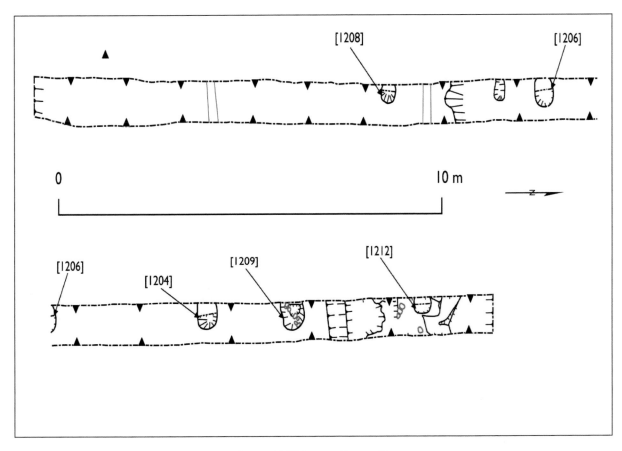

FIGURE 10.39 PLAN OF TRENCH 12.

Trench 12 was subsequently extended to the east and west by 5m in each direction in order to try and identify more postholes associated with the northern pair; but time and resources were limited and the exercise was unsuccessful.

The northern two postholes were separated by a distance of approximately 4m and are likely to be from the same structure. In view of the dating from (1209), it is conceivable that they represent elements from a building which was contemporary with occupation of the hillfort during the middle Iron Age. If so, then ploughing has removed all traces of internal floor surfaces or occupation deposits. It is conceivable that postholes (1209) and (1212) represent one side of a four-post structure, which are often associated hillforts in the northern Welsh Marches.

Trench 13 *(Figures 10.40 and 10.41)*

Trench 13, measuring 15 x 1m, was located on the hillfort's interior within the modern cultivated field and was aligned roughly northwest-southeast. It was located to test the field boundary between the large cultivated field owned by Mr Platt and the smaller field to the northwest in an area owned by the Forestry Commission. The trench was excavated using a mini-digger with a 1m wide toothless ditching bucket. The uppermost context encountered was the modern plough soil (1300) which was up to 0.4m thick. Beneath this was a layer of yellowish-brown clay-silt sub-soil (1301) up to 80mm thick

FIGURE 10.40 TRENCH 13. GENERAL VIEW LOOKING NORTHWEST (SCALE 1M).

which in turn overlay the natural clay (1302) which extended over the entire trench. At the northwestern end of the trench the modern field boundary could be seen to be formed by a low earthen bank consisting of mid-brown clay-silt (1304) covered with turf and topsoil (1303); which was approximately 3.5m wide at the base and 1m high. The southern edge of bank (1304) was seen to be overlying sub-soil deposit (1301) and was sealed by plough soil deposit (1300); this suggested that the bank was not any great antiquity. There was no evidence for a flattened prehistoric

FIGURE 10.41 TRENCH 13. VIEW OF THE SECTION THROUGH THE FIELD BOUNDARY LOOKING SOUTHWEST (SCALE 1M).

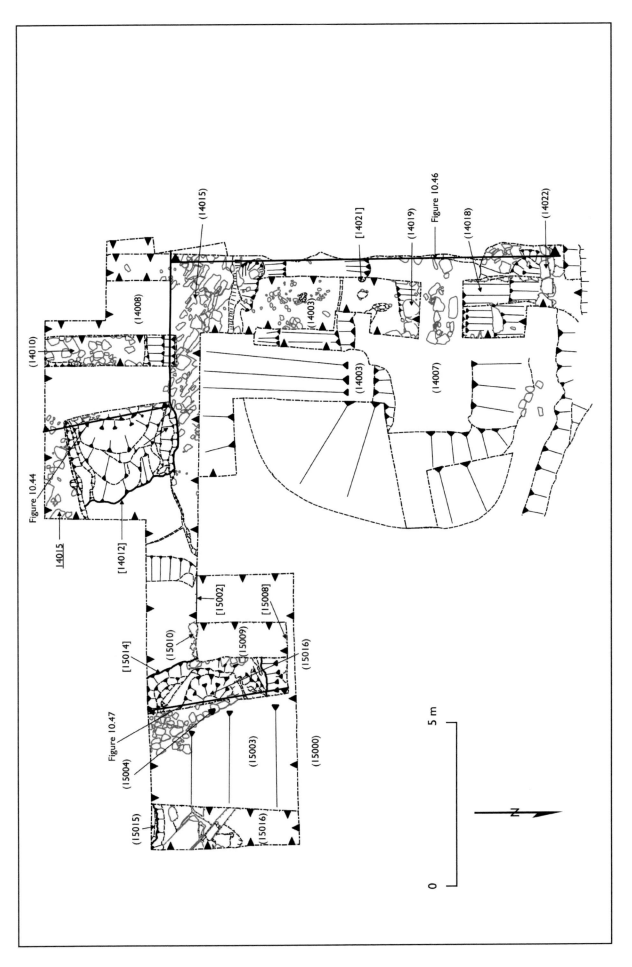

FIGURE 10.42 PLAN OF TRENCHES 14 AND 15.

171

rampart or any indication of a backfilled ditch as had been conjectured by Varley.

Trench 14 *(Figures 10.42–10.46)*

Trench 14, measuring 33 x 2m, was located within Varley's Area 2 excavation and was focused on the outer rampart and eastern terminus of the western arm to the inner ditch.

Natural Geology

Solid sandstone bedrock was identified in Trench 14 (14023), but only seen in the sides of inner ditch cut (14012). Overlying the bedrock was a layer of partially weathered mudstone (14015) which had the appearance of rows of roughly rectangular shaped blocks of mudstone within a clay matrix. This layer was the lower 'pavement of flagstones set in puddled clay' as described by Varley and shown in both his section

through the outer rampart and his plan of Area 2, which he considered was a manmade feature (Varley 1950: 23, figures 8 and 9, plate 8). Layer (14015) was covered by a layer of firm red-brown clay (14014) which was 0.3m thick and probably represented a band of fully weathered mudstone. Above this was a layer of light grey/green clay (14013) up to 0.06m thick. Varley had described this clay layer in his excavation report and attributed the colouration to a copper-compound of malachite which he noted occurred within the local Keuper rocks (*ibid.* 23). Overlying (14013) was a second layer of partially weathered mudstone (14034) up to 0.3m thick which was similar in appearance to layer (14015) with the exception that the mudstone blocks were less regular and more poorly sorted within the surrounding clay matrix.

During the original 1936–8 excavation Varley concluded that the stratigraphy described above as layers (14015), (14014), (14013) and (14034) represented the levelled

FIGURE 10.43 TRENCHES 14 AND 15. AERIAL VIEW LOOKING NORTHWEST.

remains of the prehistoric outer rampart. This can now be discounted within the development of the prehistoric hillfort as natural geology.

Pre-rampart activity

Overlying the uppermost weathered mudstone layer (10434) was a layer of buff-yellow silty clay (14017/14018) up to 0.14m thick; which had lenses of iron staining showing as rust coloured striations formed through natural mineralisation. Layer (14017/14018) had been shown on Varley's section drawing as an 'occupation deposit' and described as 'a thick deposit of carbon-flecked, bone-scattered occupation material, devoid of relics except for masses of iron slag' (Varley 1950: 23). A 60 litre bulk sample <1> recovered from layer (14017) produced a charred cereal grain which was used for radiocarbon dating, providing a date of 730–400 cal BC (BETA-317521). Layer (14017/14018) is almost certainly the same layer as encountered beneath the inner rampart in Trench 1 where it was recorded as (114).

The inner ditch (Phases 4 and 6)

Initial quarrying for the western arm of the inner ditch had apparently removed a large area of the upper natural geology as well as part of occupation layer (14017/14018) between the inner and outer ramparts; the quarried material being used for rampart construction. Within this wide quarry area a much more modest primary ditch cut (14012) was excavated through the lower weathered mudstone layer (14015) and in to the underlying bedrock (14023). Primary ditch cut (14012) was approximately 4m wide at the top, 1.5m deep with a flat base 1.9m wide (Figures 10.44 and 10.45). The eastern end of the ditch ended in a sub-square terminus, tapering to a more rounded terminus at the base of the cut. The primary fill (14011) was a red/brown clay which was very clean and was sampled (sample <2>) to recover material suitable for radiocarbon dating. It was thought probable that the top of fill (14011) had been truncated by a ditch re-cut (14033). The primary fill of re-cut (14033) was a mass of angular mudstone rubble (14010) which could either represent a sudden collapse of the inner rampart or a deliberate attempt at partially backfilling the ditch. Above this was an upper fill of red/brown silty clay (14009) containing moderate amounts of large angular stones.

The outer rampart (Phases 5 and 8)

The earliest event in the construction of the outer rampart was the sinking of a timber post in to layer (14017). This was represented by a circular posthole (14021) which was 0.68m in diameter and 0.48m deep; the posthole had a steeply tapering profile that terminated in a blunt point. The fill of the posthole (14020) was a red/brown clay, rich in angular fragments of mudstone. The matrix was

identical to the overlying rampart deposit (14016), which implied that the post had been removed shortly before the rampart material was deposited.

The primary outer rampart consisted of a single deposit of red/brown clay that was rich in small angular mudstone fragments (14016). This created a bank 4.5m wide at the base and 1.2m high. The front of the bank had a surviving face which sloped at a 45 degree angle, whilst the rear of the bank appeared somewhat truncated and may have been affected by the re-cutting of the primary inner ditch (14033). This feature may have functioned as a counterscarp bank prior to the cutting of the outer ditch as seen at the eastern end of the outer rampart in Trench 3.

Subsequently, a much larger bank was added to the outer rampart and this was probably associated with the cutting of the outer ditch. This secondary rampart began with a primary tip of angular stone fragments (14019)/(14030) on to the front of primary bank (14016). Possibly at the same time, a stone revetment wall (14022) was constructed to retain the extended rampart. Following this, a series of mudstone-rich clay deposits (14029) to (14025), was built up against the rear of the revetment wall (14022) and then the remaining gap was filled by a deposit of small angular mudstone fragments (14007). The top of this extended bank was then capped with a layer of large angular stones (14006), which were then sealed by a thin layer of red/brown clay (14005). These additions resulted in a much larger bank, 9.7m wide at the base and 2.1m high. The front of the bank would have been retained by the revetment wall (14022) of mudstone slabs, whilst the rear of the bank had a stepped profile which is perhaps suggestive of a raised walkway on the rampart interior (Figure 10.46). This enlarged outer rampart is likely to have been built at the same time as the outer ditch was initially excavated, as it is formed from a large amount of redeposited natural material which probably represents up-cast from the outer ditch excavation. Scientific dating from the primary fills of the outer ditch at Trench 3 (with a C14 date of 400–200 cal BC (NZA-36654)) provides some chronological framework for this phase of the rampart.

This larger secondary rampart had been identified by Varley, however, owing to his misinterpretation of the natural geology (as the prehistoric rampart) he attributed the enlarged outer rampart to the late Saxon refortification of Eddisbury by Aethelflaed in AD 914.

Additional material was later deposited on the inside face of the outer rampart sealing clay capping layer (14005) and removing the stepped profile of the earlier bank. This was represented by successive deposits of red/brown silty clay (14004) and (14003) with a combined thickness of up to 0.5m, containing angular fragments of mudstone. The additional material would have served to

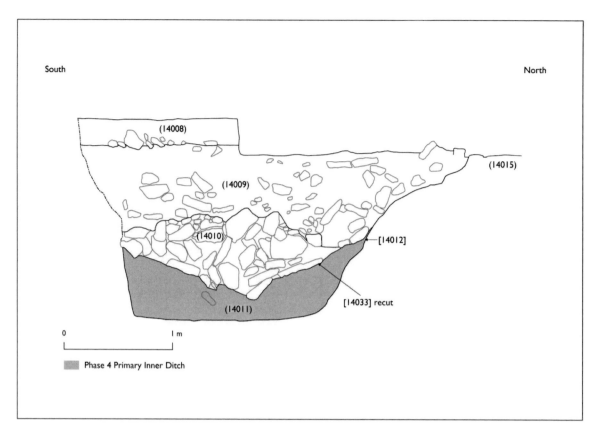

FIGURE 10.44 TRENCH 14, EAST FACING SECTION THROUGH INNER DITCH [14012].

FIGURE 10.45 TRENCH 14, SECTION THROUGH DITCH [14012] LOOKING WEST.

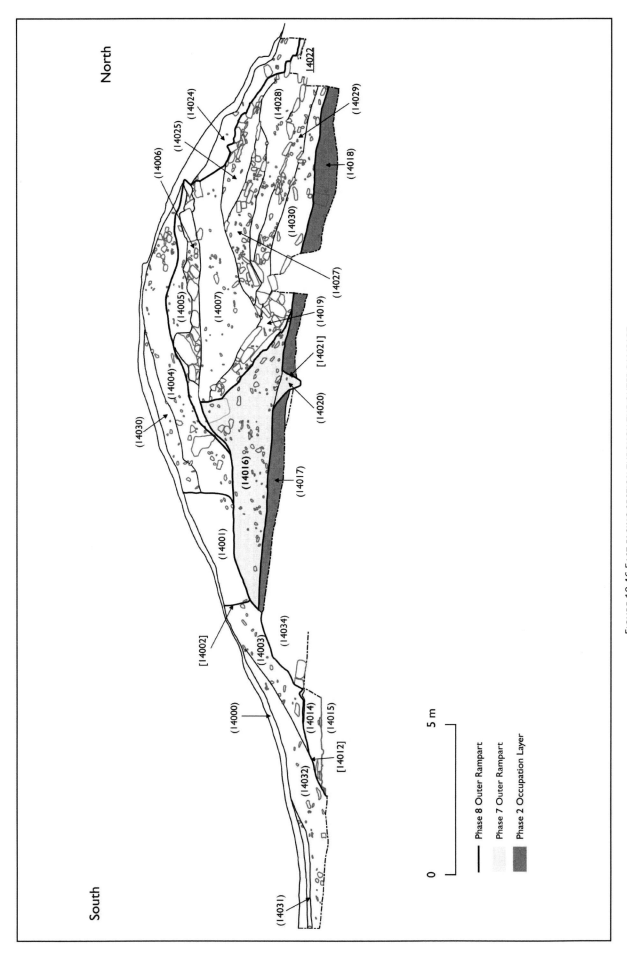

North

South

(14024)

(14025)

(14006)

(14028)

(14029)

(14018)

(14030)

(14027)

(14005)

(14007)

(14019)

[14021]

(14020)

(14004)

(14030)

(14016)

(14017)

(14001)

[14002]

(14003)

(14034)

(14000)

(14014)

(14015)

[14012]

(14032)

(14031)

14022

5 m

0

— Phase 8 Outer Rampart

Phase 7 Outer Rampart

Phase 2 Occupation Layer

FIGURE 10.46 EAST FACING SECTION THROUGH THE OUTER RAMPART.

increase the size of the outer rampart further, to a bank 11.9m wide at the base and 2.5m high. It is not possible to attribute a firm chronological framework for the last phase of rampart improvement in Trench 14, however, it may have coincided with the re-cutting of the outer ditch as observed at Trench 3. Scientific dating from the secondary fills of the re-cut outer ditch at Trench 3 (with a C14 date of cal AD 10–130 (Beta-319724)) may suggest some chronological framework for this last phase of the rampart.

The outer rampart and inner ditch (Phases 9)

The stone retaining wall (14022) must have eventually collapsed outwards and downslope towards the outer ditch. This event would have promoted the destabilisation of the outer rampart core, leading to further erosion and collapse which was represented by red clay deposit (14024).

The inner face of the outer rampart also appears to have eroded leading to the gradual infill of the quarried area occupied by the inner ditch with orange/brown silt-clay deposits (14032)/(14008) and (14031), which contained fragments of mudstone.

Varley excavations (Phase 14)

The various excavation trenches undertaken by Varley between 1936 and 1938 were given a group context number for the cut of (14002) and the backfill of (14001). The backfill itself was subsequently sealed by the modern turf and topsoil (14000) which covered the whole area.

Trench 15 (Figures 10.42, 10.43, 10.47 and 10.48)

Trench 15, measuring 33 x 2m, was located within Varley's Area 2 excavation and was focused on the western terminus of the eastern arm to the inner ditch.

The inner ditch (Phases 4 and 6)

Initial quarrying for the eastern arm of the inner ditch had apparently removed a large area of the upper natural geology between the inner and outer ramparts; the quarried material being used for rampart construction. Within this wide quarry area, a much more modest primary ditch cut (15014) was excavated through the lower weathered mudstone layer (15015) and in to the underlying bedrock (15016). Primary ditch cut (15014) was at least 3.8m wide at the top, 1.4m deep, with a concave base 0.6m wide. The western end of the ditch ended in a sub-square terminus, tapering to a more rounded terminus at the base of the cut. The primary fill (15013) was a red/brown clay-silt which was very clean and was sampled (sample <3>) to recover material suitable for radiocarbon dating. It was thought probable that the top of fill (15013) had been truncated by a ditch re-cut (15012), which had a more 'V' shaped profile being at least 3.28m wide at the top and 1.3m

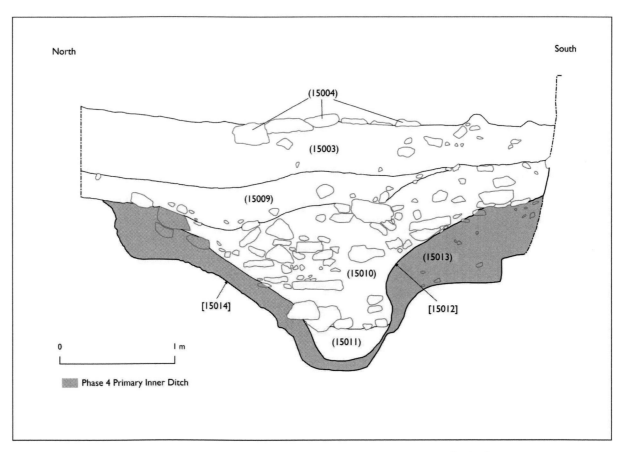

FIGURE 10.47 TRENCH 15, WEST FACING SECTION THROUGH INNER DITCH [15014].

176

FIGURE 10.48 TRENCH 15, SECTION THROUGH DITCH [15014] LOOKING EAST.

deep. The primary fill of re-cut (15012) was a red/brown clay-silt (15011), up to 0.28m thick. This was sealed by a mass of angular mudstone rubble (15010) which could either represent a sudden collapse of the inner rampart or a deliberate attempt at partially backfilling the ditch. Above this was an upper fill of red/brown silty clay (15009) containing moderate amounts of large angular stones.

Despite the area between ditch terminus (15014) and ditch terminus (14012) having been disturbed in to the natural subsoil by Varley's excavations, it was still possible to ascertain that the gap between the tops of the two ditch terminals was 2.9m. This distance would seem more than adequate to allow for an entrance through the inner ditch and is of comparable size to the width of the eastern entrance as seen at Trench 4.

The inner ditch (Phases 9 to 11)

The inner face of the outer rampart appears to have eroded leading to the gradual infill of the quarried area occupied by the inner ditch with orange/brown silt-clay deposits (15003); which was up to 0.55m thick and contained fragments of mudstone.

Subsequently a sandstone structure (15004) was inserted above the inner ditch fills. This structure consisted of a course of roughly-dressed sandstone blocks forming a possible wall foundation on a northwest - southeast alignment. Unfortunately, the structure had been partly removed by Varley when he cut a section across the inner ditch terminus; there is no reference to the structure in his report. Structure (15004) remains undated, however, a possible sunken-featured building was recorded by Varley

overlying the inner ditch fills by the northern entrance. A loom weight recovered by Varley from this structure suggests that it is likely to be associated with Anglo-Saxon occupation of the hillfort (see Chapter 4, this volume).

Varley excavations (Phase 14)

The various excavation trenches undertaken by Varley between 1936 and 1938 were given context numbers for the cut of (15002) and (15008) and the backfill of (15001), (15005), (15006) and (15007). The backfill itself was subsequently sealed by the modern turf and topsoil (15000) which covered the whole area.

The finds

General

In spite of careful cleaning and excavation of most archaeological horizons by trowel, accompanied by on site sieving and bulk sampling from most contexts for palaeoenvironmental analysis, finds retrieval was minimal.

The pottery

Prehistoric pottery

David Mullin

Summary: A total of 13 sherds of possible prehistoric pottery and three small pieces of fired clay were recovered from five contexts during the excavation. On examination, four (from context 14001) appear to be of Anglo-Saxon date and are discussed below. Of the remaining nine sherds, all could be of late Bronze Age date, although the relatively small sherd size and rolled nature of some of these suggest they could be residual within the contexts from which they were recovered.

Method: The total numbers of sherds and weight were quantified by context. Fabrics were assessed macroscopically by x10 hand lens.

Results: Due to the small amount of pottery recovered from each context, and the small sherd size, caution must be exercised in the interpretation of this material. No diagnostic sherds were present in the assemblage and no vessel profiles could be reconstructed. Due to the small sherd size, no thin-sections were taken and fabric analysis was only undertaken macroscopically.

Context 513: two sherds (43g), both of which have a poorly sorted fabric containing irregular inclusions of crushed rock. Both have wiped outer surfaces which contain some mica. The larger sherd (32g) is possibly from the upper section of a fairly thick-walled (10mm) vessel, whilst the smaller may be from the same vessel, although the sherds do not conjoin.

Context 442: four sherds were recovered from this context. Three sherds (9g) have the same fabric and may be from the same vessel. The fabric contains quartz sand. Vessel walls are relatively thin (5mm) and could form part of a hemispherical bowl/cup. One sherd (5g) has angular rock inclusions and is a somewhat coarser, thicker vessel (wall thickness 10mm) with a wiped outer surface. This has more in common with the two sherds from context 513.

One small fragment of fired clay (2g) was also recovered from this context.

Context 701: two small fragments of fired clay (2g).

Context 718: three sherds were recovered from this context. Two sherds (11g) have abundant finely crushed rock temper which is different to that of the sherds from context 513, in that it is well sorted and of smaller size. The interior of the larger sherd (10g) appears to have been eroded and the smaller sherd (1g) is small and rolled, suggesting they may be residual. One sherd (27g) has a sand fabric with moderate inclusions of larger pieces of rock. The inner and outer surfaces are smoothed and contain mica. The vessel wall is 9mm thick and curving and the breaks are old and weathered.

Discussion: The rock tempered pottery from context 513 may be of late Bronze Age date, the larger sherd has much in common with the slack-shouldered, bucket-shaped jars recovered from Beeston Castle (Royle and Woodward 1993, figure 47), which also had large rock clasts within their fabric. The rock tempered sherd from context 422

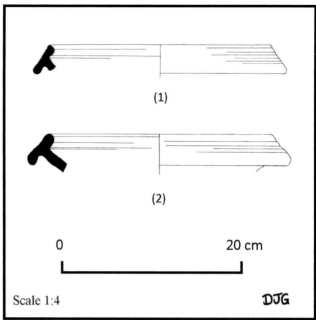

FIGURE 10.49 THE ROMAN POTTERY

is very similar in fabric and form to those from context 513, but may be residual, especially given the Iron Age radiocarbon dates from this context (see below).

The three sherds with a sandy fabric recovered from context 442 appear to be from a small, fine bowl although interpretation is difficult due to the small proportion of the vessel which is represented. A similar bowl, in a very different fabric, was recovered from a Late Bronze Age context at Beeston Castle (Royle and Woodward 1993, figure 48 (49)) and similar vessels were also recovered from contexts of a similar date at the Breiddin (Musson *et al.* 1991, figure 52: (65) and (71)). The two radiocarbon dates (NZA-36656 and NZA-36591) from this context at Eddisbury are, however, early Iron Age, suggesting the pottery may be residual.

The radiocarbon date from context 718 (NZA-36648) spans the late Bronze Age to early Iron Age. Due to the small size and eroded/rolled nature of the more abundant rock tempered sherds from this context, these appear to be residual. The larger, rock and sand tempered sherd is similar to the sherds from contexts 422 and 513, but the rock inclusions are of a different material. Again this would not be out of place in the late Bronze Age, but some caution should be exercised in its stratigraphic interpretation as the weathered breaks suggest it too may be residual.

Roman pottery

Dan Garner

A rim sherd from a Mancetter-Hartshill (MAH WH) hammerhead mortaria weighing 30 grams was recovered from plough soil context (1000) in Trench 10 (Figure

10.49 (1)). The form can be dated *c*. AD 280–360 (Gillam 1970: 69).

This sherd represents the first evidence for later Roman occupation of the hillfort. Interestingly, a second rim sherd from a Mancetter-Hartshill (MAH WH) hammerhead mortaria was recovered during a fieldwalking exercise undertaken by the Sandstone Ridge Trust in 2013 (Figure 10.49 (2)). This sherd is of similar form and date to the find from Trench 10 but is not from the same vessel, indicating that the late Roman pottery is unlikely to be from casual loss and is more likely to be derived from occupation of the site.

Anglo-Saxon pottery

Dan Garner

A single body sherd of early Anglo-Saxon pottery weighing 16 grams was recovered from context (14001) in Trench 14. The sherd came from a layer overlying the backfilled inner ditch, which was attributed to the Varley excavation backfill from the 1930s. Unfortunately, the sherd was broken during excavation, and of the four fragments recovered, only the two larger fragments can be re-joined.

Fabric: The sherd is from a handmade vessel and the fabric is fired to a black/dark grey colour with the internal surface being a uniform orange/buff colour. The clay has frequent inclusions of white mica and sub-rounded quartz sand. There are larger poorly sorted inclusions of angular dark red/brown and black fine grained rock up to 5mm in size which are probably a deliberately added temper.

Surface Treatment: The external surface has been deliberately rusticated by pinching the wet clay prior to firing. Vessels exhibiting this type of surface treatment are sometimes referred to as 'pinched pots'. The technique is usually associated with Anglo-Saxon domestic pottery of the 5th and 6th century AD where it is found on lugged vessels and bucket-shaped cooking pots (Kennet 1985: 28). Pottery with this style of surface treatment is well represented on pagan Anglo-Saxon settlement sites such as Mucking (Hamerow 1993) and West Stow (West 1985), where it is clearly part of the domestic ensemble. It has been suggested that this rustication was not a form of decoration, but rather to facilitate the handling of slippery containers or large storage vessels (Hamerow 1993: 35).

The recovery of pagan Anglo-Saxon pottery in Cheshire is unprecedented as the area is considered to be aceramic from the end of the Roman period until the 10th century AD. The closest comparable find of pottery of this date is from Red Bank in Manchester (Morris 1983: 7). The context from which the sherd was recovered makes the find a residual object; however, it does provide another tantalising piece of evidence for re-use of the hillfort prior to its documented refortification in AD 914.

Post-medieval pottery

Dan Garner

A total of 194 sherds of post-medieval pottery weighing 2.356 kg were recovered from the excavations (Figure 10.50). A key to the fabric codes used in the post-medieval pottery catalogue is provided below in Figure 10.51. All of the post-medieval pottery was recovered

FABRIC / CONTEXT	BASALT	BBG	BISCUIT	BRWST	CREAM	MIDP	MIDY	MOCHA	MOTTW	PEARL	SCBW	SLIPW	STONEW	TORTO	WSGST	Total
100		3						2		2						7
101		5			5											10
105		2	1		3					10		1				17
300		1								1						2
400		5														5
403	1	6	1	1	1	1				4	3	1	1		1	21
422		6														6
445			2													2
501		20			3			3		14	9	6			3	58
506		1								1						2
509		1		1	1		1		1	1	1	1				8
700		2			1					2				1		6
800		6					1			1						8
14000					2					10						12
14001		3		1	6		1			9					1	21
15000				1	1		2			4					1	9
Total	**1**	**61**	**3**	**5**	**23**	**1**	**2**	**8**	**1**	**59**	**13**	**8**	**1**	**1**	**7**	**194**

FIGURE 10.50 POST-MEDIEVAL POTTERY BY CONTEXT AND SHERD COUNT.

Fabric Code	Fabric	Date
BASALT	Agate ware	c. AD 1740+
BBG	Black & brown glazed ware	16th to 19th century
BISCUIT	Biscuit-fired ware	18th/19th century
BRWST	Brown stoneware	17th to 19th century
CREAM	Cream ware	c. AD 1760+
MIDP	Midlands Purple	16th to 18th century
MIDY	Midlands Yellow	17th to 18th century
MOCHA	Mocha ware	19th/20th century
MOTTW	Mottled ware	c. AD 1680+
PEARL	Pearl glazed earthenware	c. AD 1780+
SCBW	Slip-coated buff ware	c. AD 1740+
SLIPW	Slip ware	17th to 19th century
STONEW	Stoneware	19th/20th century
TORTO	Tortoiseshell decorated ware	c. AD 1740+
WSGST	White salt-glazed stoneware	c. AD 1720+

FIGURE 10.51 KEY TO POST-MEDIEVAL POTTERY FABRIC CODES.

from demonstrably modern contexts which were mainly associated with the backfilling of Varley's excavations or the modern topsoil.

The post-medieval pottery assemblage from the Eddisbury excavations 2010-11 can be seen as typical of material recovered from post-medieval deposits in Cheshire and is probably derived from midden spreading on the adjacent ploughed field. However, much of the earlier 17th and 18th century material occurs residually in 20th century contexts and as such has little potential for further study beyond providing basic site chronology.

The glass

Dan Garner

A total of 61 fragments of glass were recovered from seven of the evaluation trenches and these included: 52 fragments of post-medieval vessel glass; eight fragments of post-medieval window glass; and one fragment of possible Roman window glass. The glass recovered from the evaluation trenches is summarised in Figure 10.52.

Trench	Context	Colour	Vessel	Date	Comment
1	100	Clear	Mould-blown Bottle	c. 1900+	2 base and 6 body fragments
1	100	Clear	Mould-blown Bottle	c. 1900+	5 decorated body fragments
1	100	Blue	Mould-blown Bottle	c. 1900+	1 neck fragment
1	100	Green	Hand-blown Bottle	Post-medieval	1 body fragment
1	101	Brown	Hand-blown Bottle	Post-medieval	1 body fragment
1	101	Green	Window	Post-medieval	1 fragment
1	105	Clear	Mould-blown Bottle	c. 1900+	1 decorated body fragment – same vessel as (100)
1	105	Clear	Mould-blown Bottle	c. 1900+	1 body fragment
1	105	Green	Hand-blown Bottle	Post-medieval	1 body fragment
3	300	Clear	Mould-blown Bottle	c. 1900+	4 base fragments
3	300	Green	Hand-blown Bottle	Post-medieval	1 body fragment
3	300	Clear	Window	Post-medieval	1 fragment
4	400	Clear	Indeterminate	Post-medieval	1 body fragment
4	400	Blue/green	Window?	Roman	1 fragment
4	403	Clear	Window	Post-medieval	1 fragment
4	403	Green	Window	Post-medieval	1 fragment with partial graffiti scratched on to 1 surface ' ...narc...'
4	403	Green	Window	Post-medieval	2 fragments
4	403	Green	Hand-blown Onion Bottle	Early 18th cent	1 neck fragment
4	403	Green	Hand-blown Bottle	Post-medieval	2 body fragments
4	403	Clear	Bottle	c. 1900+	1 body fragment
4	422	Green	Hand-blown Bottle	Post-medieval	1 base and 1 body fragment
7	700	Clear	Window	Post-medieval	1 fragment
8	800	Clear	Window	Post-medieval	2 fragments
8	800	Green	Hand-blown Bottle	Post-medieval	2 body fragments.
14	14000	Green	Hand-blown Bottle	Post-medieval	4 body fragments
14	14001	Brown	Hand-blown Bottle	Post-medieval	3 body fragments
14	14001	Clear	Mould-blown Bottle	c. 1900+	5 body fragments. Hexagonal form
14	14001	Clear	Mould-blown Bottle	c. 1900+	1 rim and 2 body fragments. Partial legend '...RO...'.
15	15003	Blue	Mould-blown Bottle	c. 1900+	3 body fragments. Square form
15	15003	Clear	Mould-blown Bottle	c. 1900+	1 base fragment with partial legend '...ME'. Torpedo form

FIGURE 10.52 THE GLASS BY CONTEXT.

FIGURE 10.53 POST-MEDIEVAL GLASS WINDOW FRAGMENT WITH PARTIAL GRAFFITO FROM CONTEXT (403).

Trench	Context	Stem	Bowl	Mouthpiece	Stamp	Comments
1	100	1	-	-	-	
1	101	1	5	-		Moulded leaf and branch decoration, 19th century
3	300	-	2	-	-	Join
4	403	4	2	1	-	
4	427	-	1	-	-	Moulded in to the shape of a boot, 19th century
5	501	3	-	-	-	
8	800	1	1	-	-	
14	14001	2	1	-	-	Leaf moulding down the mould joint, Chester 1810–40
15	15000	-	-	1	-	
15	15007	-	1	-	-	Chester 1640–80
	Totals	12	13	2	-	

FIGURE 10.54 CLAY TOBACCO PIPE BY CONTEXT.

The 52 post-medieval vessel glass fragments recovered from the evaluation were all thought to be from bottle forms with the exception of one indeterminate fragment. From this material 17 fragments were from vessels manufactured using the hand-blown technique; only one large fragment of bottle neck from context (403) was closely identifiable as an 'onion' bottle form, dateable to the early 18th century. The remaining 35 fragments were derived from a maximum of nine vessels all of which were manufactured using the mould-blown technique associated with later post-medieval/modern mass production. None of the later vessels were complete enough to make any suggestions as to their original contents.

FIGURE 10.55 DECORATED 19TH CENTURY CLAY TOBACCO PIPE BOWL FRAGMENTS FROM CONTEXTS (429), (14001) AND (101) (LEFT TO RIGHT).

Among the eight fragments of post-medieval window glass there was one fragment from context (403) which had a graffito scratched on to its surface. The graffito was executed in small neat hand writing and appears to read '…(m)arc(h)…' or '…mewc …' which is clearly incomplete but may indicate part of a date (Figure 10.53).

There was also a single fragment of possible Roman window glass from context (400), which was blue/green in colour and had rough pitted surfaces in keeping with manufacture using the casting technique, favoured in the earlier Roman period. Whilst the fragment was recovered from a modern context there are other Roman artefacts from the hillfort interior and ditch fills which support a Roman presence at Eddisbury.

The clay tobacco pipe

Dan Garner

A total of 27 fragments of clay tobacco pipe were recovered from the excavations and are summarised in Figure 10.54.

The 13 bowl fragments in the assemblage included three bowls with moulded decoration of 19th century type. Two of the examples had common 19th century decorative

Trench	Context	Type	Date
1	100	Nail (round section)	Post-medieval
1	105	Nail (round section)	Post-medieval
1	105	Barbed wire x2	Modern
4	400	Wire staple	Modern
4	403	Wire	Modern
4	403	Strap hinge (door)	Post-medieval
4	403	Nail (square section)	Post-medieval
4	403	Wire staple	Modern
4	403	Rod of triangular section	
4	422	Nail (round section) x2	Post-medieval
4	422	Indeterminate	
14	14000	Harness fitting	Post-medieval
14	14000	Nail (square section) x4	Post-medieval
14	14000	Lever with plastic handle	Modern
14	14001	Nail (square section) x5	Post-medieval

FIGURE 10.56 IRON OBJECTS BY CONTEXT.

styles, but the third was a novelty item shaped in to the form of a boot (Figure 10.55).

One pipe bowl form was of a 17th century type with a small spur with no evidence for a maker's stamp. The form is comparable to pipes from the Chester series dated c. 1640 to c.1680 (such as Rutter and Davey 1980: 219 figure 79 (56)).

The clay pipe assemblage mainly serves to provide additional dating material for the site narrative. Unfortunately, all of the contexts which produced dateable tobacco pipe fragments are modern and the objects are therefore residual.

The metalwork

Dan Garner

Iron

A total of 24 iron objects were recovered from the excavations at Eddisbury during 2010–11 and these are summarised in Figure 10.56. All of the objects were recovered from demonstrably modern contexts, which were mainly associated with the backfilling of Varley's excavations or the modern topsoil. Fourteen of the objects were identifiable as nails, with a further five being sections of wire which are probably associated with previous episodes of livestock fencing and repair. The most unusual object came from Trench 14 and was an iron lever which still had a black plastic handle attached to one end. The object is thought to be from a mechanism for launching clay pigeons and it was associated with the finding of many fragments of ceramic clay pigeon (ceramic discs used as the target in clay pigeon shooting) in topsoil context (14000). None of the ironwork was thought to relate to activity on the hillfort in antiquity.

Copper-alloy

A total of ten copper-alloy objects were recovered from the excavations between 2010 and 2011. All but one of the objects were associated with the use of firearms. Seven of the objects were complete or nearly complete .303 gun cartridges and of these four exhibited the crimped ends usually associated with blank rounds. This included one from Trench 1 context (100); two from Trench 4 context (403); and four from Trench 14 context (14001).These items strongly suggest military training on the hilltop after the backfilling of Varley's

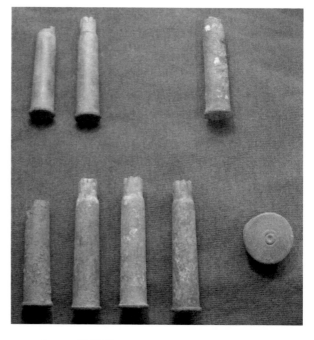

FIGURE 10.57 COPPER-ALLOY GUNSHOT CARTRIDGES.

FIGURE 10.58 COPPER-ALLOY DISC BEARING A CHI-RHO SYMBOL ON ONE SIDE.

excavations and the most likely context for this would be during World War II (1939–45).

Two of the objects were the base caps from shot gun cartridges, one from Trench 3 context (300) and one from Trench 14 context (14001), which had been stamped with the name of the manufacturer 'ELEY BROs LONDON' and the gauge 'No 12'. The rest of the cartridge would most likely have been paper, which has subsequently perished. These objects may be associated with military training or alternatively it may have a sporting association (as indicated by the fragments of clay pigeon described above) (Figure 10.57).

The final copper-alloy object from Trench 1 context (105) is more unusual. It appears to be either a bronze disc or a very worn coin. Both surfaces of the disc/coin have been marked in antiquity by a number of scored lines: on the obverse the scoring has created a fairly distinctive 'P' above an 'X' which is apparently centred within the circumference of the object. This combined symbol is a Chi-Rho, an early Christian symbol usually associated with late Roman Christianity of the 4th century AD. The reverse of the disc/coin is less easy to explain as it consists of a series of between four and six parallel vertical lines, with a pair of horizontal lines running along the top and bottom of the verticals (Figure 10.58).The design appears deliberate but the meaning remains uncertain. This object is a rare indication of

early Christianity in the region as a whole; it is certainly the first example of a late Roman/sub-Roman Chi-Rho to have been published in Cheshire.

The worked flint

Dan Garner

A total of eight pieces of worked flint were recovered from the excavation trenches and these can be ascribed a broad earlier prehistoric date. The individual pieces are described below by trench and are illustrated in Figure 10.59.

Trench 1, context (102):

1: A broken end from a plano-convex knife in a light grey flint. Probably of Neolithic/early Bronze Age date.

2: A waste flake in a dark grey flint with white cortex surviving on one surface. Retouch at one end and along one edge suggests it was utilised as a side scraper. Neolithic/early Bronze Age in date.

Trench 3, context (302):

A waste flake in a light grey flint with white surface patination. There is no evidence of secondary working and it is unlikely to have been utilised as a tool (not illustrated).

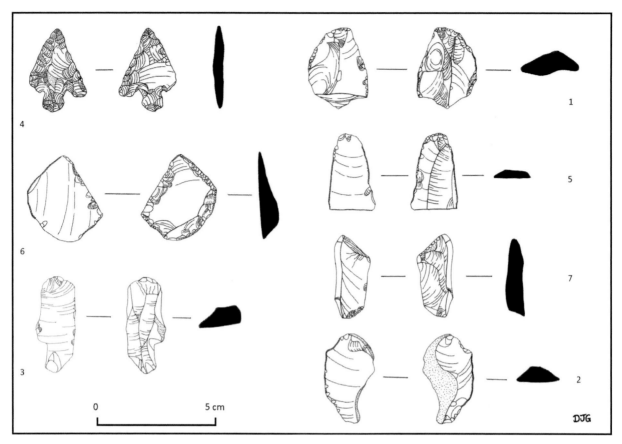

FIGURE 10.59 THE WORKED FLINT

Trench 7, context (700):

3: A flake in a honey-coloured flint with a small patch of cortex surviving on one surface. Retouch along one edge suggests it was utilised as a side scraper or blade. Neolithic/early Bronze Age in date.

Trench 10, plough soil context (1000):

4: An almost complete barbed and tanged arrowhead. The arrowhead is manufactured from a pale grey flint with pressure flaked invasive retouch covering the entire surface of both sides. The object can be classed as a 'fancy barbed and tanged arrowhead' of Ballycare type 13 (Butler, 2005: 163). Early Bronze Age (2500–1500 BC) in date.

Trench 14, context (14001):

5: A broken end from a plano-convex knife in a light grey flint. Probably of Neolithic/early Bronze Age date.

Trench 15, context (15001):

6: A complete gunflint in a dark grey flint. The object appears to be a gunflint used in the firing mechanism of a flintlock firearm. A second gunflint was recovered from the interior of the hillfort during fieldwalking by the Sandstone Ridge Trust in 2013. Post-medieval in date.

Trench 15, context (15003):

7: A flake in a dark grey flint. Retouch at one end and along one edge suggests it was utilised as a blade. Neolithic/early Bronze Age in date.

Whilst most of the worked flint objects can only be ascribed a broad date and were retrieved as residual items in later contexts, it is notable that four of the pieces (from Trenches 1, 14 and 15) came from the vicinity of an *in situ* early Bronze Age hearth feature in Trench 1. However, the possibility that some of these objects date from the Neolithic period cannot be entirely ruled out as previously recorded objects from Eddisbury of Neolithic date (such as fragments from a grooved ware urn) point to earlier periods of prehistoric activity on the hill top. The occurrence of one later flint object in the form of a gunflint highlights the use of flint as a specialist tool on the Eddisbury hilltop during the post-medieval period.

The decorated sandstone boulder

George Nash

An Old Red Sandstone boulder, recovered from the excavation within the entrance area of Eddisbury hillfort in the summer of 2010, contained on one of its surfaces multiple cupmarks. The likely date of these engravings is between the late Neolithic and the late Bronze Age (*c.* 3000–700 cal BCE). The original provenance of the

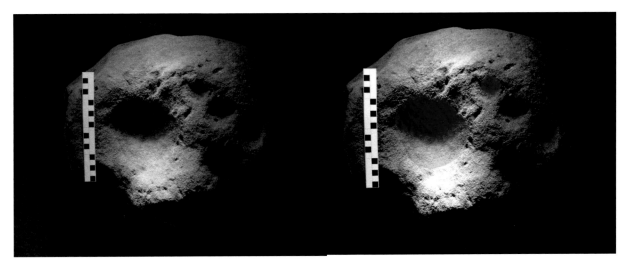

Figure 10.60 Decorated sandstone boulder from Trench 4.

boulder is unknown as it was recovered from within the backfill deposit of W. J. Varley's excavation trench in 1936. According to the current excavator and based on Varley's excavation notes, the stone may have originated from a blocking/collapse deposit/feature from within the southeast entrance of the hillfort (Garner personal communication).

The irregular-shaped boulder, measuring roughly 56 x 42 x 28cm, is made from local laminated course-grained Old Red Sandstone. The granular matrix contains small pebble inclusions and pebble scaring/pitting. The fractured surface of the stone shows evidence of damage, probably the result of rough handling when it was (re) deposited into the backfill.

The (presumably) upper surface contains a series of motifs that are usually associated with Neolithic/Bronze Age burial-ritual deposition (i.e. found within or close to cairns and barrows). Three deeply gouged cupmarks arranged into an equilateral triangle are located on an elevated section of the upper surface; each measuring between 5 and 6cm in diameter (shown in red on Figure 10.60). A smaller, shallower fourth cupmark measuring c. 3cm in diameter is located between the tri-group and a larger cupmark (shown in green on Figure 10.60). To the left of the tri-group is a large shallow slightly ovate cupmark that measures 19 x 16cm in diameter. This motif is gouged onto a lower section of the upper surface of the boulder.

Prehistoric rock-art from the Welsh Marches is infrequent with only three sites recorded north of the Welsh Marches: Caer Alyn hillfort (Wrexham), The Calderstones (Liverpool) and a recent discovery on the Wirral (since the publication of this report, the author along with rock art specialists Daniel Arsenault and Aron Mazel have concluded that the Wirral assemblage is not prehistoric). A further five sites are known in Herefordshire and three in Gloucestershire (Nash 2007). No sites are recorded in Shropshire and until the discovery of the boulder at

Eddisbury hillfort, no sites were recorded in Cheshire. Therefore, the Eddisbury Hill boulder is a significant discovery. Concerning context, three decorated boulders and stones originate from hillfort sites: Nottingham hillfort (Gloucestershire), Caer Alyn hillfort (Wrexham) and Eddisbury hillfort; each discovered stone possessing cupmarks. The small boulder from Nottingham hillfort comprises a large cup-and-ring with groove, whilst a recently discovered sandstone slab fragment from Caer Alyn comprised three shallow-pecked cupmarks.

The gouged cupmarks and the way they are arranged on the Eddisbury Hill boulder have similarities with cupmark arrangements on several stones from the Calderstones monument in Liverpool – Stones C and E (see Nash & Standford 2010).

Based on its size, this boulder should be classified as portable art (Watson 2009). The shape and size of the boulder suggests that it could be moved around the immediate landscape possibly as a portable shrine. The date of the Eddisbury Hill boulder is probably middle (c. 1500–1000 BCE) to late Bronze Age (c. 1000–700 BCE), although one cannot discount an earlier date (see Waddington et al. 2005). This assumption is based on many decorated boulders (with cupmarks) found elsewhere, in particular, from northern Britain (see Beckensall 2009).

In comparison to other decorated boulders and stones found in Britain, the Eddisbury Hill boulder can be considered one of a group of portable stones that contains simple multiple motifs of varying size; a rare occurrence in the northern Marches. A large number of hillforts (or hill enclosures) both inside and outside the Welsh Marches show clear evidence of earlier prehistoric activity with the survival of early and middle Bronze Age barrows and cairns for example. These earlier sites appear to have commanded respect by Iron Age fort builders and users. If this is the case, it is conceivable that further decorated stones from Eddisbury hillfort await future discovery.

Other Stone
Dan Garner

Five other worked stone objects were recovered from the excavations and whilst they can all be attributed to modern contexts associated with Varley's excavation backfills, they are likely to be derived from occupation of the hilltop in antiquity.

The objects are illustrated in Figure 10.61 and include:

1: A fragment from a pale grey sandstone saddle-quern from Trench 4 context (403);

2: A fragment from a red sandstone mortar from Trench 4 context (403);

3: A fragment of a light grey sandstone hone from Trench 4 context (403);

4: A fragment of a red sandstone hone from Trench 14 context (14001);

5: A fragment of red sandstone saddle-quern found on the surface during an initial site walkover of the Merrick's Hill area.

The two fragments of saddle-quern are likely to be derived from prehistoric activity on the hilltop but little more can be inferred from these residual objects. The stone mortar from Trench 4 is of uncertain date but would not be out of place in a prehistoric context. The hones from Trenches 4 and 14 are of uncertain date and given the modern contexts from which they were recovered it is difficult to infer anything further about their provenance. The worked stone objects mainly serve to highlight the potential for the recovery of this artefact type from the hilltop during any future investigation of the site.

Palaeoenvironmental Sample Assessment
John Carrott, Gemma Martin and Alison Foster (abridged by Dan Garner)

The following overview by phase groups is abridged from an unpublished report by Palaeoecology Research Services (Report no. PRS 2012/12) dated April 2012. The full report is available in the online appendix.

A total of thirty-three samples were assessed by Palaeoecology Research Services Limited, Kingston upon Hull (PRS), for their bioarchaeological potential. Further analysis of 18 of these sediment samples was subsequently undertaken from 16 deposits, together with four additional bulk samples and four spot samples from the excavations in 2011.

Phases 1 to 3 (pre-hillfort)

The deposits yielded little interpretable environmental evidence and the scarcity of material suggests that either the occupation activity during this phase was relatively short-lived, or that the main focus for the activity was situated away from the area under investigation. Traces of cereal residues and remains of wild/weed fruits/seeds hint at the consumption of (?hulled) barley and certain scrubland species including hazelnut, sloe/plum/cherry and bramble, which may have been growing within the locality. There was also evidence for the use of heather, which appears to have been collected for fuel.

Phases 5 to 8 (construction/use of hillfort)

The greatest evidence for crop processing activities and dietary indicators was associated with the ramparts. There was evidence for the consumption of glume wheats, most notably emmer and spelt, as well as bread wheat-type and hulled (and perhaps naked) barley, although there was insufficient material to be able to ascertain potential crop preferences or arable husbandry regimes. The cereals identified were typical of those cultivated during the Iron Age period in Britain (Greig 1991), although the traces of oat are perhaps more likely to be of a wild species, since oat is not known to be widely cultivated in England until the post-Roman periods.

The general paucity of domestic and/or crop processing residues from the main phases associated with the construction/use of the hillfort is interesting; whether this is due to the excavation strategy of targeting previous excavation trenches, or whether the composition of the assemblages are a true reflection of the scale of production/consumption, is difficult to determine. Where evidence for crop processing activities has been identified, the composition of the charred cereal residues suggests processing on a small-scale, possibly day-to-day, basis. The Bronze Age/early Iron Age site of Beeston Castle, produced a similar range of cultigens and low densities of charred remains.

There was a little evidence for the continued exploitation of certain scrubland-type species for consumption and/or domestic purposes, most notably hazel, bramble and sloe/plum/cherry-type (*Prunus*). This was substantiated by the charcoal evidence which, in the main, reflected a continued emphasis on wood from scrub/light woodland and heath being used for fuel, with only a little from more substantial tress. The exception to this was a charcoal-rich layer within the southern guardroom (Context 424), where the assemblage was exclusively of oak. This deposit and a second similar one in the same location (Context 417), were originally considered to be possibly the remnants of wattle and daub. The identifiable

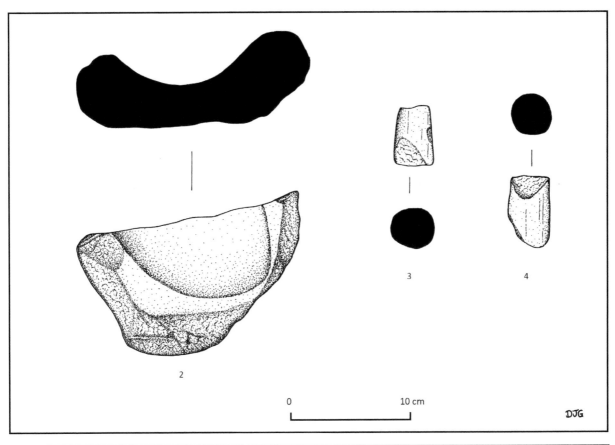

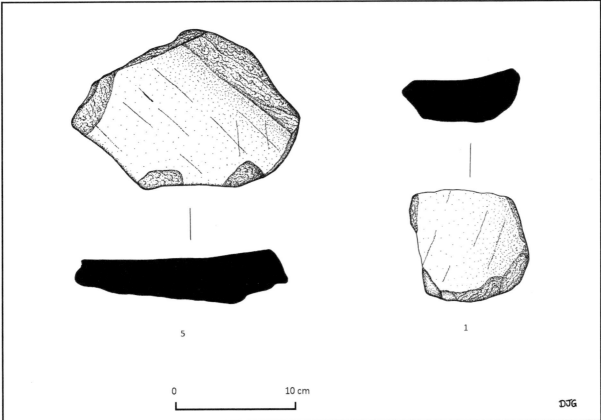

FIGURE 10.61 OTHER WORKED STONE OBJECTS.

Sample	Declination	Inclination	MAD (°)	Demagnetisation
2A	51.4	84.5	2.4	Thermal
2B	33.5	76.1		1 step 100mT
2C	90.9	58.4	8.1	AF
2D	3.4	70.6	2	AF
3A	-2.6	84	2.8	Thermal
3B	48.7	81.3	3.4	Thermal
3C	355	78.7	4.5	Thermal
4A	17.8	77	2.5	AF
4B	-40.4	68.2	8.9	AF
4C	95.8	59.9	11.3	AF
6A	6	66.9		NRM
6B	9.2	65.4		NRM
6C	11.7	63.7		NRM
6D	20	62.3		NRM
6E	19.1	63.3	3.1	Thermal
7A	66.6	69.4	4.6	Thermal
7B	83.9	71	6	Thermal
8A	14.1	65.4		NRM
8B	23.6	62.8	3.7	Thermal
8C	20.5	63.6		NRM
8D	9.5	67.9		NRM

FIGURE 10.62 DIRECTIONS OF REMANENT MAGNETISATIONS AND DEMAGNETISATION TREATMENT. MAXIMUM ANGLES OF DEVIATION GREATER THAN 5° WERE EXCLUDED FROM THE FINAL ANALYSIS. DIRECTIONS ARE NOT VARIATION CORRECTED.

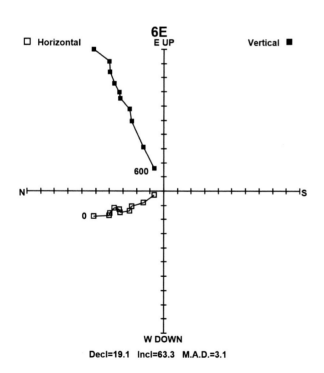

FIGURE 10.63. VECTOR ENDPOINT DIAGRAM OF THE THERMAL DEMAGNETISATION OF SAMPLE 6E, ONE OF THE DRILLED SANDSTONE CORES.

charcoal from Context 417 was mainly hazel roundwood (of less than 20 years of wood growth) and so could certainly be from a former wattle and daub construction and it is possible that, although oak is unlikely to have been used as wattle, the charcoal from Context 424 could derive from an associated structural timber.

Phase 11 (post-use/abandonment of hillfort)

This phase of activity relates to a number of Roman/sub-Roman features that cut into the ramparts/ditch fills of the (?abandoned) hillfort. A series of six samples from five deposits were taken from a feature identified as a possible clay oven (Trench 7, context 724) which was set into the top of the inner rampart. The function of the feature remained uncertain on the basis of the biological evidence; there were little or no domestic residues associated with any of the sampled deposits and consequently nothing to confirm or refute the interpretation of the feature as a possible clay oven. Overall, the charcoal assemblages reflected a continuing reliance on wood from scrub/light woodland for use as fuel; although small oak twigs could perhaps have been casually collected as kindling or, conceivably, derived from trimming of larger logs in preparation for their use as structural timbers.

Archaeomagnetic Dating Report

Neil Suttie (abridged by Dan Garner)

Introduction

Excavations at Eddisbury hillfort (53.22°N, 2.67°W) during the summer of 2010, revealed a rounded burnt feature composed of reddened clay and soil with inclusions of heated sandstone, overlying the northern ramparts of the hillfort (Trench 7, context 724). Neil Suttie of the Geomagnetism Laboratory at the University of Liverpool was invited to sample the feature for the purpose of archaeomagnetic dating and attended the site on 13 October 2010, with colleagues Florian Stark and Megan Thomas.

Archaeomagnetic Sampling and Analysis

The feature was sampled by taking oriented monoliths, 10–20cm across, set in plaster. In total eight individual monoliths were taken. Plaster of Paris was mixed and poured over a part of the feature and its surface levelled using a sheet of Perspex and a bubble level. Once dry a magnetic compass was used to mark north on the plaster. Owing to the conditions a sunsight could not be used and there is a small chance that the results given here could have been affected by the presence of local field irregularities, although there was no indication of these. Once in the laboratory, blocks 1–5 and 7 were cut into 2cm cubes and blocks 6 and 8 had one inch diameter cores drilled from sandstone inclusions. Magnetic susceptibilities of samples taken from each block were measured on a Bartington MS-2 susceptibility bridge. All samples had strongly enhanced susceptibilities, in the range $5–60 \times 10^{-3}$ (SI). The natural remanent magnetisations (NRM) were measured on an AGICO JR-6 magnetometer. The NRM were in the range of 2–10A/m for the clay and 0.1–0.5 A/m for the sandstones. In all cases the high ratio of NRM to induced magnetisation suggests a thermoremanent magnetisation acquired when the feature last cooled. Samples were stepwise thermally demagnetised or AF demagnetised to check that the magnetisation had a single component isolated by principal component analysis (Kirschvink 1980). When the maximum angle of deviation (MAD) was more than 5°, the direction

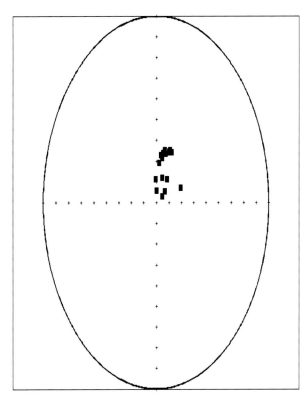

FIGURE 10.64 DIRECTIONS OF THE 17 SAMPLES USED IN THE ANALYSIS. ALL DIRECTIONS HAVE BEEN VARIATION CORRECTED.

was not used to calculate the mean. Results are shown in Figure 10.62. Blocks 1 and 5 were too unconsolidated to be measured. Only one sample from blocks 6 and 8 were demagnetised as the other samples are being kept for archaeointensity analysis. However, these exhibited a single component of magnetisation (see Figure 10.62) so the NRMs of the remaining samples have been used in the final calculation.

Dating

The International Geomagnetic Reference Field gives the local declination as 3°W at the time of sampling. Correcting the values in Figure 10.63 by this amount yields a mean direction of 21.7°E with an inclination of 71.4° and an α_{95} of 4.2°, for the 17 selected samples with MAD < 6°. Figure 10.64 shows the distribution of the directions in a circular plot.

To date the firing of the feature the mean direction is compared with the UK reference curve described in Zananiri *et al.* (2007). Results are displayed using the software of Pavón-Carrasco (2011) in terms of Bayesian confidence intervals following Lanos (2004) in Figure 10.65.

The estimated 95% confidence interval for the date of firing of the feature is

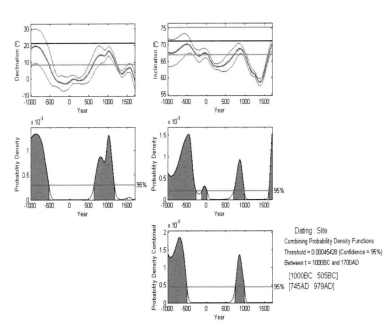

FIGURE 10.65. BAYESIAN CONFIDENCE INTERVALS FOLLOWING LANOS (2004) USING SOFTWARE OF PAVÓN-CARRASCO (2011) AND THE UK SECULAR VARIATION CURVE OF ZANANIRI *ET AL.*(2007).

745–980AD, or an earlier date spanning the first half of the 1st millennium BC. The earlier date can be considered unlikely on archaeological grounds as the feature post-dates the main phase of the hillfort. Taking this into account, the most likely date determined archaeomagnetically is 860AD ±70 years at 65% confidence.

Summary

Of the 21 individual samples taken from six independently orientated blocks, four were rejected as they failed to give single component magnetic vectors during demagnetisation. The remaining 17 samples were all used to calculate the following result.

N=17/21

Declination 21.7°	Inclination 71.4°	α_{95} 4.2°

Date of last firing   **745–980 AD (95%)**

860AD ± 70 at 65% confidence.

Trench/Context number	Sample Code	Luminescence Age (years before 2010)	Central Date	1 σ error (68% confidence)	Calendrical Bandwidth (68% confidence)	Calendrical Bandwidth (2σ, 95% confidence)
T1/Context (118). A brown clay deposit from within a possible hut or kerb cairn beneath the inner rampart	LV447	5,350 +/- 1000	3340 BC	1000 years	4340–2340 BC	5340–1340 BC
T3/Context (331). A possible counterscarp bank deposit beneath the outer rampart	LV444	2,560 +/- 230	550 BC	230 years	780–320 BC	1,010–90 BC
T4/Context (405). A primary inner rampart deposit	LV443	2,510 +/- 170	500 BC	170 years	670–330 BC	840–160 BC
T7/Context (725). A mid-grey-brown silt-clay that formed a phase of inner hillfort rampart building	LV450	2,250 +/- 580	240 BC	580 years	820 BC–340 AD	1,400 B –920 AD

FIGURE 10.66 RESULTS OF THE LUMINESCENCE DATING.

Report on luminescence age estimation

Barbara Mauz and Susan Packman

Eight samples (laboratory codes LV443-450) were taken from excavations on Eddisbury hillfort, in collaboration with Dan Garner, Project Officer (Archaeology), Habitats and Hillforts, during September 2010.

Sample preparation:
1. Removal of carbonate with 10%v/v HCl.
2. Removal of organics with H_2O_2.
3. Dry sieving to obtain 200–300 µm grains.
4. Mineral separation using heavy liquids at 2.62 s.g. and 2.76 s.g.
5. 48% HF for 40 minutes.
6. Re-sieving with 180 µm sieve.

Luminescence tests indicated poor sensitivity, thermal transfer, poor recycling ratios, presence of an ultrafast component and occasional feldspar contamination.

The reliability of the OSL ages depends upon the statistical approach which, in turn, depends on the 'depositional process' of the quartz samples. We assumed here that daylight exposure occurred when the sand from which the samples were collected was shovelled into the wall construction. Such a procedure exposes only some grains to daylight and hence the samples are composed of fully and partially bleached grains. The statistical parameters (σ, c, k) confirm this hypothesis for LV443 and LV444 (Figure 10.66). The parameters of LV450 were not conclusive and allowed, in principle, three different statistical models to be employed. The sample was described as being affected by bioturbation (crotovina) which excluded one of the three models. The age of LV450-A is derived from the assumption that grains measured are from one population and bioturbation affected only a small percentage of the grains. The age of LV450-B is derived from the assumption that the highest frequency in the histogram represents the host population of grains which obtained younger grains from the surface through bioturbation. The latter is in agreement with field observation. Within error limits LV444 and LV443 return the same age.

Radiocarbon Dating

Pete Marshall, Dan Garner and Christine Prior

Introduction

Twelve single entity samples (Ashmore 1999) were submitted for radiocarbon dating to the Rafter Radiocarbon Laboratory, New Zealand and Beta Analytic. The nine charcoal and carbonised plant remains samples dated at Rafter were processed using the acid/alkali/acid protocol of Mook and Waterbolk (1985) and measured by Accelerator Mass Spectrometry (AMS) as described by Zondervan and Sparks (1997). The three samples submitted to Beta Analytic were pretreated following the standard acid/alkali/acid procedure (Mook and Waterbolk 1985) and dated by AMS. Both laboratories maintain continual programmes of quality assurance procedures, in addition to participation in international inter-comparisons (Scott 2003; Scott *et al.* 2010) which indicate no laboratory offsets and demonstrate the validity of the precision quoted.

Results

The radiocarbon results are given in Figure 10.67, and are quoted in accordance with the international standard known as the Trondheim convention (Stuiver and Kra 1986). They are conventional radiocarbon ages (Stuiver and Polach 1977).

Calibration

The calibrations of the results, relating the radiocarbon measurements directly to calendar dates, are given in Figure 10.67 and in outline Figure 10.68. All have been calculated using the calibration curve of Reimer *et al.* (2009) and the computer program OxCal v4.0.5 (Bronk Ramsey 1995; 1998; 2001; 2009). The calibrated date ranges cited in the text are those for 95% confidence. They are quoted in the form recommended by Mook (1986), with the end points rounded outwards to 10 years or 5 years for errors less than 25 years. The ranges in plain type in Figure 10.67 have been calculated according to the maximum intercept method (Stuiver and Reimer 1986). All other ranges are derived from the probability method (Stuiver and Reimer 1993) (Figures 10.68 to 10.72).

Interpretation

The stratigraphic model

The model shown in Figure 10.68, based on the stratigraphic relationship between samples from individual trenches, shows good overall agreement (Amodel=78). It excludes NZA-36669 from beneath the hillfort rampart in Trench 1 as this pit clearly pre-dates construction of the hillfort by a considerable period of time. The model estimates that activity associated with the hillfort dates to 860–525 cal BC (95% probability; start_eddisbury; Figure 10.68) and probably 750–570 cal

Laboratory Number	Sample Number	Material & context	Radiocarbon Age (BP)	d¹³C (‰)	Calibrated date range (95% confidence)
Trench 1					
NZA-36669	[122] 26/T	Carbonised hazelnut shell fragment from the charcoal-rich fill (122) of a sub-circular feature (126 - ?hearth) sealed beneath the hillfort rampart from Trench 1.	3422±25	−26.6	1870–1640 cal BC
Trench 3					
NZA-36654	[312] 5/T	Charcoal, roundwood indet. from a lens of charcoal-rich silt [312] near the base of the outer ditch (313) in Trench 3.	2251±25	−24.9	400–200 cal BC
Beta-319723	E1076305IC	Charcoal from (305)	2260±30	−23.8	390–210 cal BC
Beta-319724	E1076309IC	Charcoal from (309)	1930±30	−24.9	cal AD 1–130
Trench 4					
NZA-36656	[442] 20/T (B)	Carbonised emmer/spelt wheat grain from a sub-circular deposit of charcoal rich silt (442) that overlay the western tail of rampart deposit (405). Initially, deposit (442) was thought to be the base of a hearth, but the lack of evidence for *in situ* burning suggest that it was a dump of burnt material derived from hearth sweepings. Trench 4.	2347±20	−22.7	410–385 cal BC

FIGURE 10.67 SUMMARY OF THE RADIOCARBON RESULTS FROM THE EDDISBURY SAMPLES. (1)

NZA-36591	[442] 20/T (A)	Carbonised emmer/spelt wheat grain from a sub-circular deposit of charcoal rich silt (442) that overlay the western tail of rampart deposit (405). Initially, deposit (442) was thought to be the base of a hearth, but the lack of evidence for *in situ* burning suggest that it was a dump of burnt material derived from hearth sweepings. Trench 4.	2297±25	−23.4	410–260 cal BC
NZA-36592	[417] 23/T	Carbonised hazelnut shell fragment from [417] a charcoal-rich silt containing large fragments of carbonised wood and lumps of burnt clay that overlay the floor deposit (418) within the southern guardroom. Trench 4.	2176±25	−25.9	360–160 cal BC
Trench 7					
NZA-36648	[718] 29/T	Carbonised barley grain from [718] a layer of mid-grey silt-sand which contained a distinct area of charred material including fragments of burnt bone, from pre-rampart activity in Trench 7.	2483±25	−23.9	770–410 cal BC
NZA-36593	[725] 35/T (A)	Carbonised emmer/spelt wheat grain from [725] a mid-grey-brown silt-clay that was flecked with charred material and sandstone fragments and formed a phase of inner hillfort rampart building in Trench 7.	2260±25	−23.9	400–200 cal BC
NZA-36646	[725] 35/T (B)	Carbonised hazelnut shell fragment from [725] a mid- grey-brown silt-clay that was flecked with charred material and sandstone fragments and formed a phase of inner hillfort rampart building in Trench 7.	2467±25	−28.0	770–410 cal BC
Trench 12					
NZA-36653	[1210] 13/T	Carbonised *Prunus* fruitstone from [1210] the secondary fill of posthole (1209) one of two eastern postholes of the posthole building in Trench 12.	2203±20	−27.7	375–195 cal BC
Trench 14					
Beta-317521	E1129140171A	Charcoal from [14017]	2410±30	−23.2	730–400 cal BC

FIGURE 10.67 SUMMARY OF THE RADIOCARBON RESULTS FROM THE EDDISBURY SAMPLES. (2)

BC (68% probability). The end of activity is estimated as occurring in 35 cal BC–cal AD 220 (95% probability; end_eddisbury; Figure 10.68) or cal AD 20–135 (68% probability).

Estimates for when the inner rampart was built can be derived for Trench 4; 625–390 cal BC (95% probability; T4_inner_rampart_built; Figure 10.68) and Trench 7; 650–420 cal BC (95% probability; T7_inner_rampart_built; Figure 10.68). Given that construction of the inner rampart is very likely to have taken place as a "single event" these estimates can be combined (Figure 10.68) to provide an estimate for when this earthwork was built of 590–415 cal BC (95% probability; Figure 10.68) and probably 525–425 cal BC (68% probability).

The archaeological phase model

An alternative model for the chronology of Eddisbury is shown in Figure 10.70. This is based on both the stratigraphic relationships between samples and the archaeological phasing (Sidell *et al*. 2007). The archaeological phase model (Figure 10.70), has poor agreement between the radiocarbon dates, OSL dates and prior information (phasing and stratigraphy); (Amodel=3). A number of measurements have low individual index of agreement; NZA-36591 (0), NZA-36656 (3) and NZA-36646 (45).

If the individual index of agreement, for a sample, falls below 60% (Bronk Ramsey 1995; 1998) the radiocarbon date is regarded as inconsistent with the sample's calendar age, if the latter is consistent with the sample's age relative to the other dated samples. This can indicate that the radiocarbon result is a statistical outlier (more than 2 standard deviations from the sample's true radiocarbon age), but a very low index of agreement may be indicative of the sample that is residual or intrusive (i.e. that its calendar age is different to that implied by its stratigraphic position).

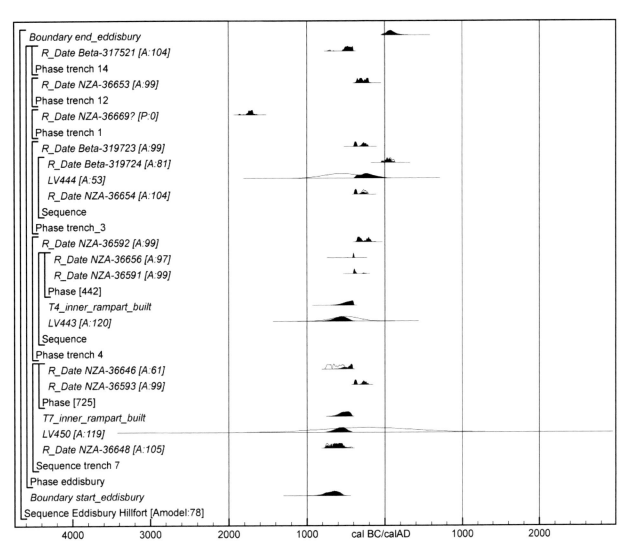

FIGURE 10.68 PROBABILITY DISTRIBUTIONS OF DATES FROM EDDISBURY (STRATIGRAPHIC MODEL): EACH DISTRIBUTION REPRESENTS THE RELATIVE PROBABILITY THAT AN EVENT OCCURS AT A PARTICULAR TIME. FOR EACH OF THE RADIOCARBON DATES TWO DISTRIBUTIONS HAVE BEEN PLOTTED, ONE IN OUTLINE, WHICH IS THE RESULT OF SIMPLE CALIBRATION, AND A SOLID ONE, WHICH IS BASED ON THE CHRONOLOGICAL MODEL USED. DISTRIBUTIONS OTHER THAN THOSE RELATING TO PARTICULAR SAMPLES CORRESPOND TO ASPECTS OF THE MODEL. FIGURES IN BRACKETS AFTER THE LABORATORY NUMBERS ARE THE INDIVIDUAL INDICES OF AGREEMENT WHICH PROVIDE AN INDICATION OF THE CONSISTENCY OF THE RADIOCARBON AND OSL DATES WITH THE PRIOR INFORMATION INCLUDED IN THE MODEL (BRONK RAMSEY 1995). THE LARGE SQUARE BRACKETS DOWN THE LEFT HAND SIDE ALONG WITH THE OXCAL KEYWORDS DEFINE THE MODEL EXACTLY.

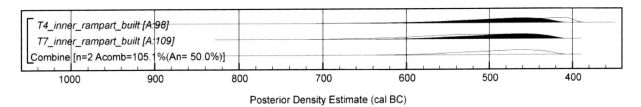

FIGURE 10.69 ESTIMATED DATE FOR THE BUILDING OF THE INNER HILLFORT RAMPART DERIVED FROM ESTIMATES SHOWN IN FIGURE 10.68.

A further alternative model is shown in Figure 10.71. NZA-36646 appears to be too old for its stratigraphic phase (Phase 6) and thus it was excluded from the model (Figure 10.71). This model shows good overall agreement Amodel=70. As well as providing estimates for the start and end of activity by assuming the archaeological phases are abutting we are able to estimate the end of one phase/start of the following (Buck *et al.* 1992). These estimates are shown in Figures 10.72 and 10.73.

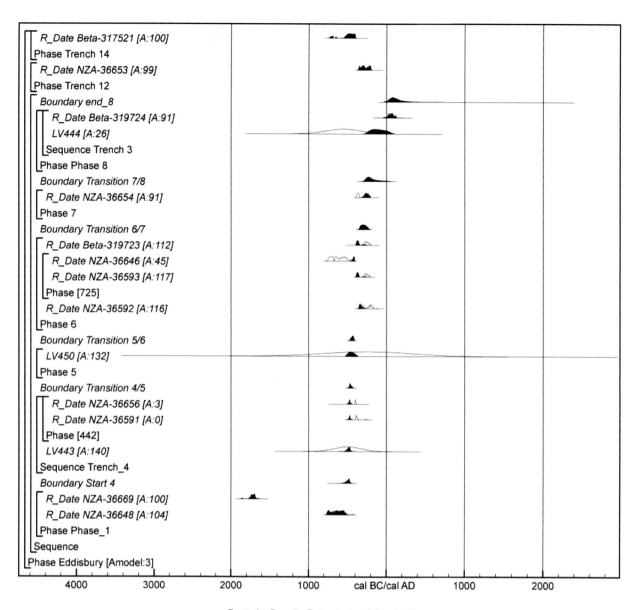

FIGURE 10.70 PROBABILITY DISTRIBUTIONS OF DATES FROM EDDISBURY (ARCHAEOLOGICAL PHASE MODEL): EACH DISTRIBUTION REPRESENTS THE RELATIVE PROBABILITY THAT AN EVENT OCCURS AT A PARTICULAR TIME. FOR EACH OF THE RADIOCARBON DATES TWO DISTRIBUTIONS HAVE BEEN PLOTTED, ONE IN OUTLINE, WHICH IS THE RESULT OF SIMPLE CALIBRATION, AND A SOLID ONE, WHICH IS BASED ON THE CHRONOLOGICAL MODEL USED. DISTRIBUTIONS OTHER THAN THOSE RELATING TO PARTICULAR SAMPLES CORRESPOND TO ASPECTS OF THE MODEL. FIGURES IN BRACKETS AFTER THE LABORATORY NUMBERS ARE THE INDIVIDUAL INDICES OF AGREEMENT WHICH PROVIDE AN INDICATION OF THE CONSISTENCY OF THE RADIOCARBON AND OSL DATES WITH THE PRIOR INFORMATION INCLUDED IN THE MODEL (BRONK RAMSEY 1995). THE LARGE SQUARE BRACKETS DOWN THE LEFT HAND SIDE ALONG WITH THE OxCAL KEYWORDS DEFINE THE MODEL EXACTLY.

Discussion

Chronological modelling suggests the hillfort at Eddisbury was initially constructed in fifth century cal BC, with the major phases of construction continuing into the late third century cal BC.

Discussion

The results of the work at Eddisbury have proved very informative, even though most of the excavation trenches constituted the re-excavation of previous archaeological

interventions on the hillfort. The work has increased our understanding of the hillfort and has provided a greater understanding of the impact that the current management regime is having on the buried archaeological remains.

Late Neolithic/early Bronze Age activity: Previously, little was known about Eddisbury hill prior to the construction of the hillfort beyond the finding of a group of urns on the eastern side of the hill in 1850. The urns are thought to have represented a group of cremation burials and one of them has now been identified as 'grooved ware' dating to the late Neolithic (CHER 832). This

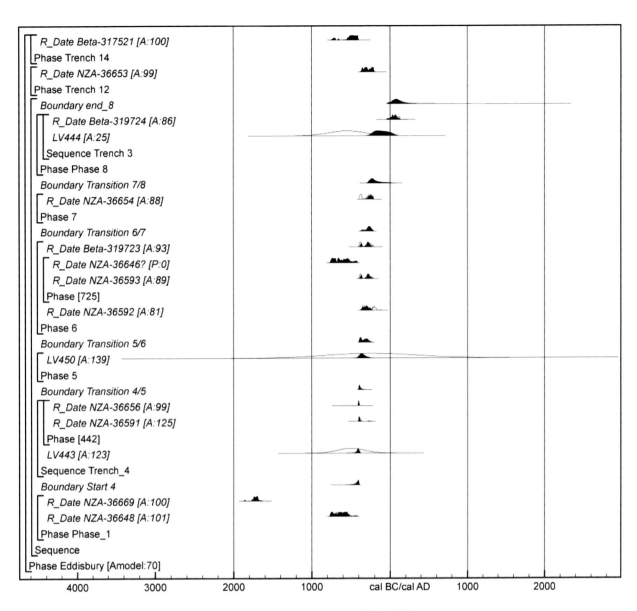

Posterior Density Estimate (cal BC/cal AD)

FIGURE 10.71 PROBABILITY DISTRIBUTIONS OF DATES FROM EDDISBURY (ARCHAEOLOGICAL PHASE MODEL): EACH DISTRIBUTION REPRESENTS THE RELATIVE PROBABILITY THAT AN EVENT OCCURS AT A PARTICULAR TIME. FOR EACH OF THE RADIOCARBON DATES TWO DISTRIBUTIONS HAVE BEEN PLOTTED, ONE IN OUTLINE, WHICH IS THE RESULT OF SIMPLE CALIBRATION, AND A SOLID ONE, WHICH IS BASED ON THE CHRONOLOGICAL MODEL USED. DISTRIBUTIONS OTHER THAN THOSE RELATING TO PARTICULAR SAMPLES CORRESPOND TO ASPECTS OF THE MODEL. RESULTS FOLLOWED BY ? HAVE BEEN EXCLUDED FROM THE MODEL FOR REASONS EXPLAINED IN THE TEXT. FIGURES IN BRACKETS AFTER THE LABORATORY NUMBERS ARE THE INDIVIDUAL INDICES OF AGREEMENT WHICH PROVIDE AN INDICATION OF THE CONSISTENCY OF THE RADIOCARBON AND OSL DATES WITH THE PRIOR INFORMATION INCLUDED IN THE MODEL (BRONK RAMSEY 1995). THE LARGE SQUARE BRACKETS DOWN THE LEFT HAND SIDE ALONG WITH THE OXCAL KEYWORDS DEFINE THE MODEL EXACTLY.

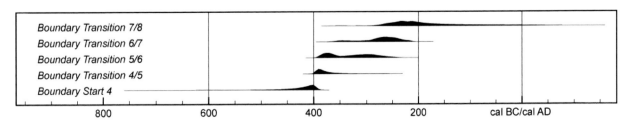

Posterior Density Estimate (cal BC/cal AD)

FIGURE 10.72 PROBABILITY DISTRIBUTIONS FOR BEGINNINGS AND ENDINGS OF ARCHAEOLOGICAL "PHASES' AT EDDISBURY. THE DISTRIBUTIONS ARE DERIVED FROM THE MODEL SHOWN IN FIGURE 10.71.

Parameter (phase)	Posterior Density Estimate (95% probability)	Posterior Density Estimate (68% probability)
Start_4	520–385 cal BC	440–390 cal BC
Transition 4/5	405–325 cal BC	400–370 cal BC
Transition 5/6	395–255 cal BC	390–355 (30%) or 330–275 (38%) cal BC
Transition 6/7	360–215 cal BC	295–225 cal BC
Transition 7/8	290 cal BC–cal AD 30	275–140 cal BC

FIGURE 10.73 POSTERIOR DENSITY ESTIMATES FOR THE DATES OF ARCHAEOLOGICAL PHASES AT EDDISBURY, DERIVED FROM THE MODEL DESCRIBED IN FIGURE 10.71.

urn has been illustrated many times since the beginning of the 20th century (Shone 1911: 59; Varley 1964: 67; Longley 1987: 66; Morgan and Morgan 2004: 39) and is held within the collections at Warrington Museum.

The most compelling evidence for pre-hillfort activity was recovered from Trench 1 where a pit (129) (or possible hearth) was identified sealed beneath the base of the inner rampart. Radiocarbon dating has suggested an early Bronze Age date 1870–1640 cal BC (NZA-36669) for this feature. This discovery may be relevant to Varley's original excavation in this area where he also identified a hearth (Varley 1950: 24) in close proximity to pit (129), but unfortunately, Varley's feature had been removed by his excavations. The stratigraphic significance of the early Bronze Age hearth/pit is crucial to understanding the later phases of the hillfort rampart and also serves to demonstrate that Varley's original interpretation of a flattened and then rebuilt inner rampart was incorrect (*ibid.*).

An early Bronze Age presence on the hilltop can be further supported by the recovery of a barbed and tanged flint arrowhead from the plough soil on the hillfort interior at Trench 10. This can be seen in the context of a growing number of other worked flint artefacts recovered from fieldwalking on the hillfort interior and from Trenches 1, 3, 7, 14 and 15. Furthermore, the decorated sandstone boulder recovered from Trench 4 is likely to date to between the late Neolithic and the late Bronze Age.

The structural evidence combined with the growing number of stray finds from the hilltop would suggest a funerary element to the late Neolithic/early Bronze Age activity. This can be seen as part of an emerging pattern of monument building within the surrounding landscape during this period, with both isolated round barrows and a significant barrow cemetery at the Seven Lows within a two mile radius of the hilltop.

Late Bronze Age/early Iron Age activity: Varley identified evidence for a pre-rampart timber palisade associated with postholes and pits on the Merrick's Hill part of the hillfort during his excavations between 1936 and 1938 (Varley 1950: 34). These features were attributed a date of *c.* 400–250 BC on typological parallels (*op. cit.*

49–52). Subsequently, a number of other hillforts such as Beeston Castle have produced evidence for pre-rampart timber palisades of late Bronze Age date (Ellis 1993: 87–91). The Merrick's Hill area was subject to reinvestigation by the Liverpool University Field School between 2010 and 2011 (see Chapter 11) and a full account of the results of this work will be published elsewhere.

Positive evidence for a pre-rampart palisade trench was not found beneath the inner rampart at Trenches 1, 4 or 7 and the evidence for this remains confined to the Merrick's Hill area. At Trench 1, the fill of pit (129) was sealed by a layer of grey silt-clay (114) that Varley had identified as an 'occupation layer' separating his original and rebuilt inner rampart (Varley 1950: 23–4). A very similar layer was identified beneath the inner rampart in Trench 7 (layer (718)) and beneath the outer rampart in Trench 14 (layer (14017)). In both instances these layers produced very similar radiocarbon dating results of 770–410 cal BC (NZA-36648) from layer (718) and 730–400 cal BC (Beta-317521) from layer (14017). At Trench 7, layer (718) produced a small assemblage of pottery that has been tentatively identified as late Bronze Age in character (see Mullin above). Furthermore, bulk samples from Trench 1 (layer 114), Trench 7 (layer 718) and Trench 14 (layer 14017) produced traces of cereal residues and remains of wild/weed fruits/seeds which hint at the consumption of (?hulled) barley and certain scrubland species including hazelnut, sloe/plum/cherry and bramble, which may have been growing within the locality. The charcoal assemblages provided evidence for the use of heather and hazel, which appears to have been collected for use as fuel. However, the scarcity of material in the samples was thought to suggest that either the occupation activity during this phase was relatively short-lived or that the main focus for the activity was situated away from the area under investigation.

At Trench 1 'occupation layer' (114) was overlain by a structure which Varley interpreted as a 'Dark Age hut' (Varley 1950: 24–7, figure 8 and plate 9). On re-visiting this structure, it was clear that it was sealed by the primary inner rampart of the hillfort and was set above 'occupation layer' (114). This structure could represent the kerb to a hut circle approximately 5m in diameter; and if so, then it may belong to pre-hillfort occupation of the hilltop in the early Iron Age. A possible internal floor surface may be represented by layer (118) but OSL dating of this layer has suggested an earlier prehistoric date of 5340–1340 BC (sample LV447). The OSL date is not wholly reliable given the range of accuracy (±1000 years) and in any event contamination from the late Neolithic/early Bronze Age activity in the vicinity of Trench 1 may have contributed to this early date. An alternative interpretation of the feature as representing a small stone kerbed mound remains a possibility, but it is difficult to push either interpretation too far without uncovering more of the structure in plan.

The combined evidence would suggest a phase of late Bronze Age/early Iron Age activity on the hilltop prior to the construction of the hillfort and this would appear to have been in the form of unenclosed settlement. The kerb of stones beneath the inner rampart in Trench 1 would suggest that this occupation was not simply a pre-cursor to hillfort construction and is more likely to represent an earlier phase of activity on the hill. However, the possibility of a small contemporary palisaded enclosure on the Merrick's Hill end of the hilltop cannot be entirely ruled out.

The First Hillfort Phase: The inner rampart was investigated in Trenches 1, 4 and 7 and in each instance there were two clear phases of rampart building; the inner ditch was investigated in Trenches 3, 14 and 15. In Trenches 1 and 7 the primary rampart appears to have consisted of a bank of redeposited natural clay and mudstone with an outer drystone revetment wall made from mudstone slabs (more clearly identified at Trench 1 than at Trench 7). The construction of this bank appears to be contemporary with the first phase of the inner ditch, which consisted of a series of inter-connected quarry pits at Trench 3. The distinct impression was that the segmental inner ditch was primarily created to quarry material for the construction of the inner rampart bank. In this respect there was little difference between the inner rampart construction at Trenches 1 and 7; strongly suggesting that the entire hilltop was enclosed by a single rampart and ditch from the beginning. The inner rampart at Trench 4 was noticeably different as the primary bank material was redeposited natural red sand. This might be partly explained by its proximity to the eastern entrance, or alternatively, might imply the absence of an external quarry ditch here.

Varley's earliest report on his Eddisbury excavations made note of a counterscarp bank associated with the primary hillfort construction, which later became subsumed by the secondary outer rampart (Varley and Jackson 1940: 65). He later abandoned this idea (Varley 1950). However, evidence for a possible counterscarp bank was identified in Trenches 3 and 14, beyond the inner ditch. In both cases the bank seems to have covered a timber post-setting which might suggest an initial timber palisade beyond the inner ditch, or that the counterscarp bank had a timber revetment. It is not

certain if this feature was part of the primary hillfort design or a later embellishment prior to the creation of the secondary outer rampart.

Analysis of the combined scientific dating results indicates that the primary rampart was constructed during the fifth century cal BC (see above) but it is uncertain if the eastern entrance was part of this initial hilltop enclosure. It now seems likely that an entrance originally existed on the northern side of the hillfort, in the location of Trenches 1, 14 and 15 (Varley's Area 2). This is largely based on the 2.9m wide gap in the inner ditch which Varley had argued was evidence for an extension to the primary hillfort defences, but which has been more recently interpreted as a possible entrance (Cocroft *et al.* 1989). The northwestern entrance in Varley's 'Area 1' was not revisited as part of the Habitats and Hillforts Project, so there are no additional insights regarding the phasing of this feature. Another possible entrance on the southwest side of the hillfort was originally postulated by Varley (Varley and Jackson 1940: 65), but this remains entirely uninvestigated at present.

Evidence for occupation of the primary hillfort is confined to the presence of a metalled surface (441/444) along the inside edge of the rampart, that was largely made from heat-shattered stone which is likely to represent a waste product from the boiling of water. This surface overlay a discrete charcoal-rich deposit (442), which produced two radiocarbon dates of 410–385 cal BC (NZA-36656); 410–260 cal BC (NZA-36591). This deposit also produced a small assemblage of pottery that has been tentatively identified as late Bronze Age in character (see Mullin above). Varley originally reported evidence for a similar 'cobbled floor' in his Area 4 (to the south on Merrick's Hill) on which lay scatters of ash containing prehistoric pottery sherds, cooking bones and a fragment of a bronze pin (Varley 1950: 34). Bulk samples from Trenches 4 and 7 produced evidence for the consumption of glume wheats, most notably emmer and spelt, as well as bread wheat-type (*Triticum aestivum* sl.) and hulled (and perhaps naked) barley, although there was insufficient material to be able to ascertain potential crop preferences or arable husbandry regimes. The cereals identified were typical of those cultivated during the Iron Age period in Britain (Greig 1991).

The Second Hillfort Phase: The outer rampart was investigated in Trenches 3 and 14 where there appeared to be one main phase of rampart building; the outer ditch was also investigated in Trench 3. At Trench 14 the earlier counterscarp bank was incorporated in to a much larger rampart bank, which was furnished with an outer drystone revetment wall of similar design to the inner rampart. The construction of the outer rampart would have required a substantial amount of quarried material and this is most likely to have been produced by the cutting of the outer ditch. Both Varley's excavations in his Area 2 and the recent excavations at Trench 3 have demonstrated that the outer ditch had a deep 'V' shaped profile quarried deep in to the natural rock to a depth of 2.5m. A secondary fill (312) of the outer ditch in Trench 3 produced a radiocarbon date of 400–200 cal BC (NZA-36654) and this remains the only dating evidence directly associated with the creation of the outer rampart.

The evidence from Trenches 1, 3, 4, 7, 14 and 15 would suggest that the inner ditch was re-cut at the time that the outer rampart was created and the up-cast from this used to increase the size of the inner rampart. Primary silting (305) of the re-cut inner ditch in Trench 3 produced a radiocarbon date of 400–200 cal BC (Beta-319723) and material associated with the enlargement of the inner rampart bank (725) in Trench 7 also produced a radiocarbon date of 400–200 cal BC (NZA-36593). Analysis of the combined scientific dating results indicates that the outer rampart was constructed between the fourth and later third century cal BC (see above). It is possible that the eastern entrance in Trench 4 (Varley's Area 3) was constructed during the addition of the outer and enlargement of the inner ramparts. This entrance was furnished with an inturned corridor and a guardroom over which there may have been a timber superstructure. The dating of the east entrance is primarily based upon evidence from the burning of the southern guardroom which produced a radiocarbon date of 360–160 cal BC (NZA-36592). The eastern entrance may have been a replacement for the postulated entrance in the area of Trenches 1, 14 and 15 (Varley's Area 2), as the addition of the outer rampart bank and ditch here, would have entirely blocked access to the hillfort interior.

Evidence for occupation of the later hillfort is confined to the presence of a posthole alignment on the hillfort interior identified in Trench 12, from which one posthole fill (1210) produced a radiocarbon date of 375–195 cal BC (NZA-36653). It is possible that the postholes belong to a number of separate structures, but without uncovering more structural components these features remain somewhat enigmatic.

Roman activity: Varley argued that the hillfort defences had been deliberately slighted and attributed this activity to the conquering Roman army in the late 1st century AD (Varley 1950: 57). In particular, he referenced the blocking of the eastern entrance, the filling of the ditches and the levelling of the ramparts. However, on investigation the evidence is far less clear, as the levelling of the inner and outer ramparts in Varley's Area 2 can now be disregarded as a mis-interpretation of the natural geology. The filling of the inner ditch in Area 2 was dated to c. AD 80–120, on the basis of one sherd of Roman coarseware (op. cit. 24); whilst the filling of the inner ditch by the northwestern entrance (Varley's Area 1) was dated by a single fragment of Roman roof tile, which Varley conjectured could be no later in date

than AD 120 (op. cit. 10). Similarly, the blocking of the eastern entrance and its northern guardroom were dated by the presence of a single base sherd of Roman mortarium (op. cit. 33).

Evidence from Trench 3 identified a re-cutting of the outer ditch and the secondary fill (309) of this re-cut produced a radiocarbon date of cal AD 10–130 (Beta-319724). This event may have been linked with the final enlargement of the outer rampart represented in Trench 14 by deposits (14004) and (14003). The dating of this event is somewhat problematic as it could be seen as a refortification of the outer rampart on the eve of the Roman conquest, by the indigenous population. Alternatively it could be an act undertaken by the Roman military, once the area was under their control. The site of the hillfort is well placed for overseeing the Roman road, on the south side of the hill, which connected the fortress at Chester (Deva) with the fort at Northwich (Condate), and it could well have been used by the military in the post-conquest period.

Excavation at Trench 10 produced a single rim sherd from a Roman hammerhead mortarium dated c. AD 280-360 (see above) and a second hammerhead mortarium rim was recovered from the hillfort interior during a fieldwalking exercise undertaken by the Sandstone Ridge Trust in 2013. This meagre assemblage of Roman material can be bolstered by a glass melon bead, which was recovered by fieldwalking on the hillfort interior in 2009 and possibly with the copper-alloy disc bearing a Chi-Rho symbol recovered from Trench 1. The general impression is that the Roman activity within the hillfort is not restricted to the period of military conquest and appears to continue in to the late Roman period. The nature of this activity remains obscure, but it does suggest the hillfort was not abandoned in the Roman period.

Early Medieval re-occupation: It has already been argued (above) that the 'Dark Ages hut' identified by Varley beneath the inner rampart in Trench 1 (his Area 2) is in fact a prehistoric feature likely to date to the late Bronze Age/early Iron Age. Likewise, his evidence for the Aethelflaedan reconstruction of the outer rampart in Trench 14 can be disregarded, in view of the clarification regarding his interpretation of the natural geology as the primary hillfort rampart. This does not entirely rule out all of Varley's assertions regarding an early medieval phase to the hillfort and indeed the recovery of a sherd of early Saxon pottery from Trench 14 (see above) supports a pre-Aethelflaedan phase to the site.

Perhaps the best evidence for this remains the 'Saxon hut' located above the fills of the inner ditch in Varley's Area 1 (by the northwestern entrance) which he describes as 'a laid floor of clay mixed with twigs and defined by a low stone kerb' (Varley 1950: 10). Varley goes on to state that the hut was oval in shape and that an entire baked clay loom weight of annular type was recovered from the clay floor (*ibid.*) which he ascribed a later 6th to 8th century date. This loom weight has been recovered during recent work by Liverpool University in to what remains of the Varley archive and its function and form can now be confirmed (see Chapter 4).

Adjacent to this hut feature, Varley also recorded the slighting of the inner rampart in order to provide a level platform for the construction of a 'small circular hut' (Varley 1950: 20). This feature has been repeatedly misunderstood since its initial uncovering, as Varley initially interpreted it as a 'Dark Ages hut' in the principal publication of his excavations (*op. cit.* 21). However, 14 years later the image of the structure was republished by Varley and is described as a 'small Iron Age Hut' (Varley 1964, plate 7). More recently, the plan of the structure was republished by Matthews as part of a composite figure to compare the plans of late prehistoric buildings from the northwest region (Matthews 2002: 12). The simple detail that has been repeatedly overlooked about this structure is that it has an internal diameter of less than 2m and is therefore unlikely to be a hut at all. Returning to Varley's original account he states that 'In and around this hut lay a thick black deposit containing vast quantities of daub bearing stick impressions, cooking bones and exceedingly crude pottery' (Varley 1950: 20). On the basis of this review it is suggested that the structure actually represents an oven (possibly a corn drier) which probably had a wattle and clay dome forming the upper part of the structure. The stratigraphic position of this structure would suggest a post-Iron Age date; however, Varley's description of the pottery as a 'thick paste stiffened with quartz grits almost the size of peas' (*ibid.*) has often been used to suggest that it was actually Iron Age briquettage (Cheshire stony VCP). In light of the early Saxon pottery sherd recovered from Trench 14, this crude pottery could be argued to be of a similar date. Unfortunately, without the pottery available for re-analysis the actual date of the structure and its associated material remains a matter of speculation.

This early Saxon activity might provide a context for the enduring name of the hilltop, Eddisbury or Eades byrig, meaning 'Ead's stronghold'. The name was already well established by the time of the founding of the Aethelflaedan burh in AD 914 and it is perhaps the case that the hillfort was simply refounded by Aethelflaed, rather than being an entirely new Mercian fort.

This inevitably brings us to the issue regarding the identification of Eddisbury hillfort with the Aethelflaedan burh established in AD 914. Higham has raised doubt over the logic of Eddisbury (in Delamere) being the location of a fort in a chain of defences, running between Chester in the west and Manchester in the east. Furthermore, he has drawn attention to the location of a second Eddisbury place-name in Rainow near Macclesfield as a possible alternative candidate

(Higham 1993: 111). This wavering doubt has been fuelled by the seeming lack of solid dating evidence for a late Saxon presence at Eddisbury hillfort. The discovery of an oven base set in to the back of the inner rampart in Trench 7, has perhaps provided the supporting evidence that has for so long eluded researchers of the site. The oven has been scientifically dated to 860 ±70 AD (cal AD 745–980) and whilst this date range could still pre-date the burh founding of AD 914, a late Saxon presence on the hilltop now seems demonstrable.

Frustratingly, establishing evidence for a late Saxon presence does little to help define what the Aethelfaedan burh might have consisted of in terms of the extant defences. However, it must be considered that some of the elements of Varley's hillfort slighting, which he attributed to the Roman military, might actually be the work of the Mercians. In particular, the blocking of the eastern entrance could well have been deliberate to make the defensive circuit of the hill more defensible with a small garrison. It also seems likely that the inner rampart and ditch had long been abandoned as defences by the 10th century and that the outer rampart and ditch was the only effective defensive barrier on the hilltop. In this context, the re-cutting of the outer ditch (Trench 3) and heightening of the outer rampart (Trench 14) could in fact be part of the 10th century refortification; the early radiocarbon date from the outer ditch re-cut in Trench 3 could be explained as being from redeposited material associated with the earlier Roman activity on the hillfort.

Management Review

The implications of the excavation results for the management of the hillfort are summarised below. A full review of management measures implemented through the Habitats and Hillfort Project has been presented in an unpublished Management Review Report (Garner 2011d). The Merrick's Hill part of the hillfort is reviewed in Chapter 11.

Plough erosion: A large part of the hillfort interior is suffering from active erosion through repeated ploughing on an annual basis; this includes occasional deep ploughing for potato crops. The ploughing is undertaken through class consent and there is no Higher Level Stewardship agreement with Natural England. Archaeological excavation has demonstrated that over much of the interior this repeated ploughing has removed any traces of vertical stratigraphy, rendering much of the surviving archaeology as plough-truncated features cut in to the natural sub-soil. The exception to this is along the eastern and northeastern edges of the inner rampart. As described above, the post-medieval alteration and maintenance of the field boundary along this stretch of the inner rampart has served to bring the entire rampart within the active plough zone. It has been noted above that the inner rampart zone preserves stratigraphy spanning from the late Neolithic/early Bronze Age periods to the early medieval period. The ongoing agricultural regime will continue to erode this valuable and limited resource and further consideration should be given to preservation by record.

Domestic occupation: The northwestern end of the hillfort has been divided in to several privately owned residences; a number of which encroach on to the monument. The largest property includes a small field occupying the area of the hillfort containing the northwest entrance. This field is currently down to permanent pasture and is grazed by livestock; however, it is demarcated by a recent double line of stock-proof fence which follows the course of the inner rampart. The primary risk in this area is that over time as properties change ownership there is a potential for inappropriate development and landuse. This has already been noted where the end of one garden was terraced in to the line of the outer rampart in order to accommodate a giant outdoor chess board.

Gorse roots: The areas of gorse established along various sections of the outer rampart were cleared by the Forestry Commission during the Project. Examination of one area at Trench 14 suggested that the gorse was relatively shallow rooted and had not contributed to destabilisation of the rampart. Continuing management of the gorse by the Forestry Commission will negate any future management problems in this regard.

Conclusions

The excavation has served to provide a greater level of knowledge regarding the form, character and level of archaeological preservation on the monument known as Eddisbury hillfort. This has identified the monument as a rare early type of hilltop enclosure, which owes its origins to the early Iron Age. The hillfort interior has no above ground features to consider; however, sub-surface structures in the form of postholes and pits have been identified within the trenches. Sampling has demonstrated that, within the confines of the excavation, artefact and ecofact recovery has been low with only hardy materials such as ceramics, stone tools and charred plant remains being identified from the prehistoric period.

The excavation has also helped to identify the monument as a multi-period site with some evidence for phases of Roman and early medieval use that were previously poorly understood or unsubstantiated. Sampling has again demonstrated that, within the confines of the excavation, artefact recovery has been low, whilst ecofact recovery has been very low with only hardy materials such as charred plant remains being identified from the early medieval period.

Chapter 11
Rescuing a scheduled monument: Recent work at Merrick's Hill, Eddisbury Hillfort

Richard Mason and Rachel Pope

Introduction

Excavations at Eddisbury hillfort, Merrick's Hill were conducted over six weeks by the University of Liverpool Archaeology Field School between 25 July–7 August 2010 and 24 July–19 August 2011, as part of a working partnership with the Heritage Lottery-funded Habitats and Hillforts Project. Merrick's Hill is a particularly badly-damaged area at the southeast tip of Eddisbury hillfort, covering c. 0.3ha, and a particular focus for activity across the years. This paper begins by outlining the work of Professor William J. Varley (then of the Geography Department, University of Liverpool) and his wife Joan, in this area between 1936 and 1938, and provides an interim statement of the archaeological resource as discovered by recent survey, excavation and archival work. It then moves on to discuss the damage sustained by the monument across the later 20th century and ongoing management issues. This paper should be treated as an interim statement ahead of the final report, to be produced on the work of the University of Liverpool at Eddisbury.

Aims/objectives

One of the aims of the Habitats and Hillforts project was to re-assess the work of the Varleys at Eddisbury in a bid to update our understanding and provide improved dating evidence of Iron Age settlement along Cheshire's Sandstone Ridge. As part of this, the excavations at Merrick's Hill (Varley's Area 4), had clearly defined aims to:

- improve our understanding of the management challenges facing this scheduled monument, which are at their most developed in the Merrick's Hill area;
- gain an understanding of the monument's archaeological potential, in what is the only unploughed area of the site;
- re-assess the conclusions of the Varley excavations, particularly regarding the origins of the hillfort, as well as the later use of the site.

These aims had to be achieved within the English Heritage (now Historic England) conditions of consent, which confined work to the re-excavation of previously excavated trenches.

Our objectives across the two years were to:

- quantify the impact of woodland regeneration on the post-medieval structural remains;
- determine the extent of recent investigations by amateur geologist Mr John Edwards;
- assess the extent of the Varleys' work to define the surviving archaeological resource;
- relocate and sample-excavate Varley trenches to obtain material for C14 dating from:
- the eastern stone-revetted Iron Age rampart and associated occupation deposit;
- the pre-rampart palisade trench;
- the southern ditch.

As a field school, the excavations also aimed at providing the practical arm to introductory teaching in archaeological methods at the University of Liverpool, with eighty first year undergraduates obtaining practical skills training in the principles of stratigraphy and formation processes, single-context excavating and recording, drawing site plans and sections, archaeological photography and illustration, finds identification and processing, geophysics and topographical survey, as well as environmental sampling and processing. Student feedback from the Eddisbury field school was hugely positive and it remains a commitment of the authors to train students in practical archaeology on research excavations.

Merrick's Hill was badly overgrown and had to be cleared of sycamore woodland, ivy, brambles, and nettles prior to excavation in 2010, but the surviving foundations of rectangular buildings could mostly still be detected. Our strategy for 2010 was firstly to conduct a topographical, walk-over, and photographic survey of Merrick's Hill to help determine the extent of John Edwards' recent excavations. It was also decided to strip and clean three large areas – over Buildings One and Two and the 1936–38 southern ditch Section 1 (Varley 1950, figure 12) – to help determine the extent of the Varley excavations and locate areas of best potential for sample excavation, and to quantify the impact of woodland regeneration. In addition it was decided to open three trenches: Area 1 in the area of the eastern rampart and occupation deposit; Areas 1 and 2 over the palisade trench; and Area 3 over the southern ditch section (Figure 11.1).

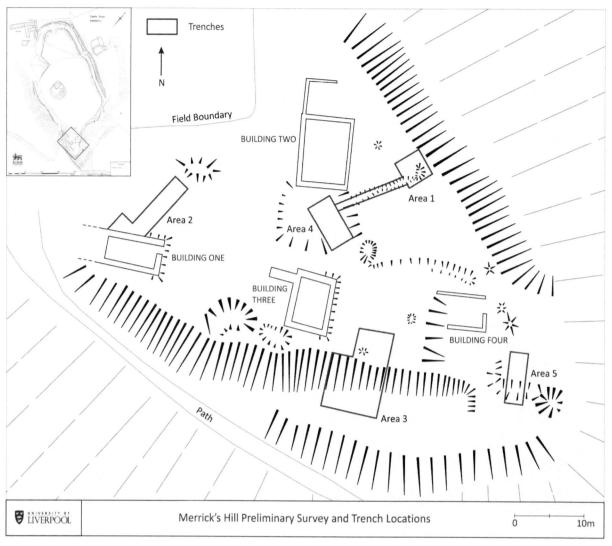

FIGURE 11.1 DRAFT SURVEY OF MERRICK'S HILL SHOWING TRENCH LOCATIONS (COURTESY OF BEN EDWARDS).

Having gained a preliminary understanding of the surviving archaeology in 2010, excavation continued in 2011. Areas 1 and 2 were adjusted in size slightly so as to achieve the aims of the project within the allotted timescale. Area 2 was extended to locate the return of the palisade trench identified by the Varleys. The aims of Area 3 were adjusted following relocation of Varley's (1950) Section 1 as it was felt unsafe to proceed with excavation to the recorded depth of 3.6m given the proximity of a very large sycamore tree, which had remained un-felled due to its large size. The revised aims of this trench were to continue with the investigation of the boundary wall surrounding the buildings and to investigate the potential for a prehistoric rampart in this area of the site.

Area 4 was opened along the southern edge of the 2010 Area 1 cleaning trench, with the intention of ensuring we located the return of the sand-filled trench that had been found inside Building Two (Varley 1950). It was also hoped to assess the damage caused by stone robbing in the later 20th century and to investigate the survival of the

archaeological resource within the interior of Merrick's Hill. In October 2010, a slot trench had been excavated in our original Area 1 by Earthworks Archaeology, at the request of English Heritage. Their backfill was re-excavated in 2011 by Liverpool students to join Areas 1 and 4. A reassessment of Earthworks' findings, including full assignment of contexts was conducted to ensure continuity with our own records. Area 5 was opened in the southeast over a 'snaking' trench recorded by survey in 2010, with the intention of characterising the nature of this feature and assessing any damage to the surviving archaeological resource.

Varley excavations 1936–1938

The Varleys' work at Eddisbury was undertaken at the suggestion of Christopher Hawkes, to investigate the Cheshire hillforts with a view to understanding their link to those of the Welsh Marches. They followed the Varley excavations at Maiden Castle, Bickerton between 1932 and 1935, as the result of a proposal to place a reservoir at Eddisbury (Historic England registry file

AA100540/1/PT2), utilising unemployed Liverpool dockworkers as the workforce (Varley 1950: 1). In line with other contemporary excavations such as those of the Wheelers and the Bersus, Varley notes that 'direction of actual excavation' was undertaken by a mixed-sex team consisting of Joan Varley, Betty Furness, Ronald Ellis, and Frank Walker. Also amongst the on-site team were a young Margaret Owen (site surveyor and planner) and Tom Jones (site photographer), married in 1940 and later of Mucking fame. Publication of the site report was delayed by the outbreak of World War II, and Bill Varley's subsequent move to Ghana. The Varleys' Area 4 was focused on Merrick's Hill, known locally as 'the chamber in the forest' and believed to be the site of a 14th century hunting lodge. Very much of their time, the Varleys were keen to fit the archaeology to the historical accounts. It is perhaps this over-riding desire, especially regarding the historical chronology of Hawkes' Iron Age, that ultimately saw Varley's work criticised by subsequent authors (e.g. Cotton 1954).

Although Varley's Eddisbury sequence has seen criticism (e.g. Forde-Johnston 1962: 38; Cocroft *et al.* 1989), our investigations revealed a fairly methodical approach to excavation itself. Initially, excavation was based around the post-medieval structural remains, with the clearing

of the interior rooms of the post-medieval buildings. The cuts of the Varley wall-chasing trenches were still visible on the ground and were identified around Buildings One and Three (Figure 11.2). This was very much akin to later 19th century chase-and-clear methods, developed particularly in the excavation of Roman forts. As the excavations progressed, however, early attempts at more modern open-area excavation appear to have been utilised, opening up the area around the culvert between Buildings Two and Four and the area south of Building Three (Figure 11.3). The opening up of large areas was in line with contemporary excavation trends more generally (cf. Bersu 1940). The Varleys also dug three sections across the southernmost ditch, Section 1 being re-located by us in excavation. The extension of the fourth, northernmost ditch section into the interior, however, seems to have been purely a device for illustrating the full structural sequence in cross section. With the area heavily disturbed by later 20th century investigations, no evidence for Section 4 into the interior was found during our excavations. A fifth section, down off Merrick's Hill, might be seen in Varley's (1950) figure 3 as Section G.

At present, it seems as if the Varley campaign was largely focused on defining the extent of the hillfort earthworks on Merrick's Hill and there is currently no evidence to suggest that, beyond excavation of the post-medieval buildings, they ventured into the lower-lying interior of the site between Buildings One and Two. It seems instead that they used the lower-lying ground in the centre of Merrick's Hill to locate their spoil heaps. Excavations in Area 2 found two episodes of dump deposits, composed of a mixture of architectural materials (largely brick, slate, and stone). At present we believe the earlier of these dumps to be associated with Varley's excavations, which had worked to effectively level the ground surface between Buildings One and Two. Our topographic and walk-over survey also located the remnants of a large turf heap in the space between the excavations of Building One and Building Two, although it remains possible that this was associated with later excavations on the site (below). Finds from our Area 1 investigations included corrugated iron shoring, and two surveyor's nails from the Varley excavations. We also identified a rock-cut posthole under the front rampart revetment, excavated by the Varleys which then seems to have been subsequently deliberately sought out in a later season, when a mixed assemblage of choice sherds were deposited in it; a Varley closing deposit of sorts. We have excavated evidence that all of the Varleys operations were fully backfilled at the end of each year's season of excavation.

In summary, the Varleys' techniques seem to have been transitional between more traditional methods of wall-chasing/clearing and the move towards area excavation to natural, a technique that was at its beginnings in the late 1930s. The authors are confident in the excavation abilities of the Varleys, which we believe were fairly

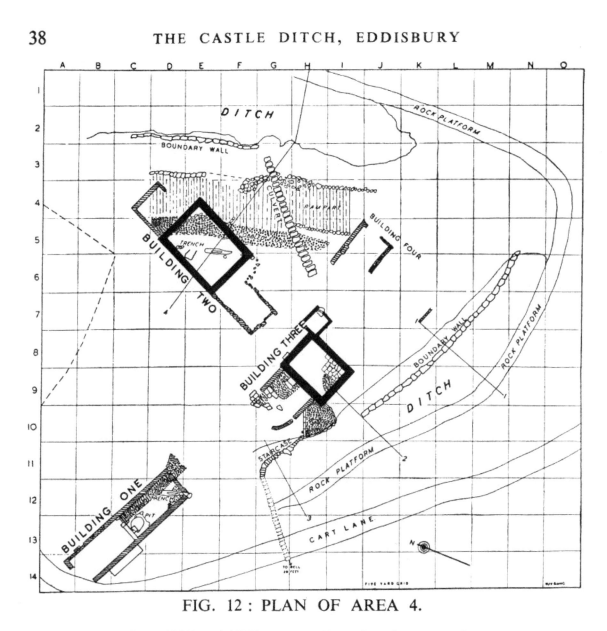

FIG. 12 : PLAN OF AREA 4.

FIGURE 11.3 VARLEY'S (1950) SITE PLAN OF MERRICK'S HILL (VARLEY AREA 4).

exemplary for their time. The only real flaw seems to have been in the final interpretation of the site, when the desire to fit the archaeology to known historical events seems to have taken precedence over the excavated evidence. Regarding excavation techniques, however, the Varleys seem to have been at the very forefront of the field in 1930s Britain. In 2011, the current authors located and secured the lost Varley archive for Eddisbury (see Mason and Pope, Chapter 4, this volume). Work is ongoing with this material and this, along with the re-evaluation of the Merrick's bones assemblage at Manchester Museum and information from the more extensive Almondbury hillfort archive, currently being worked on by Rowan May on behalf of ARCUS/YAT[1]

for the Tolson Museum in Huddersfield, will aid us in our re-interpretation of the Varleys' work at Merrick's Hill prior to full integration with the results of our own excavations.

Post-Medieval occupation of Merrick's Hill

Based on Joan Varley's work with the documentary sources and its location within the Old Pale, Varley (1950) links the buildings on Merrick's Hill to the foresters of Delamere. He reports that in 1652, two documents refer to there being four lodges or houses in Delamere forest 'called by the names of the chamber in the forest' for use by the chief forester and his under-keepers, these were 'Edesburye lodge, or the old pale lodge, the new pale lodge, Hornebyes lodge and Massyes lodge' (Varley 1950: 66). The documents suggest that

[1] Archaeological Research and Consultancy at the University of Sheffield/York Archaeological Trust

the oldest of these belonged to the keeper 'antiently a house under the hill in the old pale walks' adjoining the enclosed land; and that the Dones, the chief foresters, had a 'house upon the hill within the pale [which] was called by the name of the chamber in the forest'.[2] In the mid-17th century, the Dones apparently had two lodges, an older chamber under the hill at Old Pale, since given to the keeper, and a newer house on the hill, perhaps that named New Pale 'the said Dones in their respective times have had allowance from the kings and queens of England for repaires of the said Chamber and the house in the new pale' (Varley 1950: 66).

Varley (1950) believed that occupation of Merrick's Hill began in the medieval period, in the 14th century. The first historical references given in his 1950 report date to 1337, when Prince Edward of Wales agreed to allow Richard Doun, the forester at Delamere, to build rooms (40ft x 20ft and two storeys high) for his own convenience. Over a decade on, in 1351, the Black Prince's Register contained an order to build a lodge for the better preservation of both forest and game, and three years later the officials of Chester were ordered to remove an unroofed chamber from 'Pecforton' manor and put it on 'Edesbury' hill for the reception of the forester. Whether these separate sources ultimately refer to the same eventual building event is unknown, similarly there are few clues as to the location of this early lodge. It is only the later sources that suggest that the earliest lodge might be the 'Edesburye' lodge, under the hill at Old Pale. Further interrogation of the historical records, which now include the Arden Estate records at the Cheshire Record Office, beyond those consulted in the 1950 report, will undoubtedly reveal more on the medieval origins and post-medieval development of the Old Pale. This research, currently being undertaken by the authors, will provide an up-to-date historical background to the site.

A culvert (located between Buildings Two and Four) and the boundary wall (see Figure 11.3) were found to be of one continuous build (Varley 1950: 40).[3] Varley noted that the former was covered by 16th to 18th century building debris, and did not drain any of the buildings. As such, he believed that the culvert must be medieval and built to drain an earlier, undiscovered, timber building (*ibid.* figure 18.1). Varley accepted that even the earliest of the building foundations at the site (Buildings Two and Three) were not medieval, but late 16th or 17th century with a date of origin at about 1550 (Varley 1950: 41, 48, 66). This is the date given by our specialists for the origins of the later occupation, based on the date range of the excavated ceramics and glassware from the site. We can now confirm that the culvert is in fact post-medieval with mid-late 18th century ceramics found in the construction fill of a previously un-investigated section. We know too that the boundary wall is post-medieval, having found clay pipe from beneath the wall in Area 1. In Area 3, we located two separate phases of construction of the post-medieval boundary wall, and a period of revetment, showing repair of the feature across time. Nevertheless in 2010–11, Merrick's Hill did produce a minimum of four medieval sherds, with eight further sherds from the Varley archive also identified as medieval. Julie Edwards (Cheshire West and Chester) suggests that even this low volume (representing a minimum total of twelve vessels) may still represent occupation.

The 2010–11 excavations produced *c.* 2000 sherds of post-medieval/early modern ceramics and 6.6kg of vessel and window glass. These were predominantly from residual contexts, given our brief from English Heritage to re-examine the trenches of Varley. An initial assessment of the post-medieval ceramic assemblage was conducted by post-medieval ceramics specialist Chris Cumberpatch (independent researcher). The results of this analysis were incorporated into the preliminary data structure reports, and were used as an initial basis for dating the post-medieval deposits. The assemblage subsequently received assessment by regional expert Julie Edwards (Cheshire West and Chester) to further classify the local wares and refine dating information ahead of integration into the final data structure report. Of the 1100 sherds from our excavations that could be dated to a particular century, less than 0.1% are considered medieval and 16th century (four sherds medieval and one sherd 16th century), 5% as 17th century, 44% as 18th century, 44% as 19th century, and 6% as 20th century. An analysis of the post-medieval glass assemblage was conducted by Hugh Willmott (University of Sheffield). Initial findings suggest a few later 16th century glass vessels, with the bulk of the assemblage as 17th to 18th century in date, and an unusually low volume of glassware dating to the 19th and 20th centuries, thereby dating activity perhaps slightly earlier than the ceramic.

Beyond the ceramic and glass, the 2010–11 excavations produced 108 clay pipe fragments, 20 of which were stamped/decorated. Work by Peter Davey (University of Liverpool) suggests that these have helped to increase our knowledge of the current Chester clay pipe typologies. The earliest date represented in the pipes is 1580, with a rare 17th century peak, and the suggestion of a high status site during the 18th century, dating which is roughly in line with that of the

---

[2] This name apparently only specifically given to Merrick's Hill on the OS maps after 1839, once occupation had ceased (Oswald 2000, Appendix 3).

[3] There are issues with Varley's (1950) conflation of three distinct features: the boulder-block revetment onto bedrock on the eastern vertical face of Merrick's Hill (which Varley believed to be a medieval boundary wall, see our figure 11.2); the post-medieval boundary wall on the break of slope (which he believed to be the front facing of the hillfort rampart – but from which we retrieved clay pipe); and the additional boundary wall/rock-cut platform which holds the current fence-line around the base of Merrick's Hill. More details will be given in the final report.

glass. Work by the late Paul Courtney (University of Leicester) on the metalwork assemblage suggests that it is strongly architectural or domestic in character, and includes a 14th to 17th century iron buckle and 15th to 17th century cast bronze ring. A full assessment of the Varley faunal assemblage, held at Manchester Museum, has been undertaken by Sue Stallibrass (University of Liverpool) alongside the remains from the 2010–11 excavations. Early indications are deer and potential early 19th century selective sheep breeding. Other high status finds from the site include red deer and fish remains, oyster shells, a pewter spoon, and tin-glazed earthernware albarello jars or drug jars (excavated by John Edwards, below). Overall, the suggestion is that Merrick's Hill, Eddisbury was the site of a relatively high status 17th to 18th century rural settlement in post-medieval Cheshire.

Prehistoric activity on Merrick's Hill

Iron Age Earthworks

Varley (1950: 34) was concerned that he had not located the internal hillfort rampart at the southern side of Merrick's Hill, and this was something that the current work sought to address. The form of the overburden on the ground surface does lead one to believe that a rampart might still be extant. In Area 1, we found the post-medieval boundary wall built against the front of the prehistoric rampart. However our Area 3 trench, which was located several metres either side of the boundary wall, found no evidence for the existence of a southwestern rampart in this area. The boundary wall was at this point positioned midway down the natural slope and built onto natural (see also Varley 1950, figure 14.1).[4] It remains possible, as Varley (1950) believed, that there had originally been an internal rampart to the southwest, but that this was positioned upslope from the natural drop in rock outcrop and therefore not associated with the post-medieval boundary wall at this point. If so, this would most likely be in the area of Building Three, however it is likely in this case, as Varley (1950) concluded, that it had been entirely removed by the post-medieval activity on the site. Only a more extensive open-area excavation might be able to confirm whether this was indeed the case.

This work has, however, located what instead appears to be a new *external* rampart at the southwest side of Merrick's Hill, in an area of scrubland south of the access track (marked as 'path' on Fig. 11.1). This stretch of earthwork had not been recognised by Varley (Varley and Jackson 1940, figure 8; Varley 1950, figure 3), nor Forde-Johnston (1976, figure 73), and only partially by the survey undertaken by the Royal Commission

in 1987 (cf. Cocroft *et al.* 1989). Detailed topographic survey of this part of the hillfort earthworks has now been undertaken by Dr Ben Edwards with the assistance of the authors. This seemed to confirm to us that, in addition to the well-studied northwestern and eastern entrances to the hillfort (Varley Areas 1 and 3), there remains the possibility of a southwestern entrance, as recognised by Varley and Jackson (1940, figure 8 – labelled 'S.W. entrance'), but then subsequently rejected by Varley (1950, figure 10) and by Cocroft *et al.* (1989).

A walk-over survey has also suggested the possibility of a southeastern entrance at the southernmost tip of Merrick's Hill. Unfortunately, the removal of woodland prior to the 2010 season of excavation saw a substantial quantity of brushwood deposited in this area, making full assessment difficult. Despite recognising that the hillfort ditches around Merrick's Hill both terminate at this point, and being unable to demonstrate the continuation of the eastern rampart in this area, Varley nevertheless suggested that this was not an entrance due to the continuation of the rock-cut platform and associated walling. Varley's assumption was, however, that these two episodes of construction (ditch and wall/rock-cut platform) were contemporary. From our walkover survey, however, we are now confident that the wall surrounding the southeast tip of Merrick's – and its potentially-associated 'rock cut platform' – is actually post-medieval in date, creating what is to this day the boundary fence-line around the lower gradients of Merrick's Hill; and further, that this feature may be truncated by the path (Fig.11.1). The fact that the ditches both terminate here makes a compelling case for an entrance at this point. This suspected southeastern entrance on Merrick's Hill is directly opposed to the entrance at the northwest of the monument, suggesting that the two may have been contemporary.

Rather than Varley's 'missing internal rampart' then, the hillfort earthworks at Merrick's Hill seem to comprise: an external ditch around the base of the hill which terminates to form a southeastern hillfort entrance, directly opposed to Eddisbury hillfort's northwestern entrance; an internal rampart on and to the east of Merrick's Hill (as excavated by Varley), which lacks a corresponding internal rampart to the south of the hill; and instead the hillfort has an *external* rampart off the hill and beyond the ditch, which is perhaps broken by a further entrance at the southwest (Varley's 'S.W. entrance'). Finding the new bit of earthwork in the area of scrubland does seem to have solved Varley's issue with this section of the hillfort earthworks. Working out our understanding of the relative phasing of these earthworks and entrances will be conducted as part of the final site report.

The construction of the linear cobble surface identified at Merrick's in 2011 (Area 1) is remarkably similar

---

[4] Although health and safety restrictions meant that Area 3 was not excavated to natural.

to that found in association with the northwest hillfort entrance (Varley 1950, figure 7). At Merrick's, Varley notes a linear cobbled surface with associated postholes and an occupation horizon consisting of 'ash scatters', with prehistoric ceramic, bone, and a fragment of a bronze pin (*ibid*. 34). This horizon was relocated in 2011, with ceramic retrieved from its construction phase; it seems to be relatively late in the prehistoric sequence, having cut into, and seriously truncating, an earlier deposit containing possible Iron Age ceramic. We have been able to achieve dating material from both construction and use events associated with this cobble surface. The current authors consider that this linear stretch of cobbling leading up to the hillfort's southeast entrance might correspond to the cobbled roadway at the diametrically opposed northwestern entrance to the hillfort, found in Varley Area 1 (see Varley and Jackson 1940, figure 4). In Varley and Jackson (1940, figure 8) the cobbling is shown to curve off to the north; however this does not correspond with the excavated plan of the cobbling (Varley 1950, figure 12) which shows a short, straight stretch pointing in the direction of the northwestern entrance.

The large boulder-block wall above the inner-face of the northeastern ditch, as described by Varley and labelled 'boundary wall' (incorrectly) on the published plan (Varley 1950, Figure 12/Fig.11.3 this chapter), was located by the authors on the eastern side of Merrick's Hill in walk-over survey; whilst the rampart, again as described by Varley: earthen core (but with no timber visible), stone-revetted to front and rear, was revealed in excavation. Following our work on the site in 2010, Earthworks Archaeology completed a slot excavation of Forde-Johnston's section (below) in Area 1, to locate and establish the depth of archaeological deposits, at the request of English Heritage. We began our 2011 excavations from this point. Although severely truncated by later activity, we were able to elucidate two separate episodes of rampart construction: a primary, fairly modest earth and stone bank (surviving to 0.84m wide) augmented by an earth and stone deposit banked up against its interior face (bringing the rampart's truncated width to 1.9 m). Beneath the latter deposit lay a deposit with possible Iron Age ceramic, and perhaps broadly contemporary with the original earthwork phase. As a result of the Varley excavations, it has been difficult for us to work out the relationship between the later rampart material and the cobble roadway, the 1930s excavation having removed those stratigraphic relationships. It may be that the two were contemporary, although it is also just possible that the cobble roadway was later and cut in to rampart material. We hope that the dating programme will enable us to shed some light on this.

Palisaded Enclosure

In Area 1, we re-located the rock-cut posthole beneath the front stone revetment in Varley's (1950) Section 4

drawing, which produced the Varley closing deposit.[5] In Area 2, we located the return of the palisade trench identified by the Varleys inside Building One, which we had hoped would be undisturbed. The palisade cut had unfortunately been removed at this point by a currently unattributed 20th century intervention (Figure 11.4).[6] In Area 1, however, we located the return of the sand-filled rock-cut palisade trench, which was at this point undisturbed. Excavation revealed three separate stages of palisade construction. In Stage 2, the recut palisade was associated with a horizontal interface, with occupation smear, which was cut by several postholes. A post-pipe from Stage 3 of the palisade produced fragments of poorly fired clay (which had the appearance of sherds) – presumably indicating an episode of post decay – before ending with a final conflagration event. These three episodes of occupation have now been dated to the later Bronze Age. The excavations produced 20 dateable prehistoric contexts, including: palisaded enclosure construction Stages 2-3 and destruction, plus three contemporary occupation surfaces and postholes; two phases of hillfort construction, and the cobble roadway. We had hoped to achieve in the region of ten radiocarbon dates for the Merrick's Hill site, but are sadly still seeking funding for this.

Nine sherds of prehistoric ceramic have been sent to the National Museum of Scotland for assessment by Colin Wallace and Fraser Hunter. Two further sherds were collected by Earthworks Archaeology at Merrick's Hill, from the area of the cobble roadway. In addition to these sherds from Merrick's, a further eight have been collected from elsewhere at Eddisbury, from contexts AMS-dated to the early Iron Age (Dan Garner personal communication). Whilst this assemblage may seem rather small, it is actually relatively important, as, beyond VCP, the Cheshire Iron Age is generally considered to have been aceramic. The excavated prehistoric assemblage also includes three coarse stone tools (two pounders/hammer-stones and a whetstone), assessed by Dawn McLaren (National Museum of Scotland) and a small quantity of flint.[7] All palaeobotanical and wood charcoal remains have been assessed by Dr Ceren Kabukcu (University of Liverpool). These suggest cultivation of emmer wheat (21 grains), with some barley, oat, rye, and the occasional gathering of blackberry/nuts. The greatest assemblage of grain was from the final destruction of the palisade, suggesting that arable cultivation may have started relatively early. Importantly, our excavations revealed no evidence for the cultivation of spelt wheat.

---

[5] In the text, Varley refers to a 'palisade trench' beneath the front stone revetment (1950: 34), however on his section drawing (1950, figure 13) it is marked as a posthole. Previously, he had commented that the Merrick's Hill palisades were 'not apparently on the line of the subsequent rampart at all points' (Varley and Jackson 1940: 64).

[6] The 1987 Royal Commission survey clearly shows this area as disturbed.

[7] The latter being held by the Cheshire West and Chester Museum Service at the time of going to press.

FIGURE 11.4 AREA 2: PREVIOUSLY EXCAVATED PALISADE TRENCH BEYOND BUILDING ONE (NOTE THE MODERN BRICK AND SANDSTONE FILL IN SECTION).

Assessment of the Varley archive from the 1936–38 excavations includes a variety of prehistoric material, including 25 prehistoric ceramic sherds, four whetstones and a plant fossil used as a mortar (which we assume may be prehistoric). There is some question regarding the ceramics, however, as initial assessment suggests they do not tally with the description/sketch illustration of the prehistoric sherds from Eddisbury, as given on Varley's record cards (see Mason and Pope, Chapter 4). All that remains in the archive from Varley's work at Merrick's Hill is one late Mesolithic to early Neolithic flint bladelet. What is apparent at this stage is that the earliest occupation on the site of Eddisbury hillfort appears to have been a later Bronze Age palisaded enclosure on Merrick's Hill, which expanded to the west during the Iron Age and developed into Cheshire's foremost prehistoric monument. We can also say at this stage that the hillfort may have had at least four entranceways, with one in the Merrick's Hill area to the southeast, and one at the southwest; not all of these were necessarily contemporary, and working out the phasing of these entranceways with that of the hillfort earthworks will be a task for the final report. There is an excellent prehistoric sequence at Merrick's Hill, with the potential to re-write our understanding of prehistoric Cheshire. One of the key aspects of this work, however, as we worked to document both 20th century damage

and ongoing threats to the prehistoric remains, has been the recognition that this scheduled monument remains at significant risk.

Merrick's Hill since Varley

World War II activity

Military occupation of Merrick's Hill during World War II was represented primarily by a 0.5m deep rock-cut waste pit towards the northern end of Area 3. The main find from the pit was tin cans totalling 52kg. The pit finds suggest two main episodes of military activity. The primary, secondary, and tertiary fills contained large quantities of food/drink containers and British military World War II-issue water purification kits, the deposition of waste from military activity on the site, with an apparent 'clearing' of the site occurring during or after 1945, as indicated by a Burslem plate dated 1945 in the primary fill. The tertiary fill was less substantial and contained a higher proportion of silt, suggesting that the pit was then left open for a period. The final two deposits contained much lower quantities of tin cans and purification kits, suggesting a greater separation in time from site occupation. Instead, these largely contained communications wires, carefully bound into rolls and tied before deposition. The suggestion is that an initial site clearance episode, for which the waste pit was dug, was subsequently followed by a final 'closing' of activity on Merrick's Hill. Visitors to the site in 2011 recalled the existence of a World War II camp down off the hill, presumably the searchlight batteries which were located in the field southeast of Eddisbury Hill Farm that is said to have housed Italian POWs (Joyce and Foxwell 2011: 53), also a 'tower' on Merrick's Hill during the 1930s/1940s, perhaps an observation tower.

Possible investigations by James Forde-Johnston

Visible before de-turfing began in Area 1, a straight slot trench (0.85m wide and 0.55m deep) was apparent in the area of the eastern rampart, extending into a large 'crater' on the eastern periphery (Figure 11.5). A similar intervention was encountered in walk-over survey at the southeast tip of Merrick's Hill, but slightly less substantial than that in Area 1, at 0.5m wide and 0.20m deep. Both trenches had a U-shaped profile, associated upcast deposits, and were un-backfilled, having been left to accumulate shallow silty, humic fills. The section investigated in Area 5 certainly existed prior to the activity of John Edwards (below) who referred to it as a 'mysterious trench' (2003a). In Area 1, we initially

FIGURE 11.5 AREA 1: MID-20TH CENTURY SLOT TRENCH THROUGH THE AREA OF THE EASTERN RAMPART, WITH 'CRATER' IN BACKGROUND; LOOKING EAST.

assumed this to be the remains of the Varleys' Section 4 as it intersected all features shown in the section drawing; however it ran into the area of the southern annexe of Building Two rather than the central room. During excavation it then became clear that this trench actually cut 20th century material. Associated upcast deposits, including a well-preserved turf, were also found directly on top of Varley backfill. The passage of time between the 1930s excavations and these later interventions was demonstrated by a burrow beneath the later upcast, which cut a buried turfline overlying Varley backfill. The location of these trenches seems to be relatively archaeological, although they had not been excavated to the same depth as the 1930s excavations. Both trenches can be found on the 1987 Royal Commission survey, suggesting that they were not associated with the later 'geological' activity of John Edwards (below).

Two oral testimonies from visitors to the site in 2010 recalled excavations on Merrick's Hill in the late 1940s/1950s. We know that Varley re-excavated his own 1939 trenches at Almondbury hillfort (Yorkshire) thirty years later to obtain material for radiocarbon dating (Rowen May personal communication), so there is a possibility that this is Varley re-visiting his own work. If prior to the 1950 publication, then the activity might be placed in the late 1940s, consistent with one oral testimony (Joyce and Foxwell 2011: 52); however a second visitor placed it slightly later, in the 1950s. In 2010, we established contact with James Forde-Johnston's widow, Kathleen Forde-Johnston, who confirmed that her late husband had 'dug' at Eddisbury in the late 1950s or early 1960s; though we cannot rule out the possibility of confusion with his topographic survey at Eddisbury c.1960–2 (Forde-Johnston 1962). These trenches were not backfilled, which is unlike Varley. In Area 1, the purpose of the trench seems to have been to test the section through the rampart and perhaps its relationship with the cobbles and boundary wall. In Area 5, the intention may have been to test the idea of a southeast entrance. Our excavated evidence includes pieces of plastic sheet found below associated upcast deposits, and a crisp packet and remains of a nylon blanket from the secondary fill. At present, the weight of evidence seems to suggest that these are the activities of James Forde-Johnston, seeking to test the conclusions of Varley's (1950) report, ahead of his own article which discusses Molly Cotton's (1954) problem with Varley's discussion of the Eddisbury rampart (Forde-Johnston 1962: 38).

Prior to deturfing in Area 1, a c. 1m deep oval crater (c. 3.0 x 2.0m) was found cutting topsoil, and the fills of Forde-Johnston's linear trench, at the latter's eastern extent (Figure 11.1). Initially, during excavation, it was thought that this must then originate with the activities of John Edwards (below); however its presence on the Royal Commission survey proves that its original excavation occurred prior to 1987; although we believe there were subsequent, minor investigations inside the original cut, which may have truncated the original relationship between the linear and the crater.[8] The original aim of re-investigating the work of Varley seems clear, given its focus on the junction of the culvert exit, the boundary wall, and the hillfort rampart's external facing. It may be that this phase of Forde-Johnston activity followed his digging of the linear trench, the latter perhaps investigatory to locate the rampart, which, upon its discovery, led to the digging of the 'crater'. The archaeological location, together with the fact that it was un-backfilled, and excavated prior to 1987, suggests that this feature can most securely be attributed to James Forde-Johnston. A very similar feature found next to our Area 5, that we know was subsequently investigated by John Edwards (as his 'Collapse Feature 1'), seems also to have originated with Forde-Johnston; the fact that it was not backfilled working to attract Edwards' attention (below).

Modern archaeological investigation

Prior to de-turfing in Area 2, a rectangular trench (c. 3.0 x 1.5m) was found in the southwestern corner of the eastern room of Building One (Figure 11.6). Partially backfilled, unlike the Forde-Johnston trenches, this trench had not been re-turfed, instead being left to gather

leaf detritus from Merrick's sycamore woodland. Notably different to the activities of John Edwards (below), this intervention is much more 'archaeological', both in its character and its location. The trench is rectangular in shape and sits over the location of the Iron Age pit found and published by Varley (1950, figure 12). Its absence on the 1987 Royal Commission survey would seem to confirm the intervention as relatively recent, and the lack of vegetation growth over the exposed soil suggests that this investigation is most likely to be as recent as the early 2000s; a new and very humic topsoil was only just beginning to form from the decaying leaf matter. We are currently unable to assign this intervention to a particular individual, but a similar intention to Forde-Johnston, i.e. to re-evaluate the work of Varley, seems clear.

John Edwards' geological investigations 1995–2004

Before our own excavations began, we were aware of recent 'geological' investigations by amateur geologist John Edwards, who had reputedly found complete post-medieval vessels in the southern area of Merrick's Hill (Dan Garner personal communication). Further research into his activities revealed a substantial series of excavations over a period of no less than eight years between 1995 and 2003. The following discussion is

FIGURE 11.6 EARLY 21ST CENTURY EXCAVATION INSIDE BUILDING ONE, OVER VARLEY'S IRON AGE PIT.

---

[8] Which presumably represent activities associated with Edwards and/ or the individual responsible for the rectangular intervention into Building One during the 1990s–2000s.

FIGURE 11.7 AREA OF JOHN EDWARDS' INTERVENTIONS AT THE SOUTHERN END OF MERRICK'S HILL.

based on information from Historic England's registry file 050311, which contains Edwards' applications for Scheduled Monument Consent (SMC), correspondence, and reports. Edwards' main grounds for requesting SMC was to locate geological 'fault lines' and 'solution pockets' on Merrick's Hill. In 1995 he was granted consent to excavate a 2ft x 6ft area. Sketches in his SMC application show areas of interest that coincide with features recorded by us in survey/excavation. Edwards highlighted an area (in our Area 1) as of interest for the presence of solution pockets; whilst we know that the 'crater' pre-dates this (see above), his sketches do suggest some investigation here. We also believe that a significant depression to the east of Varley's (1950) Building Four (Figure 11.7), notably lacking in vegetation, is the result of investigations by John Edwards. Edwards' campaign at Merrick's Hill continued for seven years, until a 'deep shaft-excavation' was reported to English Heritage in 2002.

At this point, Edwards was invited to submit a new SMC application in which he asked to excavate two 'collapse features' which the farmer had suggested might be the location of fault lines. Edwards' 'Collapse Feature 1' survives as a *c*. 1.0m deep oval 'crater' (2.9 x 1.8m) immediately east of Area 5 (Figure 11.8). Cut into topsoil at the eastern extent of a Forde-Johnston trench (Figure 11.1), it had been left open to accumulate a shallow organic fill. This 'crater' had very similar dimensions to that attributed to Forde-Johnston (above), and its location at the external end of a linear, investigatory trench suggests a similar excavation strategy. This feature, however, was not recorded by the 1987 Royal Commission survey.[9] We believe it possible that this

'collapse feature' of Edwards had originated with the activities of Forde-Johnston (above). The description by Edwards (2003a) suggests an un-backfilled intervention, as characteristic of the latter's work. Edwards' description suggests that this 'collapse feature' had formed due to soil 'falling into a large unconsolidated fault'. In Area 5, we excavated/recorded the feature's upcast deposits. Finds included early post-medieval to early 20th century ceramic (predominantly 18th and 19th century), vessel glass, brick, slate, and a stone roof tile with original nail. This contradicts Edwards' (2003a) report stating that there were no finds. Edwards claims to have found 'cut steps' into bedrock, which he believed were part of 'something bigger'; unfortunately these were beyond the limits of our investigation.

Edwards' (2003b) 'Collapse Feature 2' (Figure 11.8), exposed a series of dressed stone steps, presumably those of a cellar, most likely associated with Varley's (1950) Building Four. With progress obstructed by two trees, Edwards continued excavating 8ft to the northeast against an 'upstanding stone wall', encountering the same structure. Walkover survey located only the general area of this excavation, it having been backfilled on the instruction of English Heritage (Figure 11.7). At this point, as Edwards appeared to be encountering archaeological structures, the Regional Inspector of Ancient Monuments requested archaeological supervision.[10] Between December 2003 and January 2004, the South Trafford Archaeological Group (STAG) was brought in to undertake a resistivity survey across

not to have been surveyed to the same degree of detail as the rest of the monument.
[10] In his 2003 application for SMC Edwards provides a sketch plan indicating that 'Collapse Feature 2' was located some 20m east of Building Four, and beyond 'the limits of archaeology'. In reality it was located immediately north of the north wall of that building.

[9] It is just possible that this feature was missed by the 1987 survey, its edges being home to no less than seven young sycamore trees, and we are already aware that the southeastern area of Merrick's Hill seems

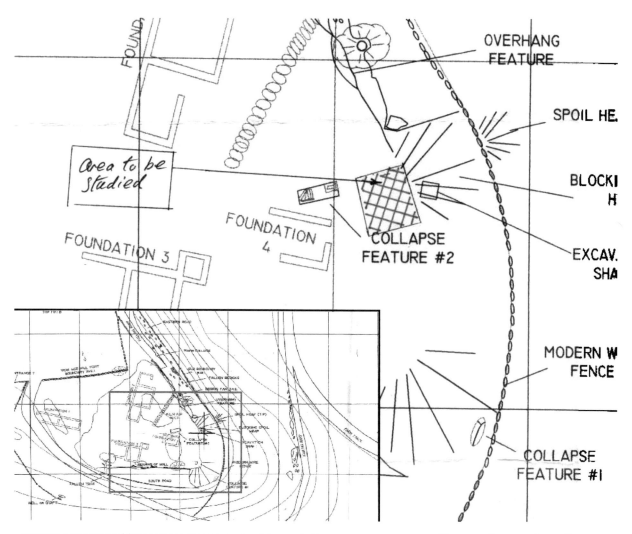

FIGURE 11.8 EDWARDS' 'GEOLOGICAL REPORT MAP' OF MERRICK'S HILL, SHOWING LOCATION OF 'COLLAPSE FEATURES 1 AND 2' AND HIS AREA TO BE STUDIED (2003).

a 20 metre square area, ahead of Edwards' proposed 2 metre square 'keyhole' trench. It was subsequently agreed that since any future work would require the professional archaeological excavation of a 3 metre square trench, prior to any further geological investigations, these activities should cease at Eddisbury.

During post-excavation research between our 2010 and 2011 seasons, we met Derek Pierce (STAG) who was in possession of Edwards' finds from the site. Edwards, after establishing a partnership in late 2003 at the earliest, had apparently deposited finds with STAG, who then worked to catalogue them. The majority of the early modern/modern material had then been disposed of, but a small assemblage of earlier material had been retained, including a Cistercian-ware mug (*c*. 1450–1600); two tin-glazed earthenware albarello or drug jars (*c*. 1600–1650); two yellow-ware copies of tin-glazed 'waisted' albarello medicine jars (*c*. 17th century); and other domestic vessels dating between the 17th and 19th centuries.[11] The

assemblage represents ten vessels. Whilst the date-range of the assemblage is consistent with material from other excavations at the site, without contextual information they offer little opportunity for interpretation, although the complete vessels were thought to have been retrieved from the Building Four cellar floor (Dan Garner personal communication). What we can state is that the presence of high status earthenware/medical provisions again implies occupation of an elevated status in the late 16th or 17th centuries.

Management issues

Tree root damage

The tree stump diameters across Merrick's Hill provide an estimated age of 30–40 years. The majority of new tree growth seems to have occurred within the areas of Varley's backfill, such as the interiors of all three post-medieval buildings, on top of the eastern bank and on the face of the southern bank/rampart; presumably as a result of the loose fills aiding root penetration. Building

---

[11] This assemblage is now in the possession of the authors.

One has encountered perhaps the most severe root damage (Figure 11.6). Here, the tree stump is wider than most on the site and had begun to fragment interior and exterior stone walls; although the problem may have been exacerbated by the recent re-excavation of Varley's backfill in this area. Elsewhere, tree roots have grown on top of built structures, but not penetrated wall cores (Figure 11.9); scrub and tree clearance by the Habitats and Hillforts project has largely prevented further damage, prior to growth becoming increasingly detrimental to the structural integrity of the post-medieval building foundations. The large sycamore in the southeast area of Merrick's Hill (adjacent to Varley's Section 1), however, is visibly penetrating the post-medieval boundary wall and will undoubtedly have a significant impact on the underlying archaeology should the tree fall. Excavation also revealed the occasional activities of burrowing animals, presumably rabbits, at the site.

Stone robbing

A 1.40m wide cut found where the eastern wall of the south extension to Building Two was recorded by Varley (1950), is the result of stone-robbing activity. This linear cut into the eastern bank, which we know is very late in the stratigraphic sequence, had an associated upcast deposit that contained 19th century ceramics and two copper alloy coins from the 1980s, providing a *terminus*

post quem for this particular intervention. Soon after the removal of topsoil, a comparison to Varley's (1950) photographs and plans revealed the extensive robbing of building stone in Areas 1 and 2. The removal of topsoil/vegetation on the wall tops of Buildings One and Two revealed exposed original mortar, caused by the removal of at least one course (in places two) of ashlar stones (Figures 11.10 and 11.11). Alongside this activity, oral testimonies from visitors to the site in 2010 recollect playing on Merrick's Hill as children in the later 20th century, notably crawling through the culvert; we understand that these activities continue to this day. Whilst the main concern here is that of public safety, such activity is likely to have a detrimental impact on any surviving deposits within the culvert, which could ultimately produce excellent evidence for the function of this structure on the site.

Soil management

Between the 2010 and 2011 seasons there had been notable movement, and an increase in the volume, of our spoil heap. This was a result of the landowner using the spoil created by the excavations to increase the shallow depth of sandy soils in fields elsewhere on the farm. The volume increase was apparently a result of spoil acquired from the eastern entrance excavations (see Garner, Chapter 10, this volume). Merrick's Hill had long been used by the landowner's family as a 'storage

FIGURE 11.9 TREE ROOT INTERACTION WITH THE REMAINS OF VARLEY'S (1950) BUILDING TWO.

FIGURE 11.10 VARLEY'S (1950) PLATE 21 SHOWING BUILDING TWO.

FIGURE 11.11 BUILDING TWO AS THE WALLS SURVIVE TODAY FOLLOWING STONE-ROBBING ACTIVITY.

area' for any available soil that could be used to improve the farm's fields. This system of soil management sees any acquired soil held temporarily at Merrick's Hill until its re-allocation, by machine, to the arable fields (Michael Platt personal communication). This practice may provide some protection for the archaeological deposits. For example in Area 2, we recorded evidence of relatively deep soil deposits above those whose finds suggest an association with Forde-Johnston's activity (*c*. 1960s). It seems that a previously lower-lying area of Merrick's Hill between Buildings One and Two has also accumulated deposits in this way, which *may* have worked to protect the prehistoric archaeology.

Metal-detecting

Prior to de-turfing, three sub-rectangular pits were identified cut into topsoil in Areas 1 and 3. Excavation of these features revealed them to be very shallow (*c*. 0.05m) and very modern. The silty, organic fills suggest that the pits were not deliberately backfilled, but had been left open to accumulate a shallow fill over time (Figure 11.12). Our interpretation of these features is that they may indicate a period of metal-detecting activity at the monument late in the 20th or early in the 21st century. Each of the three interventions was located over prominent archaeological earthworks and this represents

FIGURE 11.12 EXCAVATED METAL-DETECTING PIT.

a continuing interest in Merrick's Hill. Our Area 4 demonstrated that the bedrock was relatively close to the surface between Buildings Two and Three. Work here revealed a number of postholes, two of which were post-medieval in date (perhaps indicating a timber precursor to the Building Two stone annexe); two or three were considered more likely to be prehistoric in date, as found in association with a prehistoric surface, and with post-pipes and charcoal inclusions. The fact that potential prehistoric cut features lie so close to the surface in this area of the site, provides considerable cause for concern given the ongoing management issues.

Discussion: Re-excavating Merrick's Hill

Returning to the project aims and objectives, a key aim was to re-assess the conclusions of the Varley excavations, particularly regarding the origins of the hillfort. In line with Iron Age studies at the time, Varley recorded this at 200 BC (Varley 1950: 53), with the Merrick's Hill palisaded enclosure as either Bronze Age, or early Iron Age at c. 400–200 BC (Varley and Jackson 1940: 64; Varley 1950: 52). To achieve this aim we relocated and sample-excavated Varley's trenches to obtain material for C14 dating from the northern stone-revetted Iron Age rampart and associated occupation deposit and the pre-rampart palisade trench. Whilst we relocated his Section 1 through the southern ditch, we were unable to re-excavate this due to safety concerns. We now have a sequence of 20 dateable episodes across the 1st millennium BC, including three distinct construction phases for the palisaded enclosure (including a final conflagration event), at least two phases to the eastern hillfort rampart, and finally the cobbled roadway. These will be detailed in the final Eddisbury report. We have associated ceramics from later Iron Age deposits, and a full suite of palaeobotanical remains suggesting the dominance of emmer wheat cultivation. We were unable to locate a surviving southern rampart on Merrick's Hill, but are hoping to add to the interpretation of the 1987 Royal Commission survey with what appears to be a southern rampart off the hill south of the access track, and two potential southern entrances.

In terms of re-assessing the work of Varley, we believe that the Varleys' fieldwork strategy was of a high standard for the time, cutting-edge even, and that the problem came with his interpretation of the site, not seen in full until the 1950 report, after Varley had spent several years in Ghana. We find some of the problems with the Eddisbury report difficult to understand when they are compared with the fairly meticulous archaeological reasoning encountered in Varley's reports for Maiden Castle, Bickerton (Varley 1935; 1936). Having seen the scale of the Almondbury hillfort archive currently being worked on by Rowan May (ARCUS/YAT), the majority of the site records for Eddisbury may have been lost during World War II and Varley's (1950) report

is what could be remembered based on only the small amount of material that we have been able to retrieve (Mason and Pope, Chapter 4). This may account for some of the problems encountered regarding Varley's (1950) interpretation. Following the excavation work undertaken by Dan Garner in Varley Areas 1–3, (Garner, Chapter 10) we intend to revisit Varley's interpretation of Eddisbury hillfort, and offer new thought on this long-debated topic. This is a very exciting time to be re-evaluating the work of W. J. Varley and re-assessing his role in British hillfort studies.

In addition, largely through the Varley Archive Project as well as our own excavations, we have been able to revisit the post-medieval archaeology of Merrick's Hill, and will present the results of both projects in our final report for Eddisbury. Varley found the culvert and boundary wall to be of one build and believed that they were medieval (14th century) in date. We now know these to be post-medieval (with a later, 18th century *terminus post quem*). Assessment of the Merrick's finds suggests that the main episode of occupation began in the late 16th century, and continued throughout the 17th to 19th centuries. We also know that this was a relatively high status settlement. We have, however, identified a minimum of 12 medieval sherds which do indicate earlier activity, whether or not this constitutes occupation remains debateable. Regarding both the prehistoric and post-medieval archaeology, we now have a much better understanding of the archaeological potential of the site, with a record of the extent of interventions by not only the Varleys, but also James Forde-Johnston, and amateur geologist John Edwards. As a result, we are able to define the surviving archaeological resource as a relatively complete sequence of site occupation during the 1st millennium BC and the 16th to 19th centuries AD, with potential medieval origins, as well as activity in World War II. No definitive Anglo-Saxon evidence was found at Merrick's Hill, but was confirmed elsewhere on the site (Garner, Chapter 10).

Finally, we have also vastly improved our understanding of the management challenges currently facing this scheduled monument. Having worked to record the impact of woodland regeneration on the post-medieval structural remains, we have also recorded ongoing management problems including stone-robbing activity, the potential impact of the farm's soil management strategies on archaeological deposits, as well as evidence for metal-detecting activity. All those engaged in leading the recent work at Eddisbury consider that, as a result of the relatively fragile and truncated state of the prehistoric deposits at Merrick's Hill, combined with continuing active threats to this resource, full re-excavation of Varley's Area 4 must now be seriously considered. Only open-area excavation will solve the question of a southern rampart inside the ditch, and that of the potential for medieval occupation. Similarly, there is a real need to investigate the interior of Merrick's Hill to assess the potential for prehistoric houses, in what remains the only unploughed area of the hillfort. Whilst much prehistoric evidence was lost to the post-medieval occupation, what remained has, as a result, been afforded protection from modern agricultural ploughing. Unfortunately in some areas, prehistoric features survive below only a shallow depth of topsoil. Eddisbury has an unrivalled potential to unravel the prehistoric sequence for North West England; and, as the surviving sequence at Merrick's Hill is currently at risk, preservation by record deserves further serious consideration.

Acknowledgements

The authors would like to thank Dan Garner (Habitats and Hillforts), Ellie Morris and Jill Collens (Cheshire West and Chester Council) for funding and advice. Thanks to Derek Pierce (South Trafford Archaeological Group) for memories of the activity of John Edwards. Special thanks to Ben Edwards (Manchester Metropolitan University) for co-directing the site for two weeks in 2011 and for his survey and digital illustration work, and to Tom Lightbown for supervision, and digitization work in AutoCAD. Thanks to our other wonderful supervisors: Allison Cuneo and Jenn Danis (formerly Dickinson College), Abi Knowles and Chris Davis (University of Durham), Harvey Furniss, Esme Hammerle and Cecilie Lelek Tvetmarken (University of Liverpool), and Mhairi Maxwell and Rachael Reader (University of Bradford). Thanks also to our invaluable site assistants: Margaret Staudter (Dickinson College), Caitlin Harrison (Knox College), Nicola George, Diana Nikolova, Nicky Nielsen and Dane Spacey (University of Liverpool) and the eighty first-year undergraduates from Liverpool with whom this site became even more exciting to excavate. Grateful thanks also to the specialists on the project for their expert work and advice: Alan Braby, Paul Courtney, Chris Cumberpatch, Peter Davey, Julie Edwards, Fraser Hunter, Ceren Kabukcu, Dawn McLaren, David Mullin, Sue Stallibrass, Colin Wallace, and Hugh Willmott.

Chapter 12
Excavations at Kelsborrow Hillfort

Dan Garner

Introduction

The hillfort known as Kelsborrow Castle is situated at around 122m OD, on the western side of the Cheshire Sandstone Ridge (Figure 1.2). This chapter presents the results of archaeological excavation carried out at the hillfort between 14 November and 9 December 2011, under the overall directorship of the author. The work was conducted as a training opportunity for local volunteers under the supervision of professional archaeologists Gary Crawford-Coupe and Leigh Dodd (Earthworks Archaeological Services).

The excavation at Kelsborrow hillfort was intended to provide additional data to inform a strategy for the long-term management of the scheduled monument, in line with the findings of the Desk-Based Assessment and the Condition Assessment carried out by Oxford Archaeology (North) prior to the start of the Project (OAN 2008a; 2008b) (see Chapter 1).

The site was on the Heritage at Risk Register owing to ongoing erosion through repeated ploughing. The monument occupies two fields and is in private ownership as part of Castle Hill Farm. It is presently down to permanent pasture which is grazed by livestock (cattle) as part of a Higher Level Stewardship agreement with Natural England, as part of the Countryside Stewardship Scheme.

Site location

This part of the Ridge comprises an outcrop of Middle Triassic Sherwood Sandstone and Mercia Mudstone (British Geological Survey 1980) overlain by Bridgnorth well-drained sandy soils (British Geological Survey 1983). The site is defined by the curving arc of a bank, with an external ditch at the northern side, and steep cliffs at the southwest and southeast, which form a wedge-shaped enclosure. The site has extensive views to the south and west, while the higher ground of Birch Hill, adjacent to the site, blocks the view to the east. The land to the north of the site consists of a generally elevated and undulating section of the Sandstone Ridge which terminates to the southwest in the steep cliffs which were utilised by the builders of the hillfort. The overall area of the site is approximately 3.6ha (9 acres), with 0.7ha (1.75 acres) being occupied by the bank and ditch (Forde-Johnston 1962: 20). The bank has been spread by ploughing, over a much wider area than would originally have been covered, suggesting that the original rampart would have been quite large. At ground level, the ditch appears to

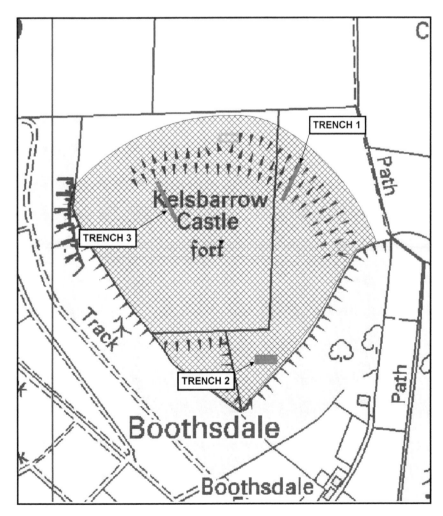

FIGURE 12.1 TRENCH LOCATION PLAN OVER-LAID ON TO THE MODERN OS MAP © CROWN COPYRIGHT. REPRODUCED BY PERMISSION OF THE CONTROLLER OF HMSO LICENCE NO 100053067.

diminish at the western side of the hillfort, although the bank continues up to the natural cliff edge. At the eastern end of the circuit, the bank and ditch appear to terminate and it is suggested that this may have formed a simple entranceway (*ibid.* 21).

Methodology

The fieldwork at Kelsborrow comprised three excavation trenches as located on Figure 12.1. In the case of all trenches the approach, as defined by the Scheduled Monument Consent, was to cause minimal disturbance to the surviving archaeological deposits by either targeting a previous excavation trench or by only removing demonstrably recent surface litter and topsoil. After mechanical topsoil stripping all excavation was therefore undertaken by hand, using appropriate hand tools; and was undertaken with a view to avoiding damage to any archaeological features or deposits which appeared to be demonstrably worthy of preservation *in situ*. Excavated material was examined in order to retrieve artefacts to assist in the analysis of their spatial distribution. All investigation of archaeological horizons was by hand, with cleaning, inspection and recording both in plan and section.

Trench 1 was excavated towards the northern apex of the main rampart arc in the location of an excavation trench undertaken by Dr David Coombs, from Manchester University in 1973 (Coombs 1988). The location of the 1973 trench was captured by an aerial photograph taken by the Potato Marketing Board (No 2982/Run G/June 1975) and was identified by a geophysical survey undertaken by Chester University in 2009 (see Chapter 6, this volume). There was no section produced in the published report (Coombs 1988) from the 1973 trench and attempts to locate the original archive at Manchester University were unsuccessful. Trenches 2 and 3 are in the locations of anomalies identified by the geophysical surveys undertaken in both 2009 and 2010 (see Chapter 6).

All three trenches were reinstated at the end of the excavation process. In each case a sheet of geo-textile (*terram*) was used to line the base of the excavation

Phase	Summary
1	Pre-hillfort activity on the hilltop
2	Construction of an earthen rampart to create a promontory enclosure
3	Early medieval re-occupation of the promontory
4	Post-medieval field boundaries
5	Modern activity

FIGURE 12.2 THE MAIN PHASES IDENTIFIED WITHIN TRENCHES 1, 2 AND 3.

and then the trench was subsequently backfilled using the excavated material. In areas where earthwork reinstatement was required there were enough large sandstone fragments within the excavated material to be able to recreate the original contour without the need for additional measures such as wire mesh gabions or sandbags. All three trenches were given a top covering of the original topsoil which had been set aside for the purpose and then re-seeded with grass in order to return the areas to permanent pasture.

Arrangements were made for the long-term storage of the physical archive with the Cheshire West and Chester Museum Service with the unique accession number CHEGM 2011.21.

Results

A broad sequence of phases was developed for the whole site, in an attempt to maintain a basic chronological framework for all excavation trenches (Figure 12.2)

Trench 1 (Figures 12.3–12.11)

Trench 1, measuring 25 x 4m, was excavated towards the northern end of the main rampart in the location of Manchester University's 1973 excavation trench. It was primarily intended as an opportunity to re-examine and record a full section through the rampart and to recover material for scientific dating where appropriate. The trench would also serve to inform some of the more general management issues regarding the effects of plough damage.

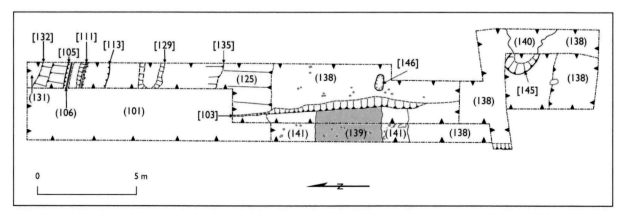

FIGURE 12.3 PLAN OF TRENCH 1

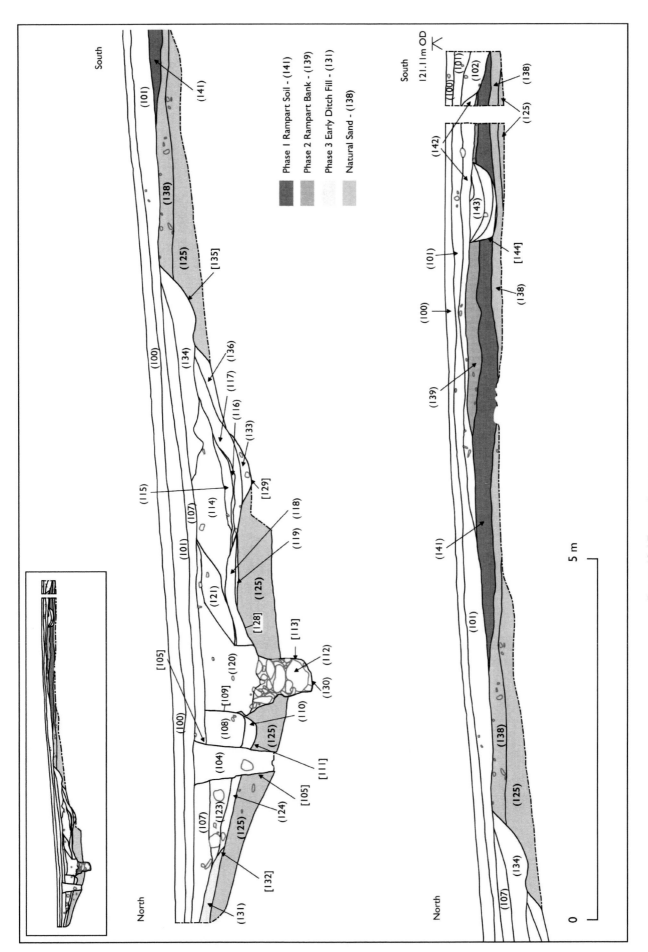

South

(101)

(141)

Phase 1 Rampart Soil - (141)
Phase 2 Rampart Bank - (139)
Phase 3 Early Ditch Fill - (131)
Natural Sand - (138)

(138)

(125)

[135]

(100)

(134)

(117)

(116)

(133)

(129)

(115)

(114)

(107)

(101)

(119) (118)

(121)

[128] (125)

[113]

(120)

(112)

[109]

(130)

[109]

[105]

(100)

(108)

(110)

(125)

[111]

(104)

[105]

(107)

(123)

(124)

(125)

[132]

(131)

North

South

121.11m OD

(101)
(100)
(102)

(138)

(125)

(142)

(143)

[144]

(138)

(101)

(100)

(139)

(141)

(101)

(138)

(125)

(134)

(107)

North

5 m

0

Figure 12.4 Trench 1 northwest facing section

219

FIGURE 12.5 REMAINS OF THE BUFF/WHITE SAND (139) OF THE RAMPART BANK. LOOKING NORTHWEST.

FIGURE 12.6 REMAINS OF THE BUFF/WHITE SAND (139) OF THE RAMPART BANK (CENTRE LEFT). LOOKING NORTHEAST.

FIGURE 12.7 POSSIBLE EARLY DITCH FILL (131) (TO LEFT) CUT BY LATER FIELD DRAINS. LOOKING SOUTHEAST.

Phase 1

The earliest stratigraphic horizon encountered in Trench 1 was a layer of dark orange/brown sand (141) with rare flecks of charcoal which measured 12.22m north-south, at least 2m east-west and was 0.23m thick. Layer (141) lay directly above natural sand (138) and was bulk sampled (sample <11>) for palaeoenvironmental analysis. The layer probably represented a pre-rampart soil horizon.

Phase 2

Above deposit (141) and towards the centre of Trench 1 were the remains of a bank (139) which had been interpreted as the base of the hillfort rampart during the 1973 excavations. The rampart deposit consisted of a buff/white fine textured sand (139), with rare sub-rounded pebbles and charcoal flecks. It measured 4m wide, 0.28m thick and was uncovered for a length of 4m (Figures 12.5 and 12.6). Deposit (139) was bulk sampled (sample< 9>) for palaeoenvironmental analysis and wood charcoal was extracted and used to attain a radiocarbon date of 1000–840 cal BC (BETA-325775).

Phase 3

At the northern end of Trench 1 it was noted that the complex sequence of post-medieval ditch and field drain cuts (described below) had removed virtually any trace of an earlier ditch which might have been associated with the hillfort rampart construction. However, the remnants of a deposit (131) were identified on the northern-most edge of the trench which possibly indicated the slight traces of an earlier ditch cut (Figure 12.7). Deposit (131) was a dark brown silt, flecked with charcoal fragments which measured 1m north-south, 1.2m east-west, and was 0.2m thick. Deposit (131) was bulk sampled (sample <4>) for palaeoenvironmental analysis and wood charcoal was extracted and used to recover a radiocarbon date of cal AD 1020–1160 (BETA-325774).

At the southern end of Trench 1, the original 1973 excavation had identified a charcoal spread on the internal side of the hillfort rampart. During re-excavation in 2011 the remains of this charcoal spread were uncovered and recorded as deposit (140). This was a charcoal-rich mid-grey sand-silt that appeared to fill a shallow pit (145). Pit (145) was a shallow bowl-shaped depression cut in to natural sand (138),

FIGURES 12.8 AND 12.9 THE ORGANIC-RICH DITCH FILLS (133) IN BOTH PLAN (TOP) AND SECTION (BOTTOM). LOOKING SOUTHEAST.

cut (128), which was aligned east-west and measured 0.5m wide, 0.2m deep and at least 1.2m long. The primary fill of ditch (128) was a thin lens of dark grey/brown clay-silt (119) over which was a deposit of grey/brown silt-sand (118) up to 0.15m thick. The uppermost fill of ditch (128) was a dark brown silt-clay (127). The full width of ditch (128) could not be established as the northern side of it had been removed during the cutting of field drain (113).

Ditch (129) was cut in to the upper fill (127) of ditch (128) and was aligned east-west, measuring 4m wide, 1m deep and at least 1.2m long. The primary fill of ditch (129) was an organic-rich mid-grey/brown sand-silt (133) up to 0.15m thick (Figures 12.8 and 12.9). Silt (133) was bulk sampled (sample <12>) for palaeoenvironmental analysis; beetle carapace from leaf-eating weevils were extracted and used to attain a radiocarbon date of cal AD 1650–1950 (BETA-317209). Overlying fill (133) was a mid-grey/brown silt-sand (117) which was up to 0.14m thick and was bulk sampled (sample <2>) for palaeoenvironmental analysis. Above fill (117) was a dark brown/black silt-clay (116) which was up to 50mm thick and was bulk sampled (sample <1>) for palaeoenvironmental analysis. Fill (116) was covered by a series of interleaved lenses of mid-grey/brown and light grey silt-sand (115) up to 0.15m thick; overlying this was a mixed deposit of red clay, light brown silt-sand and red sand (114). An iron horse shoe was recovered from the interface between the base of fill (114) and the top of fill (115); (Figure 12.10) after conservation this horse shoe was dated to c. AD 1600–1800. On the basis of the horse shoe and the radiocarbon date from fill (133) it seems probable that ditch (129) dates to the 17th or 18th century.

Field drain (113) (Figure 12.11) was cut in to the upper fill (114) of underlying ditch (129) and was an east-west aligned linear trench measuring at least 1.2m long, 1.15m wide and 1.4m deep. The lowest fill of trench (113) consisted of a grey and red/brown sandy-silt (130) that was up to 0.1m thick. Overlying silt (130) was a

measuring 1.7m wide, 0.32m deep and was at least 1.2m long. Deposit (140) was bulk sampled (sample <8>) for palaeoenvironmental analysis and wood charcoal was extracted and used to recover a radiocarbon date of cal AD 990–1120 (BETA-325776).

Phase 4

At the northern end of Trench 1, the edge of the ditch identified in 1973 was re-exposed and a full section completed across its width; revealing a complex sequence of activity. The earliest context in the sequence (deposit (131)) is described above under Phase 3. The earliest post-medieval feature in the sequence was ditch

FIGURE 12.10 THE IRON HORSE SHOE IN SITU. LOOKING
SOUTHEAST.

deposit of sub-angular sandstone blocks (112) up to 1m thick; the blocks were up to 0.4m in size and had been loosely set to allow them to function as a drain or soak-a-way. Above stone deposit (112) was a deposit of orange/brown clay (120/121) up to 0.7m thick which formed the uppermost fill of field drain (113).

To the south of field drain (113) there was a shallow ditch (135) which was aligned east-west and measured 2.5m wide, 0.3m deep and at least 1.2m long. Ditch (135) was also cut in to upper ditch fill (114) and was filled with a mixed orange/brown and grey sand (134).

Ditch (111/132) was cut in to the northern side of earlier field drain (113) and was an east-west aligned linear measuring 2m wide, 0.11m deep and at least 1.2m long. The fill (110/124) was a dark grey/brown silt-sand containing sub-rounded pebbles up to 20mm in size. Ditch (111/132) was cut by ditch (109) which was aligned east-west and measured 2.1m wide, 0.7m deep and at least 1.2m long. Cut (109) was interpreted as the re-cut of field boundary or drainage ditch (111/132) and was filled with a mixed deposit of red/brown sands and clays (108/123); which contained occasional angular mudstone fragments up to 0.2m in size. Above fill (108/123) was a deposit of red/brown silt-clay (107) which was 0.15m thick and appeared to cover an area 14m north to south and at least 2m east to west.

The most recent feature revealed within the ditch area was a linear cut (105) which was cut through deposit (107) and was aligned east-west; being exposed for a length of 1.2m, the cut was 1.1m deep, 0.45m wide at the top, tapering to 0.25m at the base. At the base of cut (105) was an iron service pipe (106) which had

FIGURE 12.11 SHOWING A SECTION THROUGH THE POST-MEDIEVAL FIELD DRAIN (113). LOOKING SOUTHEAST.

been detected on the magnetometry survey undertaken in 2010 (see Chapter 6); the survey suggested that the pipe ran from the pond located to the west of Trench 1, in a southeastern direction towards the valley known as Boothsdale. Above iron pipe (106) was a mixed backfill deposit (104) consisting of patches of red sand, light brown silt-sand and brown clay.

Phase 5

Towards the centre of Trench 1 (in the location of the rampart bank) a sub-circular pit (146) had been cut in to the natural sand (138) and then filled with the 1973 backfill deposit (102); the pit measured 0.8m long, 0.45m wide and 0.3m deep. It is possible that pit (146) is shown on the 1973 trench plan published in 1988; however, it is not described or discussed in the published account and is clearly separate from the line of three postholes thought to have been associated with the rampart construction. It is feasible that pit (146) might have been a pre-rampart feature but it is now impossible to be sure.

On the western side of the re-excavated trench a rectangular cut (144) was noted in the section, sealed beneath ploughsoil (101) and cutting rampart deposit (139); the rest of the feature seemingly removed but not recorded during the 1973 excavation. Cut (144) measured 1.3m north to south and was 0.35m deep; the fill (143) consisted of interleaved lenses of brown clay and pale brown sand. Cut (144) was sealed by a discrete deposit of mixed red/brown clay (142) which was 5.42m north to south and 0.1m thick; this was interpreted as the truncated base to the 1973 spoil heap which had seemingly survived the subsequent ploughing episode.

After the removal of ploughsoil (101) the cut and backfill of the 1973 excavation was tentatively identified. On investigation the backfill (102) was confirmed as a mixed

brown sandy clay and light brown sand-silt which varied in depth between 0.3m to the south and 0.9m to the north; the backfill produced several relatively modern finds including bits of a plastic yogurt carton and a wooden pencil. The cut (103) measured 2m wide and 25m long with a maximum depth at the northern end of 0.9m. The initial difficulty in identifying the 1973 trench was due to the fact that ploughing after the trench had been backfilled, had served to truncate the top of the backfill, leading to smudging and spreading of the trench edges.

The uppermost context within Trench 1 was turf and topsoil layer (100) which was a mid-brown loam 0.14m thick; below the topsoil was a modern ploughsoil layer (101) which was also a brown loam up to 0.2m thick. Both the topsoil and the underlying ploughsoil were removed mechanically with a toothless ditching bucket.

Trench 2 (*Figures 12.12–12.15*)

Trench 2, measuring 14 x 3m, was located to investigate circular anomaly 'I' from the 2009 Chester University survey, which was possibly also visible on the 2010 ArchaeoPhysica survey (see Chapter 6) but was not identified as an archaeological feature in the report. The trench was also located in an area of relatively low lying ground which was thought to have attracted a greater depth of soil deposition and so promoted a higher level of preservation after the previous ploughing episodes on the monument.

Phase 4

Beneath modern ploughsoil (201) a layer of mid-red/ brown sandy-clay (202) was exposed covering the entire trench; layer (202) was up to 0.2m thick and was thought to be the base of an earlier post-medieval ploughsoil. Layer (202) overlay a deposit of natural sand (205) which in turn overlay the top of sandstone bedrock (206).

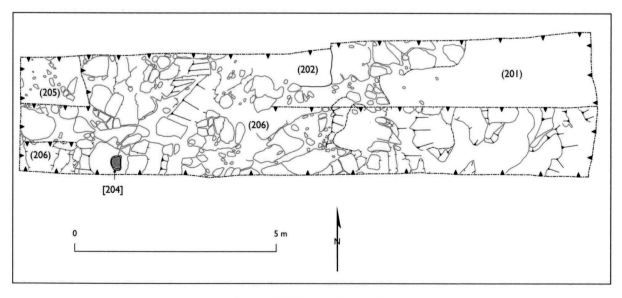

FIGURE 12.12 PLAN OF TRENCH 2.

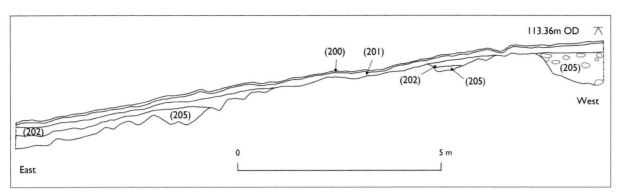

FIGURE 12.13 TRENCH 2 NORTH FACING SECTION.

FIGURE 12.14 GENERAL VIEW OF TRENCH 2. LOOKING EAST.

At the western end of the trench (where the sandstone bedrock outcropped closer to the modern ground surface) a single posthole (204) was identified cutting in to the bedrock (206). Posthole (204) was roughly square in plan and measured 0.35m long, 0.25m wide and 0.35m deep (Figure 12.5). The fill (203) was a dark brown silt-sand with occasional sandstone fragments up to 100mm in size; the fill was sampled (sample <10>) for palaeoenvironmental analysis.

Phase 5

The uppermost context within Trench 2 was turf and topsoil layer (200) which was a dark brown loam

50mm thick; below the topsoil was a modern ploughsoil layer (201) which was also a dark grey/brown loam up to 0.15m thick. Both the topsoil and the underlying ploughsoil were removed mechanically with a toothless ditching bucket.

Trench 3 (*Figures 12.16–12.21*)

Trench 3, measuring 33 x 2m, was located to investigate the southern edge of circular anomaly [19] from the 2010 ArchaeoPhysica survey which had been interpreted as a possible large pit (see Chapter 6). Anomaly [19] was one of a number of similar features running along the length of the hillfort rampart and their interpretation was

FIGURE 12.15 VIEW OF ROCK-CUT POSTHOLE (204). LOOKING WEST.

uncertain ranging from natural geology to a possible pre-rampart feature; the targeted anomaly was quite large being approximately 20m east-west and 10m north-south. Trench 3 was also located on an area of relatively high ground which may have been subject to a greater level of soil erosion after the previous ploughing episodes on the monument.

Phase 1

The earliest archaeological context identified in Trench 3 was layer (307/308) which was an extensive context covering the whole trench. Layer (307/308) was a clean orange/brown sand up to 0.25m thick which was interpreted as a natural sub-soil; however, during initial cleaning of the upper surface where it had an interface with the base of layer (302) an early Neolithic flint leaf-shaped arrowhead was recovered.

Beneath layer (307/308) was a dark grey sand (309) which was up to 0.3m thick and covered the entire trench. Layer (309) was interpreted as a natural subsoil which had become discoloured by the leaching of iron minerals from layer (307/308) above. Layer (309) overlay the natural sandstone bedrock (310).

Phase 3

At the northern end of Trench 3 there was a shallow sub-circular pit (304) measuring roughly 1m in diameter and 0.15m deep. Pit (304) was filled with a charcoal-rich deposit of dark grey silt-sand (303); this was bulk sampled (sample <6>) for palaeoenvironmental analysis and wood charcoal was extracted and used to recover a radiocarbon date of cal AD 690–890 (BETA-325777) (Figures 12.17– 12.21).

Adjacent to pit (304) was the base of a truncated posthole (306) measuring 0.2m long, 0.13m wide and 0.08m deep. The posthole was filled with a mid-grey sand-silt (305) which contained rare charcoal flecks. Both pit (304) and posthole (306) were cut in to layer (307/308).

Phase 4

After the removal of modern ploughsoil (301) a layer of mid-red/brown sandy-clay (302) was exposed covering the entire trench. Layer (302) was up to 0.1m thick and was thought to be the base of an earlier post-medieval ploughsoil.

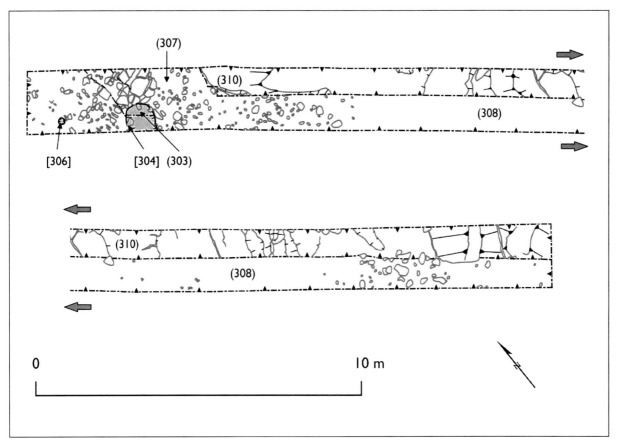

FIGURE 12.16 PLAN OF TRENCH 3.

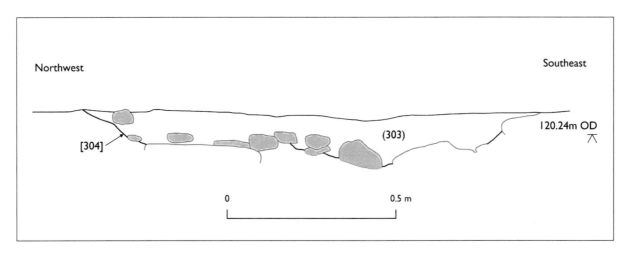

FIGURE 12.17 TRENCH 3 SOUTHWEST FACING SECTION THROUGH PIT (304).

Phase 5

The uppermost context within Trench 3 was turf and topsoil layer (300) which was a dark brown loam 70mm thick; below the topsoil was a modern ploughsoil layer (301) which was also a mid-brown loam up to 0.15m thick. Both the topsoil and the underlying ploughsoil were removed mechanically with a toothless ditching bucket.

The finds

Dan Garner

In spite of careful cleaning and excavation of most archaeological horizons by trowel, accompanied by on site sieving and bulk sampling from most contexts for palaeoenvironmental analysis, finds retrieval was minimal.

227

FIGURE 12.18 SECTION THROUGH PART OF TRENCH 3 (304). LOOKING NORTHEAST.

FIGURE 12.19 VIEW OF TRENCH 3 WITH PIT FILL (303) IN THE FOREGROUND. LOOKING SOUTHEAST.

FIGURE 12.20 SECTION THROUGH PIT (304). LOOKING NORTHEAST.

FIGURE 12.21 PIT (304) FULLY EXCAVATED. LOOKING NORTHEAST.

The metalwork – iron

A single iron object was recovered from the excavation of field boundary ditch context (115) in Trench 1. The object was a complete iron horse shoe of the so-called keyhole type (Sparkes 1976) with calkins and a fullered groove set close to the outer edge, through which the nail holes were punched. It measured 110mm long x 110mm wide, with a maximum width of 30mm. There were six sub-rectangular nail holes present. The object is dated *c.* AD 1600–1800 (Figure 12.22).

The worked flint

A single piece of worked flint was recovered from the excavation. This was a small leaf-shaped arrowhead (Figure 12.23 (1)) with a broken tip from Trench 3 context (308). The object was manufactured from a flake of dark grey flint and was of ogival form; being of Green's type 1A (Butler 2005: 123). There was invasive retouch, executed by pressure flaking, covering the entire surface of the dorsal side; with retouch on the ventral side confined to just tip and edges. The object measures 22mm from distal to proximal ends and 16mm across the medial section. This type of arrowhead is usually found in association with early Neolithic pottery and early and middle Neolithic monuments.

Approximately 12 months prior to the 2011 excavation the local land owner and his family recovered an object of worked flint from the up cast to an animal burrow, located in the field immediately east of the scheduled monument (less than 100m from the promontory fort). The object (Figure 12.23 (2)) was found broken in to two pieces (both of which were recovered) and was manufactured from a flake of pale grey flint; it measured 70mm from distal to proximal ends and 20mm across the medial section. The object has been identified as an unmodified knife blade of possible early Neolithic date.

Palaeoenvironmental Sample Assessment

Alison Foster, Lindsey Foster, Angela Walker and John Carrott (abridged by Dan Garner)

The following text is abridged from an unpublished report by Palaeoecology Research Services (Report no. PRS 2012/34) dated October 2012. The full report is available in the on line appendix.

Twelve 'bulk' sediment samples representing deposits encountered in all three trenches but predominantly from the re-excavations in Trench 1, were submitted to Palaeoecology Research Services Limited, Kingston upon Hull, for an assessment of their bioarchaeological potential.

Ancient biological remains recovered from the eight deposits which did not exhibit waterlogged preservation

FIGURE 12.22 AN IRON HORSE SHOE FROM DITCH FILL (115), TRENCH 1.

were restricted to relatively small quantities of poorly preserved and largely indeterminate charcoal, with occasional other charred plant macrofossils. The remains provided too little material for any interpretation but were, on occasion, sufficient for submission for radiocarbon dating (via AMS). Amongst the charred plant remains identified in the sample from the late Bronze Age rampart deposit (139) there were small amounts of grass and heather which perhaps hint at the presence of lowland heath in the vicinity. The early medieval deposit produced a tiny assemblage of charred plant macrofossils from context (303) which comprised a single charred grape 'pip', a glume wheat grain and a grass/oat grain, and two other indeterminate cereal/grass grains, but provided too little material for interpretation. The Saxo-Norman deposits, contexts (131) and (140), produced a few identifications and/or partial identifications for the wood charcoal fragments (heather, *Calluna*, root/rhizome fragments from Context 131 and hazel, *Corylus*, and perhaps oak, *Quercus*, from Context 140) and Context 140 also yielded charred plant macrofossils including two oat (*Avena* – perhaps from a cultivated crop but equally likely to be a wild form) grains (caryopses).

Four of the deposits assessed exhibited waterlogged preservation of organic remains. All of these were located in Trench 1 and comprised the primary, secondary and tertiary fills of post-medieval ditch 129 and the lowermost fill of land drain 113. These deposits yielded small, to quite large, assemblages of plant and invertebrate macrofossils, which provided consistent evidence for the presence of standing water within both the ditch and the land drain, with associated wetland marginal ground.

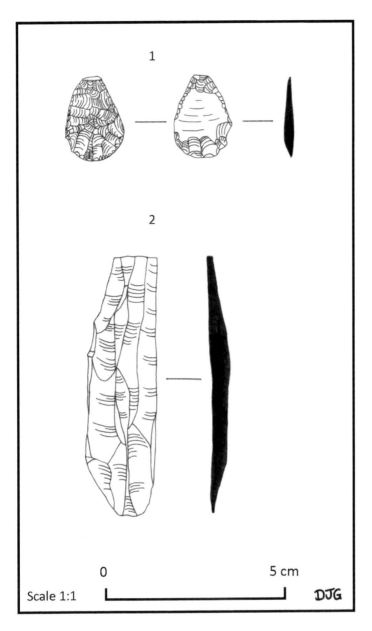

described by Zondervan and Sparks (1997). The radiocarbon results are given in Figure 12.24 and are quoted in accordance with the international standard known as the Trondheim convention (Stuiver and Kra 1986). They are conventional radiocarbon ages (Stuiver and Polach 1977).

Discussion

In spite of the minimal invasive methods used during the trial excavation the results have proved informative in both increasing our understanding of the monument known as Kelsborrow Castle hillfort and in terms of gaining a greater understanding of the impact that the current management regime is having on the buried archaeological remains.

Pre-hillfort landscape: Previously, little was known about the landscape prior to the construction of the hillfort beyond stray finds of two polished stone axes (CHER 834/0/1; CHER 834/0/2) which are attributed to the Neolithic period and a bronze palstave which was recorded as having been found within the promontory fort in 1810 (CHER 833/1) (OAN 2008a: 42). Evidence recovered from Trench 1 has identified an ancient buried soil (141) sealed beneath the base of the rampart; however, the very limited excavation of this deposit (limited to the taking of bulk sample 11) recovered no artefacts or material suitable for scientific dating. Furthermore, the early Neolithic arrowhead recovered from layer (308) in Trench 3 and the knife blade recovered from an animal burrow in the adjoining field to the east, add to the growing artefact scatter in the general vicinity of the hillfort. The suggestion that the wider site may once have been the focus of Neolithic activity remains a tantalising possibility.

Rampart form: In terms of 'understanding' the hillfort it has been informative to reinvestigate the structural form of the main rampart. This was originally interpreted by Coombs as a 'timber box-type rampart' represented by a north-south alignment of three postholes with a 'core' of fine-grained white sand about 4m wide at the base (Coombs 1988: 65–6). The 1973 excavation had removed the 'core' deposit and any underlying buried soil down to the top of the natural sub-soil within Trench 1.

The line of three postholes identified by Coombs in 1973 could not be re-located within the 2011 excavation, possibly suggesting that they had either been rather ephemeral features or that they had been inserted in to the top of the 'core' deposit and had not penetrated

These features clearly represented repeated attempts to provide drainage for the surrounding land, with elements of the plant assemblage from the land drain fill (remains of blackberry, raspberry and, perhaps, blackthorn) hinting at the establishment of hedgerows adjacent to this feature.

Radiocarbon Dating Summary

Dan Garner

Five samples were submitted to the Beta Analytic Radiocarbon Laboratory, Miami, Florida in 2012. The five samples were processed using the acid/alkali/acid protocol of Mook and Waterbolk (1985) and measured by Accelerator Mass Spectrometry (AMS) as

Laboratory Number	Sample Number	Material & context	Radiocarbon Age (BP)	d13C (‰)	Calibrated date range (95% confidence)
BETA-325774	4	Charcoal, from lower ditch fill deposit (131)	990±30	-26.2	cal AD 1020–1160
BETA-325775	9	Charcoal, from rampart deposit (139)	2790±30	-26.7	1000–840 cal BC
BETA-325776	8	2x oat (*Avena* sp.) grains (caryopses) and 1x cereal/grass grain, from pit fill (140) of pit [145]	1030±30	-26.5	cal AD 990–1120
BETA-325777	6	1x glume wheat grain, 1x oat (cf. *Avena*) grain, 2x cereal/grass grains, from pit fill (303) of pit [304]	1200±30	-23.6	cal AD 690–890
BETA-317209	2	Beetle chitin - phytophagous *Otiorhynchus* sp. weevil elytra (x4), pronota (x2) and head (x1) from fill (133) of ditch [129]	210±30	-26.1	cal AD 1650–1950

FIGURE 12.24 SUMMARY OF THE RADIOCARBON RESULTS FROM THE KELSBORROW SAMPLES

the underlying sub-soil to any great depth. The latter suggestion would indicate that the postholes were stratigraphically later than the initial formation of the rampart 'core' and could be related to a later phase of activity. Coombs' line of postholes are shown on the eastern side of his published excavation trench plan and the 2011 re-excavation exposed a slightly wider area of the intact hillfort rampart for a length of nearly 4m; being traced 2m further to the west than the 1973 excavation. This additional section of rampart was not removed during the 2011 excavation; however, the top of the 'core' deposit was closely examined without identifying any further posthole alignments. This provided a gap of nearly 4m between the posthole alignment identified in 1973 and the western edge of the 2011 excavation trench, which is a rather large spacing for structural timbers associated with a box-style rampart and so raises some doubts regarding the original interpretation of the structural evidence. The surviving evidence may suggest an original rampart consisting of a simple earthen bank with a basal width of 4m.

Date of rampart construction: The rampart 'core' within Trench 1 was bulk sampled <sample 9> for palaeoenvironmental analysis and wood charcoal was extracted and used to attain a radiocarbon date of 1000–840 cal BC (BETA-325775). The date suggests that initial rampart construction took place during the late Bronze Age. Amongst the charred plant remains identified in the sample from the rampart deposit there were small amounts of grass and heather which perhaps hints at the presence of lowland heath in the vicinity; indicating a managed landscape involving regular livestock grazing.

The rampart outer ditch: The defences have previously been described as including an outer ditch which geophysical survey has suggested extended all the way to the natural break of slope on the western and southeastern sides of the hillfort; being interrupted by a modern water-filled quarry pit roughly half way along its length. However, the southeastern extent of this ditch would not support Forde-Johnston's suggestion of an

entranceway in this location, as indicated by a terminus to the rampart bank before reaching the edge of the natural slope. Excavation of a complete section across the outer ditch in Trench 1 during 2011 has suggested that it is not contemporary with the rampart construction and in fact belongs to a much later phase in the development of the monument. The removal of the outer ditch from the prehistoric phase of the promontory fort brings the form of the defences in to line with that seen at Helsby, Woodhouse and Beeston during the late Bronze Age i.e. a single bank with no outer ditch or developed entrance.

Early medieval re-occupation: The identification of deposits and features dating to the early medieval period in both Trenches 1 and 3 during the 2011 excavation was unexpected.

The earliest feature identified for this phase was a shallow sub-circular pit in Trench 3 which contained a charcoal-rich fill that produced a radiocarbon date of cal AD 690–890 (BETA-325777). The charred plant remains recovered from the fill included fragments of grass, wheat and oats which might indicate that crop processing was taking place on the site; a single charred grape pip was also present. The pre-conquest date recovered from the charred plant remains may provide a context for the place-name 'Kelsborrow' (or 'Kelsborough Castle' as it is shown on an 1813 map of Delamere Forest (CALS 113224)) which Higham suggests combines the personal name *Kel* with the Old English element – *burh* (meaning Kel's fort) (Higham 1993: 138). The archaeological evidence points to occupation of the hillfort in a period prior to the Aethelflaedan burh building programme of the early 10th century.

Examination of the section through the outer ditch in Trench 1 identified the northern lip to the earliest surviving phase of this feature; which produced a radiocarbon date of cal AD 1020–1160 (BETA-325774). This might suggest that the promontory enclosure was re-fortified in the Saxo-Norman period with an outer ditch being added to the existing prehistoric bank. The line of postholes identified during the 1973 excavation might also belong to this phase of re-fortification. Wood charcoal from the early medieval ditch fill included fragments of heather which perhaps hints at the presence of lowland heath in the vicinity, indicating a managed landscape involving regular livestock grazing. Furthermore, on the hillfort interior in Trench 1 a charcoal-rich pit fill produced an almost identical radiocarbon date of cal AD 990–1120 (BETA-325776) (this had been first identified as a charcoal 'patch' during the 1973 excavation). The dimensions of the pit were not fully exposed during the 2011 excavation and its function remains uncertain; however, the fill suggests occupation on the hillfort interior at a time when it had seemingly been re-fortified. Charred plant remains from the pit fill included fragments of heather, cereal/grass, alder, hazel and grains of oats; the latter perhaps indicating crop processing on the site.

The scientific dating evidence suggests activity on the monument during the 11th or 12th century AD which would be much later than the Aethelflaedan burh building of the early 10th century recorded in the Anglo-Saxon Chronicle (as evidenced at nearby Eddisbury). It is tempting to suggest that Kelsborrow could have been utilised as a Norman castle in the post-conquest period and the appearance of the earthwork as recorded by Ormerod (see Chapter 2, this volume) with a large internal mound is very reminiscent of a motte and bailey design. This internal mound is now barely visible in the lidar data and could be a natural topographic feature (Chapter 7, this volume), and it was not detected in the geophysical surveys (Chapter 6); however, not all castles of this period had mottes in the design (Stanford 1991: 136–7). It is worthy of note that many of the smaller castles in the Welsh Marches have no documentary record and whilst there was a proliferation in castle building during the anarchy of Stephen's reign (1134–54), most will be earlier (*ibid.* 135). There are other examples in the Welsh Marches of prehistoric hillforts being re-used as Norman castles such as the 12th century ring-work known as the Citadel inside the Herefordshire Beacon hillfort (*ibid.* 137); closer to home there is the 13th century castle sited at Beeston. No artefacts dateable to this period have been recovered from the monument; however, an antiquarian reference to the recovery of an iron sword from within the enclosure in 1810 (CHER 833/1) might be of relevance. The three early medieval dates recovered from such a relatively small sample of the hillfort interior might suggest fairly extensive occupation during this phase of the site. The range in dates might imply several periods of use rather than a single event.

The post-medieval landscape: Examination of the complex sequence of stratigraphy identified in the outer ditch section in Trench 1 supports the presence of a well establish post-medieval boundary. The feature is likely to pre-date the enclosure award of 1819 (CALS QDE1/23/2/6) based upon the combined dating evidence provided by the iron horseshoe and the radiocarbon date

from weevil chitin. The enclosure map of 1819 does not show a boundary following this alignment and nor does any subsequent map of the area. The combined evidence would suggest that the boundary was created whilst the area was still contained with the Royal Forest of Delamere; the precise function of such a boundary remains uncertain. The environmental evidence suggests that the ditch itself may have remained filled with water for a prolonged period and it has been suggested that it may have served as much as a drain as a boundary, implying associated wetland/marginal ground. Elements of the plant assemblage from the later land drain fill (including remains of blackberry, raspberry and, perhaps, blackthorn) hint at the establishment of a hedgerow adjacent to the ditch. The most likely conclusion is that the extant hillfort earthwork had long been used as an identifiable feature in the landscape and was simply formalised during the 17th or 18th century by the creation of a field ditch and associated hedge. Whether this was simply part of an *ad hoc* field enclosure system or something more specialised associated with the management of forest animals such as deer, cannot be ascertained from desk-based research. Whatever its purpose, the boundary appears to have been abandoned and forgotten after the early 19th century enclosure award.

Management Review

The implications of the excavation results for the management of the hillfort are summarised below. A full review of management measures implemented through the Habitats and Hillfort Project has been presented in an unpublished Management Review Report (Garner 2011c).

Plough erosion: The remains of the rampart had clearly already been spread and flattened by the time of the 1973 excavation and identification of the 1973 excavation trench during 2011 proved problematical owing to truncation and smudging of the trench edges during post-1973 ploughing. The areas examined on the hillfort interior suggested that all vertical stratigraphy had been removed from the site as part of the on-going plough erosion and that even features cut in to the sub-soil had been significantly eroded by this process. The monument is now down to permanent pasture as part of a Higher Level Stewardship agreement between the landowner and Natural England, as part of the Countryside Stewardship Scheme and as such the shallow and ephemeral archaeology still present on the site should be protected from further erosion of this type.

Conclusions

The excavation has served to increase our knowledge of the form, character and level of archaeological preservation on the monument known as Kelsborrow Castle hillfort. This has identified the monument as a rare early type of hilltop enclosure, which owes its origins to the late Bronze Age rather than the previously suspected Iron Age. The hillfort interior has no above ground features to consider; however, sub-surface structures in the form of postholes and pits have been identified within all three trenches. Sampling has demonstrated that, within the confines of the excavation, artefact and ecofact recovery has been very low with only hardy materials such as stone tools and charred plant remains being identified from the prehistoric period.

The excavation has also helped to identify the monument as a multi-period site with relatively plentiful evidence for a phase of early medieval use that was previously unsuspected. Sampling has again demonstrated that, within the confines of the excavation, artefact recovery has been entirely negative whilst ecofact recovery has been very low with only hardy materials such as charred plant remains being identified from the early medieval period.

Chapter 13
Environmental changes in lowland Cheshire: Hatchmere and Peckforton Mere

Richard Chiverrell, Heather Davies and Pete Marshall

Introduction

The programme of the Habitats and Hillforts project encouraged the development of a better understanding of the timescale and nature of human impacts on the landscape of lowland Cheshire. Parallel with the investigations at the hillforts, two lakes were targeted for investigation of the palaeo-record preserved within the lake sediments. Hatchmere is situated to the east of the Sandstone Ridge and is overlooked by Eddisbury hillfort. It is a Site of Special Scientific Interest (SSSI) and comprises a eutrophic lake with an associated area of fen carr and dry woodland. The mere lies in a depression in outwash deposits of the last glaciations; today it reaches a maximum water depth of ~3.5m and is surrounded by fringing wetland and reedswamp. Peckforton Mere, also to the east of the Sandstone Ridge, lies further south and is close to the hillfort at Beeston Castle. Peckforton is a very eutrophic shallow water body, with maximum water depth of ~1.5 metres. The mere is situated in agricultural fields but is surrounded by reed and willow wetland (Figure 13.1).

Methods

Field sampling

At both Hatchmere and Peckforton Mere complete Holocene sediment sequences were sampled from the deepest sector of the lakes from an anchored floating platform. The sediments are largely organic limnic muds and extend in age back to the end of the last ice age. The cores were taken in 1m overlapping lengths using a Russian-style large capacity (0.07x1m) sediment corer, with sediment penetration facilitated using a manual hammer tapping system. Cores were wrapped and sealed in polythene and stored refrigerated until required for analysis.

Geochronology: radiocarbon dating and age-depth modelling

Six samples were selected to provide a chronology for the core taken from Hatchmere and a total of twelve samples for that from Peckforton Mere. The six samples from Hatchmere and eight of the samples from Peckforton Mere were submitted for radiocarbon analysis to the Scottish Universities Environmental

Research Centre, East Kilbride (SUERC). The samples were pre-treated using the acid-base-acid protocol (Stenhouse and Baxter 1983).The samples were converted to carbon dioxide in pre-cleaned sealed quartz tubes (Vandeputte *et al.* 1996), graphitised as described by Slota *et al.* (1987) and measured by Accelerator Mass Spectrometry (AMS) (Xu *et al.* 2004). One sample (GU-22813) produced insufficient carbon following pre-treatment and was not dated.

The remaining four samples from Peckforton Mere were submitted to Rafter Radiocarbon Laboratory, New Zealand and were processed using the acid/alkali/acid protocol of Mook and Waterbolk (1985) and measured by Accelerator Mass Spectrometry (AMS) as described by Zondervan and Sparks (1997).

Both laboratories maintain continual programmes of quality assurance procedures, in addition to participation in international comparisons (Scott 2003). These tests indicate no laboratory offsets and demonstrate the validity of the measurement quoted. Bayesian modelling approaches (Buck *et al.* 1996) were used for the age-depth modelling of the two lake sediment sequences (Blaauw 2010). Details of Bayesian age-depth modelling can be found in Blaauw and Christen (2005), Blaauw *et al.* (2007a; 2007b) and Bronk Ramsey (2009) and examples of its implementation in Blockley *et al.* (2007; 2008) and Gearey *et al.* (2009).

Pollen analysis

Pollen samples were taken from the two lake sediment sequences. Sample preparation followed standard preparation procedures, with the extracted material being stained with safranin and mounted in glycerol (Moore *et al.* 1991). Three hundred total dry land pollen grains (Moore *et al.* 1991) were counted from each slide. Samples were counted using a trinocular microscope at x400 magnification; ax1000 oil immersion lens was used for grains requiring closer scrutiny. Identifications were made using the keys of Faegri *et al.* (1989) and Moore *et al.* (1991), supported by the University of Liverpool type slide collection. Taxonomic nomenclature followed the conventions of Stace (2010) and Bennett *et al.*(1994). Relative pollen diagrams were drawn using TILIA (Grimm 2010).

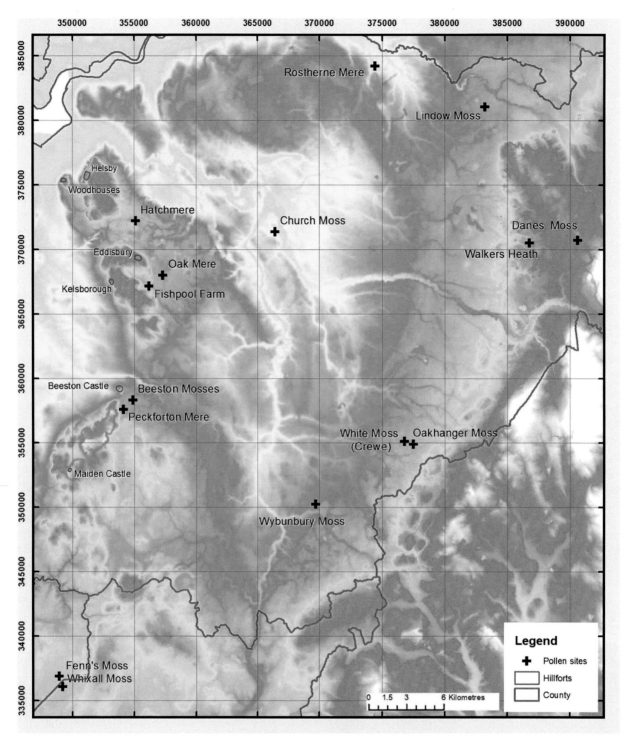

FIGURE 13.1 FIELD LOCATIONS REFERRED TO IN THE TEXT

Results

Geochronology

The results are presented as conventional radiocarbon ages (Stuiver and Polach 1977) and are quoted in accordance with the international standard known as the Trondheim convention (Stuiver and Kra 1986). The calibrations of these results, which relate the radiocarbon measurements directly to the calendrical timescale, are also given (Figure 13.2). All have been calculated using the datasets published by Reimer *et al.* (2009) and the computer program CLAM (Blaauw 2010). The calibrated date ranges cited are quoted in the form recommended by Mook (1986), with the end points rounded outward to 10 years for errors greater than 25 years and to 5 years where the error is less than 25 years. The ranges in Figure 13.2 have been calculated according to the maximum intercept method (Stuiver & Reimer 1986).

Peckforton Mere					
Laboratory Code	**Depth**	**Material**	**Radiocarbon or other age (BP)**	**δ13C (‰)**	**Calibrated date (95% confidence)**
SUERC-33258	2.3m	Bulked organics >63µm	1385±30**	-30.7	cal AD 600–680
SUERC-33259	2.5m	Bulked organics >63µm	1275±30**	-30.1	cal AD 660–810
SUERC-33260	3m	Bulked organics >63µm	1440±30**	-29.5	cal AD 560–660
SUERC-33261	3.9m	Bulked organics >63µm	1335±30**	-29.4	cal AD 640–770
GU-22813	4.7	Terrestrial macrofossils	Failed	-	-
SUERC-33262	5.5m	Bulked organics >63µm	990±30	-29.2	cal AD 990–1160
SUERC-33263	6.5m	Bulked organics >63µm	1490±25	-29.4	cal AD 530–640
SUERC-33264	7.3m	Bulked organics >63µm	2550±30	-29.4	800–550 cal BC
NZA-38006	8.11m	Fine grained gyttja	3035±20	-31.0	1390–1215 cal BC
NZA-37792	8.81m	Fine grained gyttja	3859±20	-30.0	2465–2205 cal BC
NZA-38007	9.61m	Fine grained gyttja	4654±25	-307	3520–3360 cal BC
NZA-37729	10.31m	Alnus macrofossil	5491±25	-29.3	4370–4270 cal BC
Hatchmere					
Lake surface	3.20m	Sediment water interface	-61 BP		
Pb marker	3.40m	Fall in Pb concentrations	-20 BP		
Pb marker	4.30m	Rise in Pb concentrations	110 BP		
SUERC-41872	4.50m	Plant macrofossils	643±24	-25.0	cal AD 1285–1395
SUERC-41873	5.00m	Plant macrofossils	813±23	-29.1	cal AD 1180–1270
Pending	6.10m	Plant macrofossils	Pending		
SUERC-41874	7.00m	Plant macrofossils	3769±31	-28.3	2290–2050 cal BC
SUERC-41875	8.10m	Plant macrofossils	5015±23	-26.6	3940–3870 cal BC
SUERC-41876	8.70m	Plant macrofossils	5710±23	-27.1	4615–4460 cal BC

FIGURE 13.2 CHRONOLOGICAL MARKERS AND RADIOCARBON RESULTS FROM A: PECKFORTON MERE; B: HATCHMERE

Age-depth models

The *P-Sequence* modelling in Oxcal (not shown) shows good overall agreement between the stratigraphic information and radiocarbon dates for both sequences, with the exception of the upper four ages at Peckforton, which are regarded as contaminated with older carbon and plant remains. The age-depth models shown were calculated using as LOESS locally weighted spline using CLAM (Blaauw 2010) and both sites show relatively slow rates of sediment accumulation during the early Holocene through to around 2000 BP when sedimentation rates increased sharply (Figure 13.3).

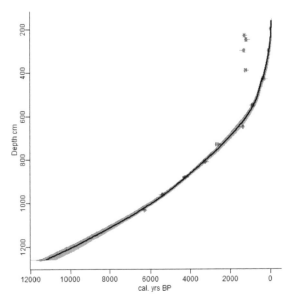
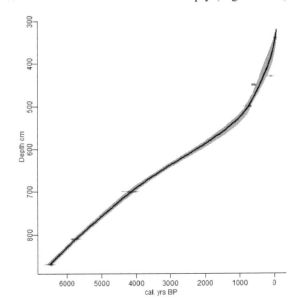

FIGURE13.3 AGE-DEPTH MODELS FOR (LEFT) PECKFORTON MERE AND (RIGHT) HATCHMERE

Pollen data

Hatchmere (HAT2011)

The results of the 44 samples from Hatchmere are presented in Figure 13.4 as percentages of TLP (total land pollen), with spores and aquatics presented as percentage of TLP plus spores and aquatics. A total of 15,155 pollen and spore grains were identified. Five pollen zones have been distinguished and are described here.

HAT2011-lpaz 1840.5–810.5cm (6140–5750 cal BP) Alnus-Quercus

The lowest pollen zone in the sequence from Hatchmere is dominated by arboreal taxa (95% TLP). The major taxa are *Quercus* (~40%), *Alnus* (~20–25%) and *Corylus* (~15–20%). Herbaceous taxa make up around 5% of the identified grains. Herbaceous diversity is low, largely comprising Poaceae. Spores and aquatic taxa are at low levels in this zone.

HAT2011-lpaz2 810.5–680.5cm (5750–3825 cal BP) Alnus-Corylus-Quercus

Zone 2 is marked by an increase in *Corylus* and a decrease in *Quercus* towards the base of the zone, followed by return to similar levels to Zone 1 at the top of the zone. *Ulmus* levels decline (3–5% in Zone 1 to <1% in Zone 2) towards the base of the zone. The diversity of aquatic species increases in this zone, and herbaceous taxa increase towards the top of the zone (from ~5% to ~10%).

HAT2011-lpaz3 680.5–640.5cm (3825–3063 cal BP) Alnus-Betula-Quercus-Corylus

Zone 3 is marked by an increase in *Betula*, with Poaceae and *Pteridium* throughout the zone. Herbaceous taxa increase from ~5% to ~10% in this zone. *Plantago lanceolata*, *Rumex acetosa* and rosaceous taxa become more constant in this zone.

HAT2011-lpaz4 640.5–500.5cm (3063–755 cal BP) Alnus-Quercus-Poaceae-Cyperaceae

This zone sees a marked increase in Poaceae and Cyperaceae. The percentage of Poaceae fluctuates throughout the zone but is highest in the centre of the zone. Herbaceous taxa peak in the centre of the zone at 40%, with arboreal taxa showing a corresponding low of ~60%, with *Quercus* in particular declining, before increasing to 75% at the top of the zone. There is an increased diversity of both herbaceous and aquatic taxa in this zone. *Calluna vulgaris* becomes more constant, at around 2–5% in this zone. Cerealia taxa become more constant in the top half of the zone, and there is also a marked increase in *Typha angustifolia*. Cannabiaceae grains appear for the first time towards the top of this zone.

HAT2011-lpaz5 500.5–415.5cm (755–235 cal BP) Cannabiaceae-Alnus

This zone is marked by a rapid increase in Cannabiaceae pollen, which peaks near the base of the zone and declines slightly towards the top, and a decline (75–50%) in arboreal taxa. Arboreal taxa then remain at a constant level (~50–65%) throughout the zone, as do Poaceae (~10%), Cyperaceae (~3–6%) and other herbaceous and aquatic taxa. *Quercus* and *Calluna vulgaris* increase slightly towards the top of the zone, whilst *Pteridium* declines. Cerealia taxa are less common in this zone than in Zone 4.

Peckforton (PEC1)

The results of the 37 samples from Peckforton are presented in Figure 13.5 as percentages of TLP (total land pollen), with spores and aquatics presented as percentages of TLP plus spores and aquatics. A total of 12,666 pollen and spore grains were identified. Five pollen zones have been distinguished and are described here.

PEC1-lpaz1 1011–916.25cm (6109–4673 cal BP) Alnus-Corylus-Quercus

The lowest pollen zone in the sequence from Peckforton Mere is dominated by arboreal species (95–99%), mainly comprising *Alnus, Corylus* and *Quercus* grains. Herbaceous and aquatic taxa are rare and diversity is low.

PEC1-lpaz2 916.25–853.75cm (4673–3869 cal BP) Alnus-Corylus-Quercus

The base of this zone is marked by a slight decrease in *Quercus* pollen and an increase in Poaceae. Arboreal pollen remains dominant (~90–95%).

PEC1-lpaz3 853.75–766.25cm (3869–2791 cal BP) Alnus-Betula-Corylus-Quercus-Poaceae-Cyperaceae

Zone 3 is marked by a decrease in arboreal taxa from ~90% to ~60% and an increase in Poaceae and Cyperaceae grains. *Tilia* disappears and the level of *Betula* grains increases and fluctuates throughout the zone. Spore taxa, particularly Pteropsida and *Pteridium* increase and fluctuate throughout this zone. The diversity of herbaceous taxa increases: Cereal taxa and *Cannabiceae* appear and *Plantago lanceolata* and *Rumex acetosa* maintain constant levels from this zone onwards.

PEC1-lpaz4 766.25–703.75cm (2791–2112 cal BP) Alnus-Corylus-Poaceae-Quercus

This zone is marked by a decrease in arboreal taxa and an increase in herbaceous taxa (from ~10% to ~3-% at the base of the zone, but then decreasing throughout the rest

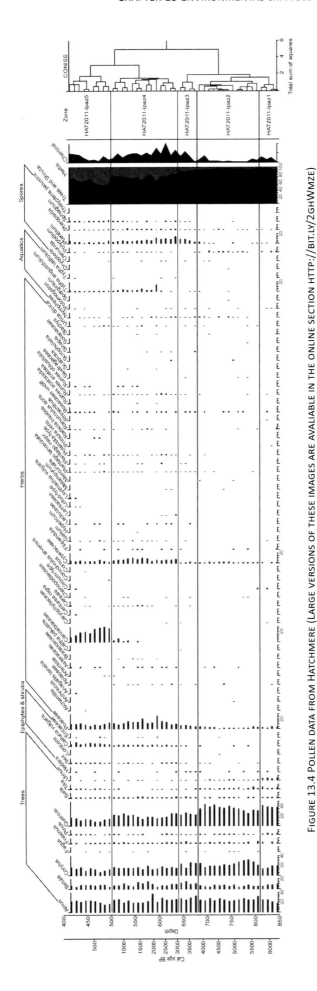

FIGURE 13.4 POLLEN DATA FROM HATCHMERE (LARGE VERSIONS OF THESE IMAGES ARE AVAILABLE IN THE ONLINE SECTION HTTP://BIT.LY/2GHWMZE)

of the zone). Poaceae pollen increases and peaks at the centre of the zone and *Alnus* decreases towards the top of the zone. *Pteridium* increases through the zone to 18% (TLP+aquatic+ spores) and then decreases to the top of the zone.

PEC1-lpaz5 703.75–560cm (2112–883 cal BP) Alnus-Corylus-Quercus-Poaceae-Betula

This zone in marked by a slight increase in arboreal taxa, particularly *Betula*, which continue to fluctuate throughout the zone between ~70 % and ~90%. Poaceae and Cyperaceae also fluctuate slightly and *Calluna vulgaris* increases slightly to around 3%.

Interpretation

Hatchmere

The palaeocological sequence from Hatchmere covers the period from the end of the Mesolithic (~6000 cal BP) up to around AD 1800. Woodland taxa – particularly oak, alder and hazel – are dominant through the Neolithic until the later Bronze Age. The paucity of open ground species supports the interpretation of a largely forested landscape during *lpaz* 1 and 2.

A decline in oak and increase in grass suggests there was some woodland clearance in the early Bronze Age (~3900 BP). This is supported by an increase in bracken, holly and birch, which are indicative of vegetation disturbance and increased light levels in woodland clearings, and by a marked increase in microcharcoal concentration within the samples. Ribwort plantain also consistently appears in all samples, indicating that land was being used for grazing animals. Furthermore, cereal pollen first appears in samples during the early Bronze Age.

Heather becomes more consistent in samples from the middle Bronze Age (~3400 cal BP). Continued low levels within samples throughout the remainder of the core indicate the development of heathland in the region from this period. Increases in sedges and wetland species (particularly bulrushes) may indicate the local development of wetter areas from the end of the Bronze Age (~2700 cal BP) onwards.

There are further fluctuations in woodland species, followed by a more marked decline in the late Bronze Age and early Iron Age, beginning around 2500 cal BP. Corresponding increases in grass and open-ground herbaceous taxa, and a peak in microcharcoal, suggest increased deforestation, which reached its height during the Iron Age. Cereal pollen also becomes a more consistent feature of the record from the later Iron Age (~2000 cal BP) until the medieval

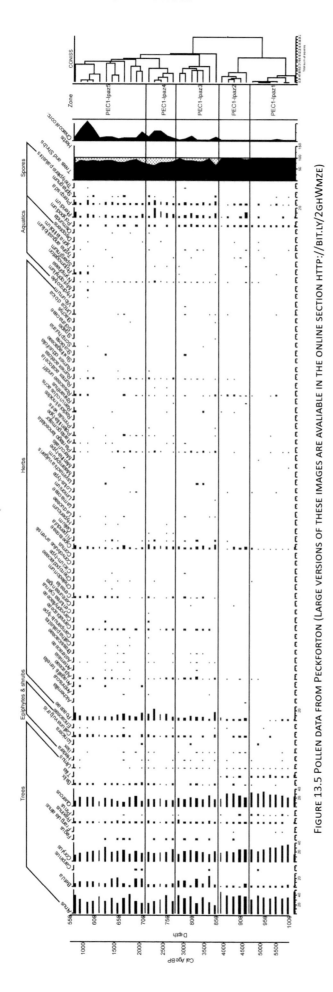

FIGURE 13.5 POLLEN DATA FROM PECKFORTON (LARGE VERSIONS OF THESE IMAGES ARE AVALIABLE IN THE ONLINE SECTION HTTP://BIT.LY/2GHWMZE)

period. There is a small increase of arboreal taxa and a decrease in grasses and sedges in the early medieval period (~900 cal BP or AD 1200), suggesting limited woodland regeneration.

Cannabiaceae pollen first appear in the record at low levels in the late Roman period (around 1500 cal BP), rapidly increasing to become the dominant taxa by the early medieval period. This dominance peaks around 600 cal BP (~AD 1400) and then declines in the post-medieval period, whilst still remaining prevalent in the upper samples (up to 235 cal BP). The dominance of Cannabiaceae pollen is indicative of hemp-retting activities in the mere; these would have been most intensive in the medieval period, but possibly extended back as far as the late Roman period in the local area. At this period, the lower levels of Cannabiaceae pollen may indicate hemp growing locally between ~1500 and 800 BP, rather than hemp retting directly in the mere. As Cannabiaceae decline during the later medieval and post-medieval periods, there is a slight increase in tree species (particularly oak and hazel) and in heather. This may indicate some woodland regeneration and heathland development, perhaps suggesting a decline in agricultural activities in the local area.

Peckforton

The palaeoecological sequence from Peckforton covers the period from the end of the Mesolithic (~6000 cal BP) to the beginning of the medieval period (around AD 1066). The Peckforton diagram shows a more consistently wooded landscape than that from Hatchmere with arboreal species, particularly alder, dominant throughout the record. The Peckforton record also covers a shorter period of time than that from Hatchmere, ending at the opening of the medieval period. However, in common with the Hatchmere record, the Peckforton results show two phases of clearance, followed by some woodland regeneration, in the early Bronze Age (~4000–3600 cal BP) and the Iron Age (~2600–2000 cal BP). At Peckforton, these deforestation phases are marked by a decline in arboreal species, particularly oak and birch but also lime in the early Bronze Age. There is also an increase in grass and sedge species, as well as bracken, and open-ground herbaceous species (e.g. docks). Corresponding peaks in microcharcoal concentration indicate local burning activities.

Cereal pollen first appears in the record in the early Bronze Age and remains at a constant low level throughout the rest of the core, indicating local agricultural activities. Ribwort plantain also becomes a consistent feature of the record from this period onwards and is indicative of animal grazing. Heather also shows a similar pattern, being recorded at consistent low levels from the early Bronze Age onwards, suggesting heathland development in the region. Cannabiaceae pollen first appear in the record in the early to middle Bronze Age (~3600 cal BP) and are found at low levels throughout the rest of the core. This may suggest local cultivation of hemp, but does not seem to indicate that hemp-retting took place in the mere before the Middle Ages.

Chapter 14
Pollen and plant macrofossil analysis of peat deposits from Ince Marshes

RSK Environment Ltd

Introduction

Ince Marshes are located in the Mersey estuary (Figure 1.2) and constitute a low-lying wetland area with islands of drier ground that have produced evidence of human activity dating back to the Bronze Age. The hillforts on Helsby and Woodhouse Hills overlook this rich environmental resource, while a Roman fortlet and medieval manorial remains on the marshes attest to the strategic importance of the area in the past. The deep peat deposits that have accumulated in the estuary since the last Ice Age were thought likely to contain records of changes to the surrounding environment brought about by human activities over the centuries.

In advance of development on the marshes, RSK Environment Ltd and Cambrian Archaeological Projects were brought in to carry out an assessment and field evaluation in 2005 and 2006. Further investigations by RSK in 2010 included the removal of cores and bulk samples from *c.* 3m deep peat deposits found on the site. The cores were taken from boreholes excavated by geotechnical engineers associated with the development.

Three sets of samples were taken from three adjacent boreholes:

- Borehole BH405 – continuous core in three sections, through the upper clay and upper peat (UP).
- Borehole BH406 – a series of bulk samples (*c.* 3 litres) from the top of the lower peat to the bottom of the peat 10.5m below ground level. Dark grey silty clay lies below the bottom sample, Bulk 6 (LP).
- BH407 – a reserve continuous core from a borehole close to BH405 and BH406. The core contains upper peat deposits. This core has been retained in reserve untouched in case additional environmental analyses are required at some time in the future.

The core taken from the upper peat was fairly small in diameter (8cm). Larger bulk samples were taken from the lower peat, because this was easier when sampling at depth. Although this meant that depth measurements were less precise, it was possible to take pollen samples, radiocarbon samples and plant macrofossil samples from the same large, intact lump of peat, thus ensuring that the data still ties together.

A multidisciplinary approach was used, with samples for pollen first being removed from the cores by Sylvia Peglar, followed by samples for radiocarbon dating, and then samples for plant macrofossils from the same locations in the cores. Sampling was kept to a minimum depth (2cm) to maximise the resolution. Samples for AMS dating were taken from intact peat at the centre of the core, so as to minimise the possibilities of contamination[1].

Assessments of pollen and plant macrofossils from the samples through the upper and lower peats, BH405 and BH406, were undertaken in April 2011 (Peglar & Carruthers 2011). Twenty samples from points *c.* 12cm apart through the upper and lower peat profiles were assessed for plant macrofossils (see Figure 14.2 for actual depth measurements). Fairly wide spacing was used in the assessment so that additional samples could be taken at a later date if specific changes needed to be studied in detail. Wherever possible, the same levels were examined for both pollen and plant macrofossils in order to maximise the level of interpretation at each depth. Radiocarbon samples were taken from seven of the sample points, as listed in Figure 14.3. Following recommendations in the assessment report, full analysis was undertaken on the samples in order to retrieve the maximum amount of information from the samples.

Analysis of Palynological Samples

Sylvia Peglar

Introduction

Pollen and spores may be transported from great distances, although most will probably be derived from close to the deposition site and either arrive from inwash or be airborne. Thus the pollen assemblages may provide evidence of the nature of the vegetation (and hence environment) around the site but also the regional vegetation and environment. The taxonomic level to which pollen and spores may be identified is usually only to family, type or genus and rarely to species, whereas macrofossils may often be assigned to species. The analysis of macrofossils provides a much more local picture as, in general, macrofossils do not travel far. Thus the two analyses are complementary to one another.

---

[1] Dates have been calculated with reference to Reimer et al. 2009.

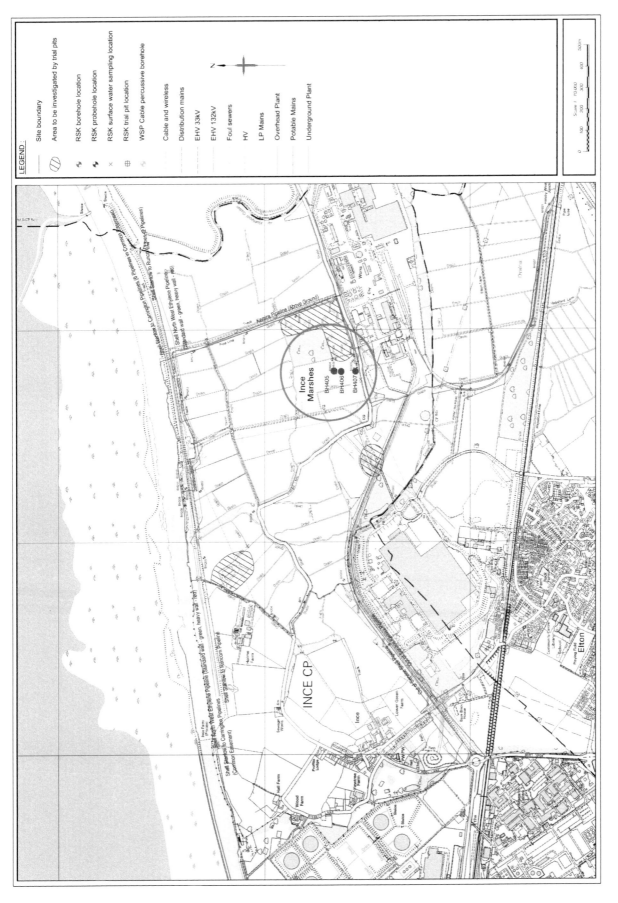

FIGURE 14.1 INCE MARSHES BOREHOLE SAMPLE LOCATION PLAN

	1	2	3	4	5	6	7	8	9	10	11	12	13	14	16	18	19	20	21	22
Sample number																				
Actual Depth	30cm	42cm	54cm	66cm	78cm	90cm	102cm	114cm	126cm	142cm	154cm	166cm	178cm	190cm	bulk1	bulk3	bulk4	bulk5	bulk6	base
herbs of grassland/heath/disturbed ground																				
Ranunculus acris/bulbosus/repens (buttercup achene) DG		1																		
Potentilla sp. (cinquefoil achene) DGMY		5																		1
Viola sp. (violet seed) EGSW											1						3			
Labiatae cf. Stachys sp. (cf. woundwort nutlet) MGD															1	1				
Valeriana officinalis L. (common valerian fruit) G																			2	
woods/scrub/fen taxa																				
Urtica dioica L. (stinging nettle achene) CDn																		1	6	
Betula pubescens Ehrh. (downy birch seed) Whawp																		12	21	7
Betula pubescens Ehrh. (downy birch female catkin bract) WHawp																		2	5	3
Betula sp. (indeterminate birch female catkin bract) WSF																			3f	
Betula sp. (poor birch seed, no wings) WSF							4									2	3	13	39	12
Alnus glutinosa L. (alder seed) WSF									1		1		1			2				
Alnus glutinosa L. (alder catkin) WSF													2							
Salix sp. (willow bud scales) WSF																		3	4	
heathland taxa																				
Calluna vulgaris (L.) Hull (heather seed) Emsp			++			[1] 2				1	1									
Calluna vulgaris (L.) Hull (heather shoot tip) Emsp			[9]																	
Calluna vulgaris (L.) Hull (heather leaf) Ep		[1]	[4]	[1]							1									
Erica tetralix L. (cross-leaved heath leaf) Mew		[1]																		
E. cinerea L. (bell heather seed) E																				
Erica sp./Calluna vulgaris (heather, ling capsules) EM		[2] 3	[6] 86		2						4									
bog/marsh/aquatic taxa																				
Ceratophyllum demersum L. (rigid hornwort achene) P																				7
Ranunculus sceleratus L. (celery-leaved buttercup achene) MP	1													1						
Ranunculus subg. Batrachium (crowfoot achenes) P										cf. 1								2		2
Myriophyllum sp. (water-milfoil nutlet) Pc							5													4
Rumex cf. hydrolapathifolium (cf. water dock achene) P																		2	3	1
Lycopus europaeus L. (gypsywort nutlet) FGwP																7	1f		1	
Mentha sp. (mint nutlet) MPG											1									
Menyanthes trifoliata L. (bog bean nutlet) MFw																1	cf.1f			
Eupatorium cannabinum L. (hemp-agrimony achene) wGHP															15+					
Hydrocotyle vulgaris L. (marsh pennywort fruit) M		1		2			5			1						1		1		
Angelica sylvestris L. (wild angelica fruit) GFMP																			1	
Lemna sp. (duckweed fruit) P				1															1	
Potamogeton sp. (pondweed fruit) M													3					2	2	8
Zannichellia palustris L. (horned pondweed achene) Mc																				2
Juncus sp. (rush seed) MPw	++	+++	+	++	+	+			+++	+	++							+		

FIGURE 14.2 INCE MARSHES PLANT MACROFOSSILS. (1)

Sample number	1	2	3	4	5	6	7	8	9	10	11	12	13	14	16	18	19	20	21	22
Typha angustifolia L. (lesser bulrush seeds) MPw																[1]				
Eriophorum vaginatum L. (hare's-tail cottongrass nutlet) Mp					11	3				1	18									
Schoenoplectus cf. *tabernaemontani* (C.C.Gmel.)Palla.(cf. grey club-rush nutlet) Mp, coastal																		cf.1		cf.1
Eleocharis sp. (spike-rush nutlet) MPw								1	3			1							3	
Cladium mariscus (L.)Pohl (great fen-sedge nutlet) FPc							31	8			2	15			1	cf.[1]f	cf.[2]f			
Carex cf. *pseudocyparus-type* (utricle with nutlet) MPw								2		1						2	3		2	2
Carex sp. (trigonous *pseudocyperus* -type sedge nutlet) MPw														2						
Carex sp. trigonous other nutlet MPw		1															4		4	3
Carex sp. (grey lenticular sedge nutlet) MPw													14			6	3	8	12	5
Indeterminate Cyperaceae nutlet					1f															
Poaceae NFI (small grass seed)						1														
main peat components																				
wood fragments	+++	++		+++	+	+	+++	[+]++	++	++	+	++	+++		++	++	++	+	++	++
roundwood		++	++	+	++	++	+	+	++	++	+	+	+			+	++	++	++	++
tree leaf fragments																		++	+++	++
wood charcoal		[+]		[++]	[+]	[+]	[+]	[+]			[+]				[+++]	[+++]		[+]	[+]	[+]
fibrous ericaceae stems and roots			+++	+																
Sphagnum spp. moss, detached leaves and shoot tips						+++	+++									+				+++
Other mosses NFI							+			++								++	+	+
Indeterminate monocotyledonous stem frags (includes Phragmites stems)	+			++	+++	+++	+++	+	[+]	+	+	+	++	+++	+++	[++]++	[+]+	+++	[+]+	++
Phragmites-type rhizomes and nodes				1	18				13		1	++[+]	+	[4]21	11	9	1	6	2	3
Insect fragments	++	+		+	+							++	+	++						++
TOTAL	1	12[4]	86[19]	3[1]	14	6[1]	40	11	4	4	29	16	20	4	17	21[2]	25[2]	44	112	58
approximate sample volume (ml)	100	100	100	100	100	100	100	100	100	100	100	100	100	100	300	300	300	300	300	300

FIGURE 14.2 INCE MARSHES PLANT MACROFOSSILS. (2)

KEY: [] = charred; no brackets = waterlogged: FREQUENCY + = 1-2 items; ++ = 3-10; +++ = >10 HABITAT PREFERENCES: C=cultivated; D=disturbed; E=heaths; F=fens; G=grassland; M=marsh/bog; P=ponds/ditches etc. S=scrub; W=woods; SOILS a=acidic; c=calcareous; p=peaty; w = wet to damp

Methods

Standard volumes (1cc) of the sediment samples were prepared for pollen analysis using a standard chemical procedure, using HCl, NaOH, sieving, HF, and Erdtman's acetolysis to remove carbonates, humic acids, particles >170 microns, silicates and cellulose respectively. The samples were then stained with safranin, dehydrated in tertiary butyl alcohol, and the residues mounted in 2000cs silicone oil (method B of Berglund & Ralska-Jasiewiczowa 1986). Tablets containing a known number of *Lycopodium* spores were added to the known volume of sediment at the beginning of the preparation so that pollen and spore concentrations could be calculated (Stockmarr 1972). Slides were examined at a magnification of 400x (1000x for critical examination) by equally spaced traverses across two slides to reduce the possible effects of differential dispersal on the slides (Brooks & Thomas 1967) until a total land pollen and spore sum (TLP) of at least 400 had been counted. Pollen identification, where necessary, was aided using the keys of Moore *et al.* (1991) and a small modern pollen reference collection. Andersen (1979) was followed for identification of cereal-type pollen. Indeterminable and unknown grains were recorded as an indication of the state of the pollen preservation. Plant nomenclature follows Stace (2010).

Results

The results are presented as a pollen diagram (Figure 14.4). Tree, shrub, dwarf shrub, herb and fern taxa are expressed as percentages of the total land pollen and spore sum (sumP). Aquatics, bog moss, algae, indeterminable and unknown pollen and spores are expressed as percentages of sumP + the sum of the group to which they belong. Taxa with values of <1% are represented by a +. Charcoal was not counted as the small (<170 microns) particles remaining on the pollen slides may be derived from great distances. The larger charcoal particles found during the macrofossil analyses are likely to have been derived locally and are therefore much more informative.

Lower peat (LP)

Six samples, LP6–LP1, were analysed from the lower peat layer (Borehole BH406). Macrofossils were also analysed from sediment below the six bulk samples from the borehole (sample <22>). They showed that wet peaty soils including bog moss (*Sphagnum*) were accumulating at the site with fen carr-type woodland with birch (*Betula*), willow (*Salix*), common reed (*Phragmites australis*) and a variety of aquatic and marsh plants (Carruthers, below). This level was dated to the early post-glacial period (10050–11610 cal BC and 9570–9550 cal BC (Beta-297299).

Sample <21> (LP 6) This was the lowermost sample analysed for pollen. The pollen assemblage is dominated by about 45% herb pollen, predominantly grasses (Poaceae), probably common reed, with about 30% tree and shrub pollen, mainly birch and willow

Laboratory Number	Sample Number	Depth	Material	Measured Radiocarbon Age	Conventional Radiocarbon Age	2 sigma calibration
Beta-297293	40501	30cm upper peat	peat	2820±30 BP	2770±30 BP	1000–840 cal BC (2940–2790 cal BP)
Beta-297294	40506	90cm upper peat	peat	4170±30 BP	4140±30 BP	2870–2610 cal BC (4820–4560 cal BP) AND 2600–2590 cal BC (4550–4540 cal BP)
Beta-297295	40510	142cm upper peat	peat	4010±30 BP	3970±30 BP	2570–2510 cal BC (4520–4460 cal BP) AND 2500–2460 cal BC (4450–4410 cal BP)
Beta-297296	40514	190cm upper peat	peat	5900±40 BP	5890±40 BP	4840–4690 cal BC (6790–6640 cal BP)
Beta-297297	40616	Bulk 1 lower peat	peat	8360±50 BP	8340±50 BP	7520–7300 cal BC (9840–9250 cal BP)
Beta-297298	40619	Bulk 4 lower peat	peat	9370±50 BP	9330±50 BP	8730–8460 cal BC (10680–10410 cal BP)
Beta-297299	40622	Base of lower peat	peat	10170±50 BP	10140±50 BP	10050–9660 cal BC (12000–11610 cal BP) AND 9570–9550 cal BC (11520–11500 cal BP)

FIGURE 14.3 INCE MARSHES RADIOCARBON DATES

with some poplar (*Populus*) and juniper (*Juniperus*). A few grains of pine (*Pinus sylvestris*) are present but represent pine growing at some distance from the site. Pine produces vast quantities of pollen and would have a much higher value if they had been growing close by. The pollen assemblage suggests that at the time of deposition, freshwater reed swamp with the telmatic taxa common reed, bulrush (*Typha latifolia*), lesser bulrush and/or bur-reed (*Typha angustifolia/Sparganium*) and sedges (Cyperaceae) were growing at the site. Other taxa of wet soils present include meadowsweet (*Filipendula*) and carrot family (Apiaceae). Willow and birch were growing on the wetter soils, with juniper on the drier soils, perhaps at some distance. There is evidence of ferns, particularly marsh fern (*Thelypteris palustris*), growing locally, and spores of horsetails (*Equisetum*) are also present. The pollen of pondweed (*Potamogeton*), spines of hornwort (*Ceratophyllum*) and the remains of the green algae *Pediastrum* and *Botryococcus* are all characteristic of fresh water. There is no evidence of any marine influence at this time.

Sample <20> (LP 5) The pollen assemblage from sample <20> is very similar to that from sample <21>. The first grains of hazel (*Corylus*) and oak (*Quercus*) are found, marking their migration into the region, but there are fewer fern spores, particularly marsh fern. The aquatic taxa present include water milfoil (*Myriophyllum spicatum/verticillatum*) and marsh pennywort (*Hydrocotyle vulgaris*), both freshwater taxa.

Sample <19> (LP 4) There is a change in the pollen assemblage of sample <19> compared with those of samples <20> and <21>. Total tree and shrub pollen increases to nearly 50%, with rises in the pollen of pine (*Pinus sylvestris*), hazel, and to some extent oak. There is a concomitant decrease in the pollen of birch, willow and poplar. This marks the beginning of the spread of pine and hazel and the migration of oak into the region. The first grain of elm (*Ulmus*) is found. The total herb value drops to 20%, mainly due to a decrease in grass pollen (reed?) but with an increase in sedges. This may register a slow change from reed swamp to sedge fen development. Fern taxa also increase, perhaps growing in the marsh/fen (marsh fern) or in the drier deciduous woodland that was approaching the site. A few grains of polypody (*Polypodium*), a fern of woodland and tree trunks are present. The spines of the freshwater taxon hornwort and the algae *Pediastrum* and *Botryococcus* are no longer found but there is no evidence of any marine influence.

This level has been dated to 8730–8460 cal BC (Beta-297298), the Mesolithic period, but there is no indication in the pollen of any human presence. However, it is interesting to note that the first grains of goosefoot (Chenopodiaceae) and cabbage family (Brassicaceae) appear, taxa associated with drier soils and often disturbed ground. Together with the decrease in aquatic taxa this suggests that the area was becoming less wet from the lowering of sea level and/or the increase in height with the accumulation of soil.

Sample <18> (LP 3) Birch and willow pollen continue to decline while sedges increase, suggesting the continued development of sedge fen and regional woodland. Fern values remain high. Large fragments of charcoal were found during the macrofossil analysis of this sample and have been identified as willow or poplar (Challinor in Carruthers, below). These genera are unlikely to have been burnt in natural fires, and it is therefore possible that human impact was being made on the local vegetation at this time (Carruthers, below).

Sample <17> (LP 2) Pine pollen is at its highest value in this sample, marking its spread in the region but, as suggested above, it was probably not growing nearby. Sedge pollen is at its maximum in this sample, indicating the occurrence of sedge fen at the site with a little hazel/oak woodland on the drier ground.

Sample <16> (LP 1) This is the uppermost sample from the Lower Peat. It has been dated to 7520–7300 cal BC (Beta-297297). It is marked by a very high value of hazel (34% TLP), slightly less pine and oak, but with slight rises in birch and willow. Sedge pollen is greatly decreased from sample <17>. Unidentifiable pollen is high and several spores of Glomus are present, a fungus found in soil, indicating erosion of sediment. This, together with the change from organic to silty clay lying above the Lower Peat suggests increased waterlogging due to a rise in sea level at this time.

The six samples from the Lower Peat therefore provide evidence for the development of the vegetation during approximately the first two thousand years of the Holocene period following the late Glacial. Reed swamp with birch, willow and poplar was growing locally during the time that the two basal samples (<21> and <20>) were being laid down. The upper four samples (<19> to <16>) show the development of sedge fen, with a succession of tree types (pine and hazel, oak and elm) migrating into the region and then spreading as the climate ameliorated and soils became favourable for their growth. Analyses from Knowsley Park, Merseyside (Innes 1994) show a similar succession and spread of trees. There is no pollen evidence for any marine influence on the vegetation during this time, nor is there any evidence of human impact on the vegetation.

Upper peat (UP)

Fourteen samples throughout the upper peat layer (borehole BH405) were analysed (samples <14> to <1>).

Sample <14> (UP 190cm) This is the basal sample of the Upper Peat. It has been dated to 4840–4690 cal BC (Beta-297296). There is thus a gap of approximately two thousand five hundred years between the two peat layers. The pollen assemblage is dominated by tree and shrub pollen, especially oak, hazel and alder (*Alnus*) with elm, lime (*Tilia*) and ash (*Fraxinus*). Oak, hazel and elm were already present in the region during the Lower Peat phase, but alder, lime and ash must have arrived during the time of silt deposition. Alder is known to have entered the region about 7500 years BP, lime about 7000 and ash about 6000 (Birks 1989; Innes 1994). The abundance of alder pollen in the assemblage, together with grasses (reed?) and other wetland herbs such as meadowsweet and meadow rue (*Thalictrum*), suggests the occurrence of alder fen carr on the site at this time. Within the region mixed deciduous woodland developed on the drier ground with oak, hazel, elm, lime, ash and birch. Spines of the freshwater hornwort are present and suggest there is no sign of any marine influence at this time.

Sample <13> (UP 178cm) The pollen assemblage from this sample is similar to that from sample <14> with the addition of bog myrtle (*Myrica gale*) and heather (*Calluna vulgaris*), both taxa which may grow on wet moorland, bogs and wet open woodland. Some sphagnum spores are also present, suggesting the occurrence of a mosaic of wetland – bogs, fen and wet woodland (alder carr) – with mixed deciduous woodland on drier ground in the region. There is also some evidence for wet grassland with the occurrence of herbs such as carrot family, daisy-type, ribwort plantain (*Plantago lanceolata*), thistle-type (*Cirsium*-type) and buttercup (*Ranunculus*-type). There is also one grain which could be a cereal but could also be from several wild grasses, including sweet grass (*Glyceria*), which grows in mud or shallow water.

Sample <12> (UP 166cm) Pollen from this sample is similar to that from sample <13> but the values are suppressed by the very high value of ferns, including marsh fern. This may be due to the incorporation of a sporangium into the sediment processed for pollen. Grains of the great fen sedge (*Cladium mariscus*) are present. There is further evidence of grassland being present with a variety of herb pollen, including ribwort plantain, dandelion-type (*Taraxacum*-type), ragged robin (*Lychnis flos-cuculi*), bird's foot trefoil-type (*Lotus*-type) and sorrel-type (*Rumex acetosa*-type).

Sample <11> (UP 154cm) The pollen assemblage from sample <11> is almost identical to that from sample <13>, with evidence of a mosaic of wet habitats including alder fen carr, bogs and wet and possibly drier grassland, with mixed deciduous woodland.

Sample <10> (UP 142cm) Similar habitats are suggested as above (samples <14> to <11>), but there is one definite grain of wheat (emmer/spelt) (*Triticum*), and an increase in herbs which could be associated with meadows and arable land. Cereal grains are large and do not travel far and suggest that there was some cultivation quite nearby at this time This has been dated to 2570–2510 cal BC and 2500–2460 cal BC (Beta-297295), although this may be incorrect (Carruthers, below) as the sample may have been contaminated by younger material. This could also have resulted in the incorporation of the wheat grain.

Sample <9> (UP 126cm) The pollen assemblage from this sample is similar but grains of heather and bog myrtle are missing, suggesting the disappearance of any heath perhaps as a result of increased waterlogging. Remains of foraminifera, planktonic organisms that are only found in brackish and salt water, are present. This is the only possible evidence from the pollen analyses of any marine influence at this site.

Samples <8> to <2> (UP 114, 102, 90, 78, 54 and 42cm) These six samples all contain similar pollen assemblages. There are variations when one taxon has a high value and depresses other values, but the taxa present remain the same. There continues to be evidence of a mosaic of habitats including alder fen carr, fens, bogs and, on drier ground, mixed deciduous woodland, grassland and heath. There is no further evidence of cereal growth or any marine influence on the vegetation. Sample <6> (UP 90 cm) has been dated to 2870–2610 cal BC and 2600–2590 cal BC (Beta-297294), in the Neolithic period.

Sample <1> (UP 30cm) A date of 1000–840 cal BC (Beta-297293), the Iron Age, has been assigned to this sample. The pollen assemblage is again similar to those from the samples below it, suggesting that the same mosaic of habitats was present. However, tree and shrub pollen is down to 45% TLP and herb pollen up to 55% TLP. The latter is mostly grass and may be indicative of pasture with slightly raised values of herb taxa which may be associated with meadows/pasture – ribwort plantain, buttercup-type, cinquefoil-type (*Potentilla*-type), sorrel-type and bracken (*Pteridium*).

The analysis of the upper peat shows that there was a variety of wetland and drier habitats present throughout, although the proportions of the different vegetation types may have varied as the site was affected by changing water table levels. There is slight evidence of some cereal growth at about 2500 cal BC and possible indications of grazing either in meadows or open woodland towards the top of the sequence.

The pollen sequences from the two peat layers at Ince Marshes are very similar to those derived from peat layers at Knowsley Park, Merseyside (Innes 1994) and Newton Carr, Hoylake, northwest Wirral (Cowell & Innes 1994). Their peat layers were associated with rises in sea level and thus the peat layers at Ince Marshes can also be correlated with sea level changes.

Analysis of Plant Macrofossils

Wendy Carruthers

Methods

The core and bulk sample sizes were quite small and this was reflected in the plant macrofossil sample volumes, amounting to *c.* 100ml peat from the core when loosened and placed in a measuring cylinder and a total of 300ml of loosened peat from each of the bulk samples.

The peat was disaggregated gently by hand in a bucket of warm water. The contents of the bucket were then washed through a graduated stack of sieves (meshes of 3mm, 1mm and 250 microns) and rinsed through with clean water, taking care not to allow the sieves to become blocked and overflow. Although not all of the compacted peat lumps were disaggregated in this way, the gentle method ensured that items such as delicate leaf fragments could be observed on the surfaces of compacted lumps, rather than being lost through the use of chemicals. Some teasing apart of peat lumps was undertaken in a Petri dish under the dissecting microscope during full analysis in order to fully characterise the deposits.

During full analysis all of the residues were sorted for wood fragments, twigs, charcoal fragments, insect fragments, fruits and seeds. The extracted material and sorted sieve residues have been stored in water.

Since large charcoal fragments were observed in bulk samples <18> and <16> at the assessment stage the remaining peat was rapidly processed in order to recover as much identifiable charcoal as possible. No other plant macrofossils were extracted from these extra samples, however, due to time constraints. The charcoal from samples <16> and <18> was dried and sent to Dana Challinor for identification. The results are given in the sample descriptions below.

Results

The results of the plant macrofossil analysis are presented as a species list in Figure 14.2 and in the sample descriptions below. Nomenclature and much of the habitat information follow Stace (2010). Hill *et al.* (1999) was also consulted for ecological information and for salinity data. The radiocarbon dates are listed in Figure 14.3 and a summary of the main changes in vegetation is given in Figure 14.5.

The following section outlines the sequence of environmental changes taking place in the area surrounding cores BH405 and BH406, starting from the base of the lower peat, sample <22>.

Lower peat (LP)

Sample <22> (base of LP) The presence of fluvioglacial deposits beneath the lowest sample suggest that the growth of the lower peat was initiated in the early post-glacial period, when the climate was warming and sea levels were rising rapidly. This was confirmed by the date of 10050–9660 cal BC and 9570–9550 cal BC (Beta-297299). Sample <22> consisted of a moss-rich peat (primarily *Sphagnum sp.*) with some evidence of woodland, including downy birch (*Betula pubescens*). Well preserved seeds and female catkin bracts confirmed the identification of this indicator of wet peaty soils. Downy birch rapidly spread across the British Isles in the Early Holocene, and it was only as climatic warming progressed that silver birch (*Betula pendula*) became the more common species of birch in Britain, as it is today (Godwin 1975). A variety of aquatic and marsh plants was present amongst the plant macrofossils at Ince, including pondweed (*Potamogeton spp.*), horned pondweed (*Zannichellia palustris*), rigid hornwort (*Ceratophyllum demersum*) and sedges (*Carex spp.*). The presence of hornwort suggests that temperatures had already risen to a level where this thermophilous aquatic species could survive (Ammann *et al.* 2007: 2479).

According to the National Vegetation Classification (NVC) species such as downy birch, willow and common reed (*Phragmites sp.*) characterise fen carr-type woodland that has become established on topogenous fen peats (e.g. W2; Rodwell 1991). The presence of sphagnum moss in this sample (though not in samples above this within the lower peat) indicates that it is the more acidic, base-poor sub-community that was represented in the sample. However, some in-wash of nutrients may have occurred from time to time, since four water-milfoil nutlets (*Myriophyllum sp.*: an aquatic plant of base-rich soils) were recovered. A few small fragments of charcoal were present, but whether or not this indicates human activity in the area is uncertain. Traces of burning were observed in all of the lower peat samples, sometimes seen as charred monocot leaves and stems and at other times present as identifiable fragments of charcoal (see samples <16> and <18> described below).

Sample <21> (LP 6) This sample produced the first confirmation from plant macrofossils that woodland existed in the immediate vicinity of the sampled area, since poorly preserved tree leaves were observed in the laminated peat. In addition, seeds and female catkin bracts of downy birch were common, and there were occasional willow (*Salix sp.*) catkin bud scales. A few fragments of moss (but not sphagnum) and a range of aquatics/marsh plants were represented, including utricles and seeds of probable Cyperus sedge (*Carex cf pseudocyparus*). In view of the dominance of grass-type pollen in samples <21> and <20> (Peglar, this report) a fairly open reedswamp with birch/willow scrub

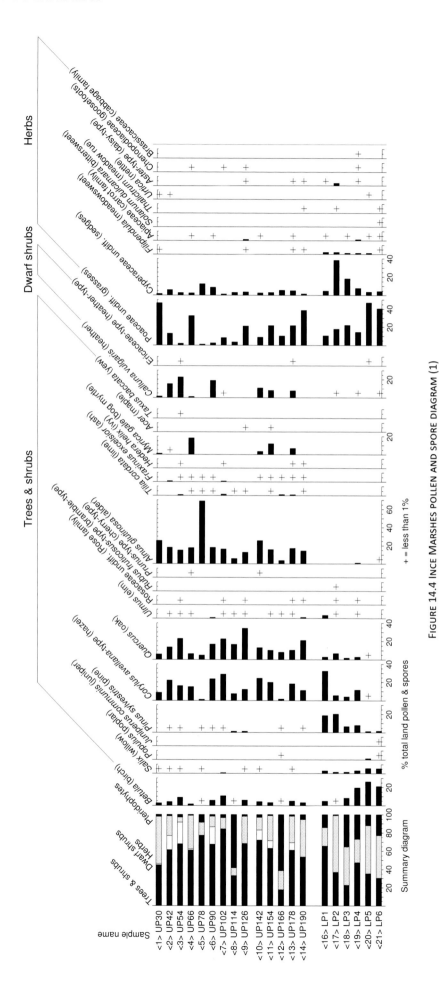

FIGURE 14.4 INCE MARSHES POLLEN AND SPORE DIAGRAM (1)

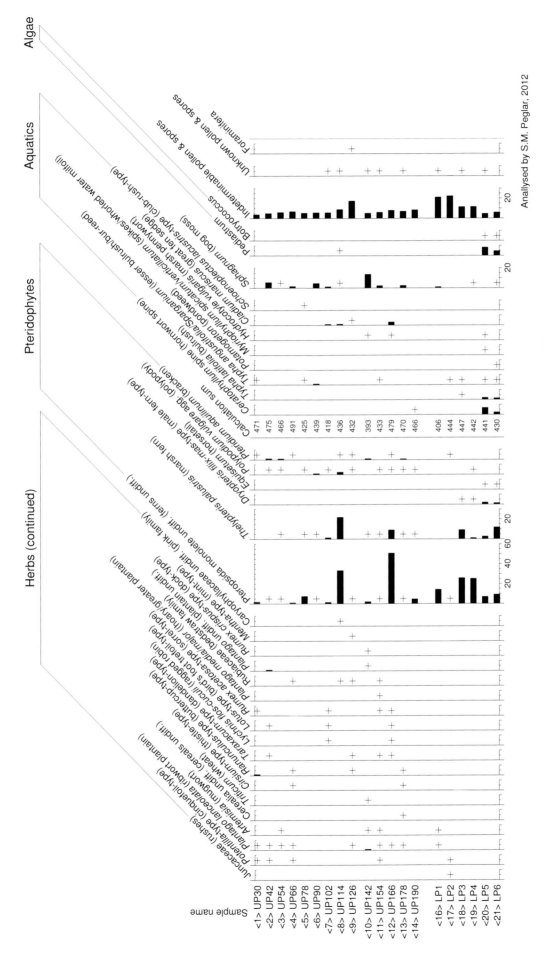

Analysed by S.M. Peglar, 2012

Figure 14.4 Ince Marshes pollen and spore diagram (2)

appears to have existed at this time, with taller wetland plants such as common reed (*Phragmites sp.*) and wild angelica (*Angelica sylvestris*) dominating some areas. The main differences between samples <21> and <22> are the absence of tree leaves in sample <22> and the absence of sphagnum moss in sample <21>. It is likely that similar habitats existed in both periods, but that tree cover was patchy, interspersed with boggier areas, and being strongly influenced by changes in water level. It is interesting to see that at no point in this lower section of the profile was there plant macrofossil evidence for marine influence, suggesting that the coast was some distance from Ince Marshes at this time.

Sample <20> (LP 5) This sample contained a similar range of downy birch seeds and catkin scales to sample <21>, as well as some leaf fragments. However, the main component appeared to be monocotyledonous stem fragments and rootlets (abbreviated to 'monocots' from here onwards). Monocots include a wide range of grass-like plants such as rushes, sedges, grasses and reeds. Seeds of rush and sedge were present in sample <20>, and common reed rhizome fragments were present, confirming the marshy nature of the vegetation. Samples <21> and <20> were very similar, although the evidence for birch/willow scrub in the immediate area was slightly reduced in sample <20>, and a smaller range of other taxa was recorded. The presence of a few water-milfoil nutlets in sample <20> indicated that some base-rich areas existed in the area.

Sample <19> (LP 4) There was plant macrofossil evidence from this sample that burning of monocot vegetation occurred, although human involvement is uncertain. Included in this charred vegetation was the first evidence for great fen-sedge (*Cladium mariscus*), along with waterlogged gypsywort (*Lycopus europaeus*), cf bogbean (cf *Menyanthes sp.*) and violet (*Viola sp.*). Together with the pollen, this suggests that open marshy vegetation was the principal habitat. Birch (not identifiable to species level) was still present in the locality but at much lower levels. Changes in the pollen (described by Peglar, above) suggested that sedge-fen was developing around this time, peaking in sample <17>.

A radiocarbon date of 8730–8460 cal BC (Beta-297298) confirmed that peat continued to accumulate through the Mesolithic period as sea levels continued to rise and warming of the climate progressed. However, no obvious marine influences were noted at this stage.

Sample <18> (LP 3) At the time that sample <18> accumulated wood had been burned in greater quantities and plant macrofossil evidence for birch was low. Large fragments of charcoal were frequent, including some roundwood. A few of the larger fragments were sent to Dana Challinor for identification with the following results:

- Sample <18>: *Salix/Populus sp.* - 15 fragments (6 roundwood, moderate or strong ring curvature, with radial cracks); Indeterminate - 18 fragments.
- There were notable heterogeneous rays which suggests *Salix* rather than *Populus*, but this is not considered to be a reliable characteristic, so the identification is left as *Salix/Populus sp.* The roundwood suggests some smallish branches (Dana Challinor personal communication).

Willow bud scales were present in samples <20> and <21> but virtually no traces of these two taxa were present above sample <18>. The pollen evidence also demonstrated that birch / willow scrub was in decline from sample <20> onwards. Birch is a good fuel wood, and the sap, leaves, bark and timber have a variety of uses. Willow and poplar, on the other hand, do not burn well as unseasoned wood, so the possibility of the charcoal having been created by natural fires within a wetland situation are extremely unlikely (Dana Challinor personal communication). In fact, in his book about Hatfield forest, Oliver Rackham (1989) suggests that 'trees like oak and lime burn like wet asbestos, and nobody has ever succeeded in burning down a native wood'. Although the reduction in willow and birch undoubtedly relates to climatic warming to some extent, it is also likely that human activities played a part in their decline at Ince Marshes around ten thousand years ago.

Increases in the range of marsh/aquatic taxa (including hemp-agrimony (*Eupatorium cannabinum*), marsh pennywort (*Hydrocotyl vulgaris*) and charred bulrush (*Typha angustifolia*) and the presence of possible common reed stem fragments, nodes and rhizomes suggest that more open marshy conditions existed on the site, perhaps in part due to the removal of tree cover by humans. Sedge-fen was the dominant vegetation, with taller species such as bulrushes and common reeds probably dominating the landscape.

Sample <17> (LP2) Very few identifiable plant macrofossils were present in sample <17>.

Sample <16> (LP 1) The uppermost bulk sample examined from the lower peat consisted primarily of monocot stem fragments and stem bases (including common reed). However, several fragments of wood and wood charcoal were also present. The charcoal was identified by Dana Challinor as follows:

- Sample <16>: *Salix/Populus sp.* - 16 fragments (4 roundwood -faint ring curvature); Indeterminate - 11 fragments.

A radiocarbon date of 7520–7300 cal BC (Beta-297297) was obtained from this level, confirming that the lower peat accumulated throughout the Mesolithic period as a result of climatic warming. The thick deposit of light grey brown silty clay lying above the lower peat presumably signifies a further rise in sea level leading to flooding episodes. However, as before, no definite evidence for marine influence on the vegetation was found in the peat on either side of the clay. Very few identifiable plant macrofossils were present in sample <16>, although frequent fragments of hemp agrimony seed amounting to about 15 achenes were present. Hemp agrimony grows in a range of damp habitats but is currently only coastal in distribution in Scotland (Stace 2010). It is possible that habitat preferences have gradually changed over such a long period of time. Silt deposition occurred at the end of the Mesolithic period, with accumulation of the upper peat beginning around 4840-4690 cal BC (Beta-297296).

Upper Peat (UP)

Sample <14> (UP 109–111cm) This sample, located at the base of the upper peat, consisted of a fairly open, *Phragmites*-rich peat. Common reed nodes and monocot stem fragments were abundant, and some of them were found to be charred. Common reed occurs in both freshwater and saline habitats, from fens and bogs to the edges of salt-marshes and estuaries. Some marine influence may have persisted as the peat started to accumulate, although no obligate halophytes have been found in any of the pollen or plant macrofossil samples from Ince. Very few identifiable fruits or seeds were recovered from this sample, the only taxa recorded being sedges (*Carex sp.*) and celery-leaved buttercup (*Ranunculus sceleratus*). These taxa are fairly widely found in freshwater and marshy habitats, as well as coastal areas in Scotland, Wales and Ireland for the latter species (Stace 2010). A radiocarbon date of 4840–4690 cal BC (Beta-297296) was obtained from this level, demonstrating that the upper peat started to accumulate in the early Neolithic period. By this time the climate had warmed to the extent that lime, alder and ash had spread to the area (Peglar, this report).

Sample <13> (UP 178–180cm) Wood fragments dominated the plant macrofossil assemblage from sample <13>, and the first traces of alder fruits and cones were recorded. The few other identifiable macrofossils included pondweed and several sedge nutlets. Occasional monocot stem fragments and rhizomes were also present. Alder carr was growing close to the sampling point at this time, although the fact that at no point in the profile were alder fruits and seed abundant suggests that a patchwork of open sedge fen and alder scrub probably existed, rather than a dense tree cover.

Sample <12> (UP 166–168cm) This sample contained frequent fruits of great fen-sedge (*Cladium mariscus*), and the main component of the peat was monocot stem fragments (including common reed, but also possibly fen-sedge). The growth of fen-sedge (a plant of wet, base-rich sites) could indicate soil disturbance

on the surrounding slopes, perhaps causing an influx of nutrients. However, burning can also bring about a release of nutrients. Traces of burnt common reed indicated that human activity may have been taking place in the area, although natural fires are also a possibility. The peat at this level was subject to oxidation, resulting in poor preservation. Perhaps the establishment of fen woodland in some areas caused drying of the surface levels of the peat. The only other identifiable plant macrofossil present was a nutlet of club-rush that was morphologically most similar to grey club-rush (*Schoenoplectus cf tabernaemontani*). This form of club-rush is most often found near the sea, although it also grows in marshes and dune-slacks (Stace 2010). Because only one tentatively identified seed was recovered it is not possible to confirm that marine influences affected the area at this time, but it is a possibility, particularly since tree pollen fell, maybe due to a raised water table (Peglar, this report).

Sample <11> (UP 154–156cm) Major changes in the nutrient-status of the peat appear to have occurred between samples <12> and <11>, since ericaceous plant macrofossils made a brief appearance at this point (154cm), not being found again as plant macrofossils until sample <6> (90cm). Ericaceous roots and twigs were present, giving the peat a fibrous, felty texture. Traces of heather seed and a leaf (*Calluna vulgaris*), and a few ericaceous fruits were also found. Heather and bog myrtle pollen were also fairly frequent (Peglar, this report). Rapid soil deterioration leading to heathland development can occur as a result of clearance and repeated grazing on poor soils (Godwin 1975), though no evidence for human activity on the site was found. In addition to heathy vegetation, wet ground taxa were also present, such as bulrush (*Typha angustifolia*), rushes (*Juncus sp.*), and great fen-sedge. Either a patchwork of marsh and heathland existed at this time, or two successive vegetation types have been compacted into the two centimetres of peat examined in the sample. Once established, dense rooted heathers would have dried out the upper surfaces and lead to oxidation and the loss of softer plant tissues, such as monocot stems.

Sample <10> (UP 142–144cm) The peat core at this point was very hard, dry, and crumbly. The sample contained very poorly preserved plant remains including small fragments of wood, mosses and occasional wetland taxa such as marsh pennywort (*Hydrocotyle vulgaris*), sedge and bullrush. Reedswamp and fen are the likely vegetation types represented. Because a pollen grain of hulled wheat was recorded from this sample – the only cereal-type grain observed in any of the samples (Peglar, this report) – a sample was submitted for radiocarbon dating. However, the dates obtained of 2570–2510 cal BC and 2500–2460 cal BC (Beta-297295) are problematical as an earlier date was recovered from a better preserved sample higher up the profile (see sample

	Borehole no.	Depth from top of core (cm)	Actual depth (cm)	Pollen code	Sample no.	2 sigma calibrated date (cal BP)	Summarised vegetation description (pollen and macrofossil evidence)	
UPPER PEAT	405 (i)	30	30	UP 30	1	2940 to 2790	The sequence ends in the Late Bronze Age with a more open, damp meadow/pasture pollen assemblage, but with alder carr still present locally and oak/hazel woodland slightly reduced on drier land. Evidence for heathland had almost disappeared in this sample and Poaceae was the dominant pollen group. Unfortunately the drier, more oxidised peat produced very few macrofossils.	PASTURE/MEADOW WITH ALDER CARR AND OAK WOODS IN THE AREA
		42	42	UP 42	2		Heathland was still being burnt locally and some drier areas now supported herbs such as buttercup and cinquefoil (macros). Wetter areas contained sedges and reeds and the same mix of alder carr and deciduous woodland existed in the wider area.	HEATH AND ALDER CARR
		54	54	UP 54	3		This sample was primarily composed of matted, felty ericaceous vegetation, including abundant heather/heath capsules and some burnt shoots. Heather pollen was also frequent. Further afield the same mixture of alder carr and drier woodlands on higher ground existed (pollen), though there was less evidence for marshy, wet vegetation (pollen and macros).	HEATH WITH SIGNS OF BURNING, ALDER CARR
	405 (ii)	4	66	UP 66	4		Alder carr, heath and reedswamp continued in the area (pollen and macros). Wood fragments and occasional burnt heather occurred throughout samples 6 to 2.	REEDSWAMP, HEATH AND ALDER CARR
		16	78	UP 78	5		Tall monocot vegetation including bulrushes (seeds) occupied the site with heathy areas (heather capsules) and abundant alder carr in the area (pollen).	REEDSWAMP, HEATH AND ALDER CARR
		28	90	UP 90	6	4820 to 4560 and 4550 to 4540	Heathland returned to the site (pollen and macros) but sphagnum moss was still frequent, suggesting that a patchwork of dry and wetter areas existed.	HEATH, SPHAGNUM BOG AND ALDER CARR
		40	102	UP 102	7		A similar mosaic of fen, bog and deciduous woodlands on drier land (pollen) existed. Frequent sphagnum moss made up much of the peat matrix in samples 7 and 6, and abundant great fen-sedge nutlets and several marsh pennywort fruits in this sample demonstrated that wetter fen pools and marsh existed on the site. There was a minor increase in birch pollen and a few poorly preserved seeds suggesting that either silver or downy birch were growing on the peaty soils that had by now turned acidic.	SPHAGNUM BOG WITH ALDER CARR AND LOCAL WOODLAND
		52	114	UP 114	8		Charcoal fragments and/or burnt ericaceous material (samples 6 to 2) become a constant factor from this point upwards, indicating probable low-level human exploitation of the area. Ferns were frequent (spores) and a mosaic of alder fen carr, sedge-fen (in particular, great fen-sedge; macros), bogs and oak/lime/hazel woodland on drier ground (pollen) existed in the area.	ALDER CARR, SEDGE-FEN, PROBABLE LOW-LEVEL HUMAN ACTIVITY
		64	126	UP 126	9		Pollen (foraminifera) and macros (grey club-rush) suggest possible marine influence in the area causing a loss of heathland. Macro preservation was poor but rushes and Phragmites (a plant of saltmarsh and estuaries as well as inland bogs) were dominant. Oak woodland was at its peak (pollen) in the wider region.	ALDER CARR, OAK WOODS, PROBABLE MARINE INFLUENCE

FIGURE 14.5 INCE MARSHES SUMMARISED VEGETATION CHANGES (TO BE READ FROM THE BASE UPWARDS). (1)

Borehole no.	Depth from top of core (cm)	Actual depth (cm)	Pollen code	Sample no.	2 sigma calibrated date (cal BP)	Summarised vegetation description (pollen and macrofossil evidence)	
405(iii)	4	142	UP 142	10	4520 to 4460 and 4450 to 4410	The only definite cereal pollen grain (hulled wheat) from Ince was recorded and herb pollen increased, possibly indicating small-scale arable cultivation. However, the peat was very loose and crumbly at this point (the top of the third section of core from borehole 405) and the radiocarbon date conflicts with the date from sample 6. Only four identifiable macros were present, all of which were from marshy taxa. A question remains over this sample as to whether contamination occurred or not.	REEDSWAMP, ALDER CARR, HEATH, TRACE OF ARABLE CULTIVATION OR CONTAMINATION?
	16	154	UP 154	11		This sample contained the earliest macrofossil evidence of heathland on the site, though it was not frequent or charred (unlike in samples 2 to 6). Ericaceous pollen was also frequent as was bog myrtle. Tree pollen recovered to its previous levels but the dominant vegetation type on site was probably a patchwork of reedswamp (including frequent bulrush; seeds) and drier grassland with heathy vegetation and some ruderal weeds (pollen).	HEATH AND REEDSWAMP ON SITE, ALDER CARR
	28	166	UP 166	12		The main taxa were open, marshy fenland plants including great fen-sedge (frequent nutlets and pollen), Phragmites rhizomes and ferns (incuding marsh fern spores). The fall in tree pollen at this point (in particular, alder and hazel) could relate to human activity in the area, since some evidence of burning marsh vegetation was present. There were also smaller amounts of wood in the peat sample than in sample 13. Elm pollen frequency was too low at Ince to identify the elm decline but it has been dated to 5120±50 BP on the Wirral (Cowell & Innes 1994, 204) so probably occurs between samples 14 and 6. The uncertain identification of a grey club-rush nutlet, which mainly occurs near the sea, provides possible evidence of marine influence. A marine incursion close to the site could be another explanation for the short-lived drop in tree pollen, though the evidence is tentative.	SEDGE-FEN, SHORT-LIVED REDUCTION IN SCRUB. MARINE INFLUENCE?
	40	178	UP 178	13		Frequent wood fragments (including branchwood), an alder seed and catkin fragments indicated that alder carr was now present on, or very close to, the site. Several sedge nutlets, sphagnum spores, bog myrtle and heather pollen indicate that a mosaic of wet, open, drier heathy and scrubby areas existed. Heathland macrofossils were not present until sample 11 so this may have been a short distance from the site at the time sample 13 accumulated.	ALDER CARR LOCALLY DOMINANT
	52	109	UP 190	14	6790 to 6640	During the 2500 year gap between the end of the LP and start of UP development alder, lime and ash spread to the area. Together with oak, hazel and elm these trees dominated the pollen assemblage. Poaceae were also abundant and the few macrofossils surviving in the compacted peat indicated that sedge-fen interspersed with alder-carr dominated the area, with larger trees on drier ground.	SEDGE-FEN AND ALDER CARR WITH OAK/LIME/ASH/HAZEL WOODS
CLAY BELOW UPPER PEAT	57-59			15			

FIGURE 14.5 INCE MARSHES SUMMARISED VEGETATION CHANGES (TO BE READ FROM THE BASE UPWARDS). (2)

255

Borehole no.	Depth from top of core (cm)	Actual depth (cm)	Pollen code	Sample no.	2 sigma calibrated date (cal BP)	Summarised vegetation description (pollen and macrofossil evidence)	
LOWER PEAT							
406	Bulk 1		LP1	16	9840 to 9250	A significant rise in hazel pollen and fall in sedge pollen occured at this level. The monocot peat contained high levels of large charcoal (with willow/poplar identified) but few identifiable macrofossils were recovered from the poorly preserved compacted peat. The presence of silts above this level indicates sea level rises and silt inundation, but no definite evidence for marine taxa was found in the pollen or macros either side of the clay deposit.	REEDSWAMP, SEDGE-FEN, HAZEL AND ELM RISE
	Bulk 2		LP2	17		(Pollen only) Sedge-fen was present with a little oak/hazel woodland on drier ground and pine growing further afield. Pine was at its highest in this sample and sedge pollen was abundant.	SEDGE-FEN
	Bulk 3		LP3	18		Sedge-fen was present with regional oak/hazel woodland and declining birch/willow scrub. Pine was present. Significant numbers of large charcoal fragments including willow/poplar (a species unlikely to burn in natural fires) suggested human activities in the area.	WILLOW/POPLAR CHARCOAL - POSSIBLE HUMAN ACTIVITY
	Bulk 4		LP4	19	10680 to 10410	Tree pollen dominated (nearly 50%) with significant levels of pine, hazel and oak and decreasing birch and willow. The first trace of elm pollen was found. Poor peat preservation and the presence of tree rootlets, together with some pollen from disturbed ground taxa suggested the drying out of some areas. Two burnt great-fen sedge nutlets and sedge/grass-type vegetation could indicate low-level human activity in the area or natural fires. A change from reedswamp to sedge-fen is likely.	SEDGE-FEN, PINE/OAK/HAZEL WOODS, FIRST ELM POLLEN
	Bulk 5		LP5	20		The pollen and macro samples were similar to sample 21 with reedswamp and some birch and willow scrub but the peat mainly consisted of of sedge/reed stems rather than tree leaves. The first pollen from hazel and oak were recorded. The absence of juniper from this point onwards is likely to be due to climatic warming.	BIRCH/WILLOW SCRUB, FIRST ARRIVAL OF HAZEL AND OAK
	Bulk 6		LP6	21		Freshwater reedswamp occurred with the pollen assemblage dominated by Poaceae (grasses, including Phragmites). There was evidence for birch, willow, poplar and juniper growing nearby (presence of downy birch leaves, seeds and remains of catkins; 30% tree pollen). Pine probably grew some distance away. Ferns and horsetails (particularly marsh fern) were present.	REEDSWAMP AND BIRCH/WILLOW/ JUNIPER SCRUB
	Tub (base)			22	12000 to 11610 and 11520 to 11500	The sequence starts in the early post-glacial period when climatic warming enabled plant species to gradually migrate across the British Isles. (Macros only) A fairly open landscape existed at Ince with sphagnum bog and freshwater reedswamp. A variety of submerged and emergent aquatic plants grew in wetter areas. Downy birch was growing nearby but no leaves were present so the seeds and catkin fragments may have been blown a short distance to the site.	SPHAGNUM BOG, REEDSWAMP AND BIRCH SCRUB
CLAY BENEATH LOWER PEAT	Tub (clay)			24			

FIGURE 14.5 INCE MARSHES SUMMARISED VEGETATION CHANGES (TO BE READ FROM THE BASE UPWARDS). (3)

<6>). Because sample <10> was located at the top of the third section of core 405 and because it was very loose in texture it is more likely that contamination had occurred in sample <10> than sample <6> (where the radiocarbon sample was taken from within an intact, firm section of peat). However, the fact that the pollen grain was from a hulled wheat is important, as discussed below. Whilst it may have been displaced it is clearly not from a modern species of wheat, so it confirms arable cultivation as having taken place in prehistoric times.

Sample <9> (UP 126–128cm) Monocot stem fragments and common reed nodes dominated sample <9> and rush seeds were frequent. Some of the monocot stem was charred, perhaps suggesting management for grazing during the Neolithic period, or the flushing out of game. Natural fires are also a possibility. Poorly preserved wood fragments were infrequent and an alder seed was present. Three seeds of *cf* grey club-rush (*Schoenoplectus cf tabernaemontani*) were present, possibly indicating some marine influence at this time. This suggestion was backed up by the identification of foraminifera characteristic of brackish or salt water in the pollen samples (Peglar, this report). Some of the other macrofossil genera contained species that are found in saltmarsh habitats, for example *Phragmites*, some species of rush (*Juncus sp.*) and some species of spike-rush (*Eleocharis sp.*), so it is possible that the extent of marine influence is difficult to detect in the samples and has been underestimated.

Sample <8> (UP 114–116cm) This peat sample was fairly humified. Decayed wood and monocot stems were roughly equal in frequency. Some small fragments of wood charcoal were present. Great fen-sedge fruits were the most frequent macrofossil. The presence of sedge and spike-rush suggests sedge-rich, open fenland vegetation. No clear evidence was found to determine whether tree re-growth was being suppressed by grazing or periodic burning, but tree pollen was temporarily lower in this sample than in those above and below it (Peglar, this report).

Sample <7> (UP 102–104cm) Wood fragments dominated sample <7>, including some twigs. Sphagnum moss leaves were also abundant, as were great fen-sedge fruits. The scarcity of heather pollen and frequency of sphagnum suggested increased wetness at this time. A few poorly preserved birch (*Betula sp.*) seeds were present, perhaps suggesting a period of fen scrub re-growth.

Sample <6> (UP 90–92cm) A radiocarbon date of 2870–2610 and 2600–2590 cal BC (Beta-297294) was obtained, placing this level in the late Neolithic period/ early Bronze Age. This date (90cm depth) is slightly earlier than that from 142cm depth (sample <10>), as described above. This slight inversion of dates, with *c.* 50cm of peat between the two samples, is probably due

to a problem with the date from sample <10>, since the core at sample <6> was intact and not compacted or loose. However, it is also possible that this date was at fault.

Sample <6> contained frequent sphagnum leaves although these were probably of a different species than those in sample <7>, being much smaller. The main component of the peat was decaying monocot stems and possibly heather roots. Occasional heather (*Calluna vulgaris*) seeds were present, including a burnt seed, and heather pollen was recorded (Peglar, this report). This marks the start of an extended period of heathland development on the site, with ericaceous plant macrofossils being recovered from all of samples <6> to <2>. The nutrient-poor acidic conditions indicated by sphagnum enabled heathers to become established on the drier areas, and this probably led to drying out and the exclusion of fenland taxa from this point onward. At first common reed and bulrush continued to occupy wetter areas (samples <6> and <5>), but by the time samples <4> to <2> were forming rushes and one or two wetland herbs were the only taxa other than heathers.

Sample <5> (UP 78–80cm) The main component of sample <5> was fibrous, decaying monocot stem bases and stem fragments. Some of the fibrous material might have been derived from heather roots and shoots, since *Erica/Calluna sp.* fruits were present. A few burnt ericaceous twigs were present, suggesting occasional burning may have been taking place. As noted above, bulrush, rush and sedge were also present.

Sample <4> (UP 66–68cm) An increase in the growth of woody vegetation was indicated in sample <4>, as wood fragments were the main component of the peat. Although some of this was heather-type roundwood, most of it came from larger trees. Small fragments of charcoal indicated that burning was taking place, so it is possible that the unburnt wood fragments also relate to clearance. The plant macrofossil evidence suggest that a mixture of wet areas with sphagnum and a few aquatics (pondweed, marsh pennywort, rushes) and drier areas with heather and possibly scrub existed. The presence of fine white silt in the plant macrofossil sample suggested that flooding or inwash from the cultivation of land nearby may have occurred at this time.

Sample <3> (UP 54–56cm) The loose, matted felt-type structure of the peat in sample <3> and presence of frequent ericaceous roots, fruits, charred heather (*Calluna vulgaris*) shoot tips and a few seeds indicated that heathland was the dominant vegetation type in the location of borehole 405. Heather pollen was also frequent (Peglar, this report).

Sample <2> (UP 42–44cm) This sample contained a similar mix of habitat indicators as was found in sample

<4>, including wood fragments, heather (occasionally charred) and frequent rush seeds. The presence of buttercup (*Ranunculus acris/bulbosus/repens*) and cinquefoil (*Potentilla sp.*) seeds suggests that some drier, grassy areas existed at this time, perhaps providing grazing for livestock. The pollen assemblage was similar to sample <3>. Woods and heath still dominated the area.

Sample <1> (UP 30–32cm) At the top of the upper peat, below a thick deposit of grey/brown silty sandy clay, Sample <1> consisted of poorly preserved, soft wood peat. The only identifiable plant macrofossils to survive were frequent wood fragments, several rush seeds, an aquatic crowfoot-type buttercup (*Ranunculus subg. Batrachium*) and some fragments of insects. Grass pollen was the principal type present, with alder, oak and hazel indicating the continued presence of woodland and alder carr (Peglar, this report). Since monocot seeds and stems are unlikely to survive where oxidation of the peat has taken place it is possible that grasses, common and rushes had originally been the main components but that only the more resistant, woody remains have survived. Inundation and burial of the peat by silt occurred after 1000–840 cal BC (Beta-297293) according to the radiocarbon date from the top of the peat, making the accumulation of peat end in the late Bronze Age.

Discussion

The analysis of both pollen and plant macrofossils from identical sample points in the same cores has greatly enhanced the quantity and quality of data being retrieved. This is because each source of evidence has provided a slightly different type of data. Pollen mainly provides information about local and regional vegetation changes, whilst plant macrofossils give a more detailed picture of vegetation changes at the site itself. Differences in levels of identification can also be useful, for example fruits, seeds and vegetative material can often be identified to species level, providing the maximum ecological information, whilst some pollen is only identifiable to a broad group of species. Pollen, however, is often present in much larger quantities in peat than identifiable plant macrofossils, so can be used to demonstrate environmental changes in a more statistically significant form.

Summarised changes in the vegetation are presented in Figure 14.5. A classic sequence of succession was found to be present in the lower peat deposits: from the early Holocene fairly open reedswamp with willow, birch and juniper, to gradual colonisation of the area by pine. Following an increase in hazel, mixed deciduous woodland became established on the drier ground, with oak, elm and later, lime moving into the area. Pollen from the upper peat showed that there was a remarkable persistence of deciduous woodland through time, although alder carr probably dominated the area close

to the sampling point for most of the time that the upper peat was accumulating. Because of the low frequency of elm pollen at Ince it has not been possible to define the elm decline, but according to work carried out by the North West Wetlands Survey on Merseyside the date in this region is around 4034–3790 cal BC (5120±50 BP; SRR 2929) This is the date obtained at Park Road, Meols, on the north Wirral coast (Cowell & Innes 1994: 204). This puts the elm decline between samples <14> and <6> (bearing in mind possible problems with the radiocarbon date from sample <10>).

The plant macrofossils demonstrate that at times drier heathland was the dominant vegetation type in the immediate area (upper peat only), whilst at other times wetter sphagnum bog, *Phragmites* reedswamp or sedge-fen were present. Evidence for small-scale burning was common, being recorded in eleven of the twenty plant macrofossil samples. Although large fragments of charcoal were only common in two samples, <16> and <18> in the lower peat, it is clear that coastal areas of the Liverpool basin were being heavily exploited by humans in the Mesolithic period (Cowell & Innes 1994: 173). It is often difficult to recognise small-scale clearances in pollen diagrams of this period, particularly when the woodland was probably located some distance from the site on drier, higher ground. However, the fact that willow/poplar charcoal was identified on the site suggests that deliberate burning rather than natural fires had been taking place at Ince. As noted above, these very sappy woods do not easily catch fire in a wetland location, so it is likely that fires from transient camps were represented in the samples or some sort of deliberate clearance and burning.

In the lower part of the upper peat (sample <10>) a single pollen grain of hulled wheat hinted at arable agriculture taking place in the area. As described above, there are questions over the integrity of this deposit, particularly in the light of the inversion of dates in samples <10> and <6>. However, it is significant that the pollen grain was from a hulled wheat (either emmer or spelt) rather than one of the free-threshing wheats grown today. This means that the grain had not come from a modern source but had possibly been transported down the profile from later Neolithic or Bronze Age levels. Therefore, its presence at least confirms that some arable cultivation was taking place in the area in prehistoric times, or perhaps that cereals had been brought to the area, since pollen can be transported on the chaff of hulled wheats (Robinson & Hubbard 1977). More substantial evidence from sites such as Bidston Moss on the Wirral confirms that cereal cultivation was taking place in at least some parts of the Liverpool basin from the earlier Neolithic period onwards (Cowell & Innes 1994: 39). In the late Prehistoric period, however, areas such as Ince would have become very wet as climatic deterioration spread across the country. Very little evidence for arable cultivation was found in peat from the central mosslands of Merseyside by Cowell and Innes (1994: 131) and few other sites in the area have provided deposits that continued, untruncated, into this period. The archaeological evidence suggests that settlement occurred away from wetland areas, on drier sandstone soils and along river valleys.

It is interesting to note that evidence for marine influence was minimal and tentative, with no obligate halophytes being identified in the pollen or plant macrofossil assemblages and at best only a few 'salt-tolerant' taxa such as grey club-rush and *Phragmites* being present in any quantity. This suggests that the area was not affected by the tidal waters of the River Mersey, perhaps because the peat basin was physically isolated from the estuary. Further investigations at Ince Marshes might change this picture, particularly in the upper part of the sequence when sea levels were at their highest.

Comparisons with other sites in the area

Very few sites in the immediate area of Ince Marshes have been examined for plant macrofossils, particularly sites that cover the Mesolithic to late Bronze Age periods, but several sites in the Mersey estuary and wider region have been analysed for pollen, particularly sites studied by the North West Wetlands Survey. At Walker's Heath, Cheshire (Leah *et al.* 1997) it was suggested that human activities had modified the vegetation from the early Mesolithic period, as appears to have been the case at Ince Marshes. Pollen analysis at Knowsley Park, Merseyside (Innes 1994) produced a similar succession to that found at Ince, suggesting that the spread of tree species occurred in a fairly uniform fashion across the region as the climate ameliorated and soils became capable of supporting their growth.

Excavations at Ditton Brook on Merseyside revealed late Mesolithic temporary hunting camps with evidence of fires and frequent stone tools (Cowell & Philpott 2000). Pollen analysis produced evidence for alder wood and areas of wetland (Innes 2000), as was found in much of the upper peat sequence at Ince. It is clear that the Mersey estuary was an important hunting area in the early post-glacial period, providing accessible locations for hunting and fishing along the coast and allowing easier access inland to more heavily forested landscapes along the river valley.

Evidence from later periods suggests that, in places, more easily worked, drier soils may have been used for small-scale arable agriculture from the Neolithic period onwards. Palaeoenvironmental analysis of palaeochannel sediments near Mickle Trafford, *c.* 5 miles to the south of Ince Marshes, produced a Neolithic to early medieval pollen profile with some evidence for small-scale arable cultivation (Elizabeth Huckerby personal communication). Although only an evaluation with two radiocarbon dates, three possible clearance phases linked to cereal cultivation and pastoral farming were identified; one in the Neolithic period, one possibly in the Bronze Age, and a major clearance with extensive farming that probably dated to the late Iron Age/early Roman period.

As farming methods and tools improved in later prehistoric times it became possible to grow arable crops on heavier loams and clays in the Liverpool basin. Excavations at Brook House Farm, Bruen Stapleford, east of Chester, produced low levels of charred cereal remains in roundhouses dating from the Bronze Age to late Iron Age, demonstrating that mixed farming (including the cultivation of hulled wheats and barley) was taking place close to the Mersey estuary, albeit probably at a low level (Carruthers 2002a). Similar low levels of charred cereal remains were also found in a small Romano-British rural settlement at Birch Heath, Tarporley, to the southeast of Ince Marshes (Carruthers 2002b). It is unfortunate that few peat deposits in the area continue into the Iron Age and later periods as combined pollen and macrofossil evidence may help to determine whether arable agriculture was as limited as the charred evidence suggests, or whether the poor survival and recovery of macrofossils in clay soils is an important factor that needs to be taken into account. Future excavations in the Cheshire and Merseyside area may be able to throw some light on these questions.

Acknowledgements

Sylvia Peglar would like to thank Sandra Bonsall (Oxford Archaeology North) for the pollen preparation and the Geography Department, Lancaster University for the use of their laboratory.

Wendy Carruthers is very grateful to Elizabeth Huckerby at Oxford Archaeology North for access to her unpublished Mickle Trafford evaluation report and for helping to locate reports from the Merseyside area.

Chapter 15
Emerging Themes

Dan Garner

This volume has provided a detailed account of the archaeological work undertaken during the Habitats and Hillforts Project. The evidence presented in some chapters has allowed us to develop a more detailed understanding of certain topics. However, in other chapters it has only been possible to demonstrate what little knowledge we have of certain aspects of the Cheshire hillforts and their place within the surrounding landscape. This chapter will not attempt to re-write our understanding of the first millennium BC in Cheshire (for a recent review of this see Philpott 2010: 169–186), nor will it try to make exhaustive comparisons between the Cheshire hillforts and hillfort development across the wider region of the Welsh Marches. It will instead try to explore some emergent themes within the mid-Cheshire hillfort group, in order to provide a solid base for future research priorities within what is clearly a rich prehistoric landscape.

Concise summaries of the history of hillfort studies have recently been published (Harding 2012: 29–52; Driver 2013: 1–10) and it seems unnecessary here to attempt yet another review. Perhaps of particular relevance to the Cheshire hillfort group was Forde-Johnston's detailed analysis of the hillforts of England and Wales (1976). This study identified eleven types of Iron Age hillfort which were grouped in to the 'Wessex tradition' and the 'Western tradition' with a distinction being made between single-enclosure sites and multiple enclosure sites (Forde-Johnston 1976: 258–261). More recently, Cunliffe (2005) has attempted to break down the chronological development of hillforts on the basis of the structure of the defences and the style of the entrances; acknowledging regional differences in their planning and siting. Hillforts of the Wessex region were divided between earliest hillforts (c. 800–600 BC), early hillforts (c. 600–400/300 BC) and middle hillforts (c. 400/300–100 BC). A chronological regional development was argued from large poorly defended hilltop enclosures, through smaller and better defended enclosures to fully 'developed hillforts' like Danebury (Cunliffe 2005: 378–396).

It is worth establishing how the chronology of the Iron Age will be dealt with in this chapter. In recent years there has been increasing debate regarding the definition of what is meant by the Iron Age in Britain and Ireland. Traditional approaches which involved the division of the period in to the early, middle and late Iron Age have been questioned on the basis that these divisions are primarily relevant to the southern part of England; and that this is not necessarily relevant to other regions of Britain. The established approach provides the chronological framework presented in Figure 15.1.

It has recently been proposed that the period should simply be divided in to an Earlier and Later Iron Age, with a transitional phase c. 400–300 BC (Haselgrove and Moore 2007: 2). This point of transition during the 4th century BC is marked in many areas of Britain by a break in the settlement evidence, new site types and a move towards occupation of marginal areas (Haselgrove and Pope 2007: 8). Whilst this development is acknowledged here, the Iron Age periods in this chapter will be referred to within the parameters of the established date ranges presented in Figure 15.1.

Pre-hillfort hilltop activity

A recent review of hillfort studies has summed up the chronological range for this form of field monument as covering the two millennia of the 'long Iron Age', between 1000 BC and AD 1000 (Harding 2012: 151). It must be acknowledged, however, that the phenomenon of hilltop enclosure in Britain extends back in to the early Neolithic, with the emergence of causewayed enclosures and fortified sites such as Crickley Hill (Gloucestershire), (ibid. 151–3). It is generally accepted that these earlier monuments are not precursors to hillforts, on the grounds of there being no tradition of continuity through the second millennium BC and there being a relatively low occurrence of hillforts physically overlying causewayed enclosures (ibid. 154). Harding draws parallels between the development of hillforts in Britain and the progression from enclosed 'hill settlement' to fully fledged 'hillfort' in central and

Late Bronze Age/earliest Iron Age transition	c. 800–600 cal BC
Early Iron Age	c. 600–400/300 cal BC
Middle Iron Age	c. 400/300–100 cal BC
Late Iron Age	c. 100 cal BC to the Roman conquest

FIGURE 15.1 DIVISIONS AND ACCOMPANYING DATE RANGES APPLIED TO THE BRITISH IRON AGE (AFTER CUNLIFFE 2005: 32).

eastern Europe during the early Bronze Age, which is characterised by the erection of substantial stone walls or timber framed ramparts (*ibid.*). In Britain, Harding suggests an intermediate class of middle/late Bronze Age enclosure, using the site at Rams Hill (Berkshire) as an example of a 'simple dump bank', later enhanced by a timber framework and then palisade with a timber-lined passageway entrance (*ibid.* 155).

The sites of the six Cheshire hillforts studied as part of the Habitats and Hillforts Project demonstrate, to a varying degree, pre-hillfort activity stretching back in to early prehistory. This is most notably seen at the site of Beeston Castle, where diagnostic lithic artefacts indicate human activity as early as the Mesolithic period (Smart 1993: 56–9). More significantly, the site at Beeston produced structural elements and occupation deposits dating to the early Neolithic, which were in the vicinity of the later hillfort rampart and ditch. These features produced a C14 date of 4340–4003 cal BC (HAR-6461) and included circular terraces, hollows and an embankment, which it has been suggested could represent evidence for a defensive enclosure (Ellis 1993: 19–20). Amongst the associated artefact assemblage there were five leaf-shaped flint arrowheads of Neolithic type and pottery sherds from early Neolithic Grimston-style bowls (1993: 76). Later Neolithic activity was not clearly demonstrated, but sherds of Beaker pottery were recovered from the site, as well as six sherds from early Bronze Age Collared Urns or accessory cups (Royle and Woodward 1993: 76). Early Bronze Age lithics were also recovered from the Beeston site and included a tanged arrowhead, a possible barbed and tanged arrowhead and three knives (Smart 1993: 59). It was suggested that the early Bronze Age material was likely to be derived from a funerary context and probably indicated the presence of burials on Beeston crag and possibly even round barrows (Ellis 1993: 87). Finally, evidence for a pre-hillfort timber palisade was found beneath the late Bronze Age rampart, but was not firmly dated.

The sequence from Beeston Castle represents the most extensive range of evidence for pre-hillfort activity in the Cheshire group, but this is almost certainly due to the fairly extensive excavations undertaken there between 1968 and 1985. The more limited recent excavations at Eddisbury hillfort (see Chapter 10) have begun to suggest an equally complex narrative of pre-hillfort activity on the Eddisbury hilltop. The earliest activity so far demonstrated relates to a possible late Neolithic cremation cemetery on the northern side of the hill, from which part of a single Grooved Ware vessel has been published (see Chapter 2). Early Bronze Age activity is clearly demonstrated by the presence of hearths or pits sealed beneath the primary hillfort rampart, from which a C14 date of 1870–1640 cal BC (NZA-36669) was produced. Activity of this period is supported by stray finds on the hilltop including a barbed and tanged flint

arrowhead and a piece of early Bronze Age portable rock-art. The hillfort ramparts at Eddisbury have also preserved a buried soil horizon which has produced pottery of late Bronze Age type. The latter may be associated with a pre-hillfort timber palisade, but evidence for this is so far confined to the Merrick's Hill area of the hilltop.

The identification of pre-hillfort deposits at Helsby is, so far, confined to the lower cliff edge of the hillfort interior. These deposits, with evidence for extensive burning, have produced a C14 date of 3950–3780 cal BC (NZA-35504) and are clearly related to early Neolithic activity on the hilltop. This might well be supported by stray finds recovered from below the cliff edges, which include a leaf-shaped arrowhead and a polished stone axe. A possible timber palisade slot has also been identified in front of the primary rampart at Helsby, but this feature is currently undated and its interpretation remains tentative. Neolithic activity is also indicated at Kelsborrow hillfort where stray finds from the hillfort interior include a leaf-shaped arrowhead and fragments from two polished stone axes. The hillfort at Woodhouse Hill has produced a small assemblage of twenty flint artefacts of a largely late Neolithic or early Bronze Age date, although a backed blade is probably early Neolithic in its associations; the surrounding landscape appears to be rich in early prehistoric lithic finds, including diagnostic objects of Mesolithic, Neolithic and early Bronze Age date (see Chapter 3). The southernmost hillfort in our group, at Maiden Castle, has possible evidence for a pre-hillfort timber palisade slot and an early Bronze Age barbed and tanged arrowhead has been recovered from the environs of the hilltop.

More broadly, evidence from the western side of Oakmere indicates early prehistoric activity, where field walking during the Cheshire Wetlands Project recovered a small assemblage of Neolithic and early Bronze Age flint tools, including a flint axe and a chert arrowhead (Leah *et al.* 1997: 112–3). Similarly, a Neolithic leaf-shaped arrowhead was recovered during field walking to the north of Peckforton Mere during the Habitats and Hillforts Project (Garner 2012: 16).

The combined evidence is strongly suggestive of the importance of these promontory sites in the preceding millennia leading up to the establishment of the hillforts themselves, and this trend has been noted elsewhere in the Anglo-Welsh borderland (Mullin 2012: 87–8). However, it is not clear how the role of these hilltops might have been preserved, changed or evolved over this long period. The evidence from Beeston and Eddisbury suggests that during the late Neolithic and early Bronze Age some hilltops were being used for burial practices and may well have contained burial monuments, which can no longer be discerned in the surface topography. The recurrence of material culture dating to the early Neolithic at many of the hillfort sites is particularly intriguing, given the almost complete lack of evidence for either occupation sites or monuments of this period in the surrounding landscape. Indeed, palaeoenvironmental evidence from the mere sites and Helsby hilltop suggests that the Neolithic landscape was still heavily wooded and that widespread clearance on the Cheshire Ridge did not commence until the early Bronze Age (Chapter 14). It has recently been argued that the scarcity of early Neolithic monuments in the Anglo-Welsh borderland should not be seen as a lack of community coherence or organisation; but rather a selective adoption/rejection of certain elements of the Neolithic 'package' by the regional population (Mullin 2012: 87).

Hillfort architecture

Following earlier hillfort studies, Harding breaks down the 'anatomy' of hillfort enclosure in to various constituent parts by categorising the nature of the perimeter works as follows:

1. Palisaded or stockaded enclosure
2. Timber-framed and timber-faced wall-ramparts
3. Stone-faced timber-framed ramparts
4. Stone-faced and stone-built walls
5. Dump (or *glacis* type) ramparts

Harding acknowledges that there are so many variations in rampart design that virtually every site could be designated a distinctive type (Harding 2012: 59). The palisade enclosure is seen, however, as a feature of the earlier first millennium BC and is generally (though not exclusively) interpreted as a free-standing stockade as opposed to the front face of an earthen rampart (*ibid*. 54–7). Wall ramparts of timber, timber and stone, and stone (as well as possibly turf) are seen as being designed to revet the front and rear faces of a core, in order to present a steeper, taller and more impressive obstacle (*ibid*. 58).

Hillfort ditches are only briefly considered by Harding on the basis that they are rarely excavated over any great length. However, he suggests that the profiles of ditches associated with wall ramparts are often steeply 'V' or 'U' shaped, whilst dump ramparts tend to be fronted by broader, shallower ditches (*ibid*. 74). It is suggested that generally the ditch was only interrupted at the entrance, where a solid causeway gave access to the gates. Entrances can range from relatively simple, to ostentatiously elaborate designs and are usually limited to one or two; Forde-Johnston distinguished simple entrances from those with inturned or out-turned, looped or overlapping ramparts (1976: 75). Harding breaks down the anatomy of the entrance in to the component parts of the entrance passage, guard chambers, bastions, barbicans and complex outworks. Hillforts without entrances are treated separately, with two possible solutions being advanced; either that access was gained by timber stairs over the wall, or that the entrance was so

narrow that the collapsed walls had totally obscured its location (*ibid*. 87).

Driver has questioned the outmoded typologies for Iron Age hillforts and enclosed settlements, such as basic categorisation by size (in hectares), the number of ditches present or vallation, from uni- to bi- and multivallate and the generalised morphology (pear-shaped, rectangular etc).This also includes the general set of topographical models in common use with terms such as 'contour' and 'promontory' forts. He suggests that the use of rank size analysis to interrogate settlement hierarchy, with the largest settlement being ranked number one, can lead to heavy bias in regions where certain types of soils and geology have adversely affected archaeological discovery. Enclosure size cannot be used as a reliable indicator of strength or power and taking command of exceptionally prominent hills and outcrops may have been the central, important social statement. He argues that it is the complexity of the defences which signal power, political competence to harness communal labour, and the incorporation of cultural traditions (Driver 2013: 4–5).

Driver advances the suggestion that mainly during the middle and late Iron Age, there existed a concept of complex, largely non-utilitarian architecture. Architectural complexity was identified:

> "…as a suite of constructional elements whose purpose was apparently to aggrandise and monumentalise key parts of the gateways and defences of certain hillforts above and beyond the requirements for basic enclosure and defence, to project certain symbolism to those viewing or approaching the fort."(*ibid*. 129).

One significant discovery:

> "… has been the recognition of shared 'facade schemes', interpreted as being the construction or remodelling of a given hillfort along certain required architectural lines, governing the overall spatial arrangement of defences and gateways, and also the details of defensive style and technical characteristics. This results in a hillfort with an appearance and structural arrangement that apparently belongs to a distinct architectural tradition, regardless of the physical constraints of topography." (*ibid*.)

Driver identifies two main regional facade schemes for North Ceredigion, addressing issues such as the response of hillforts to topography, as well as assessing the landscape settings of hillforts which share architectural schemes (Driver 2013: 129).

In Chapter 7 a brief attempt was made to review the architectural elements of the Cheshire hillfort group and it is clear that both similarities and differences can be seen amongst, what is essentially, a relatively small group of monuments. The results of the various excavations and the subsequent programmes of scientific dating, mean that a chronological framework can now be suggested for some of these commonalities. The first distinct architectural style (hereafter the Helsby façade scheme) can be seen at potentially the earliest monument in the group. The style can be demonstrated in the primary enclosure wall at Helsby which comprised a stone-faced front revetment to a stone rampart, with no apparent external ditch or obvious entrance. The line of this enclosure wall appears to follow an architectural design which ignores the local topographical constraints, to form a simple semi-circular or crescent-shaped enclosure, created from a series of four short linear sections. The Helsby enclosure wall was sealed by a colluvial deposit, which produced a C14 date of 1435–1320 cal BC (NZA-37729). Whilst this early date must be treated with some caution, a second horizon from slightly higher up the sequence of colluvial deposits produced a C14 date of 1250–1050 cal BC (NZA-35493), which implies stratigraphical integrity of the dating results. The dating evidence would suggest that the primary phase of monument building at Helsby dates to the middle Bronze Age (1500–1140 BC).

Amongst the monuments in the group, the closest parallel to the architectural design of Helsby can be seen at Kelsborrow hillfort. Here, the primary enclosure bank appears to have been constructed as a simple earth bank (though a timber-framed wall-rampart has previously been suggested) with no external ditch or obvious entrance. Even though the rampart has now been heavily eroded by decades of ploughing, the lidar data and geophysical survey results show the line of this enclosure bank forms a simple semi-circular or crescent-shaped enclosure, also created from a series of four short linear sections. The Kelsborrow enclosure bank can be dated by material from the rampart core, which produced a C14 date of 1000–840 cal BC (BETA-325775) placing its construction firmly within the late Bronze Age. Whilst a period of over 300 years appears to separate the construction of the monuments at Helsby and Kelsborrow, it is interesting to note the finding of a bronze 'celt' (or palstave axe) within the hillfort at Kelsborrow in 1810, as this suggests a middle Bronze Age presence on the site, prior to the construction of the enclosure bank.

The second architectural style to be noted (hereafter the Bickerton façade scheme) can be illustrated first with the smallest hillfort in the group, at Maiden Castle on Bickerton Hill. The primary enclosure wall consists of a stone-faced timber-laced rampart with a shallow external quarry ditch, a possible counterscarp bank and a monumental inturned entrance. The external quarry ditch was characterised with localised deepenings and irregularities which gave the ditch a cellular appearance (see Chapter 2). The design of Maiden Castle's inner rampart is not as semi-circular or crescent-shaped as earlier commentators have suggested (see Chapter 2). The inner rampart is more of a reversed 'L' shape and mirrors the natural shape of the adjacent cliff edge, to create an enclosed space which is more like a parallelogram in appearance. The scientific dating for Maiden Castle is in need of revisiting, but it will suffice here to state that on the available information, the inner rampart is dated to 860–330 cal BC at two sigma (Matthews 2002: 5). The outer rampart is likely to be a later addition and a secondary embellishment of the original architectural design, with a simple gap entrance opposite the earlier inturned entrance of the inner rampart. The construction differs from the inner rampart and consists of a stone-faced wall without timber lacing and an outer quarry ditch which has not been investigated through excavation. The line of the outer rampart does appear more curvilinear in shape, but it is unclear whether this is a deliberate adaption, or simply an artefact of extending the line of the enclosure further out from the cliff edge. The outer rampart has produced two C14 dates of 770–400 cal BC (2435±70 BP; UB-2615) and 380–10 cal BC (2130±70 BP; UB-2614) at two sigma as calibrated by Matthews (2002: 5). The available evidence places the origins of this architectural style within the early Iron Age and possibly indicates development of the monument during the middle Iron Age.

The closest parallel to the architectural design of Maiden Castle can be seen at Eddisbury hillfort. The primary enclosure consists of a stone-faced rampart with an external 'U' shaped quarry ditch, a possible counterscarp bank and a monumental inturned entrance. The base of the external quarry ditch was characterised by a series of lozenge-shaped slots, which gave the ditch a cellular appearance (see Chapters 2 and 10). The intention of the architectural design at Eddisbury has been obscured by a certain level of modification to the natural topography of the hilltop during the post-medieval period. This is primarily associated with terracing in to the hillslope on the western side of the hillfort during the development of Old Pale Heights Farm and an adjacent stone quarry. However, geophysical survey (see Chapter 6) has successfully traced part of the line of the inner rampart in this damaged section of the hilltop; these results should be compared to the earliest plan of the hillfort by Ormerod (Chapter 2). It can therefore be suggested that the inner rampart forms two sides of the enclosure in a reversed 'J' shaped line, which broadly mirrors the natural shape of the adjacent cliff edge to create an enclosed space which is sub-rectangular or lozenge-shaped in appearance. The presence of Merrick's Hill at the southeastern end of the hillfort presents an incongruity to the overall design, but this part of the hilltop may have had special significance to the hillfort builders. The scientific dating for the construction of the inner rampart at Eddisbury is from two C14 dates of 770–410 cal BC (NZA-36648) and 740–390 cal BC (Beta-317521).

At Eddisbury, the outer rampart is a later addition and a secondary embellishment of the original architectural design, with a simple gap entrance opposite the earlier inturned entrance of the inner rampart. The construction is very similar to the inner rampart and consists of a stone-faced wall revetting an earthen bank and an outer quarry ditch with a continuous steep 'V' shaped profile. This later modification of the design probably includes the blocking of a secondary entrance on the northern side of the hillfort and the construction of a new monumental inturned entrance on the southeastern side. The scientific dating for the construction of the outer rampart at Eddisbury is derived from a C14 date of 400–200 cal BC (NZA-36593). The rampart and ditch around Merrick's Hill and along the southern cliff edge, remain undated at present. The steep 'V' shaped profile recorded in sections of the ditch around Merrick's Hill would suggest, however, that this belongs to the secondary embellishment of the hillfort. The outer end of the new southeastern entrance was possibly furnished with a pair of bastions, leading to a long stone and timber-lined passage, which had one semi-circular guard chamber on the southern side. This guard chamber had been destroyed by fire and this event can be dated by C14 dating to 360–160 cal BC (NZA-36592). The available dating evidence suggests that the design, construction and later development of Maiden Castle and Eddisbury are broadly contemporary within the early and middle Iron Age periods.

Having established two distinct architectural styles within the Cheshire hillfort group, it has been possible to suggest, using a programme of scientific dating, that the difference in designs is related to when the monuments were built. However, the remaining two hillforts in the Cheshire group do not entirely fit the argument for a preconceived design, even if there are some broadly comparable architectural elements within their construction.

The hillfort on Woodhouse hill has a stone-faced front revetment to a stone rampart, with no apparent external ditch or obvious entrance. The line of this enclosure wall appears to make use of the natural topography of the hilltop and is paralleled internally by a series of shallow quarry pits of varying size. The wall forms two sides of the enclosure in a reversed 'J' shaped line, which broadly mirrors the natural shape of the adjacent cliff edge, to create an enclosed space which is lozenge-shaped in appearance. The construction of the wall has been dated using the OSL dating technique to 1311–471 BC (LV387) (see Chapter 8) which spans the middle Bronze Age to early Iron Age periods. The lack of an external ditch or obvious entrance is in keeping with the Helsby façade scheme and the stone-revetted stone rampart wall construction is very reminiscent of the wall at Helsby. However, the characteristic semi-circular or crescent-shaped enclosure design is absent and the adherence to the natural topography, with the rampart mirroring the cliff promontory, is more in keeping with the hillforts of the Bickerton façade scheme. Whilst the dating of the Woodhouse hillfort is quite broad, its architectural design demonstrates an almost hybrid quality between the two proposed façade schemes. It is tempting, therefore, to suggest that Woodhouse represents a transitional design between the hillforts of the middle/late Bronze Age tradition and those of the early Iron Age.

The earliest phase of rampart construction at Beeston Castle superseded evidence for a timber palisade and consisted of an earth bank with no external ditch or obvious entrance. The evidence from Beeston is rather fragmentary, owing to the medieval castle outer bailey wall and gateway being sited directly on top of the prehistoric hillfort ramparts. However, the dating of the primary rampart construction is provided by a C14 date of 1300–840 cal BC (HAR-4405) and two late Bronze Age ribbed socketed axes. These have been interpreted as deliberate foundation deposits within the rampart and are of Ewart Park type, dated c. 900–700 BC (Needham 1993: 44–5). The lack of an external ditch or obvious entrance is in keeping with the Helsby façade scheme and the simple earth bank (with a possible timber-framed wall-rampart) construction is very reminiscent of the wall at Kelsborrow hillfort. However, the line of the enclosure wall does not have the characteristic semi-circular or crescent-shaped enclosure design of the Helsby façade scheme; instead it respects the natural topography of the hillslope to create a slightly sinuous line, cutting off the lower end of the hill. The natural contours of the hill dictated the location of the medieval castle gateway and this also appears to have been the case in later phases of the prehistoric hillfort. There is no evidence that this was the case with the original architectural design of the late Bronze Age fort. The design for Beeston remains unique in the Cheshire hillfort group, however, the Beeston crag is such a distinctive and prominent part of the Cheshire landscape that it might have demanded a unique design solution.

A further observation regarding the identification of the Helsby and Bickerton façade schemes can be made with regard to the later modification of two hillforts in the Cheshire group. Firstly, it can be noted that at Helsby, the original enclosure wall was modified with the addition of a new stone revetment on the internal face. The style of construction of this new wall was not in keeping with the earlier construction style of the outer revetment, but it was similar to the construction of the inturned entrance at the western end of the hillfort rampart. Beyond the original enclosure wall there is a secondary earthwork, which is either a counterscarp bank or outer rampart for which a ditch might be indicated on the geophysical survey results (see Chapter 6). This secondary earthwork does not extend on to the lower ledge of the promontory at the northern end of the original enclosure wall. The addition of an inturned entrance and outer counterscarp bank are design elements associated with the Bickerton façade scheme and it suggests that the hillfort at Helsby was deliberately adapted to this architectural style.

During the early Iron Age, at Beeston Castle the primary rampart was enhanced by the cutting of an external ditch and the creation of a formal entranceway. The detailed design of the entrance was not recovered from the excavation; however, later alterations to the rampart and entrance during the middle Iron Age suggest a timber-built inturned entrance. The most precise dating for the timber refurbishment at Beeston is offered by an archaeomagnetic date of 360–240 cal BC, from burnt sandstone in the modified rampart (Ellis 1993: 32). The addition of an inturned entrance and outer ditch are design elements associated with the Bickerton façade scheme and it suggests that, like the hillfort at Helsby, Beeston was deliberately adapted to this architectural style during the early/middle Iron Age.

The identification of distinct architectural trends within the Cheshire hillfort group might assist the analysis of other assumed late prehistoric enclosures of the mid Cheshire Ridge. The enclosure at Oakmere is perhaps the best case study, as it appears to have a design reminiscent of the Helsby façade scheme. The recent geophysical survey at Oakmere has demonstrated that the gap entrance shown on earlier earthwork surveys is likely to be a modern modification, associated with the installation of a pipe or drain (see Chapter 6). Once this is appreciated, it can be seen that the Oakmere site has many of the key features of the Helsby façade scheme, such as a simple semi-circular or crescent-shaped enclosure, created from a series of short linear sections, with no obvious entrance. The presence of an external ditch at Oakmere is suggested, but this has not been investigated through excavation and the precise sequencing of the development for the enclosure wall and ditch are not known. The adherence to elements of the Helsby façade scheme might argue for a Bronze Age origin to the Oakmere enclosure, but this now awaits confirmation through excavation. In contrast, the Peckforton Mere enclosure, with an almost completely enclosing bank and ditch, corner entrance and secondary counterscarp bank, is far more in keeping with the Bickerton façade scheme; possibly indicating an early/mid Iron Age date.

The landscape context

A number of regional hillfort studies have been published in recent years highlighting the work of individual research projects, such as the Wessex Hillforts Project (Payne *et al.* 2006), the hillforts of the Northumberland National Park (Oswald *et al.* 2006) and the Hillforts of North Ceredigion (Driver 2013). In the main, these studies bring together campaigns of non-invasive survey and pre-existing excavation data to place specific hillfort groups within their landscape settings. In the case of the Wessex Hillforts Project, aerial photography and geophysical survey were major components of the survey work, as the prevailing geology provided good results using these techniques. The aerial photography supplied the wider prehistoric landscape context and the geophysical survey the fine grained detail of individual sites. The Wessex study offers a regional model for hillfort development, beginning in the late Bronze Age/ earliest Iron Age with slight hilltop enclosures emerging in parallel with systems of linear earthworks. During the early Iron Age, the site at Danebury developed in to a primary hillfort and underwent a new phase of construction with a stronger rampart and ditch. Subsidiary hillforts established on the periphery of its territory were possibly for strategic purposes. By the middle Iron Age, Danebury had become a developed type of hillfort and was possibly the only hillfort in the region remaining in use. Final hillfort abandonment in the region is suggested to have taken place by the middle of the 1st century BC (Payne *et al.* 2006: 10–13).

The landscape context of the Cheshire hillfort group has been particularly elusive and this is in no small part due to the well-known difficulties associated with non-invasive survey techniques in the region. The combination of intensive agricultural land use and the prevalent soils of the drift geology have rendered large areas of the Ridge a seemingly blank canvas, in terms of the prehistoric landscape. This poor survival is most starkly illustrated in Chapter 7 where the lidar data has been used to show the marked difference at Manley Common, between the remaining area of forestry, with the preservation of medieval field systems and the adjoining agricultural land, where no trace remains of earlier field systems. Whilst aerial photography in Cheshire does occasionally reveal cropmark enclosure sites which have been attributed a late prehistoric/Romano-British date, these are generally isolated features with little accompanying evidence for contemporary field systems or larger territorial boundaries (Collens 1999: 36–41).

The only significant prehistoric monument type which can be discerned in the landscape of the mid-Cheshire Ridge, other than the hillforts themselves, is the scatter of early Bronze Age burial mounds noted by previous commentators (Leah *et al.* 1997: 150). This includes the barrow cemetery known as the Seven Lows, which is located in the Delamere area to the southwest of the promontory site at Oakmere (see Chapter 7). The presence of these burial mounds demonstrates a tradition of monument building in the landscape of the mid-Cheshire Ridge, prior to the construction of the hillforts, but it does not explain the lack of Neolithic monuments, stone circles or henges in the area. The lack of evidence for other late Bronze Age earthworks such as cross-ridge dykes or 'ranch boundaries' which are often associated with territorial boundary markers is also notable.

Much of the earliest fossilised pre-1600 AD fieldscapes identified within the Cheshire Historic Landscape Characterisation Project (Edwards 2007: 63) can only be attributed as 'Ancient,' with little means of establishing their precise antiquity. Recent large area excavation work at Saighton near Chester, has identified a Romano-British field system and associated trackways, which had apparently replaced an earlier field system of prehistoric date. Neither of these field systems had influenced the post-medieval ordering of the landscape, nor could they be discerned through historic map regression or aerial reconnaissance. They were essentially invisible until chance discovery by excavation (Northern Archaeological Associates 2013). The example at Saighton is likely to be a wide spread phenomenon within the Cheshire landscape and a similar discovery has been made to the south of the Roman settlement at Middlewich (Dodd 2004). The only probable piece of identifiable prehistoric field system within the Cheshire Ridge landscape is an area of co-axial field boundaries represented by broad banks, or lynchets, on the slopes of the mid-Cheshire Ridge to the north of Longley Farm at Kelsall (Longley 1987: 104; 112).

Evidence for Iron Age settlement sites, apart from hillforts, in the historic county of Cheshire is limited, but this is beginning to change with the excavation of sites such as Irby, Wirral; Bruen Stapleford; Chester; and Poulton. Neighbouring areas mainly to the north of the Mersey have also begun to investigate other Iron Age enclosure sites including excavations at Brook House Farm, Halewood (Cowell and Philpott 2000); Great Woolden Hall (Nevell 1999), Salford and Mellor, Stockport (Nevell and Redhead 2005). Philpott considers that the growing body of evidence from Cheshire and neighbouring areas in the Iron Age is beginning to suggest differences in function between sites, as well as the variety of sites at a sub-regional level (Philpott 2010: 170).

Recognition of these settlement sites is difficult, however. Although aerial reconnaissance has revealed a small but significant number of cropmark enclosure sites, few have been systematically excavated. Most of the recently discovered settlement sites dating to the first millennium BC in western Cheshire have been chance discoveries. The unenclosed settlement at Bruen Stapleford, near Chester (Fairburn et al. 2003) was located during a commercial pipeline development; the settlement evidence at Chester Amphitheatre was revealed whilst investigating the Roman amphitheatre (Wilmott and Garner forthcoming); and the settlement at Poulton, south of Chester, was discovered whilst excavating a medieval chapel and cemetery (Cootes 2015). The excavated settlement sites at Bruen Stapleford, Chester and Poulton have all produced C14 dates in the middle Iron Age (c. 400-200 cal BC). They are all located within major river valleys (Chester and Poulton in the Dee valley and Bruen Stapleford in the Gowy valley) on the

glacial clay drift geology, as opposed to the light sandy soils of the Cheshire Ridge. In this sense, comparisons can be made with settlement patterns in Eastern England where clusters of open agricultural settlement were not evenly spread, but occurred quite densely in the major river valleys, in the middle Iron Age (Hill 2007: 21). There must be a relationship between these river valley settlements of the Dee and Gowy, with some of the adjacent hilltop enclosures of the mid-Cheshire Ridge; as the chronology now shows that they are contrasting elements of a contemporary landscape. Whilst the evidence is still far too sparse to suggest a model for the relationship between these settlements and the hillforts, it is tempting to see evidence for a 4th century BC Earlier to Later Iron Age transition; with the emergence of new settlement sites and occupation of marginal areas on the heavier clay soils (Haselgrove and Pope 2007: 8).

In lieu of a fossilised prehistoric landscape, it is only really possible to discuss the siting of the hillforts within the natural landscape; this was briefly attempted with reference to the lidar data in Chapter 7. The first feature to note is that all of the prehistoric enclosures on the mid-Cheshire Ridge, including both the hillforts and mere-side enclosures, are located to exploit promontory sites. This is perhaps no surprise, given the prevailing natural landscape of the area, where such promontory locations are so common in the Cheshire hills. However, it does not so easily explain why certain promontories have been singled out in favour of other, equally suitable, locations. For example the hilltop promontory at Harthill (formerly enclosed as Harthill Park) would make a prime hillfort location, but seems to have been passed over in favour of the adjacent cliff-top site of Maiden Castle (Bickerton Hill). The use of promontories can be seen as a labour saving device, where the natural cliffs and scarps can be utilised as part of the creation of an enclosed space; however, this does not always seem to have been the primary driver for the design of the Cheshire enclosures. The answer may have more to do with the earlier prehistoric focus which these particular hilltops appear to have had.

The second feature of note is that the hilltop promontories which were enclosed appear to occupy only part of the highest ground on upland hills or ridges. This is most notable in the hillforts of the Bickerton façade scheme and at Maiden Castle the hillfort nestles on the northwestern side of a very clearly defined wider area formerly known as Bird's Hill. Similarly, Eddisbury hillfort sits at the southeastern end of the wider hilltop, which was later used to define the limits of the Old Pale deer park. It is tempting to see these larger areas as the territorial hinterland of their particular hillfort; and the alignment of the inturned monumental hillfort entrances (facing towards the wider hilltop) may lend some support to this. Unfortunately, these wider hilltops have not, as yet, yielded any evidence for contemporary land use;

other than the suggestion at Helsby that there was long established heathland which could have been exploited for livestock grazing.

The Cheshire hillfort group has been the subject of a wider study in to hillfort intervisibility in the northern Welsh Marches using a combination of field observation and GIS based viewshed analysis (Matthews 2014: 9). The results of this work have suggested a pattern of intervisibility between neighbouring hillforts, which could be used to infer socio-political connections and thus distinguish tribal identities. The research has been used to suggest that the Cheshire hillfort group can be equated with the western hub of the pre-Roman tribal territory of the Deceangli, which had its heartland in northeast Wales (*ibid*. 25). Whilst these results provide a significant dimension to the landscape in which the Cheshire hillforts were located and built, there are limitations to the approach. The most significant restriction is an assumption that all of the hillfort sites represent contemporary monuments that were in use at the same time (*ibid.* 7). Furthermore, the evidence for the tribal territories of the Deceangli and Cornovii which we possess is Romano-British and dates to the 2nd century AD; it cannot, therefore be reliably used to suggest the Iron Age administrative arrangements of the 4th/3rd centuries BC (Matthews 2002: 35).

The palaeoenvironmental investigation of the landscape

It was recognised that one way to investigate the contemporary landscape of the hillforts was to build upon earlier palaeoenvironmental work undertaken by the Cheshire Wetlands Project in the 1990s. In particular, two mere sites at Peckforton and Hatchmere were targeted (Chapter 14) for comparison with a sequence from Helsby hillfort (Chapter 13) and some timely developer-funded work at Ince Marshes (Chapter 15). It should be noted that, as with any palynological study, the catchment for the fossilised pollen could be very localised and represent vegetation within 10-20m of the sample collection point. In the case of the mere sites, the expectation was that the pollen captured within the mere would represent activity within the area bordering the watercourse which fed it; thus indicating land use in the fields adjacent to the meres.

The conclusions of the Cheshire Wetland Survey for early prehistory were heavily focused on artefact recovery from field walking and the ability of the wetland sites to provide indicators for early human activity/settlement. The primary indicator under discussion from the palaeoenvironmental data, was the presence of charcoal in the prehistoric peat stratigraphy and whether this could be used as a reliable indicator for human activity; either through accidental or deliberate firing of woodland (Leah *et al.* 1997: 150). The period of the second and first millennia BC was primarily discussed with reference to

the distribution of early and middle Bronze Age burial mounds clustered along the Sandstone Ridge (*ibid.*). It was acknowledged that the palaeoenvironmental evidence for later prehistory and the Romano-British period was relatively scarce and lacked independent dating of specific archaeological events. In general, it was concluded that there was extensive deforestation in the region from the late Iron Age and an increase in farming activity continuing in to the Romano-British period. This was followed by widespread regeneration of woodland during the early medieval period and a further period of woodland clearance and agricultural activity, which was broadly attributed to after the Norman Conquest (*ibid.* 154). In particular, the survey noted the increasing presence of cannabis-type pollen (probably hemp) in upper segments of some pollen diagrams, which was attributed to the 'historic' period (notably at sites at Hatchmere and Fishpool Farm) (*ibid.* 153–155).

The main contribution of the palaeoenvironmental work undertaken as part of the Habitats and Hillforts Project has been to provide a more precise chronological framework for some of the trends previously noted in earlier work. Despite the fact that Peckforton and Hatchmere are separated by a distance of 16km, there were some chronological trends which appeared to be repeated. Woodland taxa (particularly oak, alder and hazel) are dominant through the late Mesolithic and Neolithic until the early Bronze Age; the paucity of open ground species supports the interpretation of a largely forested landscape. Woodland clearance appears to be indicated during the early Bronze Age, with cereal pollen and species indicators (such as Ribwort plantain) suggesting livestock grazing. The presence of heather was also thought to indicate the development of heathland in the area; the beginning of this vegetational change is dated at Hatchmere to 2290–2050 cal BC (SUERC-41874) and at Peckforton Mere to 2465–2205 cal BC (NZA-37792). Whilst the pollen record fluctuates during the Bronze Age, with some indicators for episodes of woodland regeneration, there is a continued presence of cereal, ribwort plantain and heather. Further woodland clearance is indicated during the early Iron Age at both mere sites and this is dated at Peckforton Mere to 800–550 cal BC (SUERC-33264). Cereal pollen also becomes a more consistent feature of the record from the later Iron Age until the medieval period.

Cannabiaceae pollen (hemp) first appears in the record at Peckforton Mere in the early to middle Bronze Age and is found at low levels throughout the rest of the core; this may suggest local cultivation of hemp. The presence of *Cannabiaceae* pollen appears in the record at Hatchmere, with low levels in the late Romano-British period, rapidly increasing to become the dominant taxa by the early medieval period. This dominance peaks around AD 1400 and then declines in the post-medieval period, whilst still remaining prevalent in the record in the upper samples. The dominance of *Cannabiaceae* pollen is indicative of hemp retting activities in the mere, taking place most intensively throughout the medieval and post-medieval periods. Lower levels of *Cannabiaceae* pollen may indicate hemp growing locally prior to the medieval period, rather than hemp retting directly in the mere. Hemp was sown in spring and harvested about four months later (Adams 1976: 137). It benefitted the crops grown after it, such as winter cereals, owing to its high weed suppression and the ability of its large root system to loosen the soil. Hemp could be used for a variety of products, including the manufacture of cordage, durable clothing and nutritional products (the oil from the seeds is similar to linseed oil, and is sometimes used for cooking). The occurrence of hemp at both mere sites corroborates earlier work discussed in the Cheshire Wetlands Survey and suggests that the cultivation of hemp as a crop may have had a long tradition in Cheshire, stretching back in to prehistory.

Early Medieval re-use of the Cheshire hillforts

From the outset of the Habitats and Hillforts Project it was suspected that Eddisbury hillfort had been re-occupied or re-fortified as a Mercian burh by Aethelflaed in AD 914. Higham had expressed some doubt over Eddisbury (in Delamere) being the location of a Mercian fort in a chain of defences, running between Chester in the west and Manchester in the east. Furthermore, he had drawn attention to the location of a second Eddisbury place-name in Rainow near Macclesfield as a possible alternative candidate (Higham 1993: 111). The discovery of an oven base set in to the back of the inner rampart and scientifically dated to 860 ±70 AD (cal AD 745–980) (see Chapter 10) has perhaps provided the long awaited supporting evidence for the Mercian occupation of the site. However, there appears to be a small but significant amount of evidence for earlier Saxon occupation of the hilltop and the place-name itself has clear antiquity. The name Eddisbury or *Eades byrig*, meaning 'Ead's stronghold' (Dodgson 1971: 213) was already well established by the time of the founding of the Aethelflaedan burh in AD 914 and it is perhaps the case that the royal burh was simply refounded by Aethelflaed, as opposed to the refortification of a long abandoned prehistoric monument. Varley had suggested this possibility in his 1950 report (see Chapter 2) but much of his evidence was questionable and some of his stratigraphic interpretations have been shown to be incorrect (Chapter 10).

There was no expectation of uncovering similar evidence from any of the other Cheshire hillfort sites at the beginning of the Project. However, at Kelsborrow hillfort, the earliest internal feature identified was a shallow sub-circular pit containing a charcoal-rich fill that produced a radiocarbon date of cal AD 690–890 (BETA-325777). The pre-conquest date recovered from the charred plant remains may provide a context for the place-name 'Kelsborrow'

(or 'Kelsborough Castle' as it is shown on an 1813 map of Delamere Forest (CALS 113224)) which Higham suggests combines the personal name *Kel* with the Old English element – *burh* (meaning Kel's fort) (Higham 1993: 138; Dodgson 1971: 212). There is some debate about the 'Kel' element of the place-name as it also occurs in the nearby village of Kelsall, where it is considered to be derived from the Middle English personal name 'Kel(le) (Dodgson 1971: 277). However, a less popular interpretation suggests the personal name is derived from Old English Cel(i), Cael(i) or Ceol with the 'K' resulting from later Scandinavian influence (*ibid.*). Kelsall is not firmly identified in the Cheshire Domesday survey, although it has been suggested that the unidentified manor of 'Cocle' possibly refers to Kelsall (Sawyer 1987: 360). The earliest documentary reference to the Kelsall place-name is from 1257 (Dodgson 1971: 277). Regardless of the origins of the place-name, the archaeological evidence points to occupation of the hillfort in a period prior to the Aethelflaedan burh building programme of the early 10th century.

The stratigraphic evidence from the hillfort at Helsby also suggests sub-Roman/early medieval occupation of the site; the uppermost colluvial deposits associated with the main rampart producing a radiocabon date of cal AD 400–530 (NZA-35494). The place-name Helsby is recorded in the Domesday survey of 1086 as *Helesbe* meaning 'village (byr) on a ledge (hjallr)' (Dodgson 1971: 236). The site of the ledge is taken to refer to the narrow shelf at the foot of Helsby Hill, which forms the location of the modern village (*ibid.*); however, the hillfort could in fact be the original 'village on the ledge' alluded to in the place-name.

The importance of prehistoric hillforts as monuments in the Anglo-Saxon landscape has been highlighted by recent research. There is strong evidence linking the re-use of some hillforts as places of royal assembly and council, with some monuments being used as places of execution, or for the settlement of disputes and feuds. It has been suggested that:

> "certain hill forts retained a supra-regional value as symbolic markers of earlier territories or territorial identity, resulting in their adoption and use in Late Anglo-Saxon England for a variety of purposes but especially for activities relating to royal presence and status" (Semple 2013: 204).

Sites such as Yeavering, suggest the structured use of prehistoric monuments in the creation of elite sites of power and authority during the 7th and 8th centuries AD (*ibid.* 207).

Returning to the site of Kelsborrow hillfort, examination of the section through the outer ditch identified the northern lip to the earliest surviving phase of this feature; which produced a radiocarbon date of cal AD

1020–1160 (BETA-325774). This might suggest that the promontory enclosure was re-fortified in the Saxo-Norman period with an outer ditch being added to the existing prehistoric bank. The line of postholes identified during the 1973 excavation might also belong to this phase of re-fortification. Furthermore, on the hillfort interior a charcoal-rich pit fill produced an almost identical radiocarbon date of cal AD 990–1120 (BETA-325776). The dimensions of the pit were not fully exposed during the 2011 excavation and its function remains uncertain; however, the fill suggests occupation on the hillfort interior at a time when it had seemingly been re-fortified. Charred plant remains from the pit fill included fragments of heather, cereal/grass, alder, hazel and grains of oats; the latter perhaps indicating crop storage/processing on the site.

The scientific dating evidence suggests activity at Kelsborrow during the 11th or 12th century AD would be much later than the Aethelflaedan burh building of the early 10th century recorded in the Anglo-Saxon Chronicle (as evidenced at nearby Eddisbury). As suggested in Chapter 12 (this volume) Kelsborrow could have been utilised as a Norman castle in the post-conquest period, as seen in the 13th century castle sited at Beeston. No artefacts dateable to this period have been recovered from the monument; however, an antiquarian reference to the recovery of an iron sword from within the enclosure in 1810 (CHER 833/1) might be of relevance. The three early medieval dates recovered from such a relatively small sample of the hillfort interior might suggest fairly extensive occupation during several periods of use rather than a single event.

Conclusions

The archaeological research undertaken as part of the Habitats and Hillforts Project has provided a greater depth of understanding of a group of monuments, which should form the basis for any broader discussion of Cheshire during the first millennium BC. It is clear that each individual hillfort has its own distinct character and unique chronological narrative. The deployment of modern scientific dating techniques at four of the hillfort sites has allowed a more complex chronological

framework to be constructed. This framework does not, as yet, suggest unbroken lines of occupation and use, spanning the two millennia from 1000 BC to AD 1000 at any of the hillforts. However, this approach has allowed an analysis of the hillfort architecture and the identification of two distinct architectural styles, dating to the middle/late Bronze Age and the early/middle Iron Age. It has led to a clearer understanding of the landscape surrounding the hillforts, with woodland clearance and the appearance of cereal pollen from the early Bronze Age and both becoming more consistent features from the late Iron Age. It has suggested a long tradition of hemp cultivation in Cheshire, probably from the prehistoric period. It has also provided firm evidence for the far more extensive early medieval re-use of some of the Cheshire hillforts.

These results need to be seen within the context of what was essentially a series of small-scale and low impact excavations, which were targeted on areas of previous disturbance. Future large-scale and well-resourced campaigns of research and excavation at any of the hillfort sites will undoubtedly add further depth to the chronological narrative and perhaps serve to fill current gaps in knowledge. Whilst the work reported on in this volume has not led to the recovery of notable assemblages of material culture, there is however, enough limited material from sites such as Eddisbury, to suggest that significant assemblages could still be recovered during larger programmes of excavation.

The Cheshire hillforts have demonstrated a capacity to provide new evidence of occupation during the late prehistoric and early medieval periods, for which there is a limited known archaeological resource in the North West region generally. In 2001, in a working paper on Iron Age Britain which set out an overall framework for the improvement of archaeological research strategies at a regional level in Britain, Cheshire was categorised as a 'black hole' in terms of the current state of regional knowledge (Haselgrove et al. 2001). Work in the region since the publication of this paper has gone some way to address this shortcoming. It is hoped that the results from the Habitats and Hillforts Project have contributed to this growing body of evidence.

Bibliography

Adams, J. 1953. *Harrol Edge, Frodsham*. Unpublished note in the Cheshire Historic Environment Record.

Adams, I. H. 1976. *Agrarian Landscape terms: a glossary for historical geography*. Institute of British Geographers Special Publication Nine. London.

Ainsworth, S. and Barnatt, J. 1998. A scarp-edge enclosure at Gardom's Edge, Baslow, Derbyshire. *Derbyshire Archaeological Journal* 118: 5–23.

Ammann, B., Birks, H. H., Walanus, A. and Wasylikowa, K. 2007. Late Glacial Multidisciplinary Studies. In S. A. Elias (ed.), *Encyclopedia of Quarternary Science*: 2475–2486. Amsterdam, Elsevier.

Andersen, S. Th. 1979. Identification of wild grasses and cereal pollen. *Danmarks geologiske Undersøgelse* (1978): 69–92.

Anon. 1953. Stray Finds. *Journal of the Chester Archaeological Society* 40: 63

Anon. 1975. Stray Finds. *Cheshire Archaeological Bulletin* 3: 59

Anon. 1977. Stray Finds. *Cheshire Archaeological Bulletin* 5: 53

Ashmore, O. 1982. *The Industrial Archaeology of North-West England*. Manchester, Manchester University Press.

Ashmore, P. 1999. Radiocarbon dating: avoiding errors by avoiding mixed samples. *Antiquity* 73: 124–30.

Barnatt, J., Bevan, B. and Edmonds, M. 2002. Gardom's Edge: A Landscape Through Time. *Antiquity* 76: 50–56.

Bartlett, A. 1981. *Beeston Castle, Cheshire* (AML Rep No 3369).

Beckensall, S. 2009. *Prehistoric Rock Art in Britain*. Stroud, Amberley Publishing.

Behre, K-E. 1981. The interpretation of anthropogenic indicators in pollen diagrams. *Pollen et Spores* 23: 225–245.

Bennett, K. D., Whittington, G. and Edwards, K. J. 1994. Recent plant nomenclatural changes and pollen morphology in the British Isles. *Quaternary Newsletter* 73: 1–6.

Berglund, B. E. and Ralska-Jasiewicsowa, M. 1986. Pollen analysis and pollen diagrams. In B. E. Berglund (ed.), *Handbook of Holocene Palaeoecology and Palaeohydrology*: 455–484. Chichester, Wiley.

Berridge, P. 1994. The lithics. In H. Quinnell, M. R. Blockley, and P. Berridge, *Excavations at Rhuddlan, Clwyd 1969-73. Mesolithic to Medieval*: 95–114. Council for British Archaeology Research Report 95. London, Council for British Archaeology.

Bersu, G. 1940. Excavations at Little Woodbury, Wiltshire, part I. *Proceedings of the Prehistoric Society* 6: 30–111.

Bertsch, K. 1941. *Handbucher der practische vorgeschichtsforschung*. Stuttgart, Fruchte und Samen.

Birks, H. J. B. 1989. Holocene isochrone maps and patterns of tree-spreading in the British Isles. *Journal of Biogeography* 16: 503–540.

Blaauw, M. and Christen, J. A. 2005. Radiocarbon peat chronologies and environmental change. *Applied Statistics* 54: 805–816.

Blaauw, M., Christen, J. A., Mauquoy, D., van der Plicht, J. and Bennett, K. D. 2007a. Testing the timing of radiocarbon-dated events between proxy archives. *The Holocene* 17: 283–288.

Blaauw, M., Bakker, R., Christen, J. A., Hall, V. A. and van der Plicht, J. 2007b. A Bayesian framework for age modeling of radiocarbon-dated peat deposits: case studies from the Netherlands. *Radiocarbon* 49: 357–368.

Blaauw, M. 2010. Methods and code for 'classical' age-modelling of radiocarbon sequences. *Quaternary Geochronology* 5: 512–518.

Blockley, S. P. E., Blaauw, M., Bronk Ramsey, C. and van der Plicht, J. 2007. Building and testing age models for radiocarbon dates in Lateglacial and Early Holocene sediments. *Quaternary Science Reviews* 26: 1915–1926.

Blockley, S. P. E., Bronk Ramsey, C., Lane, C. S. and Lotter, A. F. 2008. Improved age modelling approaches as exemplified by the revised chronology for the Central European varved lake Soppensee. *Quaternary Science Reviews* 27: 61–71.

Brennand, M. (ed.) 2006. *The Archaeology of North West England. An Archaeological Research Framework for the North West Region. Volume 1: Resource Assessment*. (*Archaeology North West* volume 8 (issue 18, for 2006)). Council for British Archaeology North-West.

Brennand, M. (ed.) 2007. *Research and Archaeology in North West England. An Archaeological Research Framework for North West England. Volume 2 Research Agenda and Strategy*. (*Archaeology North West* volume 9 (issue 19, for 2007)). Council for British Archaeology North-West.

British Geological Survey 1980. Digital solid geology data supplied by Cheshire Historic Environment Record (CHER)

British Geological Survey 1983. Soil survey of England and Wales 1:250000 soil map. Harpenden.

Bronk Ramsey, C. 1995. Radiocarbon calibration and analysis of stratigraphy: The OxCal program. *Radiocarbon* 37: 425–30.

Bronk Ramsey, C. 1998. Probability and dating. *Radiocarbon* 40: 461–74.

Bronk Ramsey, C. 2001. Development of the radiocarbon calibration program OxCal. *Radiocarbon* 43: 355–63.

Bronk Ramsey, C. 2009. Bayesian analysis of radiocarbon dates. *Radiocarbon* 51: 337–360.

270

Brooks, D. and Thomas, K. W. 1967. The distribution of pollen grains on microscope slides. The non randomness of the distribution. *Pollen Spores* 9: 621–629.

Brooks, I. P. 1989. *The viability of micropalaeontology to the sourcing of flint*. Unpublished PhD thesis, University of Sheffield.

Brooks, I. P. 2011. *Maiden Castle Geophysical Survey (May 2011)*. Engineering Archaeological Services Client Report 2011/08. Unpublished report.

Brooks, I. P. and Laws, K. 2009. *Beeston Castle Geophysical Survey (November 2009)*. Engineering Archaeological Services Client Report 2009/22. Unpublished report.

Brooks, I. P. and Price, J. 2010a. *Beeston Castle Geophysical Survey (June 2010)*. Engineering Archaeological Services Client Report 2010/11. Unpublished report.

Brooks, I. P. and Price, J. 2010b. *Beeston Castle Geophysical Survey (August 2010)*. Engineering Archaeological Services Client Report 2010/15. Unpublished report.

Buck, C. E., Litton, C. D., and Smith, A. F. M. 1992. Calibration of radiocarbon results pertaining to related archaeological events, *Journal of Archaeological Science* 19: 497–512.

Buck, C. E., Cavanagh, W. G. and Litton, C. D. 1996. *Bayesian Approach to Interpreting Archaeological Data*. Chichester, Wiley.

Bu'lock, J. D. 1956. The Hill-Fort at Helsby, Cheshire. *Transactions of the Lancashire and Cheshire Antiquarian Society* 66: 107–10.

Butler, C. 2005. *Prehistoric Flintwork*. Stroud, Tempus Publishing.

Cappers, R. T. J., Bekker, R. M. and Jans, J. E. A. 2006. *Digitale Zadenatlas van Nederland*. Eelde (NL), Barkhuis.

Carrott, J., Foster, A., Foster, L. and Ranner, H. 2010. *Helsby*. Report no. PRS 2010/40. Unpublished report.

Carrott, J., Martin, G. and Foster, A. 2012. *Eddisbury*. Report no. PRS 2012/12. Unpublished report.

Carruthers, W. J. 2003a. Plant remains. In N. Fairburn et al, II: Brook House Farm, Bruen Stapleford. Excavation of a First Millennium BC Settlement. *Journal of the Chester Archaeological Society* 77: 34–39.

Carruthers, W. J. 2003b. Plant remains. In N. Fairburn et al, III: Birch Heath, Tarporley. Excavation of a Rural Romano-British Settlement. *Journal of the Chester Archaeological Society* 77: 90–96.

Carruthers, W. J., and Peglar, S. 2011 *Ince Resource Recovery Park, Cheshire: Pollen and macrofossil analysis of peat deposits from the Ince Marshes*. Unpublished report. CHER R3374.

Challis, A. J. and Harding, D. W. 1975. *Later Prehistory from the Trent to the Tyne*. Oxford, British Archaeological Reports British Series 20.

Cocroft, W. D., Everson, P., Jecock, M. and Wilson-North, W. R. 1989. Castle Ditch hillfort, Eddisbury, Cheshire reconsidered: the excavations of 1935–38 in light of recent field survey. In M. Bowden, D. Mackay and P. Topping (eds), *From Cornwall to Caithness: some aspects of British field archaeology*: 129–35. Oxford, British Archaeological Report British Series 209.

Collens, J. 1999. Flying on the Edge: Aerial Photography and Settlement Patterns in Cheshire and Merseyside. In M. Nevell (ed.), *Living on the Edge of Empire: Models, Methodology and Marginality. Late-Prehistoric and Romano-British Rural Settlement in North West England*. Council for British Archaeology North-West: 36–41. (*Archaeology North West 3* (Issue 13 for 1998)).

Coombs, D. G. 1988. A note on the rampart of the hillfort of Kelsborrow, Cheshire. *Manchester Archaeological Bulletin* 3: 64–67.

Cootes, K. V. E. and Emery, M. M. 2014. *The Excavation of Ring-Ditches Two and Three at Poulton, Cheshire. 2010-2013. An Interim Report*. Poulton Research Project. Unpublished report.

Cootes, K. V. E. 2015. One field, 10,000 years: the Poulton Research Project. In *British Archaeology* November-December 2015: 52–7.

Cotton, M. A. 1954. British camps with timber-laced ramparts. *Archaeological Journal* III: 26–105.

Countryside Commission. 1998. Countryside character volume 2: North West. Cheltenham.

Cowell, R. W. 1992. Prehistoric survey in North Cheshire. *Cheshire Past. An annual review of archaeology in Cheshire* 1: 6–7.

Cowell, R. W. and Innes, J. B. 1994. *The wetlands of Merseyside*. North West Wetlands Survey 1, Lancaster Imprints 2. Lancaster, Lancaster University Archaeological Unit.

Cowell, R. W. and Philpott, R. A. 2000. *Prehistoric, Romano-British and Medieval Settlement in Lowland North West England: Archaeological excavations along the A5300 road corridor in Merseyside*. Liverpool, National Museums & Galleries on Merseyside.

Coxhead, A. D. and Bevan R. M. 2008. *The story of Delamere House and Delamere Park*. Chester, Cheshire County Council.

Crutchley, S. and Crow, P. 2009. *The Light Fantastic: Using airborne laser scanning in archaeological survey*. Swindon, English Heritage.

Davies, M. G. 1990. *The Castle Ditch, Eddisbury, a report of recent fieldwork and a reconstruction of occupation phasing*. Unpublished report.

Dodd, L. J. 2004. *Residential Development on Land at Centurion Way, Middlewich, Cheshire: A Programme of Archaeological Excavation*. Earthworks Archaeological Services Ltd Client Report E614. Unpublished report.

Dodgson, J. McN. 1971. *The Place-Names of Cheshire Part III: The Place-Names of Nantwich Hundred and Eddisbury Hundred*. Cambridge, Cambridge University Press.

Driver, T. 2013. *Architecture, Regional Identity and Power in the Iron Age Landscapes of Mid Wales: The Hillforts of North Ceredigion*. Oxford. British Archaeological Reports British Series 583.

Edwards, B. 2011. *Topographic and Geophysical Survey of Helsby Promontory Fort, Cheshire*. Unpublished report.

Edwards, J. 2003a. *Report on findings from excavation of collapse feature no. 1 on Merrick's bank – Eddisbury Hill – Monument number 25692*. Unpublished report.

Edwards, J. 2003b. *Report on findings from excavation of collapse feature no. 2 on Merrick's bank – Eddisbury Hill – Monument number 25692*. Unpublished report.

Edwards, R. 2007. *The Cheshire Historic Landscape Characterisation*. Cheshire County Council and English Heritage. Unpublished report.

Ellis, P. (ed.) 1993. *Beeston Castle, Cheshire: excavations by Laurence Keen and Peter Hough, 1968–85*. London, English Heritage (Archaeological Report 23).

English Heritage. 2000. *Old Pale Farm, Delamere, Vale Royal, Cheshire*. Unpublished report.

Faegri, K., Kaland, P. E. and Krzywinski, K. 1989. *Textbook of Pollen Analysis* (4th edition). Chichester, Wiley.

Fairburn, N et al. 2003. II: Brook House Farm, Bruen Stapleford. Excavation of a First Millennium BC Settlement. *Journal of the Chester Archaeological Society* 77: 9–57.

Feachem, R. W. 1966. The Hill-Forts of Northern Britain. In A. L. F. Rivet (ed.), *The Iron Age in Northern Britain*: 59–87. Edinburgh, Edinburgh University Press.

Feachem R. W. 1971. Unfinished Hill-forts. In M. Jesson and D. Hill (eds), *The Iron Age and its Hill-forts*: 19–39. Southampton, University of Southampton.

Forde-Johnston, J. 1962. The Iron Age Hillforts of Lancashire and Cheshire. *Transactions of the Lancashire and Cheshire Antiquarian Society* 72: 9–46.

Forde-Johnston, J. 1964. Letter to Miss Ireland, 2 October 1964. Held by National Trust North West Region.

Forde-Johnston, J. 1967. Letter to Mr Gripwell, National Trust Agent, 27 January 1967. Held by National Trust North West Region.

Forde-Johnston, J. 1976. *Hillforts of the Iron Age in England and Wales: A survey of the surface evidence*. Liverpool, Liverpool University Press.

Foster, A., Foster, L., Walker, A., and Carrott, J. 2012. *Assessment of biological remains from excavations undertaken at Kelsborrow Castle Hillfort, near Willington, Cheshire. Report No. PRS 2012/34*. Unpublished report.

Frere, S. S. (ed.) 1983. Roman Britain in 1982 1. Sites explored. *Britannia* 14, 297-9.

Furness, R. 1978. *The soils of Cheshire*. Harpenden, Rothamsted Experimental Station.

Garner, D. 2011a. *A management review of work undertaken between October 2008 and July 2011 at Woodhouse hillfort (SM 25694). Report no. HH006*. Unpublished report.

Garner, D. 2011b. *A management review of work undertaken October 2008 and July 2011 at Helsby hillfort (SM 25689). Report no. HH008*. Unpublished report.

Garner, D. 2011c. *A management review of work undertaken October 2008 and July 2011 at Kelsborrow hillfort (SM 30375). Report no. HH013*. Unpublished report.

Garner, D. 2011d. *A management review of work undertaken October 2008 and July 2011 at Eddisbury hillfort (SM 30375). Report no. HH014*. Unpublished report.

Garner, D. 2012. *Hillforts of the Cheshire Sandstone Ridge*. Chester, The Habitats and Hillforts Landscape Partnership Scheme, Cheshire West and Chester Council.

Gearey, B. G., Marshall, P. and Hamilton, D. 2009. Correlating archaeological and palaeoenvironmental records using a Bayesian approach: a case study from Sutton Common, South Yorkshire, England. *Journal of Archaeological Science* 36: 1477–1487.

Gillam, J. P. 1970. *Types of Romano-British Coarse Pottery in Northern Britain* (Third Edition). Newcastle-Upon-Tyne, Oriel Press.

Godwin, H. 1975. *The History of the British Flora*. Cambridge, Cambridge University Press.

Gondek, M. 2010. *Report on the Geophysical Survey at Kelsborrow Castle, Iron Age hillfort, near Kelsall, Cheshire. Report No.1/2010 (June 2010)*. Unpublished report.

Green, J. A. 1979. *Forests*. In B. E. Harris (ed.), *A history of the county of Chester II*. 167–187. Oxford University Press for London University Institute of Historical Research.

Green, S. 1984. Flint arrowheads, typology and interpretation. *Lithics* 5: 19–39.

Greig, J. 1991. The British Isles. In W. van Zeist, K. Wasylikowa and K-E. Behre (eds), *Progress on Old World palaeoethnobotany; a retrospective view on the occasion of 20 years of the International Work Group for Palaeoethnobotany*: 299–334. Rotterdam, Balkema.

Griffiths, D. 2001. The North-West Frontier. In N. J. Higham and D. H. Hill (eds), *Edward the Elder 899–924*: 167–187. London, Routledge.

Grimm, E. C. 2010. TILIA. Illinois State Museum, Springfield, IL.

Hamerow, H. 1993. *Excavations at Mucking: Volume 2: The Anglo-Saxon settlement*. English Heritage.

Harding, D. W. 2012. *Iron Age Hillforts in Britain and Beyond*. Oxford, Oxford University Press.

Harris, B. E. and Thacker A. T. (eds) 1987. *A history of the county of Chester 1: physique, Roman, Anglo-*

Saxon and Domesday. Oxford University Press for London University Institute of Historical Research.

Haselgrove, C., Armit I., Champion, T., Creighton, J., Gwilt, A., Hill, J. D., Hunter, F and Woodward, A. 2001. *Understanding the British Iron Age: An Agenda for Action*. Salisbury, Trust for Wessex Archaeology Ltd.

Haselgrove, C. and Moore, T. (eds) 2007. *The Later Iron Age in Britain and Beyond*. Oxford. Oxbow Books.

Haselgrove, C. and Pope, R. (eds) 2007. *The Earlier Iron Age in Britain and the Near Continent*. Oxford, Oxbow Books.

Henson, D. 1985. The flint resources of Yorkshire and the East Midlands. *Lithics* 6: 2–9.

Higham, N. J. 1993. *The Origins of Cheshire*. Manchester, Manchester University Press.

Higham, N. J. and Hill, D. H. (eds) 2001. *Edward the Elder 899–924*. London, Routledge.

Hill, J. D. 2007. The Dynamics of Social Change in Later Iron Age eastern and south-eastern England c. 300 BC – AD 43. In C. Haselgrove and T. Moore (ed.), *The Later Iron Age in Britain and Beyond*: 16–40. Oxford, Oxbow Books.

Hill, M. O., Mountford, J. O., Roy, D. B. and Bunce, R. G. H. 1999. *Ellenberg's indicator values for British plants. ECOFACT Volume 2, Technical Annex*. Huntingdon, Institute of Terrestrial Ecology.

Hind, D. 1998. Chert use in the Mesolithic of Northern England. *Assemblage* 4.

Hodgson, J. and Brennand, M. 2006. Prehistoric Period Resource Assessment. In M. Brennand (ed.), *The Archaeology of North West England. An Archaeological Research Framework for the North West Region. Volume 1: Resource Assessment* (*Archaeology North West* volume 8 (issue 18, for 2006)): 23–58. Council for British Archaeology North-West.

Hodgson, J. and Brennand, M. 2007. Prehistoric Period Research Agenda. In M. Brennand (ed.), *Research and Archaeology in North West England. An Archaeological Research Framework for North West England. Volume 2: Research Agenda and Strategy* (*Archaeology North West* volume 9 (issue 19, for 2007)): 31–54. Council for British Archaeology North-West.

Hughes, G. 1996. Old Oswestry Hillfort: Excavations by W. J. Varley 1939-1940. *Archaeologia Cambrensis* 143 (for 1994): 46–91.

Innes, J. B. 1994. Knowsley Park Moss Palaeoecological survey. In R. W. Cowell and J. B. Innes, *The wetlands of Merseyside*. North West Wetlands Survey 1, Lancaster Imprints 2: 139–151. Lancaster, Lancaster University Archaeological Unit.

Innes, J. B. 2000. Pollen Analysis, in Ditton Brook, Ditton. In R. W. Cowell and R. A. Philpott, *Prehistoric, Romano-British and Medieval Settlement in Lowland North West England: Archaeological excavations along the A5300 road corridor in Merseyside*: 19–23. Liverpool, National Museums & Galleries on Merseyside.

Jecock, M. 2006. *A Rapid Survey and Archaeological Assessment of the Hillfort on Woodhouse Hill, Frodsham, Cheshire*. Archaeological Survey and Investigation Internal Report, English Heritage. Unpublished report.

Jones, D. M. (ed.) 2008. *Luminescence Dating: Guidelines on using luminescence dating in archaeology*. London, English Heritage.

Jordan, D. 2007. *Evaluating Aggregate in North West England. The Effectiveness of Geophysical Survey. Final Project report*. English Heritage.

Joyce, D. and Foxwell, B. 2011. *Captured Memories across the Hillforts of Cheshire*. Chester, Cheshire West and Chester Council.

Kennet, D. H. 1985. *Anglo-Saxon Pottery* (2nd edition). Shire Publications Limited.

Kirschvink, J. L. 1980. The least square line and plane and the analysis of palaeomagnetic data. *Geophysical Journal of the Royal Astronomical Society* 62 (3): 699–718.

Konstram, A. 2006. *The forts of Celtic Britain*. Colchester, Osprey.

Krawieki, A. 1982. *The burning of the hillfort at Maiden Castle, Bickerton Hill, Cheshire*. Unpublished dissertation. University of Liverpool.

Lanos, Ph. 2004. Bayesian inference of calibration curves: application to archaeomagnetism. In C. E. Buck and A. R. Millard (eds), *Tools for Constructing Chronologies*: 43–82. London, Springer-Verlag,

Latham, F. A. 1987. *Frodsham, the history of a Cheshire town*. Whitchurch, Local Historians.

Leah, M. D., Wells, C. E., Appleby, C. and Huckerby, E. 1997. *The Wetlands of Cheshire. North West Wetlands Survey 4*. Lancaster Imprints 5. Lancaster, Lancaster University Archaeology Unit.

Longley, D. 1979. *Prehistoric Sites in Cheshire*. Unpublished report.

Longley, D. 1987. Prehistory. In B. E. Harris and A. T. Thacker (eds), *A history of the county of Chester 1: physique, Roman, Anglo-Saxon and Domesday*: 36–9. Oxford University Press for London University Institute of Historical Research.

Mackintosh, D. 1879. Results of a systematic survey in 1878, of the directions and limits of dispersion, mode of occurrence and relation to drift-deposits of erractic blocks or boulders of the west of England and east of Wales, including a revision of many years' previous observations. *The Quarterly Journal of the Geological Society of London* 53: 425–455.

Macphail, R. 1993. The soils and pollen. In P. Ellis (ed.), *Beeston Castle, Cheshire: excavations by Laurence Keen and Peter Hough, 1968–85*: 84–5. London, English Heritage (Archaeological Report 23).

Matthews, D. 2014. Hillfort Intervisibility in the Northern and Mid Marches. In T. Saunders (ed.), *Hillforts in the North West and Beyond*. (*Archaeology North West* new series Volume 3 (Issue 13 for 1998)). Council for British Archaeology North-West.

Matthews, K. J. 2002. The Iron Age of north-west England. A socio-economic model. *Journal of the Chester Archaeological Society* 76: 1–51.

Mayer. A. 1990. Fieldwalking in Cheshire. *Lithics* 11: 48–50.

Mellars, P. 1976. Settlement patterns and industrial variability in the British Mesolithic. In G. de G. Sieveking, I. H. Longworth and K. E. Wilson (eds.), *Problems in economic and social archaeology*: 137–153. London, Duckworth.

Milln, J. 1996. *Maiden Castle, Bickerton, Cheshire. Application for Consent for Battle Area Clearance Operation. Project Brief.* National Trust. Unpublished report.

Mook, W. G. 1986. Business meeting: Recommendations/Resolutions adopted by the Twelfth International Radiocarbon Conference. *Radiocarbon* 28: 799.

Mook, W. G. and Waterbolk, H. T. 1985. *Radiocarbon Dating, Handbook for Archaeologists 3.* Strasbourg (European Science Foundation).

Moore, P. D., Webb, J. A. and Collinson, M. E. 1991. *Pollen Analysis* (2nd edition). Oxford, Blackwell Scientific Publications.

Morgan, V. and Morgan, P. 2004. *Prehistoric Cheshire.* Ashbourne, Landmark Publishing Ltd.

Morris, E. 1996. Old Oswestry hillfort: the prehistoric pottery and salt containers. In G. Hughes, Old Oswestry hillfort: excavations by W. J. Varley 1939-40. *Archaeologia Cambrensis* 143: 65–74.

Morris, M. 1983. *Medieval Manchester: A Regional Study.* Manchester, Greater Manchester Archaeological Unit.

Mullin, D. 2012. *A Landscape of Borders: The Prehistory of the Anglo-Welsh Borderland.* Oxford, British Archaeological Reports British Series 572.

Musson, C. R. with Britnell, W. J. and Smith, A. G. 1991. *The Breiddin Hillfort: A later prehistoric settlement in the Welsh Marches.* Council for British Archaeology Research Report no. 76. London, Council for British Archaeology.

Myers, A. M. 1989. Lithics, risk and change in the Mesolithic. In I. Brooks and P. Phillips (eds.), *Breaking the Stony Silence: Papers from the Sheffield Lithics Conference 1988*: 131–160. Oxford, British Archaeological Reports British Series 213.

Nash, G. H. 2007. A Scattering of images. The Rock-Art of Southern Britain. In A. Mazel, G. H. Nash and C. Waddington (eds), *Art as Metaphor: The Prehistoric Rock-Art of Britain*: 175–203. Oxford, Archaeopress.

Nash, G. H. and Stanford, A. 2010. Encryption and display: Recording new images on the Calderstones in Liverpool. In T. Barnett and K. Sharpe (eds), *Carving a Future for British Rock Art, New directions for research, management and presentation*: 11–24. Oxford, Oxbow Books.

Needham, S. 1993. The Beeston Castle Bronze Age metalwork and its significance. In P. Ellis (ed.), *Beeston Castle, Cheshire: Excavations by Laurence Keen & Peter Hough, 1968-85*: 41–50. London, English Heritage (Archaeological Report 23).

Nevell, M. 1999. Great Woolden Hall: A Model for the Material Culture of Iron Age and Romano-British Rural Settlement in North West England? In M. Nevell (ed.), *Living on the Edge of Empire: Models, Methodology & Marginality. Late Prehistoric and Romano-British Settlement in North-West England.* (*Archaeology North West* volume 3 (Issue 13, for 1998). CBArchaeology North-West.

Nevell, M. and Redhead, N. 2005. *Mellor: Living on the Edge. A Regional Study of an Iron Age and Romano-British Upland Settlement.* Manchester Archaeological Monographs Volume 1. University of Manchester.

Northern Archaeological Associates, 2013. *Saighton Camp, Chester. The Roman and Medieval Archaeology.* Client report. Unpublished report.

Ormerod, G. 1882. *The history of the county palatine and city of Chester,* revised and enlarged by T. Helsby. 2nd edition, 3 volumes. London.

Oswald, A. 2000. *An Archaeological Assessment of Old Pale Farm, Delamere, Cheshire. English Heritage Survey Report.* York, English Heritage.

Oswald, A., Ainsworth, S. and Pearson, T. 2006. *Hillforts: Prehistoric Strongholds of Northumberland National Park.* London, English Heritage.

Oxford Archaeology North, 2008a. *Habitats and Hillforts of the Cheshire Sandstone Ridge: Archaeological Desk Based Assessment.* Oxford Archaeology North. Unpublished report.

Oxford Archaeology North, 2008b. *Habitats and Hillforts of the Cheshire Sandstone Ridge: Archaeological Condition Assessment.* Oxford Archaeology North. Unpublished report.

Pavón-Carrasco, F. J., Rodríguez-González, J., Osete, M. L. and Torta, J. M. 2011. A Matlab tool for archaeomagnetic dating. *Journal of Archaeological Science* 38 (issue 2): 408–419.

Payne, A., Corney, M. and Cunliffe, B. 2006. *The Wessex Hillforts Project: Extensive survey of hillforts in central southern England.* London, English Heritage.

Petch, D. F. 1987. The Roman Period. In B. E. Harris and A. T. Thacker (eds), *A history of the county of Chester 1: physique, Roman, Anglo-Saxon and Domesday*: 115–236. Oxford University Press for London University Institute of Historical Research.

Pettitt, P. and White, M. 2012. *The British Palaeolithic. Human Societies at the edge of the Pleistocene World.* Routledge, Abingdon.

Philpott, R. A. 2010. The Iron Age. In R. A. Philpott and M. H. Adams *Irby, Wirral. Excavations on a Late Prehistoric, Romano-British and Medieval Site, 1987-96*: 169–186. Liverpool, National Museums Liverpool.

Pierce, D. C. 2004. Written communication to A. P. Davison at English Heritage, dated 20th February 2004.

Pollington, M. 2009. *Woodhouse Hill, Frodsham, Cheshire. Archaeological Topographic Survey.* Archaeological Services WYAS unpublished report no. 1997.

Pollington, M. 2012a. *Helsby Hillfort, Helsby, Cheshire. Archaeological Survey and Investigation.* Archaeological Services WYAS unpublished report no. 2355.

Pollington, M. 2012b. *Maiden Castle, Bickerton, Cheshire. Archaeological Survey and Investigation.* Archaeological Services WYAS unpublished report no. 2385.

Pope, R. E. 2011. Processual archaeology and gender politics: the loss of innocence. *Archaeological Dialogues* 18 (1): 59–86.

Quinnell, H., Blockley, M. R. and Berridge, P. 1994 *Excavations at Rhuddlan, Clwyd 1969-73. Mesolithic to Medieval.* Council for British Archaeology Research Report 95. London, Council for British Archaeology.

Rackham, O. 1989. *The Last Forest: The story of Hatfield Forest.* London, Dent.

Rawson, S. 1997. *Helsby Hillfort, preliminary report.* Unpublished report

Rawson, P. F., Curry, D., Dilley, F. C., Kennedy, W. J., Neale, J. W., Wood, C. J. and Worssam, B. C. 1978. *A correlation of Cretaceous rocks in the British Isles.* Geological Society of London Special Report No. 7.

Reimer, P. J., Baillie, M. G. L., Bard, E., Bayliss, A., Beck, J. W., Blackwell, P. G., Bronk Ramsey, C., Buck, C. E., Burr, G., Edwards, R. L., Friedrich, M., Grootes, P. M., Guilderson, T. P., Hajdas, I., Heaton, T. J., Hogg, A. G., Hughen, K. A., Kaiser, K. F., Kromer, B., McCormac, F. G., Manning, S. W., Reimer, R. W., Richards, D. A., Southon, J. R., Talamo, S., Turney, C. S. M., van der Plicht, J. and Weyhenmeyer, C. E. 2009. IntCal09 and Marine09 radiocarbon age calibration curves, 0–50,000 years cal BP. *Radiocarbon* 51: 1111–1150.

Robinson, M. and Hubbard, R. N. L. B. 1977. The transport of pollen in the bracts of hulled cereals. *Journal of Archaeological Science* 4: 197–199.

Rodwell, J. S. (ed.) 1991. *British plant communities 2: mires and heath.* Cambridge: Cambridge University Press.

Roseveare, M., Roseveare, A. and Lewis, D. 2010a. *Eddisbury Hillfort, Cheshire: Geophysical Survey Report EHC091 (10 May 2010).* Unpublished report.

Roseveare, M., Roseveare, A. and Lewis, D. 2010b. *Kelsborrow Hillfort, Cheshire: Geophysical Survey Report KHC091 (10 May 2010).* Unpublished report.

Roseveare, M. J. 2012a. *Peckforton Mere, Cheshire: Geophysical Survey Report PMF121 (08 October 2012).* Unpublished report.

Roseveare, M. J. 2012b. *Oakmere Promontory Fort, Cheshire: Geophysical Survey Report ODF121 (23 November 2012).* Unpublished report.

Royle, C. and Woodward, A. 1993. Prehistoric pottery. In P. Ellis (ed.), *Beeston Castle, Cheshire: excavations by Laurence Keen and Peter Hough, 1968–85*: 63–78. London, English Heritage (Archaeological Report 23).

Rutter, J. A. and Davey, P. J. 1980. Clay pipes from Chester. In P. Davey (ed.), *The Archaeology of the Clay Tobacco Pipe III: Britain: the North and* West: 41–274. Oxford, British Archaeological Reports British Series 78.

Saunders, T. (ed.) 2014. *Hillforts in the North West and Beyond.* (*Archaeology North West* new series Volume 3 (Issue 13 for 1998)). Council for British Archaeology North-West.

Sawyer, P. H. 1987. The Cheshire Domesday: Translation of the Text. In B. E. Harris and A. T. Thacker (eds), *A history of the county of Chester 1: physique, Roman, Anglo-Saxon and Domesday*: 36–9. Oxford University Press for London University Institute of Historical Research.

Scott, E. M. 2003. The Third International Radiocarbon Intercomparison (TIRI) and the Fourth International Radiocarbon Intercomparison (FIRI) 1990–2002: results, analysis, and conclusions. *Radiocarbon* 45: 135–408.

Scott, E. M, Cook, G, and Naysmith, P. 2010. The fifth international radiocarbon intercomparison (VIRI): an assessment of laboratory performance in stage 3, *Radiocarbon*, 53: 859–65.

Semple, S. 2013. *Perceptions of the Prehistoric in Anglo Saxon England: Religion, Ritual and Rulership in the Landscape.* Oxford, Oxford University Press.

Shaw, M. and Clark, J. 2003. *Cheshire Historic Towns Survey: Eddisbury, Archaeological Assessment.* Cheshire County Council and English Heritage. Unpublished report.

Shone, W. 1911. *Prehistoric Man in Cheshire.* Minshull & Meeson.

Siddell, J, Thomas, C, and Bayliss, A. 2007. Validating and improving archaeological phasing at St Mary Spital, London, *Radiocarbon* 49: 593–610

Sitch, B. 2012. Rediscovering a long-lost battlefield assemblage from Heronbridge, near Chester. *Museum Archaeologists News* 52: 1–4. Society of Museum Archaeologists. Available at http://www.socmusarch.org.uk/docs/SMA-Newsletter-52-Spring-2012.pdf (accessed March 2016).

Slota Jr, P. J., Jull, A. J. T., Linick, T. W. and Toolin, L. J. 1987. Preparation of small samples for 14C accelerator targets by catalytic reduction of CO. *Radiocarbon* 29: 303–6.

Smart, R. 1993. The flint. In P. Ellis (ed.), *Beeston Castle, Cheshire: Excavations by Laurence Keen & Peter Hough, 1968-85*: 56-59. London, English Heritage (Archaeological Report 23).

Sparkes, I. G. 1976. *Old Horseshoes.* Shire Album 19, Aylesbury

Stace, C. 2010. *New Flora of the British Isles*. 3rd edition. Cambridge, Cambridge University Press.

Stanford, S. C. 1991. *The Archaeology of the Welsh Marches*. 2nd revised edition. S. C. Stanford.

Stenhouse, M. J. and Baxter, M. S. 1983. 14C dating reproducibility: evidence from routine dating of archaeological samples. *PACT* 8: 147–61.

Stockmarr, J. 1972. Tablets with spores used in absolute pollen analysis. *Pollen Spores* 13: 615–621.

Stuiver, M. and Kra, R. S. 1986. Editorial comment. *Radiocarbon* 28(2B): ii.

Stuiver, M. and Polach, H. A. 1977. Reporting of 14C data. *Radiocarbon* 19: 355–63.

Stuiver, M. and Reimer, P. J. 1986. A computer program for radiocarbon age calculation. *Radiocarbon* 28: 1022–30.

Stuiver, M. and Reimer, P. J. 1993. Extended 14C data base and revised CALIB 3.0 14C age calibration program. *Radiocarbon* 35: 215–30.

Taylor, J. J. 1980. Maiden Castle, Bickerton Hill, interim report. *Cheshire Archaeological Bulletin*, 7: 34-6.

Topping, P. 1997. Different realities: the Neolithic in the Northumberland Cheviots. In P. Topping (ed.), *Neolithic Landscapes*: *Neolithic Studies Group seminar papers 2*: 113–23. Oxford, Oxbow Books.

Vandeputte, K., Moens, L. and Dams, R. 1996. Improved sealed-tube combustion of organic samples to CO2 for stable isotopic analysis, radiocarbon dating and percent carbon determinations. *Analytical Letters* 29: 2761–74.

Van Geel, B., Buurman, J. and Waterbolk, H. T. 1996. Archaeological and Palaeoecological indications of an abrupt climate change in The Netherlands, and evidence for climatological teleconnections around 2650 BP. *Journal of Quaternary Science* 11: 451–460.

Varley, W. J. 1935. Maiden Castle, Bickerton. Preliminary Excavations, 1934. *Annals of Archaeology and Anthropology University of Liverpool* 22: 97–110.

Varley, W. J. 1936. Further Excavations at Maiden Castle, Bickerton, 1935. *Annals of Archaeology and Anthropology University of Liverpool* 23: 101–112.

Varley, W. J. 1950. Excavations of the Castle Ditch, Eddisbury 1935-1938. *Transactions of the Historic Society of Lancashire and Cheshire* 102: 1–68.

Varley, W. J. 1964. *Cheshire before the Romans*. Edition 1. Chester, Cheshire Community Council.

Varley, W. J. and Jackson, J. W. 1940. *Prehistoric Cheshire*. Chester, Cheshire Community Council.

Waddington, C., Johnson, B. and Mazel, A. 2005. Excavation of a rock art site at Hunterheugh Crag, Northumberland. *Archaeologia Aeliana* 5th series 34: 29–54.

Watson, E. 2009. *Portable art or re-used rock carving? A re-analysis of the concept of portability*. Unpublished thesis, University of Newcastle.

Welfare, H. 2002. The Uplands of the Northern Counties in the First Millennium BC. In C. Brooks, R. Daniels and A. Harding (eds), *Past, Present and Future: The Archaeology of Northern England*, Architectural and Archaeological Society of Durham and Northumberland Research Report 5, 71–78.

West, S. 1985. *West Stow. The Anglo-Saxon Village. Volume 1: Text*. East Anglian Archaeology Report no. 24. Ipswich, Suffolk County Planning Department.

Wigley, A. 2007. Rooted to the spot: 'smaller enclosures' of the later first millennium BC in the central Welsh Marches. In C. Haselgrove and T. Moore (eds), *The Later Iron Age in Britain and Beyond*: 173–189. Oxford, Oxbow Books.

Wilmott and Garner (forthcoming). *Excavations at Chester's Roman Amphitheatre volume 1: The Prehistoric and Roman Archaeology*. Oxbow Books.

Xu, S., Anderson, R., Bryant, C., Cook, G. T., Dougans, A., Freeman, S., Naysmith, P., Schnabel, C. and Scott, E. M. 2004. Capabilities of the new SUERC 5MV AMS facility for 14C dating. *Radiocarbon* 46: 59–64.

Zananiri, I., Batt, C. M., Lanos, Ph., Tarling, D. H., and Linford, P. 2007. Archaeomagnetic secular variation in the UK during the past 4000 years and its application to archaeomagnetic dating. *Physics of the Earth and Planetary Interiors* 160: 97–107.

Zondervan, A. and Sparks, R. J. 1997. Development plans for the AMS facility at the Institute of Geological and Nuclear Sciences, New Zealand. *Nuclear Instruments and Methods in Physics Research* B 123: 79–83.

Online Appendices avaliable at http://bit.ly/2ghWmze